GROWING TOGETHER

Resources, Programs, and Experiences for Jewish Family Education

Jeffrey Schein and Judith S. Schiller, Editors

A.R.E. Publishing, Inc.

Denver, Colorado

Published by:
A.R.E. Publishing, Inc.
Denver, Colorado

Library of Congress Card Number 00-101921
ISBN 0-86705-046-2

Printed in the United States of America
10   9   8   7   6   5   4   3   2   1

DEDICATION

To my wife, Deborah, and our children, Ben, Jonah, and Hanna.

and

To my husband, Rick, and our children, Amy and Sam.

and

To all the families who will learn and grow together. May they go
from strength to strength.

ACKNOWLEDGEMENTS

We wish to thank the following:

Our editorial committee — Rob Spira, Enid C. Lader, Julie Jaslow Auerbach, and Mark Davidson — for their help in conceptualizing the scope, structure, and content of this volume.

The many JFE "talent scouts" across North America, who directed us to new and creative developments in Family Education.

Our commentators — Leora and Ron Isaacs, Betsy Katz, and Sally Weber — for the creative programmatic spins they provided for many chapters.

Frank Maris, Pam Folbaum, and Sheryl Goldfein for their invaluable secretarial and administrative support.

Rabbi Raymond A. Zwerin and Audrey Friedman Marcus, our editors and publishers, for both supporting us and constantly challenging us to revise and improve this volume.

CONTENTS

BETWEEN LEARNING TOGETHER AND GROWING TOGETHER

CONTRIBUTOR: JANICE P. ALPER
ADDRESS: Jewish Educational Services
4549 Chamblee Dunwoody Road
Atlanta, GA 30338
PHONE: (770) 677-9480
E-MAIL: execdir@jesatlanta.org

In the late 1970s and early 1980s, Jewish educators were drawn to Family Education as a means of bringing congregational families closer to participation in synagogue life. There was an underlying assumption that Jewish Family Education (JFE) would create a partnership between the families and the synagogue. Programs were discrete, focusing on specific grade levels and specific life cycle events, such as Bar/Bat Mitzvah, and/or they were integrated.

Eventually, JFE became a major focus of synagogue school programs. Synagogue brochures promoted family programs as a unique feature of their education curricula. Great care was given to time constraints and lifestyles. Programs took place during school hours. Materials were sent home to encourage continued practice, but there was minimum follow-up or consistency to these "one-shot wonders."

The precursor to this volume, *Learning Together: A Source Book on Jewish Family Education,* edited by Janice P. Alper (now out of print), is a compendium of programs that can be replicated in institutional settings, primarily synagogues, as a means of bringing families together for Jewish learning. Most of the volume consists of one-time programs that

can be integrated into an existing curriculum or can stand alone as a means of bringing families together for Jewish learning in a limited way. Even the extended time programs resemble single efforts because they focus on retreats and overnight happenings. There was virtually no attention to sustained learning over a given period of time to affect or change practice. It was assumed that if educators utilized several programs during a given school year, they would be transforming the institution, and creating the desired partnership between home and school. In some instances, this transformation undoubtedly occurred. But the challenges of JFE are no different in this respect from the challenges of Jewish education in general. The "conserving" forces of the status quo are at least as powerful as the desire for positive change. Hence the need for new methods and fresh approaches to Family Education.

The annual conference sponsored by the Coalition for the Advancement of Jewish Education (CAJE) became a catalyst for bringing people together to discuss and learn about Family Education. At first, there were a few sessions that focused on how to bring families together for Jewish learning. The presenters were often practitioners who had successful programs to share. CAJE provided a venue for people to network and talk about Family Education and the direction it might take. Such interchange continues to this day.

All of this background explains the need for this volume, *Growing Together: Resources, Programs, and Experiences for Jewish Family Education.* Its contents address the needs of today's Jewish family, which is seeking a way to become involved in Jewish life and to practice in a more serious and intense manner. The contents reflect the desires of the authors and editors to have clients/participants regard what they do through a prism of Jewish thought, ideas, and practice. Attention has been given to changing family structures, lifestyles, and learning styles. Many of the programs presented have participants move outside the walls of the institution, thus helping them recognize that one can be Jewish in the market, on the playground, and when planting trees.

In this work, the editors have enlisted leading Jewish Family Educators to provide wisdom and comments about the programs and ideas presented. They offer a number of alternative ways to implement the content of many of the chapters. They also stimulate the reader to consider his/her own culture when thinking about a program in order to make it relevant for themselves and their institution.

The introductions to each part of this volume discuss the rationale for choosing each program in that section and what may be gleaned from it. Each section can form the basis of a Family Education model for a learning environment. The programs can be used discretely, one at a time, or a number of them can be utilized over a period of time to create a Family Education curriculum.

Another feature of this work is in the inclusion of Family Education programs in Israel. Chapter 41 by Sally G. Klein-Katz describes the current trends in bringing families to Israel to reinforce their Jewish identity and their connection with the Jewish people. This effort, which began in the mid-1990s, has spawned numerous programs and projects between communities in Israel and North America, and especially on *kibbutzim* in Israel. Such programs have fostered strong links and partnerships beyond the confines of American Jewish life. Chapter 42 by Barbara Levin and Etti Serok describes the first and only center for Jewish Family Education in Israel.

The editors have also tapped into a number of other models for family integration in Jewish learning. Models from the community form the basis for adapting what we know from other environments to create a Jewish spin on family learning. This is evident in Chapter 38, "The Joyce Epstein Framework for Family-School Partnerships" by Meryl Wassner, and Chapter 39, "TIPS: Interactive Homework in a Jewish Context" by Enid C. Lader. These authors have shown how one can create Jewish learning in ways that are comfortable and familiar to participants.

This book is unique in that it provides many different ways for bringing families together to learn, to celebrate, and to function as Jewish families. Programs directed at Day School families may be adapted to *havurot;* programs for families with preschool children will also be effective with intergenerational participants. Above all, there are numerous suggestions and ideas about how to include Jewish talk and Jewish practice into everyday life. New dimensions have also been given to tried and true methods of bringing families together. This is indeed a strength of the book.

It is evident that the changing structure of Jewish families, the demands on everyone's time, and the desire to have meaningful Jewish experiences have all had a profound influence on JFE. Jewish Family Education is an evolving discipline. At the very least, it has thus far succeeded in bringing interested individuals together for meaningful Jewish experiences. At its most intense, it has succeeded in helping people recognize the value of living a Jewish life in today's world. I am proud to have had some very small part in this enterprise.

So, let us "grow together!"

INTRODUCTION

WHY THIS VOLUME?

Over the past decade, Jewish Family Education (JFE) has taken hold in institutions across the country. Many fine programs have been created and implemented in a variety of settings. Educational programs to train Family Educators and national certification in JFE are now in place. A perusal of offerings at the annual CAJE Conference over the last several years reflects a growing emphasis on Family Education. The Whizin Institute of the University of Judaism stages an annual, multi-dimensional JFE conference.

Clearly, Jewish Family Education is no longer a new frontier, but rather an endeavor that has matured from a "fad" to a "field" of inquiry. It is worthy not only of more creative programming, but also of sophisticated research and evaluation. Different philosophies, concepts, and distinctive methodologies have evolved and new venues have developed. Perhaps most importantly, JFE continues to be a means for enriching Jewish family life.

As the editors of *Growing Together,* we have tried to place this volume in its historical context the development of JFE as a significant aspect of Jewish education worldwide. Yet, *Growing Together* was not revealed at some educational Mt. Sinai and JFE was not born in a particular day. Rather, both are part of a continuing process, evolving over many years and in many places. Thus, we begin this volume with the reflections in Chapter 1 of Janice P. Alper about the changes in JFE over the last decade, a decade which, among other things, has taken us from her book *Learning Together* to our *Growing Together.* In Chapter 2, "Aytzahs and Chochmahs: Practical and Philosophical Advice from the

Experts," we have turned to some leading Jewish Family Educators (Julie Jaslow Auerbach, Ellen Brosbe, Sandy Dashefsky, Jo Kay, Joan Kaye, Vicky Kelman, Esther Netter, and Ron Wolfson) to capture the evolving programmatic *chochmah* (wisdom) of JFE as we move into the decade of the 60s (5760s, that is) in Jewish life.

The word "Growing" rather than "Learning" in the title of this volume reflects the changes in the field of JFE. We believe that Jewish education is part of a more intricate weave of living, learning, believing, and acting Jewishly. "Growing," as John Dewey well understood and asserted, is a generic term that cuts across the entire educational process. When Jewish Family Education was young, it was sufficient simply to get the process started. A one-time program focused on Jewish learning was itself something of a *nes gadol* (big miracle) given all that the Family Educator had to learn about working with multi-generational audiences and the newness of learning together (at least in formal settings) for Jewish families.

As many contributors to this volume note, we have made a great deal of progress. Still, we need a new stretch as Family Educators. To us, the challenge is to make sure that every new program in JFE addresses the following question: Will families participating in this program grow in their knowledge of Judaism and in their ability to sustain meaningful patterns of Jewish celebration and observance as a result of this program? We hope that the resources in this volume will help Rabbis and educators answer the question in the affirmative.

WHAT'S IN THIS VOLUME? THE CONTENT

Growing Together is divided into 13 parts and concludes with a selected bibliography of resources for Jewish Family Education. The 13 parts are: The Present Moment in Jewish Family Education; Family and Adult Learning; Retreat Programs; Community JFE Programs; Day School JFE Programs; Jewish Identity and Heritage; Early Childhood JFE Programs; Family Torah Study; Families, Schools, and Community Partnerships; Israel and Jewish Family Education; Intergenerational Jewish Family Education; Families and Prayer; Ritual for the Jewish Family.

For each section of this volume, Judith Schiller and Jeffrey Schein had the assistance of a member of our editorial committee consisting of Cleveland colleagues Julie Jaslow Auerbach, Mark Davidson, Enid Lader, and Rob Spira.

WHAT'S IN THIS VOLUME? A GUIDING METAPHOR

Many programs in this volume appear with a section of commentary at the end. These contributions come from invited "Rashis": Leora Isaacs (LI), Rabbi Ronald Isaacs (RI), Betsy Katz (BK), and Sally Weber (SW), as well as general commentary of the editors and editorial committee (EC). The appropriate initials by each comment indicates the person who submitted the comment.

The invitation to commentators was issued as a result of the early discussions of the editorial committee. We were searching for a metaphor for the volume. Naturally, as a Jewish group, our thoughts turned to food. We decided that we wanted to collect for this volume a selection of "gourmet" programs, appealing to our most sophisticated educational tastes. But as we all know, culinary artistry is not simply a formula. The creative chef must season to taste, anticipate his audience, etc.

In inviting guest commentators, we hoped to initiate even within this volume a process of programmatic "*midrash*," of helping the reader adapt these programs to the unique context of his or her own learning community. For similar reasons, we have worked with our contributors to emphasize the importance of the evaluation section of their programs. As each contributor re-imagines his/her program in a fuller way, the reader is offered a window to thinking about adapting that program to a different setting as well.

HOW DO I READ THIS VOLUME?

As an anthology, *Growing Together* is intended for multiple readerships. We believe that most readers will find the greater part of this volume valuable, but we also know the wisdom of guided reading as a pedagogic strategy. Below we have suggested the best initial reads we can imagine for different audiences.

For Rabbis: Part I, "The Present Moment in Jewish Family Education"; Part II, "Family and Adult Learning"; Part XII, "Families and Prayer"; Part XIII, "Ritual for the Jewish Family."

For lay leaders and parents: Part IX, "Family, School, and Community Partnerships"; Part XIII, "Ritual for the Jewish Family".

For teachers in synagogues: Part VI, "Jewish Identity and Heritage"; Part IX, "Family, School, and Community Partnerships."

For Day School teachers: Part V, "Day School JFE Programs"; Part IX, "Family, School, and Community Partnerships."

For community personnel (JCC Educators, Central Agency and Jewish Family Service staff, etc.): Part I, "The Present Moment in Jewish Family Education"; Part III, "Retreat Programs."

For Principals and Education Directors: Programmatic selections in each of the parts that are of special interest; Part IX, "Family, School, and Community Partnerships."

For Family Educators: Naturally, the entire volume!

We also note in this regard that many readers of this volume began their involvement in JFE with their own families. Continuing to nurture and enrich our own family and communal lives is a critically important factor in guarding against Family

Educator burnout. For instance, in Part XIII, "Ritual for the Jewish Family," we have included materials that those who are involved in Family Education might find interesting with regard their own informal role as parent, grandparent, or mentoring friend.

GROWING BEYOND GROWING TOGETHER

Programs included in this volume are the result of a three-tier scouting process. We began with letters to over 30 leaders in the field of Jewish Family Education, requesting recommendations for JFE programs that reflect Jewish substance and creativity. Based on their recommendations, initial letters of invitation were sent to potential contributors, requesting preliminary program information. Our editorial committee reviewed all submissions and made determinations about programs that best fit the goals and purposes of the book. Confirming letters were then sent, asking contributors to develop a more detailed write-up of their respective programs, based on specific guidelines. We are certain that at this very moment, programs are being developed that belong in *Growing Together*, but that did not come to our attention.

But God always sends the *refuah* before the *makeh* (the remedy before the plague).

We suggest that those engaged in Family Education in a particular community might want to form a reading/programming support group. Reading selections from *Growing Together* might get you started, but surely in the course of time, your own fine programs would become the basis for sharing and discussion. In that way, we will indeed continue the process of growing together.

A FINAL WORD

Looking back over the past years of ingathering, editing, brainstorming, writing, and refining, we are pleased to see our efforts gel into a cohesive work. The programs contained here present some new directions and points of engagement for families as the next steps in their JFE journeys. We hope our readers enjoy the mix of flavors and spices and feel inspired to add their own touches to this tasty sampling of Jewish Family Education.

Batayavon! B'hatzlachah.

THE PRESENT MOMENT IN JEWISH FAMILY EDUCATION

CONTRIBUTOR: JUDITH S. SCHILLER
ADDRESS: Retreat Institute of the Jewish
Education Center of Cleveland
26001 South Woodland Road
Beachwood, OH 44122
PHONE: (216) 831-0700
E-MAIL: torahmom@aol.com
jschillerri@aol.com

We begin this journey into Jewish Family Education by reflecting on what we have learned about the field over the past several decades. Important questions, from the philosophical to the practical, come to the fore. How has our understanding of JFE and the families with whom we work changed and evolved? What types of experiences and experiments have shaped our thinking? Where have we gained greater clarity about our work, and what still remains a mystery? In what ways have we developed a repertoire of professional skills and techniques with which to engage families in Jewish learning? In this section of *Growing Together,* these questions are addressed by several master educators who have been involved with JFE from its first steps.

Janice P. Alper begins this section. In Chapter 1, "Twenty-five Years of JFE: A Personal Reflection," she reflects on JFE from its infancy to the present. Janice reminds us that we are standing on the shoulders of many trailblazers. She honors the *chalutzim*/pioneers who forged a path for us, and shares a context for understanding how JFE has evolved in its thinking, structure, and practice.

In Chapter 2, "Aytzahs and Chochmahs: Practical and Philosophical Advice from the Experts," we

move to a more *tachlis* mode, with comments by Julie Jaslow Auerbach, Ellen Abrahams Brosbe, Sandy Waldman Dashefsky, Jo Kay, Joan Kaye, Vicky Kelman, Esther Netter, and Ron Wolfson. Each of these experts has logged countless hours in developing and implementing JFE programs. We are delighted that they have been willing to share their insights and practical advice on such matters as techniques on opening and closing a program, how to engage multi-generation audiences, transferring learning to the home, selecting the five key ingredients for a successful program, handling transitions, and more.

In Chapter 3, "From Consecration To Hagigat Limud: Partnerships in JFE," Jeffrey Schein presents his ongoing dilemma about the traditional Consecration service. While Consecration offers a natural opportunity for rich JFE programming, Schein feels that this sacred induction in Jewish learning is too often disconnected from its core meaning and values. This chapter poignantly illustrates how our very conceptualization of JFE has evolved via a bumpy road marked with many unforeseen obstacles. Fortunately, there is light along this complicated path, as Jeffrey leads us toward a new synthesis and resolution that captures the celebration of Jewish learning.

Finally, one turns in this section to the ultimate question. What difference is Jewish Family Education making in the lives of Jewish families? The answer to this question seems to vary from community to community, in part in response to a community's will and capacity to evaluate their Family Education programs in some systematic way.

We are pleased to include here the results of a sophisticated evaluation of JFE by the Chicago community in Chapter 4, "Parents Talk Back To Family Educators: Results of the Chicago Community-wide Survey" by Sharon Seidman Milburn and Marilyn Vincent.

CHAPTER 1

TWENTY-FIVE YEARS OF JFE: A PERSONAL REFLECTION

CONTRIBUTOR: JANICE P. ALPER
ADDRESS: Jewish Educational Services
4549 Chamblee Dunwoody Road
Atlanta, GA 30338
PHONE: (770) 677-9480
E-MAIL: execdir@jesatlanta.org
TARGET : All Readers

My interest in Jewish Family Education was ignited more than 25 years ago when I began my career as a professional Jewish educator. I had the good fortune to meet two people who were truly *chalutzot* (pioneers) in the field — Cheri Koller-Fox and Sherry Blumberg. At the time, Cheri Koller-Fox was the educational director of the Harvard Hillel Children's School in Boston. She initiated a program that provided families, regardless of their backgrounds or professional careers, with opportunities to participate in Jewish learning experiences in a meaningful way.

Sherry Blumberg, who was director of a synagogue school in Sacramento, California, started a "family school." Families — children and adults — came together on a regular basis to learn, study, and celebrate. This was offered as an option to the regular Religious School program.

In both of these models, the participants eventually became responsible for planning their own Jewish learning. The programs were designed to lead to self-reliance and self-direction with regard to Jewish practice. Families became more conscious of the Jewish calendar and cycle of the year. They also began to take responsibility for their own learning and to mobilize others to learn.

One of the other important developments was the Whizin Institute for Jewish Family Education at the University of Judaism. The brainchild of Dr. Ron Wolfson, the Whizin Institute has probably had the greatest impact on the largest number of people in the field. In the early years, the program brought together the leading practitioners in Jewish Family Education to deliberate and develop a lexicon and vocabulary about this field of endeavor. These practitioners, representing a variety of disciplines, became the teachers and mentors of others.

The Whizin Institute has led the way in providing models for training Jewish Family Educators. This week of courses combines serious text study with learning about the family as a system, the process of facilitating change, and objective evaluation. Participants leave the Institute with the confidence to implement and initiate programs in their respective institutions.

Training Family Educators has been at the forefront of a number of community initiatives across the country. The Sha'arim Program in Boston represents a partnership between Hebrew College and the Federation to provide funding for Jewish educators to obtain a certificate in Jewish Family Education. Graduates are placed in Boston area educational facilities as Jewish Family Educators. In Cleveland, 12 full-time Family Educators who graduated with a Masters Degree focused on Family Education now serve area congregations. Courses in Jewish Family Education are included in the graduate programs of Gratz College and the other four communally based institutions of higher Jewish learning, as well as several Rabbinic seminaries.

The National Board of License awards a Certificate in Family Education to those who meet the criteria outlined in its brochure.

One outgrowth of this new consciousness about Family Education was the establishment of Family Education coordinators in central agencies. Another was recognition by national professional organizations, such as the National Association of Temple Educators, which resulted in an active Family Education Task Force. Concurrently, Jewish Family Service agencies began to establish Jewish Family Life Education (JFLE) departments. JCCs also came on board by hiring Family Educators as part of their staffs.

As we moved into the 1990s, more attention was given to evaluation of programs. Questions were formulated as to what the learning outcomes should be, what Jewish practices we were looking at, what environmental factors were involved, and the like. The family was regarded as a dynamic system, ever changing in structure, needs, and values, and as the primary conveyor of Jewish life and living. We began to look for ways to intervene and impact that system in a positive way. The volume *Targilon: Charting a Course in Jewish Family Education* by Leora Isaacs and Jeffrey Schein (JESNA and JRF, 1999), provided significant models for engaging in JFE evaluative work.

Jewish family retreats played a major transformative role in Jewish life. Jewish Experiences for Families (J.E.F.F.) programs, under the guidance of Harlene Appelman, considered nuclear families as clients. Vicky Kelman, author of *Jewish Family Retreats*, introduced the concept of family camp to the Camp Ramah system. Several UAHC camps have also added family camp to their offerings.

The "new" element in family retreats is the interactive learning that takes place. The fun elements of a family going away together to hike, swim, and bicycle are now coupled with the enjoyable process of learning together. Family retreat programs assist families in taking Judaism back to their daily lives as well as connecting them with other families with whom they can celebrate and network. Above all Jewish learning, especially learning leading to practice, becomes more accessible.

Today, Jewish Family Education has taken on dimensions different from those of 20 or even ten years ago. Programs still abound for specific populations, or on certain themes. Now, however, facilitators also look at the family as a unit within the larger system of the community. They are concerned with how the programs can affect practice and connection to Jewish life.

The seeds for more intensive learning began with P.A.C.E. (Parents and Children for Education), initially developed by Jo Kay in the late 1970s. Parents were invited to study the same content (on an adult level) that their children were learning in school. An important part of the program was the interaction between parents and children based on their common knowledge and learning. This program laid the groundwork for intensive Family Education that is consistent with the contemporary lifestyles of participating individuals. It has been replicated in a number of synagogue and Day Schools in a variety of ways.

Over the years, articles and publications have emerged which were designed to help families interact. One of the earliest champions of JFE was *Alternatives Magazine*, edited by Audrey Friedman Marcus, which featured a regular column that showcased creative Family Education programs. Another early effort was *Together*, a series of family magazines, published by the Melton Research Center, edited by Vicky Kelman. Ongoing efforts of this kind continued with *Shofar*, a magazine, which contained suggestions for family activities with each issue (now, regretfully, no longer being published). On the Internet one can turn to JewishFamily.com, a webzine designed for family use. Additionally, many recent Jewish educational materials include suggestions on how to use curricular materials for Family Education.

Perhaps the most charismatic person to work with families is Joel Lurie Grishaver. He has the gift of bringing people together for serious Jewish study in a manner that is both enjoyable and challenging. His programs, such as "Family Bet Din," have been presented to thousands of people in North America and abroad. These presentations have been critical in helping families recognize how much Judaism has to offer them. Grishaver has demonstrated that serious Jewish learning can take place across the generations in all kinds of environments. His publications encourage interaction between school/educational setting, the home, and the synagogue. When the materials are used appropriately, families come together to assess what they have learned, whether it be skills or content, and to interact with others to see how this learning affects their lives and their practices.

Dr. Jeffrey Schein, co-editor of this volume, pioneered thinking about Family Education as part of a larger education system. His guidance of the Cooperating School Network of the Reconstructionist Movement has brought a new dimension to the place of Jewish Family Education in today's Jewish education curriculum. This project has demonstrated that one can influence systemic change by using families as a vehicle for transformation. Dr. Schein, too, learned from the *chalutzot* mentioned earlier. Collectively, we have come an enormous distance since the first surge of excitement about a new kind of education that put the family in the center of the educational process.

CHAPTER 2

AYTZAHS AND CHOCHMAHS: PRACTICAL AND PHILOSOPHICAL ADVICE FROM THE EXPERTS

Responses from: Julie Jaslow Auerbach, Ellen Abrahams Brosbe, Sandy Waldman Dashefsky, Jo Kay, Joan Kaye, Vicky Kelman, Esther Netter, Ron Wolfson

Anyone involved in Jewish Family Education knows that great programs are the result of careful planning and detailed follow-up. However, through experience, Family Educators develop a repertoire of techniques, approaches, and guiding principles, as well as philosophies that become, in a sense, "tricks of the trade." As any great chef knows, those special ingredients and garnishes greatly enhance the dish.

To satisfy our curiosity about what contributes to programmatic quality, we consulted with experts in the field of JFE. We presented questions to them and sought their *aytzah* (advice) and *chochmah* (wisdom). Their responses follow.

Engaging, stimulating beginnings and endings are essential to good JFE programs. What kinds of approaches or techniques do you find helpful in beginning and closing these programs?

Jo Kay

When working with intergenerational groups or with adults in a parallel parent program, I have found it extremely helpful for the parents to know what will be happening. What is the plan? Where will this lesson be going? What will be expected of the parent in the class? Sometimes, the opening activity may not be one a parent finds particularly comfortable or engaging. Knowing what will happen next can keep that parent from turning off completely, or even from getting up and leaving the class.

Writing your plan for the day — your agenda or outline — on the board before the class starts (and reviewing it with the group) is also a great way to help manage your time. An agenda also enables you to guide and curb in a gentle fashion those parents who would like to monopolize the session. By referring back to the agenda, you can stay on track. It is also effective to use the agenda to move the class along by saying, "We still have several items to cover . . . ."

Finally, whether working with class-size groups, grade-wide groups, or even larger groups, I have generally found it helpful to begin and end with a story. It focuses the group at the start, and refocuses the group at the end. It can be a way of summing up, reviewing the points taught, and helping the group to remember and take those points home. Stories personalize the experience and help make what is being taught, or experienced, relevant to the lives of the students (parents and children alike).

Joan Kaye

I always begin JFE programs by congratulating people on coming, and on the effort they made to be there. I tell them how wonderful, special, etc., they are for spending time on Jewish education. I do the same thing again at the end.

At the beginning of a program, I make sure to let people know exactly what is going to happen, and when, during our time together. If it is a parallel program, I tell parents what their children are doing.

In addition to congratulating people again for choosing to spend their time on Jewish education, it is really important to end a program with questions such as, "What have you learned today?" and "Where do you go from here?" These can range from questions about what kinds of conversations they plan to have with their youngsters (on the topic discussed in a parallel program) to packets of materials that might support enriched Jewish celebration (after a holiday workshop). It is essential that each program have built into it both the follow-up for the students to use at home on the material covered that day, as well as suggestions for where they can go to deepen or explore the topic further either on their own or in future programs planned by the institution.

Vicky Kelman and Ellen Abrahams Brosbe
Openings:

Greet 'em at the door. A bunch of balloons tied on the outside or at the door is a great mood setter.

Have name tags ready (or a set-up for people to make their own).

When applicable, have a sign-in sheet to collect names, addresses, and how people heard about the program.

Have activities ready for people to engage in as soon as they arrive (including food, graffiti walls, puzzles, crafts related to the day's theme). Let them work at these until the program actually begins.

If it can be avoided, don't seat participants "lecture style" for study or discussion. Circles almost always work best, as people can see one another and hear one another. Such an arrangement sets an expectation that everyone has something important to say. If participants are sitting on the floor, sit on the floor with them.

Closings:

Conclude with an appreciation circle (each person or family says a "thank-you" or an "I appreciated _____" or "One *brachah* I/we will try to say is _____."

Do a walk-through of the participants' written work or art work, or use some other way to show

off everyone's completed work (including ideas, resolutions, plans).

Evaluation:

Evaluate informally (an appreciation circle is a form of informal evaluation).

Set aside time for written evaluations before everyone leaves (doing this prior to the appreciation circle works well).

Thank everyone for coming and contributing to a successful event.

Write thank-you notes to staff, custodian, and volunteers within 24 hours.

Announce the next date — give out "save the date" postcards.

Sit down and reflect on the program and write your own evaluation. (If you have no time for sitting and writing, record your reflections into a tape recorder as you drive home. Listen to the tape before planning the next program.)

Ask for staff evaluation.

Follow up with a committee/staff debriefing.

Esther Netter

There are key things to do at the beginning and end of JFE programs. Such things as great introductions, personal greeters as people enter, clear handouts or descriptions of what will happen next all make a huge difference. Closing should include a take-home piece to enable the family to "do" something they learned or to "use" something they made. I suggest that families themselves do a closing piece, and then the whole group. Whole group closures can include (depending on size) a whip ("One thing our family learned today is _____."), completing a group mural or project, doing a page in a family journal, singing a concluding song.

Julie Jaslow Auerbach

Music is a natural way to bring people together, to focus them on a topic in a gentle, understated manner and in a non-threatening way. Similarly, a good song can provide excellent closure — and food for lingering melodic thought! Words should always be provided in a song sheet, attached if possible to a packet handed out to the attendees as they arrive at the program. The same song can be introduced at the beginning of the program and then reprised at the end.

Directions and goals should be clearly stated at the outset, giving people a glimpse of what they can expect and setting their thinking on the programmatic path.

At some point during closings, a take-home piece should be provided to participating families. This should include adequate instructions to enable participants to carry on the learning after the program is over. Sometimes that connective thread to the home is as important as the event itself!

In a JFE program, there are often learners of all ages. What kinds of techniques do you find helpful in teaching a multi-generational group (ages six to 60)?

Jo Kay

When planning a multi-generational program, it is very important to think on several levels. What do I want the children to learn? the parents? the younger siblings? Once you have established the goals, you can begin to plan the activities. If there is a text to be studied, the parent might read it to the child, and questions can be answered with pictures or with words. Young children can draw their feelings in reaction to a story, and parents can discuss or write their reactions to the same text.

When encouraging intergenerational groups to think about their families, it is helpful to provide an activity in which even the youngest child can participate, e.g., making a family symbol from pipe cleaners. Such an art project is concrete enough for young children to do, and the discussion can be abstract enough to engage the adults. In both cases, thoughtful work is being done and, consequently, learning will result.

Of course, if you are working with a parallel parent group, it's much easier to address the topic covered in the child's class — on a much higher level — in the parent class. After the groups have studied the same topic on their respective intellectual levels, parents and kids can then come together for an experiential program, which draws on what each group has studied.

Joan Kaye

Our most successful technique, especially when working with parents and teenagers, is to provide a problem to solve or project that enables both groups to accomplish a concrete task together. It is really important in doing this that the project be one that allows all participants to make meaningful contributions, as well as being an inherently worthwhile activity. For example, in a program on "Why be Jewish?", we asked small groups of parents and teens to create an ad to convince a teenager of why he/she should want to be actively Jewish. This technique enabled participants to share their thoughts without risking exposure and led to the creation of a wonderful set of "advertisements."

Esther Netter

To reach learners of all ages, always have activities, written materials, resources on multiple levels — adult and child. Weave activities throughout the program that require adult involvement so that children need to pull their parents and/or grandparents in to participate. Allow for activities that children can do on their own, and even add something that adults may enjoy on their own, too.

Julie Jaslow Auerbach

In the design of JFE programs, I like to work with a committee made up of a cross-section of parents and teachers and representing all the ages we expect to attract.

An interactive program, such as a *Scavenger Hunt* or *Treasure Hunt*, works well to keep generations focused on learning and engaged with each other. During such programs, the children can in fact be "showing and telling" while their parents provide layers of education. Or, the children themselves can become the teachers.

A follow-up take-home piece allows the learning to continue at home, and allows parents to take charge of the education themselves. It is often easier for parents to do things at a convenient time at home on their own, rather than at the event.

We all agree that continuous Jewish learning is a goal of JFE. How can we promote learning beyond the program and transfer of learning into the home?

Ron Wolfson

Provide Scaffolding:

The "take-home" materials help provide what Vicky Kelman has called "scaffolding," the temporary structures that enable parents to build Jewish experiences in the home. Families need encouragement, time, physical and psychological supports, materials, instructions, tapes — all sorts of things that can help them engage in Jewish sources and doing rituals.

Encourage Small Steps:

For many parents, engaging Jewish tradition is frightening and intimidating. For those who live full Jewish lives, it is hard to remember how really difficult and challenging many aspects of Judaism can be, especially to beginners. For this reason, I encourage families to take "small" steps. I want to give them a few things to do so they can get started celebrating Shabbat, get started in providing a home that is a Jewish learning environment. By encouraging small steps, we are saying "Judaism is a lifelong journey."

Jo Kay

It has been my experience that parents are most likely to want to continue studying when they have participated in an ongoing JFE experience. One-shot programs and extravaganzas, which are often exciting and bring families together to experience Jewish activities, in a Jewish setting, with other Jewish families, can be truly valuable and meaningful. However, those same families, although they have had a good time and perhaps created some special memories, will most likely not have had a transformative experience.

To change one's behavior from little or no Jewish study to continuous Jewish study requires an involvement in study over a period of time. It is this process that is ultimately valued, because one can assess, over time, whether meaningful learning has occurred and ascertain a family's desire to continue. Parents studying in a yearlong Family Education program feel that they want to continue what "we have only just begun." I have had parents ask, "Where can I go to continue this study?" "Can you recommend additional books for me to read?" "What classes are offered at the synagogue or elsewhere that would constitute a next step for me?"

Regarding the transfer of learning into the home, it, too, requires a process, learned and experienced over time. JFE classes that are ongoing and intensive have a greater chance of being brought into a family's home life. If Jewish ritual observance is to be sustained, it has to become something that is practiced and supported on a regular basis, and that takes time and a community of learners. A Family Education class that studies over an extended period of time, can naturally become a Havurah, and thereby continue to support one another's study and growth.

Joan Kaye

Here are some ways to promote learning beyond the program and into the home: materials, questions, follow-up phone calls (from professionals and/or peers), pairing novices with more experienced Jewish families, individual (family) goal setting, follow-up programming to share results of attempts at new practices, opportunities for people to "show off" what they have learned, and programs designed specifically to promote home observance.

Esther Netter

Always include a take-home piece (skill, object for use) in each program. Other ongoing ways to support and teach families are encouraging Havurot or twinning families with mentor families.

Sandy Waldman Dashefsky

Continuous learning in JFE is certainly a central and critical goal in meaningfully empowering parents to be able to teach their children. In order to promote learning beyond "the program," we need to create JFE integrated curricular structures that provide layering opportunities beyond "the program." These structures could take a variety of forms. Occasions for ongoing thematic learning for adults and families in our institutions could be provided, as well as diverse opportunities for learning and experiencing Judaism in the home. Initiatives could be divided into various components. For example, a research piece that I am exploring includes a four-part family Shabbat workshop series as part one, with part two consisting of an optional menu of Jewish family/adult education opportunities from which families could choose to participate.

An optional menu might include:

- A four-part JFE series with a focus on parallel adult and children's text study
- A family matching Shabbat program in which families could participate in Shabbat dinners in each other's homes, thus transferring back to the home the Shabbat dinner experience and empowering parents to take a leadership role
- A bi-monthly Friday night young family service consisting of music, storytelling, and Israeli dance
- An individualized Shabbat home learning kit prepared and distributed to families (also available on e-mail)
- A monthly Shabbat Havurah program in the community
- An adult education series
- A community family center library which circulates on a weekly basis, books, magazines, computer resources, and ritual objects
- A *chevrutah* study night or morning
- A project in which the Family Educator guides various families through an individualized plan of learning and action.

As we build an initiative with many points of entry, as well as many directions for continued growth for parents and their children, we must pay careful attention to offering a high quality of instruction and materials. In addition, if parents are to be empowered to teach their children, we must provide many opportunities for positive adult experience with Jewish living and learning. Our families deserve no less.

Julie Jaslow Auerbach

Some techniques for home connections: take-home activities for the entire family, a reading list for further study, questions for thought at home, a follow-up program, pairing families before or after. One thing is clear — the learning must be transferred from the program site to the individual home.

Sometimes it takes a few programs to alert parents to the *possibility* of changing their behavior or expanding on what they are already doing. We often think we've started at the beginning, but it's really the middle, as so many small steps must be taken in advance! Just as Shabbat provides us with a taste of *Olam Haba*, so, too, can carefully crafted connectives, designed for the individual program, provide us with a taste of the learning yet-to-be.

In the four years I have been at Solomon Schechter Day School, I have written *parashah* commentaries for our weekly *Yellow Sheet*. Each commentary has a theme appropriate for families or adults, sometimes connected to an upcoming or recently completed program. Activities are labeled "As a Family" or "As an Adult." These hook the theme of the commentary to things that families can do on their own and outside of school. This on-your-own learning has reached and motivated the community and heightened their awareness of family and adult learning experiences.

If a Family Educator's life and livelihood was on the line and they absolutely had to produce an excellent (program), what winning program would you recommend?

Ron Wolfson

Build programs around what families already like and know how to do.

This principle is best illustrated by the wonderful "reading aloud" programs for Jewish families: "*Sefer Safari*," the "Parent Connection," "Sulam" (see Chapter 14), and others. Most Jewish parents read stories aloud to their young children. It is something every parent already knows how to do, so he/she does not have to learn a new skill. It is also something every parent knows it is important to do. So, by providing good Jewish children's literature to the parent, we are empowering the parent to teach the child simply by the act of reading and discussing the book.

The second aspect of this principle is evident in the popular "extravaganza" programs in Jewish Family Education that take place at venues families enjoy. A great example is "Havdalah at the Zoo," during which families gathered to celebrate Havdalah and then visited the animals at nighttime.

The great power in Jewish Family Education is the ability to engage the family in activities that encourage communication and experiential learning together. I would play this angle up, even in the advertising for family programming. For example, when I called a Shabbat workshop "Turn Friday Night into Family Night," I attracted the highest attendance of any such workshop I offered. Although I was interested in teaching the rituals of Shabbat observance, the perceived benefit of the program was teaching families how to spend family time together. Of course, making time for families to engage each other is precisely one of the most powerful aspects of ritual.

Jo Kay

This is a very difficult question to answer. There is no *one* single program that will be great in every community or equally well facilitated by every Family Educator. Communities differ vastly, as do their educators. What I would recommend is that the Family Educator do a community assessment. Who are your constituents? What do they know and like? What do *they* want from the synagogue, school, or Jewish community? What do they do professionally and for leisure? Then I would recommend that those answers be brought together, side by side, with answers to questions that address the Jewish institution's agenda. What do we want our constituents to learn?

Programs have been extremely successful when educators know their community and those same educators have a hand in creating the program for that community. The best programs are those created by the people running them (or at least, those that have been carefully adapted by the people running the programs).

This is not to say that there are no ready-made programs that can be recommended. Rather, unless the educator has figured out what his/her community is all about, and what he/she as an educator is most comfortable teaching, those ready-made programs will not be as successful as they might be.

Everything requires thought, planning, and hard work. There are no simple, easy, ready-made answers.

Joan Kaye

Forgive me for sounding self-serving, but the "Parent Connection," which I developed, is the program I would recommend. It is easy to do, inexpensive, focused on the home, and, unlike other programs which might be terrific, it exists in written, easy to follow form. It also fits my criteria of being not a one-time program, but an ongoing curriculum. "Parent and Child Education" (PACE) is another excellent choice but, to my knowledge, it doesn't exist in written form.

Esther Netter

I am, of course, biased, but my recommendation for a winning program is a JFE program modeled on what works at the Zimmer Children's Museum of Jewish Community Centers of Greater Los Angeles (of which I am Executive Director). This museum offers an ongoing, safe, encouraging, multilevel Jewish environment for families. Special JFE events, as well as weekly and monthly programs, complement its exhibits. It has built in follow-up programming, and a leadership development track for adults and children. It is pluralistic, creative, and positive. It is relatively new, which gives it the flexibility to be responsive to the needs of families.

The Zimmer Children's Museum maintains a philosophy focused on teaching through discovering. Unlike any other museum, this one allows children to learn in a unique atmosphere and setting in which virtually all of the numerous exhibits encourage the children to touch, explore, and play.

Julie Jaslow Auerbach

In the weekly *parashah* commentary that I write for our *Yellow Sheet*, I include things for families to do at home. This provides a connection between classroom learning and the home, and with their life away from school.

I also have found that programs that hook directly to the classroom are winners. Parents want to know what their children are learning; children want to share. Adding an "adults only" layer — or a family event that all can share — serves to increase each generation's pleasure.

You are the master chef of JFE, but you are limited to five ingredients that make for a gourmet JFE program. What are those five ingredients?

Jo Kay

1. Choose what you love to teach, something that you are personally passionate about.

   If you are excited about a subject, then you will be excited about researching it, learning more about it, and ultimately about sharing it with others. Your personal excitement will be contagious and will be transmitted to your group. Nothing substitutes for genuine love and interest in the subject matter.

2. Know who your community (or class) is and what they are most interested in learning.

   If your community is excited about what is being taught, more than half of your job is already done. The motivation is intrinsic. It comes naturally from them. They are invested in what is being presented, almost as if they have as much at stake in seeing it succeed as does the educator.

3. Set up a non-judgmental system whereby everyone is protected.

   No one is permitted to judge or evaluate others. Participants are taught to speak in "I" and not "You" phrases. Once an atmosphere of trust can be established, open discussions can happen and participants can feel free to ask those "embarrassing" questions that enable them to move ahead.

4. Plan activities that meet the varied levels of experience in the group.

   Everyone should be able to walk away having learned or having relearned something. Take into consideration the fact that parents who are experts in Jewish knowledge and practice may be novice parents, and veteran parents may be at the beginning of their Jewish learning. In this way, you can begin to think about all you should consider in your plans.

5. Plan activities that address the various age levels in your group.

   Have you thought about the children, younger and/or older siblings and the parents, or perhaps even grandparents? How might each age group be able to participate in what you have planned? Are there activities available which young children can realistically do? Are there ideas being presented which will challenge and engage the adults?

Joan Kaye

My five ingredients are: Fun, Safety, New Learning, Emotional Connection, and Empowerment.

Vicky Kelman and Ellen Abrahams Brosbe

Our five ingredients are: a great Jewish text, some thought provoking questions about the selected text, bubbles, knowledge about your participants, and flexibility. The first two ingredients ensure that the program will be built around an important Jewish idea. Bubbles represent fun and a sense of play. Knowing about your participants (i.e., numbers, ages, Jewish backgrounds, family structures, etc.) enables the choice of text and questions and fun to be on target, and nothing works without flexibility.

Esther Netter

The five ingredients for a gourmet JFE programs are:
1. Make it safe and nonjudgmental.
2. Make it multilevel and at levels appropriate to both adults and children.
3. Anchor the JFE program in Jewish tradition, text, and learning. Identify what is Jewish.
4. Make it a positive experience.
5. Build in follow-up. Build in next steps.

Sandy Waldman Dashefsky

My five ingredients for a gourmet JFE program would be:
1. A mixture of a welcoming and non-threatening environment
2. A connecting with families through quality listenings, trying to meet their needs, and using their experiences as a base for the recipe

3. A creative, high quality, caring Jewish space and programming that is at various times inspiring, spiritual, intellectually stimulating, and fun

4. A combination of quality family time and adult learning time, as well as time and opportunity to connect families one to another to help them feel rooted with a growing sense of community

5. Ongoing opportunities for empowering Jewish learning and living, for adults and children, at home and in their community, through materials such as books, videos, magazines, computer resources, and ritual objects, as well as the use of ongoing workshops and classes.

Julie Jaslow Auerbach

Here are my five ingredients for a "gourmet JFE program":

1. Relevance. Every program should include aspects that are relevant to the family's life.

2. Stretch. Something that stretches the adults ever so slightly should always be included.

3. Fun. At least one piece of the event should be fun — play time — for each family member.

4. Arts. Some art form should be included to give participants a chance to express themselves.

5. Lay committee involvement. This is the "secret" ingredient, and its importance cannot be overestimated.

Of which accomplishments of JFE as a field over the past ten years are you most proud?

Jo Kay

As I reflect on the field of JFE over the last ten years, I marvel at how far we have come. When I began working in JFE programs 20 years ago, I felt really alone. There were so few educators experimenting with this work, and we were spread out all over the country. Today, we have Family Education networks, think tanks, institutes, newsletters, program banks, etc., and we have truly begun to collaborate as colleagues in an emerging field. Thus, the things about which I feel most proud are as follows (not in any special order):

• That more and more agencies, bureaus, universities, institutes, etc., are training Family Educators.

• That more and more positions for Family Educators are being created.

• That more and more synagogues, Day Schools, Community Centers, Jewish agencies, etc., see Family Education as an important and necessary form of education to be seriously included in how they teach and how they think.

• That clergy, lay leaders, and educators have begun to see Family Education not as a separate field, but as a framework for thinking about all education.

• That Family Education is spilling over into Israel (see Chapters 41 and 42). That training programs are taking Family Educators to Israel, and that Family Educators are taking families to Israel, and that Israeli educators are involved in developing JFE programs for Israeli families.

• That articles, studies, books, and programs are being written, collected, and published. This body of work will form the baseline research for the field. Not until we have some serious research and writing in this area will this field truly move forward to take its rightful place in the world of Jewish education.

Joan Kaye

In 1986, I was the only Jewish Family Educator working in a central agency. Now there are several dozen and counting. There were no synagogue positions. Now several cities have programs to train and employ full-time synagogue Family Educators. The Whizin Institute currently features a track just for those whose primary synagogue work is Family Education. And a recent look at the employment section of the *Boston Jewish Advocate* revealed more ads for Family Educators than for Hebrew teachers!

I believe the greatest accomplishments are the training programs that have been developed for Family Educators at colleges of Jewish studies, at central agencies, and at the Whizin Institute. What I find most amazing, however, is the way JFE has spread and taken hold in everything from continuity commissions to synagogues to Jewish Community Centers. Unfortunately, there has not been sufficient research (or, probably, time) to measure the actual effects of JFE on families.

Esther Netter

Over the last ten years, JFE has produced the most creative programming. JFE has taught that the child must be viewed in the context of family. JFE has also made "the family" an entity to be dealt with as a whole. JFE focuses our attention on the adult as a learner and gives institutions a new lens through which to view the family.

Sandy Waldman Dashefsky

It has been my good fortune to have been encouraged by my community to create a vision and dream, as well as to plan and oversee a major JFE initiative in Greater Hartford, Connecticut. This was aided by support and funding from 1993 to 1998 from the Jewish Federation's Council on Jewish Continuity. In addition, I have had the honor of teaching and mentoring many professionals and lay leaders in JFE. From my early years in JFE, I strongly believed that for true change to take hold in community institutions, training for professionals and lay leaders in the areas of Family and Adult Education was a critical component. I recognized that new JFE initiatives would demand a high caliber of skilled professionals and lay leadership. Funding of programs would be ineffective if personnel were not in place to design and execute projects. I, therefore, developed a two-year formal academic Family Educator's Certificate Program, through Hebrew College-Hartford Branch, which included courses and day institutes for professional and lay community members. The Certificate Program embodies a broad vision of JFE, which includes: needs assessment, establishment of goals which linked to creative ongoing family and adult educational programming, as well as structures for coaching and mentoring. Moreover, the JFE Training Program worked closely in tandem with other funded projects, especially the Family Educators Initiative (which provided Family Educators to seven synagogue schools and two Day Schools), and produced many avenues for building community and institutional collaboration.

The collaborative work of building partnerships in JFE within and between institutions, a requirement of the Continuity grants and a strong focus in the JFE Certificate Program, has been a most challenging, yet gratifying, achievement for me. This cooperative focus has given rise to many shared resources in the community — shared scholars, artists, and storytellers, as well as a cross-fertilization and support of an array of ideas and joint projects. Moreover, these partnerships have set the stage for broader synagogue change programs within our institutions by forging new structural links among families, congregations and their committees, agencies, and the Federation.

Julie Jaslow Auerbach

I am most proud of how JFE has pushed Jewish educators to think out-of-the-box, to move education beyond the classroom walls and into many unusual and usual settings. Jewish education is no longer in the exclusive domain of the classroom or the synagogue; it has begun to surround us.

Incorporation of the arts is also a source of pride. Many a family program has involved a storyteller, musician, puppeteer, dancer, or graphic artist.

What are the "new frontiers" of JFE? What is the "current wilderness"?

Jo Kay
Frontiers:

There are JFE programs which have made their way to synagogue and Day School boards, curriculum committees of these schools, into the curriculum of Jewish colleges and universities, into the work of Jewish bureaus and agencies, creating new energy and new thinking. JFE programs are addressing the Russian immigrant population, the grandparent populations (those nearby and those living too far away to be part of such programs). They are being used as outreach opportunities to unaffiliated families and interfaith families. They have been used to bring several segments of one community together or to bring several communities together. They have even begun to address the need for *K'lal Yisrael*. JFE programs, in one form or another, are finding their way into teen programs, teen trip programs, and teen Israel programs. They have focused on family issues and family life issues and how Judaism relates to them.

Wilderness:

Still waiting to be addressed, in a serious manner, are the same issues with which many of our congregations are struggling today. How can Family Education help us to meet the needs of our gay and lesbian populations and their children? What kinds of JFE programming can help sensitize our greater population to the needs of this community? Are there new rituals, which families can begin to create to address the needs of this population? How are they as families welcomed into our JFE programs today?

Has JFE programming been a support vehicle for the many divorced and/or intermarried families? Has our attention to family sensitized us to the non-traditional family in a way, which attempts to lessen their "load"? Or, have we added pressures to their already difficult situations? (Family Bar/Bat Mitzvah programs, when there is a divorce involved, can sometimes cause more pain than intended.) What JFE programs have been created to address the needs of battered wives, abused children, families struggling with drug and alcohol problems? The areas in which JFE can, and perhaps one day will, have a positive impact are still uncharted. When we realize that even within the areas where inroads have been made there are still miles to go, we can appreciate just how much wilderness is still to be cultivated.

Joan Kaye
Frontiers:

The new frontiers of JFE involve both breadth and depth. In the first category are:

• Taking successful programs in one community and reformatting them for another community (J.E.F.F. is a good example of this)
• Development of programming for special populations, such as single parents, teens, grandparents, and intermarried
• Partnerships with secular organizations, such as those taking place in Cleveland. In terms of depth, I see: moving parent evaluation from the institu-

tion to the home, as St. Louis is doing; moving from one-shot programs to parallel or ongoing learning for families; development of family schools, both within and instead of supplementary schools; increasing demand for evaluation; intensive adult education; and, finally, synagogue change as a result of JFE.

Wilderness:

The current wilderness, I believe, is the result of a field that has burgeoned without the appropriate underpinnings. Despite some excellent training programs, the demand for trained Family Educators greatly exceeds the current supply. I foresee this becoming even more of a problem as more and more people jump on the JFE bandwagon. We have lots of hunches, but we still don't really know how JFE affects Jewish identity; we need funding for longitudinal research studies. There is a tremendous dearth of written Family Education programs and curricula. While, for instance, there are probably hundreds of parallel programs for third graders taking place, I see in my work most third grade family teachers creating family programs from scratch. There are no functional mechanisms for sharing materials, no financing for people who could develop them for others. Finally, there is no clear understanding of what JFE is, or could be, among the great majority of practitioners. In too many cases, JFE programs are added to synagogue or JCC offerings because they are currently in vogue and not because the institution sees the tremendous potential of working with families as units. One family program per grade becomes the goal rather than the starting point for creating true family learning and involvement.

Vicky Kelman and Ellen Abrahams Brosbe
Frontiers:

• Professional Development
• Case studies of Family Education (for example, a group of Family Educators from the BJE in San Francisco is developing a set of ten case studies in Family Education for which a facilitator's guide is also being developed)

- Collaborative study groups (for example, monthly, three-hour collaborative study groups for educators involved in Family Education)
- Israel (for example, study seminars in Israel for Family Educators, subventions for family trips to Israel)

Wilderness:
- Professional development that is driven by goals and thinking about the big picture, and not just program driven
- Big Jewish Ideas need to be the core of what we provide for families.
- Israel trips for families should be subsidized to the same extent as trips for teens and adult missions.
- Recognition that Family Educator is a professional position and career goal
- The impression is that Family Education is for families with young children; more needs to happen for families with teens.
- The need for community professionals (Rabbis, Cantors, educators, etc.) to take a "family perspective" when dealing with family life cycle events. For example, they should include all family members and think about the impact the event (whether happy or difficult) might have on each family member and on the family as a unit.
- The need to develop the kinds of Family Education programs that address the tough times in family life, as well as the happy/holiday times. (For example, four agencies in the San Francisco area co-sponsor "Grief & Growing," a weekend retreat for bereaved families.)

Esther Netter

JFE new frontiers include focusing more on the adult as learner, on creating an advanced level, and training for JFE professionals. The wilderness still includes too many one-shot quick programs that lack follow-up. We also know that institutional change takes time and that educators need to be committed and patient.

Sandy Waldman Dashefsky

As we reflect on the future, a second component within this new JFE infrastructure could be a focus on developing a closer, personal connection with families, meeting with constituents one by one, in order better to satisfy needs, as well as providing opportunities for community building. Suggestions for establishing more personal bonds with individuals might include developing Family Educators as "JFE guides" to connect with individuals/families through personal meetings (possibly in homes), to meet to develop individual Jewish family blueprints, as well as to link families with other households in the community. In addition, as part of the new JFE frontier, we may need to think about a broader, more individualized menu approach in order to provide for the manifold needs of our constituents. Creation of Havurot and/or study groups of newly marrieds, expectant parents, single parent families, divorced parents and their children, parents with teens, might meet these distinctive life cycle based needs.

In addition, all of our JFE work needs to be grounded in the area of evaluation. Evaluation, in my view, is an important new frontier, as well as a current wilderness. Only recently are serious components and funding for evaluation of JFE initiatives receiving attention in some communities. Moreover, there needs to be an increased awareness of the significance of evaluation, as well as training provided in the areas of pre-testing and in formative and summative evaluation procedures. As we move forward in new JFE frontiers, the words of Theodor Herzl impel us: *Im tirzu, ayn zo agadah*" (If you will it, it is no dream).

Julie Jaslow Auerbach
Frontiers:
These are the new frontiers we need to address:
- How best to educate Day School parents and kids
- How to bring parents with scant knowledge up to the level of their peers — and even of their children
- How to create widespread literature programs in which elementary school kids and parents read and discuss together (see Chapter 14, "Sulam: Ladders To Literature," for one such program).
- How to make use of — and connect parents to — Jewish texts, both in family learning situations and as sources of family strength

The biggest frontier, which is also a wilderness, is finding the right time for busy parents to engage in learning on their own.

Typically, in a JFE program, there are learners of different backgrounds and experience. How do we create a level playing field that enables everyone, from the uninitiated to the yeshivah graduate, to participate comfortably?

Jo Kay

There are several techniques that might be helpful in dealing with this issue. It is, first of all, important to provide all participants with copies of the text being studied in Hebrew, English, and in transliteration. These texts can be reviewed together as a class.

We need to be careful about how we phrase our questions. None should require a great deal of background to answer, nor should they prohibit someone with an extensive background from responding. Everyone in the class should feel that they have something valuable to contribute and that each has something to learn from one another.

Family Educators can present the class with new and creative commentaries/interpretations of the texts, alongside the traditional ones, which perhaps the *yeshivah* graduate may not have confronted. As teachers, we must value all responses and perspectives as meaningful and worthy of being heard and held. Everyone has a right to his/her own perspective. Family Educators can teach the pluralistic values of respect, tolerance, and understanding.

If we look at texts both as Jewish religious writing and as literature to be analyzed, everyone can find a way into the material. If we relate the texts being studied to our lives today, we can ask such questions as: What does this text have to say about our society? about our work? about our families? about ourselves? Ask members of the class to share their personal expertise. How does being a lawyer help you better understand this Talmudic case? What would our court system today have to say about how to decide this case? How does Jewish law differ from civil law? How does your education

as a doctor, philosopher, psychologist, etc., shed light on what we are studying?

Esther Netter

Through the Zimmer Children's Museum, we have learned that in order to be inclusive of Jews of all backgrounds and knowledge levels, things should be presented that require no previous knowledge, but still provide depth. There are also materials available for the advanced learners.

Julie Jaslow Auerbach

This is a tough question! Perhaps it can be answered by providing a novel twist to an old theme. We level the playing field when the JFE program hooks into the classroom and allows families to work on their own with the subject matter. When those with greater skills become planners for those with lesser skills, once again the field is leveled.

A program often has different pieces to it. Yet, we want participants to experience the program as flowing. What are some techniques for handling transitions within a program?

Jo Kay

Generally, what I have tried to do is to have planned transitions and segues. That is, as we move from one segment to the next, a task is presented which initiates the move. Following are a series of techniques I have used at one time or another:
- Count off from 1 to 4 (all number 3s go to this space, etc.)
- Distribute colored task cards. All blue cards go to table number 1, etc.
- Find someone with the same color card and form a group.
- Parents and kids have each been studying a text. Turn the page over and if you have "Rebecca" written on the back, go to the left corner. If you have "Sarah" written on the back, go to the right corner, etc.
- Parents and kids have been studying various prayers. After some discussion in family groups, form groups of three or four families each. Place

signs on each table around the room that indicate various types of prayers (prayers of thanksgiving, of petition, of peace, etc.). As a family, decide into which category your prayer fits, then go and sit at that table. Share your thoughts with the other families at your table.

Vicky Kelman and Ellen Abrahams Brosbe

Pacing and organizing: If an event involves lots of movement and many things going on, it helps to have staff members wear special hats (the wilder or the more obvious the better) so they can be located in the crowd. Identifiable T-shirts work too, but hats are more effective.

Esther Netter

Programs do not need to be perfectly choreographed; they need to allow for different families and ages to be flexible and to be accommodated. Programs do not need to be linear in sequence. Children can pick and choose activities in a more random way if, at the end, all the activities come together. As long as distinct program components make sense on their own, it is fine to move from one thing to the next. Timing and scheduling are important, but, in my opinion, perfect transitions are not.

Julie Jaslow Auerbach

A schedule given out at the beginning of a program prepares people for what will follow. Announcements and directions are very important, too. At a recent family program at Solomon Schechter Day School, we used the hall bells to signal transitions and made preparatory announcements over the loudspeaker.

Like any good classroom teacher, a skilled Family Educator can pick up on cues from students and segue with ease into the next part of a program. Often the transition words are right there!

CONCLUSION

These are but a few of the questions addressed to our experts, and this has been but a summary of their responses. Questions arise out of planning and carrying out JFE programs. So do answers and insights and new techniques.

CHAPTER 3

FROM CONSECRATION TO HAGIGAT LIMUD: PARTNERSHIPS IN JFE

CONTRIBUTOR: DR. JEFFREY SCHEIN
ADDRESS: Cleveland College of Jewish Studies
26500 Shaker Boulevard
Beachwood, OH 44122
PHONE: (216) 464-4050
E-MAIL: jschein@ccjs.edu
TARGET : Rabbis, Cantors, Principals, and
Family Educators

I am not a fan of the Consecration service. I'm guessing anyone reading a volume about Family Education would share my reservations about Consecration ceremonies during which children are separated from their parents, recite the *"Shema,"* and receive a miniature Torah. Consecration is a highly symbolic moment, which underscores in a dramatic way the nature of the partnerships that guide Jewish education. Parents "watching," "applauding," or *"shepping nachas"* is, to the taste of most Family Educators, a far too passive form of ritual enactment to set the stage for all future Jewish education. I will happily note later new adaptations of the Consecration ritual, and share some of my own efforts to come to terms with the ceremony.

My struggles with Consecration span the several decades since my ordination. Even as I have observed colleagues adding family elements to the ceremony (parents and children shopping for material together and then making a Torah mantle, parents as well as children reciting the *"Shehechiyanu,"* grandparents being invited to the *bimah*), I remained less than satisfied. I think there are four

separate "problems" with Consecration. Each of these is outlined below.

1. The name. In truth, "Consecration" seems to be a Christian term brought into Jewish usage. I have learned to live with it. It's more palatable to me than "Confirmation." The etymology of "connecting to the sacred" or making "sacred" is powerful. I love the world "consecrate" when I hear it in the Gettysburg address. But the best of old French is still not Hebrew. I have often wondered whether *"Hakdashat Banim"* (sanctifying the children) could, after some initial awkwardness, take root as the Hebrew equivalent of Consecration.

2. The setting. Neither Simchat Torah (too *fraylich*/joyous and too crowded with other activities) nor Chanukah (with its dual etymology of education and commitment) work well for me as a time of Consecration, though I am hard pressed to explain why.

3. The tiny *Sefer Torah*. I tire of the adult reminiscences of having kept the Torah under a pillow for a few weeks and then rediscovering it 12 years later when they were getting ready to leave for college.

4. As mentioned before, the staging of the ceremony — Rabbi at the center and parents at the periphery — is very complicated symbolically. This past year, my own Havurah in Cleveland had grown enough young children for us to consider some sort of "Consecration" ceremony. I haven't come to peace with the ceremony yet, but thinking along with some of the parents about what kind of ceremony would be appro-

priate has at least moved me to another level of concern. Below you will find a description of our ceremony.

Called "*Hagigat Limud*" (celebration of Jewish learning), our ceremony took place on Tu B'Shevat. We began the planning process too late to do the ceremony on either Simchat Torah or Chanukah. But, as a group, we became attached to Tu B'Shevat and its tree imagery as the spiritual locus for honoring our children's learning. Children as trees, capable of growth on their own with the proper nurturing soil, pleased the John Dewey in me. And our theme for the Friday service became the lovely line from the Kabbalat Shabbat Psalm 92, "*Tzadik k'tamar yifrach*" (the righteous will grow like a palm). That *pasuk* (verse) helped choreograph the service as well. Children were taught to jump up and blossom every time they heard the word *yifrach* in the song. In the family Shabbat gathering the week before the *Hagigat Limud*, parents took some time to share with their children one way the children had — in their parents' eyes — grown in righteousness since Rosh HaShanah. Families then make a *tzadik k'tamar* tree with the whispered expressions of parent to child of how the child has grown in righteousness this past year serving as the leaves of the tree.

The committee planning the event gave careful thought to the gift that would be given to the parents. If we wanted the ceremony to symbolize partnership, we needed to address directly the parents' role as nurturer of the family unit. We ended up presenting parents with a copy of *Shirim Uvrachot*, the volume in the Reconstructionist *Kol*

Haneshamah series dedicated to home celebration.

We also wanted to make sure that the whole congregational, intergenerational family was included in this event. In small part, this came from their singing Debbie Friedman's "*L'chi Lach*" to the children and families. More powerfully, it came about because following the *Hagigat Limud* (itself a complex event of Kabbalat Shabbat, potluck Shabbat dinner, and an "early service"), there was a study session for the entire community called "Your Metaphoric Children: Community Responsibility for Jewish Education." Thirty-five congregants — none directly related to the children who had been honored as part of the *Hagigat Limud* — stayed to engage in the text study. This study introduces the *Targilon: A Guide to Charting a Course in Family Education* by Leora Isaacs and Jeffrey Schein.

And what of the miniature Torahs? We did give them to the children. But we made it known immediately that these should be brought each Shabbat to services. We have several round tables in the back of the sanctuary and, on each Shabbat, the children roll their Torah scrolls to the section of Torah we are reading from that Shabbat. After they locate the beginning of the portion in their scrolls, we talk and read about the Torah portion — a wonderful kind of parallel to what the adults are doing at the same time.

The transformation of Consecration into *Hagigat Limud* will undoubtedly present us with new challenges and limitations. But, for now at least, it feels like a more spiritually and Jewishly authentic expression of what we want for our children and families.

CHAPTER 4

PARENTS TALK BACK TO FAMILY EDUCATORS: RESULTS OF THE CHICAGO COMMUNITY-WIDE SURVEY

CONTRIBUTOR: DR. SHARON SEIDMAN MILBURN
ADDRESS: **Department of Child and Adolescent Studies California State University, Fullerton 800 North State College Drive Fullerton, CA 92834**
PHONE: **(714) 278-2930**
E-MAIL: smilburn@fullerton.edu

CONTRIBUTOR: MARILYN VINCENT
ADDRESS: **Community Foundation for Jewish Education of Metropolitan Chicago 618 S. Michigan Avenue Chicago, IL 60605**
PHONE: **(312) 913-1818, ext. 311**
E-MAIL: malkahv@aol.com

BACKGROUND

The Community Foundation for Jewish Education of Metropolitan Chicago (CFJE) was one of the first Jewish education organizations to recognize the tremendous importance and impact of family-based programs. Consequently, CFJE has given a high priority to Jewish Family Education programs: those activities in which children and parents participate together to acquire Jewish learning and enhance Jewish family life. The CFJE has spent almost a decade developing an extensive set of curricular materials and a Jewish Family Education program bank for Family Educators. In addition, the CFJE Department of Family Education provides professional support to Principals and Jewish educators through professional growth sessions and planning support, in order to promote understanding of the unique practices, principles, and issues associated with facilitating Jewish family life.

Subsidies are provided by the CFJE to affiliated schools in order to assist in the creation of JFE programs and experiences. The CFJE is a support foundation of the Jewish Federation of Metropolitan Chicago, and individual synagogues receive Congregational Enrichment Grants from the Federation that may also be used for JFE.

COMMUNITY-WIDE EVALUATION OF FAMILY EDUCATION PROGRAMS

As is often the case in educational settings, past evaluation of JFE programs in Chicago was largely based on anecdotal comments and responses from parents to brief questionnaires. These informal evaluations were successful in demonstrating that many parents enjoyed Family Education, and that some programs were appreciated more than others. However, these did not answer the basic question, "What impact has JFE had on families?"

The appointment in 1996 of William J. Rubin as the Executive Director of the CFJE brought a new commitment to evaluate agency programs through independent studies and analysis, and the Department of Family Education was the first to begin the program evaluation process. Marilyn Vincent, the Director of the CFJE Department of Family Education, engaged in discussions about this project with Jewish educators and researchers throughout the nation (including professionals from the Whizin Institute, JESNA, the Network for Research in Jewish Education, CAJE and the Merkava Institute). In addition, Ms. Vincent created the CFJE Family Education Survey Principals Task Force to contribute to the evaluation process. Ultimately, the CFJE commissioned the Merkava Institute, a non-profit organization dedicated to "Researching the Jewish Future," to conduct a detailed survey of CFJE affiliated synagogue schools. Linda Seidman, the director of the Merkava Institute, engaged Dr. Sharon Milburn to serve as the principle investigator for this project.

Dr. Milburn, Ms. Seidman, and Ms. Vincent worked with the CFJE Principals Task Force, to develop a unique questionnaire assessing experiences with JFE, resulting attitudes and behaviors, and priorities for Jewish beliefs and practices. (The latter set of survey items was derived from previous research on the relationship between Jewish educational practices and parents' values and priorities conducted by Dr. Milburn and the Merkava Institute. For more information, see "Which Comes First: Jewish Values or Jewish Education?" in the Spring 1999 volume of the *Journal of Jewish Education*).

All 46 CFJE affiliates with ongoing Family Education programs for elementary school students were invited to participate in the survey process. Thirty-eight schools from the Reform, Conservative, and Reconstructionist movements undertook this commitment. The enthusiasm with which the Principals and parents approached this project is evidenced by the unusually high response rate for surveys of this type. Over 2000 surveys were returned, with an average response-rate for participating organizations of 32%.

SURVEY RESULTS

We were very excited by the findings of this study, which clearly indicate parents' high regard for Jewish education. Parent responses to the Chicago survey reflected their strong desire for quality religious education for their children. In fact, parents' most frequently stated reason for joining a synagogue was their children's need for reli-

gious education. Ninety-six percent of the parents believed that religious education is an important part of their children's life, and over three-fourths agreed that JFE was an important part of Jewish education.

Family Education Overall

The central goal of JFE, like any other Jewish educational program, is to promote continuity of Jewish values and practices. Therefore, the most exciting finding in the Chicago Family Education Survey was that 85% of the parents agreed, based on their own experiences, that "Family Education is an effective way to pass Jewish values and practices on to their children." Seventy-nine percent of these parents reported that "JFE shows their children that Judaism is valuable because it allows parents and children to participate in Jewish activities together."

Past work on Jewish continuity has consistently emphasized the importance of identification with Jewish organizations and synagogues. Consequently, a central goal of JFE is the strengthening of participants' ties to the synagogue and greater Jewish community. The findings show that Chicago's JFE programs are effective at meeting this goal for both parents and children. Seventy-three percent of the parents reported that their children feel a greater sense of connection to the Jewish community as a result of JFE, and 62% reported an increase in their own sense of belonging. In a related finding, the majority of parents believe that JFE has made both their children and themselves more comfortable in synagogue settings.

Specific Family Education Topics

One of the central goals of most JFE programs is to enhance participants understanding and observance of Jewish holidays. Therefore, it was particularly gratifying to note that 80% of the parents believed that JFE had made the holidays more meaningful to their children. In fact, two-thirds of the parents agreed that these programs had also made the holidays more meaningful for themselves, and had actually expanded or enhanced their holiday observances.

In addition, when participants were asked about their interests for future JFE activities, they were most interested in additional programs regarding Jewish holidays. This is despite the fact that the holiday calendar is already well represented in Chicago JFE curricula. This desire corresponds to participants' personal priorities (assessed in the Jewish practices and beliefs section of the survey), which demonstrated the importance that these parents placed on family-based life cycle and holiday activities.

Similarly, we were pleased with our finding that 73% of the parents reported that JFE programs improved their children's understanding of the meaning of becoming Bar/Bat Mitzvah. We were surprised and delighted to find that 63% of the parents also reported that these programs had enhanced and expanded their understanding of the meaning of becoming Bar/Bat Mitzvah. Even more exciting, the majority of parents agreed that these JFE programs encouraged their children to continue their Jewish education after becoming Bar/Bat Mitzvah. This suggests that JFE may be an effective way to address Jewish educators' ongoing challenge of retaining students through the high school years and beyond.

Chicago JFE programs consistently incorporate Hebrew words and phrases. However, there was previously no concrete evidence that this strategy was effective. In this survey, 73% of the parents agreed that JFE increased their family's knowledge of common Hebrew expressions.

In an educational setting, there is always concern about the application of learning beyond the classroom. One of the original reasons for creating family-based educational programs was to promote the integration of Jewish learning into daily life. The survey suggests that JFE is generally effective in this area, as the majority of parents agreed that JFE expanded the family's ability to relate Jewish knowledge to everyday life. These parents also agreed that JFE encouraged the family to engage in further discussion and study of Jewish issues.

NEXT STEPS

The CFJE Family Education Survey clearly documents the effectiveness of JFE programs,

both in improving participants' emotional connection to Jewish organizations and practices and in increasing Jewish knowledge and understanding. This supports the continuation and expansion of these programs, and the allocation of communal funding to them. Findings such as these should continue to prioritize JFE on the community agenda.

At the end of the survey, parents were invited to comment about any aspect of their JFE experiences. These anecdotal comments clearly support the positive perceptions described above, and emphasize the sense that shared parent-child learning embodies the best of both Jewish religious practice and learning. As one respondent stated, "The best part of Family Education is learning side by side with my children, and using this knowledge over and over again at home." Future JFE activities will seek to increase this impact of Family Education on personal practice.

While the findings demonstrated that most programs were effective, parents' responses to some topics (such as holidays and Bar/Bat Mitzvah) were overwhelmingly positive. Other programs, such as those addressing Israel, received moderately positive responses. Fifty-five percent of the parents believed that JFE had increased their family's knowledge of Israel. Currently, there are many excellent JFE Israel programs, some of which focus on Tu B'Shevat and Israeli Independence Day. We believe that an emphasis on integrating Israel through the year may make a greater impact.

However, real trips to Israel are more effective than simulated programs for families about Israel. The CFJE Department of Family Education is taking steps to encourage specialized JFE Israel Trips. A recent Melitz publication about the difference between a *Family* Trip to Israel and a *JFE* Trip to Israel will be disseminated to Chicago Rabbis, Family Educators, and Principals. (See Chapter 41 in this volume, "Why Is This Israel Trip Different from All Other Trips?") Resources, materials, and workshops will also be developed in order to prepare and encourage Chicago congregations and day schools to plan JFE trips. The CFJE Department of Family Education is working in conjunction with experts in Israel who specialize in this new and exciting area of JFE Israel trips.

Responses regarding social action were the most disappointing and puzzling portion of the survey. Only 43% of the respondents believed that JFE programs had enhanced their families' awareness of community needs, and 40% that JFE programs had expanded family participation in *Tikkun Olam*. Chicago hosts many high quality JFE programs related to social action. In part, these statistics may reflect the fact that only some schools currently incorporate these topics in their JFE programs. However, this is clearly a curricular area that requires additional attention.

SHARING THE FINDINGS WITH THE JEWISH COMMUNITY

One of our most important goals is to share these exciting results with the greater Jewish community. Initially, Dr. Milburn and Ms. Seidman presented the preliminary findings to CFJE affiliated Principals and the CFJE Board of Directors. In October 2000, the final written report was completed and was then widely distributed to Jewish educators and institutions. (For a copy of the report, contact Marilyn Vincent.) In addition, the Merkava Institute created individualized reports for specific congregations detailing the responses from their congregants, and explaining the similarities and differences between their population and the general Chicago responses. (These reports were available to the Principals upon request.)

Marilyn Vincent, the Director of the CFJE Department of Family Education, will continue to utilize these results in the department's work with school Principals, congregation lay committees, boards of directors, and other educators. This survey will guide the development of future curricular materials and decisions about JFE programming. At a time of concern about the future of Judaism in America, the CFJE continues to develop a critical path to reestablish and strengthen the family as the center of Jewish identity formation. Jewish Family Education can meet the challenges of engaging both parents and children in the integration of Jewish values and practices into the lifestyle of the family.

FAMILY AND ADULT LEARNING

CONTRIBUTOR: DR. JEFFREY SCHEIN
ADDRESS: 26500 Shaker Boulevard
Beachwood, OH 44122
PHONE: (216) 464-4050
E-MAIL: jschein@ccjs.edu

Betsy Katz begins her chapter "What We Know about Adult Education" with the following vignette:

One hundred years ago and more, a man would approach his Rebbe and say, "Rebbe, don't you worry about my children. I'll take care of them. I can teach them. I want you to teach me." For decades of this century, the man and woman approaching the Rabbi would say, "Rabbi, don't worry about me. Just take care of my children. Teach them." More recently there is a new type of exchange taking place. "Rabbi," the man and woman would say, "teach my children and teach me, too. I want to learn, and I want to help you teach my children and grandchildren." (*What We Know about Jewish Education*, edited by Stuart L. Kelman, Torah Aura Productions, 1992, p. 97)

Of course, every tale has its *midrash*. In this instance, the *midrash* belongs to the Rabbis and educators who need to work with this new generation of more willing, receptive children and adults who are looking to "learn together." In this part of *Growing Together*, we explore several different levels of the complex relationship between family and adult learning. We note initially how different conceptualizations of Family Education can either underscore or minimize the relationship between adult education and Family Education. Approaches to Family Education that emphasize the importance of parallel learning sessions for children and adults will challenge the Family Educator to think clearly about the learning needs of adults. Approaches to Family Education that keep the family unit learning together *as a unit* will be less immediately attuned to the distinctiveness of the adult learner.

The challenge of having learners from ages three to 60 all being part of family programs has been addressed by our experts in Chapter 2, "Aytzahs and Chochmahs: Practical and Philosophical Advice from the Experts." There, leaders in the field each shared a technique that triggers intergenerational chemistry, while the learning still remains accessible to participants at different levels. We expand these insights now by adding that there are at least three different responses to the challenge of multiple age groups in Family Education:

1. Separating the learners for significant periods of time.
2. "Splitting the development difference" (e.g., finding ways of communication that might be appropriate for a 12-year-old and when ten-year-olds and their parents are learning together).
3. Utilizing "transparent" methodologies (storytelling, music, art, etc.) that are less conceptually dense, and that allow different age learners to read their own meanings and interpretations into what is being offered. The volume *Intergenerational Religious Education* by James W. White (Religious Education Press, 1988) is particularly helpful in developing appropriate methodologies for intergenerational learners.

There is a significant policy level at which the impetus for family and adult learning also intersect. In Chapter 5, "Between Continuity and Renaissance: Adult and Family Jewish Learning," Jeffrey Schein explores the origins of family and adult learning and discusses the present status of JFE within the broader context of evolving Jewish policy. That chapter examines the sometimes subtle, sometimes blatant shifts in communal priorities for Jewish education, and how these shifts might affect JFE.

At a programmatic level, the editors believe that family, adult, and children's learning can in theory be blended together successfully. For this reason, we are particularly excited to present Chapter 6, "Integrating Family, Adult, and Children's Learning: The Bnai Keshet Program," in which David Weinstein shares in great detail this values-centered approach to spiritual peoplehood. Each of the individual programs that make up this curriculum begins in the child's classroom, involves the adults in independent learning, and culminates in a set of three family programs for students in Grades 3 to 7. The successful integration of family, adult, and child-centered learning is the hallmark of this program.

In Chapter 7, "Reflections on Adults in the Bnai Keshet Program," Rabbi Dan Ehrenkrantz considers the differences between adult learning that is situated within a school and within the Family Education context and the more familiar synagogue contexts for adult learning.

Finally, in Chapter 8, "A Minyan of Techniques for Engaging the Adult Jewish Learner," Lois Zachary, one of the leaders in the field of adult Jewish learning, offers practical advice on how the Family Educator might more effectively engage the adults who are part of Family Education programs. Her techniques will help the Family Educator further develop his/her craft.

CHAPTER 5

BETWEEN CONTINUITY AND RENAISSANCE: ADULT AND FAMILY JEWISH LEARNING

CONTRIBUTOR: DR. JEFFREY SCHEIN
ADDRESS: Cleveland College of Jewish Studies
26500 Shaker Boulevard
Beachwood, OH 44122
PHONE: (216) 464-4050
E-MAIL: jschein@ccjs.edu
TARGET: Rabbis, family educators, community planners

What will be the place of Jewish Family Education on the Jewish communal agenda of the twenty-first century? Will it be considered as significant a priority — worthy of investing communal energy and funds — as it clearly has been throughout the 1980s and 90s? Such questions are natural for Jewish Family Educators to ask. Concern about future *parnassah* (funding), an ongoing opportunity to perfect a craft that requires decades of practice, and a deeply ingrained skepticism that Jewish priorities and funding patterns can be "faddish," all add a touch of gray to the heads of advocates for Jewish Family Education.

To refine our sense of context, we note that Jewish Family education in no small measure flew into Jewish education on the wings of the continuity agenda between 1985 and 1995. The documents of the continuity agenda were punctuated by words such as "identity" and "journey." Family Education was easily and naturally aligned with these concerns.

But what happens when the communal agenda itself changes? Within the last few years, many changes in communal structure (witness the replacement by the United Jewish Communities of the old Federation structure, the continued maturation of JESNA, etc.) have led to the unfurling of a new banner for communal Jewish life: that of Renaissance. Jonathan Woocher, Executive Vice President of JESNA, suggests that the primary goal of the Renaissance agenda is "not a program, much less a department in an organization, but a vision of Jewish community built out of Torah, *chesed,* and *tzedek.*"

Family Education does not jump from the pages of these "Renaissance" documents the way it did from "Continuity" planning tomes. As evidenced in the above statement by Jonathan Woocher, there is even a degree of suspicion about the value (or at least the impact) of programs. "Literacy" and "adult learning" are the more frequent catchphrases. In a way, this is unsurprising and even pleasing to any Jewish educator. The mark of a Renaissance person is wide knowledge, and what better challenge for Jewish educators than to create the conditions and resources for such wide and deep Jewish knowledge.

Does a typical JFE program provide a depth of knowledge and literacy? The honest answer is no. We came into Jewish education brandishing new programmatic ideas. Our calling card was our ability to connect with and engage Jewish families through new, exciting programs, both formal and informal. Perhaps we didn't ask tough enough questions about what actual knowledge people walked away with from our programs. Nor were we yet sophisticated enough in evaluation theory and practice (though recent studies in Chicago, Cleveland, and Boston have changed this dramatically) to demonstrate that these programs made a difference in the lives of Jewish families beyond the pleasant hour or so they might spend with us on a Sunday morning.

There is a conceptual challenge as well to which the better part of this chapter now turns. That challenge is to map out the relationship between family learning and adult learning. Are they separate concerns? What kind of links are created between family and adult learning within the rubric of "lifelong Jewish learning"?

FAMILY AND SEEKER DRIVEN ADULT LEARNING

We can begin to develop a more sophisticated sense of the relationship between adult and family learning if we follow the lead of the 1995 Jewish Community Federations study of Jewish identity and continuity. The study distinguishes between two different kinds of adult Jewish learning: family driven adult learning and seeker-motivated adult learning. The former kind of learning is often initiated by parent participation in Jewish Family Education. Parents often return to Jewish learning through a family program, particularly if they are participating in a kind of Family Education that builds in parallel learning sessions for adults and their children. This form of adult learning readily contrasts with seeker-motivated adult learning. This adult learning typically comes in the fifth and sixth decade of life. More inward, this kind of adult learning builds upon an already strong Jewish identity and helps the learner achieve "a Jewish heart of wisdom."

One can put this in a more traditional frame as well. The Rabbis encourage us to try new Jewish practices without caring too terribly much about the purity of our motivations because *b'toch lo b'shma ba l'shma* — sometimes something will begin with extrinsic motivation but end with intrinsic appreciation. In the context of JFE, parents will sometimes come to Family Education programs simply because they want to be good parents. With enough good experiences, however, perhaps their desire for independent adult learning will be sparked.

Jonathan Woocher captures some of these dynamics in his analysis of the "vicious" and "virtu-

ous" cycles of Jewish living. The "vicious" cycle phenomena appears to function in the following way. Since parents are doing this "*fur der kinder*" (for the children), kids soon realize that their Jewish education is not very important beyond Bar/Bat Mitzvah. Parents figure out that the goals of the synagogue are not so much perpetuating Jewish life as perpetuating the synagogue as an institution. Every point in the triangle of the personal Jewish journey, partnerships for education, and Jewish parenting collapses in a subtle conspiracy to minimize the impact of Judaism on the lives of Jewish families.

The reality of this "vicious cycle" challenged Jewish planners to find initiatives that could break the cycle of failure. As a result of those initiatives and other subtler shifts in the Jewish and general American environment, Woocher believes that we are beginning to see (and just learning how to document) the presence of a "virtuous cycle."

In regard to our three interactive forces of parenting, partnership, and journey, the virtuous cycle looks something like this. Parenting, as Nancy Fuchs-Kreimer describes it, is itself a spiritual revolution in people's lives. The receptivity to new ways of understanding oneself and tradition is enormous during this period. This leads to new openness to tradition on a personal level, but even more in terms of a concern for making religious tradition part of the family. Parents do indeed then enter synagogues and other communal institutions. And when the synagogues and Jewish Community Centers are receptive to those needs and creative in their programming, real partnerships are formed. Parents attend Family Education programs because they are slowly coming to understand how mutually intertwined are their own and the community's responsibilities in raising a Jewish child.

Jewish parenting leads to Jewish partnerships. Then, if the virtuous cycle is in place, the third force of Jewish Family Education — journey into new learning emerges. In the course of these Family Education programs, Jewish parents engage in some form of adult learning. New questions are raised and old questions revisited. Their personal relationship to Judaism is questioned. A desire for independent adult learning — thus furthering one's personal

Jewish journey — begins to emerge. The transition from family-driven to seeker-motivated adult Jewish learning begins.

A series of questions emerges as we find ourselves going through this next transformation in Jewish communal life: Will Jewish Family Education change dramatically when we begin working with the parents who have emerged from a "virtuous," rather than "vicious" circle of educational forces? What new opportunities will emerge when we already have more confident adult learners (and hence likely more confident child learners as well) working with us? Will this raise the bar of what is expected of our Family Educators in terms of Jewish knowledge, background, and sophistication? Will we find parents lamenting that if only our educators showed more commitment, we could do so much more with our children?

CONCLUSION

Jewish Family Education — the darling of the continuity revolution — has exciting educational challenges it must meet if it is not to become the orphaned child of the newer Renaissance agenda. This will require Family Educators to face head-on some of the challenges suggested in volumes such as this one and *First Fruit* (Whizin Institute, 1998). At the same time, funders and planners — given some of the extraordinary content of these volumes — will need to do a reality check on the lingering perception that JFE is all fluff, fun, and games. The same individuals will also do well to develop a more refined appreciation for the distinction between "programming" with a small "p" (individual programs) and capital "P" Programming that is the sum total of all these programmatic initiatives.

Most of all, we all need patience. Significant long-range changes come about through the intersecting social, spiritual, and educational forces in Jewish life. Those who have watched Jewish Family Education touch the lives of Jewish families for several decades now believe with a complete and perfect faith that JFE is indeed good for the Jews.

CHAPTER 6

INTEGRATING FAMILY, ADULT, AND CHILDREN'S LEARNING: THE BNAI KESHET PROGRAM

CONTRIBUTOR: DAVID WEINSTEIN
ADDRESS: Bnai Keshet Congregation
      99 South Fullerton Avenue
      Montclair, NJ 07042
PHONE: **(973) 746-4889**
E-MAIL: dhweinstein@home.com
TARGET: **Grades 3-7**

BACKGROUND

This chapter describes a program that has evolved over ten years. It was originally conceived and written as a collaboration between Dr. Jeffrey Schein and Rabbi Dan Ehrenkrantz of Bnai Keshet, a Reconstructionist Congregation in Montclair, New Jersey, under a grant from the Covenant Foundation. Since becoming the Family Educator at Bnai Keshet, I have added new programs and modified existing ones with the consultation of Dr. Schein and Rabbi Ehrenkrantz. This chapter represents only a portion of their original work. In addition, Leah Mudell, former education intern at the Jewish Reconstructionist Federation, contributed greatly to the editing and compilation of this chapter. Some of the programs here are also adaptations of programs designed by other educators. They have been credited where appropriate. Finally, credit is due the families of Bnai Keshet. Their enthusiastic participation in this program, helped it evolve into a successful model of Jewish Family Education.

DESCRIPTION OF THE PROGRAM

This Family Education program focuses on five or six important Jewish values. An emphasis on these values is woven into the weekly Religious School curriculum, parent and Family Education programs, and family projects outside of Religious School. The goal here is the integration of these values into the family life of the participants. According to Dr. Schein, "the emphasis on core Jewish values as constituting the essence of 'spiritual peoplehood' is implicit in all the activities of this curriculum." Over the past years, we have seen the program influence the life of the Religious School, the families involved, and the synagogue community as a whole. We believe that a fully integrated, values-based curriculum can be a meaningful approach for any community seeking to educate, challenge, and influence the Jewish lives of students and their families.

The program began in the mid-1990s with the introduction of the *Hiddur Mitzvah* curriculum in the *Gimel* (third grade class). Each year, another value was added to the next grade until we had a comprehensive Family Education curriculum spanning third through seventh grade. The fourth grade focuses on the interconnected values of *Kedushah* and *Menchlichkeit* (holiness), the fifth grade on *Tzionut* (Zionism), the sixth grade on *Tikkun Olam* (repair of the world), and the seventh grade explores the value of *Chochmah* (wisdom). The program includes four interconnected components:

(1) a weekly one-hour class for students based on the value, (2) adult education, (3) Family Education, and (4) family projects. Driving the process at all levels are four or five essential questions. (These have been provided at the beginning of each section below)

Each week, one hour of Religious School instruction is dedicated to a particular value. Teachers have textbooks and curricular materials which accompany the program. Three to four times a year, we expect parents to join us for both adult and Family Education. During these mornings, which are interwoven with the week to week studies, parents usually spend the first hour studying relevant aspects and texts connected to that year's value with either the Family Educator or the Rabbi. This provides parents with a number of important opportunities. First of all, they are involved in the study of the same value that their children are also studying. This helps to create a shared exploration of ideas and increased family communication around Jewish ideas and Jewish values. Second, parents are prepared during adult education for the family component of the morning.

We are seeking to change the idea of who is a Jewish educator. In many of the programs described here, parents are transformed during this first hour into the educators. They might be running a Pesach activity for the children, taking on the role of a candidate in a debate for an election in Israel, or becoming interviewers of their own children for an oral history project. Third, parents need education, too. Parents who would rarely join an adult education class are there at 9:00 a.m. ready to learn. And parents have been overwhelmingly grateful not only for being able to spend time with their children on these mornings, but for their own intellectual and spiritual growth. Finally, the adult education component creates bonds among parents, and therefore more links in the synagogue community. Important friendships have formed and synagogue members who might not otherwise feel a part of the community are involved alongside members who know everyone and who are actively involved in synagogue activities. These adult education activities are described below.

The third component of the program is the Family Education programs themselves. These programs (usually two hours in duration) are an opportunity for parents and their children to be actively engaged in the exploration of the particular value. As much as possible, we try to create an environment in which families have the time, space, and tools to explore being Jewish together in meaningful ways. This is time that most parents tell us would never exist in their hectic worlds if not for the program. Discussions and activities during these mornings are often springboards for affecting Jewish family life at home. We hear numerous stories of discussions continuing in the car on the way home or at dinner that night. Parents have told us of new rituals and ways of thinking about old rituals that resulted from the program. These mornings are usually active, challenging, thought provoking, and not easily forgotten. Most important, they are not about parents having the opportunity to watch their kids at school. They are about parents and kids going through the experience of school together. Very little can be more important to a child than seeing his/her own parent struggling to understand what it means to be Jewish and human. It tells the child that it is quite acceptable and normal to have doubts and questions and skepticism about this whole endeavor. Their parents may still be struggling, but they are still present.

A fourth component involves family experiences at home, such as the family *Tikkun Olam* project or work on the Bnai Mitzvah *Brit*. Ongoing projects in every class create continuity between the Family Education programs. They also place these values where they belong — outside of school and in the home.

In this chapter we have included three programs from Grades *Aleph, Bet,* and *Gimel,* and four programs for the *Daled* class, along with the corresponding adult education programs. While this is a recipe for a successful program in our synagogue, it is important for other communities first to go through a process of identifying those values most meaningful to them. This process has the potential to bring together disparate elements of the community and to energize the entire curriculum.

Teachers, community leaders, and parents should all take part in this process.

Very often, we have more than three programs per grade each year. In some years, adult education has been extended into an actual course that meets on a regular basis. For several years, we extended our program to include a *Bet* class Havdalah program and an *Aleph* class Shabbat program. We are also planning on starting a teen Family Education program for families of post Bnai Mitzvah students who have continued their formal Jewish education, as well as for those who have not.

The program as it is presented here represents only our current thinking about Family Education at Bnai Keshet, which is in a constant state of evolution. Just this year, we have decided to uncouple the values of *Kedushah* and *Menchlichkeit* and combine *Menchlichkeit* with *Tikkun Olam*. While we saw a natural connection between these values, we didn't feel that we were effectively helping families experience that connection. We also began to see so much overlap between *Menchlichkeit* and *Tikkun Olam* that it became confusing to us as we planned activities.

Kedushah is probably the most engaging value here, but it is also the most difficult for educators, parents, and children. While we started out having this as our value in sixth grade, we moved it to fourth grade a few years ago because we thought fourth graders might be more open to the unknown and to the mystery of *Kedushah* than our very skeptical sixth graders. We are still evaluating and experimenting with how best to teach this value, as well as all other values.

We have also had to struggle with the homework component of the program. Originally, we sent home small family activities every week with the children. We found that very few assignments were returned. This is probably part of a larger problem of homework in Religious School. So two years ago, we decided to move to large family projects for each grade with lots of instructions, forms to fill out, pressure, constructive performance, and celebration at the end. These projects have been very successful, but have required the efforts of the

teacher, the Family Educator, and the principal to help make sure that families complete their work.

We continue to face many challenges. We are starting to see many parents go through the program more than once. And while everything is new to their children, for some parents the repetition, especially in adult education, has become problematic. We are also trying to find ways to have our teachers become more integral to the program. Those who feel comfortable are being prepared to run the Family Education component of the program. This allows for a new dynamic between parents and teachers. The largest challenge remains integrating all of the threads of the program. Finding appropriate classroom materials for each value, preparing teachers for teaching this value, scheduling classroom activities to connect to family and adult programs, and helping children to make all of the connections is not always an easy task. Each year, we continue to work on meeting these challenges.

Many of the forms and texts that have guided the study programs are reproduced in the Appendixes at the end of this chapter.

GIMEL: HIDDUR MITZVAH AND JEWISH SYMBOLS

Essential Questions

These are the essential questions to be covered in this unit:

- How have the Jewish people employed symbols to express important thoughts and feelings about life?
- What are some of these symbols, and how do we use them as Jews?
- How do rituals and symbols help us express things we could not otherwise express?
- Why does *Hiddur Mitzvah* (the beautification of ritual ceremonies and ritual objects) enhance the performance of *mitzvot?*
- How can we continue to add this element of *Hiddur* to the deeds we perform as Jews?

Family Education Program #1

Adult Education Pre-Program Segment: Jewish Family Museum

Before beginning our first Family Education program, an hour is spent with just the adults. This gives us an opportunity to introduce the Family Education program and the essential questions which will guide our study of *Hiddur Mitzvah* and Jewish symbols during the year.

After this introduction we begin to explore the Jewish symbols in their home. Parents are asked to make a list of five to ten "telltale" items that would have to be removed from their house if they wanted to hide their Jewishness. This is a lead-in to our discussion of the important role Jewish symbols and objects play in our families' lives. Parents are also asked to decide what they would do with an anonymous gift of $10,000 if the only stipulation was that the money was to be used to beautify the Jewish rituals already observed by the family. This has often led to interesting discussions about the different ways we approach *Hiddur Mitzvah*. But it also has led to possibly more significant discussions about the relative importance of money in this process. Finally, parents are given a copy of the introduction to *The Encyclopedia of Jewish Symbols* by Ellen Frankel and Betsy Platkin Teutsch (Jason Aronson Inc., 1992). This introduction explores the important cultural functions of symbols and lays a foundation for our future study. (Parents are encouraged to order this book as an invaluable companion to our studies during this year.) We discuss how the societies we live in, both American and Jewish, use symbols "to represent the world around them." In some years, we have also spent time exploring the significance of *Hiddur Mitzvah* throughout Jewish civilization. One way we look at this is to study biblical texts describing all of the intricate details in the design of the Tabernacle. Since this is an early example of *Hiddur Mitzvah,* we ask: Why is *Adonai* so specific and detailed in the commandments surrounding the Tabernacle? Why is every object so ornate? And what does this tell us about the importance of *Hiddur* in Jewish life? Finally, we explore other examples of this dynamic embrace of *Hiddur Mitzvah* as we take a look at the objects parents have brought in for the Family Education part of the morning.

Family Education Segment: The Museum Explored and Expanded

After about an hour or so, the children join their parents for the Family Education program. During this program, families explore together the importance that symbols and objects play in the continuity and meaning of Jewish life. Children begin to take on the role of oral historians of their family and thus become contributors to Jewish continuity. Families are asked in advance of this program to bring their oldest Jewish object to school on the day of the Family Education activity. The objects that families have brought have often had great significance and meaningful stories attached to them. They have connected parents with their own childhoods, children with their grandparents, and families with their experiences throughout the last century in Russia, Poland, Israel, and wherever else these families have originated. They have even sometimes brought up age-old disputes about which child was supposed to get *Bubbe's* candlesticks or *Zeyda's* Bar Mitzvah *Siddur.* (In some years, families have also been asked to bring in their newest Jewish object. This encourages and sanctifies the beginnings of new traditions alongside the old.) Some additional Jewish objects should also be brought from the synagogue to fill out the museum.

Procedure

Following is the procedure for the morning:

1. The Rabbi or Educator begins the morning by telling the story of the oldest or most significant object that belongs to the synagogue. Time is allowed for questions and discussion.

2. Each family is given time to discuss as a family the history and significance of each of their objects. Parents prepare their children to tell the story of these objects and to explain their significance.

3. Each family places their objects on a table that is covered with a tablecloth (best if it is one that also has great significance). Families explore

this museum of Jewish symbols together. Some objects might be mysteries to some of the children (and adults), and they are encouraged to ask questions during this time. Before answering all of these questions, the children often are asked to formulate their own hypotheses as to the uses of these mysterious objects.

4. Everyone sits down and each family, one by one, comes to the table. Children begin to tell the story of their object. This is their opportunity to take on the role of storytellers and oral historians of their families. Parents may also add their insights to the story.

5. After everyone has told their stories and there has been plenty of time for questions and discussion, families are asked to find a little space for themselves. These stories often evoke strong emotions, memories, tears, and laughs. We want these feelings not to be locked away after the program is done, but to be recorded.

6. We move from the oral tradition to the written tradition in one of two ways before the program ends. The first way is for each family to write a letter to future generations telling once again the stories of these objects. These letters are then placed somewhere near the objects so that they, too, will be passed down to future generations. The second way is to write a "page of Talmud" for this object. A Polaroid picture of each family's object is given to the family, along with a blank sheet arranged like a page of Talmud. The picture is placed in the center. The family then writes an explanation of this object and its significance underneath it. Around the sides of the page are places for each member of the family, acting as the Rabbis, to write their feelings, stories, anecdotes, reminiscences, etc., that pertain to or are inspired by this object. Additional room might be left on the page for brothers and sisters or grandparents to add their thoughts and commentary. This page of Talmud might go home with the family, or might become the first entry into an ongoing Family Education portfolio. (A blank *daf talmud* can be found in Appendix A.)

Family Education Program #2: The Seder Plate
(Note: This program is based on a program called "Exploring Jewish Symbols with Guest Artists and Scholars." The authors Ellen Frankel and Betsy Platkin Teutsch, as guests at Congregation Bnai Keshet, helped families explore Jewish symbols. It is possible to modify certain aspects of this program and to create a very meaningful Family Education experience without guest artists.)

Introduction

Pesach offers us one of the most important Jewish educational experiences. The *Seder* itself is a rich learning experience not only for children, but for all present. The central element of the *Seder* is the *Haggadah,* or telling/teaching of our story of liberation. Symbols are used extensively in this experience. Parents have the responsibility of bringing their children into this story through a variety of rich pedagogical techniques (song, story, symbols, foods, etc.). This adult and Family Education program, which is planned for the week before Pesach, is designed to help parents in their role of educators, as well as to prepare the family for the Pesach *Sedarim.*

Procedure

Following is the procedure for the morning:
1. Parents spend the first hour learning about the symbols of the *Seder* plate — egg, *charoset, matzah,* etc. They are then divided into small groups, each group responsible for becoming experts and teachers for one of these symbols. Many different varieties of *Haggadot* are available, as well as copies of appropriate pages from *The Encyclopedia of Jewish Symbols.* All of the ingredients for each of these edible symbols are also available.

2. After parents have become "experts" on their symbol, they design an educational and fun activity for the kids so they can learn about the symbol and its significance. These activities might include: a game show, an arts project, cooking, learning a new song, etc. Each activity usually ends with the appropriate blessing for

that symbol. Lots of arts and crafts supplies (as well as help and inspiration) are also available. Parents are given another hour in which to prepare.

3. The room is set up in the shape of the *Seder* plate with signs at each station. The children come into the room and are divided into small groups and given copies of a blank *Seder* plate. They travel from station to station, participating in each of the activities prepared by the parents. They also are given the opportunity to try each of the foods. When they complete an activity, they are given a picture of the symbol to put on their blank *Seder* plate (these pictures are prepared in advance). The goal for each student is to garner all of the symbols on his or her plate.

4. After all of the children have completed their *Seder* plate exploration, the whole group is brought back together again to discuss the *Seder* plate. Parents and children then share with each other the activities in which each participated and their feelings about each symbol. We also get to see the exhausted looks on the faces of the parents after an hour or two of teaching a whole class of third graders. (This might give the parents an added appreciation for the classroom teacher's task!) Finally, we conclude with the singing of Pesach songs. Before leaving, children are encouraged to utilize some of their new knowledge by explaining the significance of these symbols at their own *Sedarim*.

This program is a nice example of changing the definition of a Jewish educator. Once the activities begin, parents become the teachers. One note, however. In the past, parents have asked for time in advance to conceive their educational activities. This year, we plan on assigning groups of parents their symbols in advance.

Family Education Program #3: Trip To the Jewish Museum

Our final Family Education program for *Gimel* is a family trip to the Jewish Museum in New York. (Other large cities might have appropriate museums or exhibits. Parents travel through the permanent exhibit with their children, searching for the items on a *Scavenger Hunt* activity sheet. We are always sure to emphasize to parents how important it is that they stay with their children discussing the items, raising questions, and helping to answer their children's own questions. It is also beneficial to have an educator available to help with these explorations. (It is usually appropriate to make a reservation with the museum in advance. However, in some years, we have arrived as individual families and have not needed a reservation.) During the next regular class, students share their *Scavenger Hunt* findings.

Since this event usually takes place in the spring, we have often planned it to coincide with the Israel Day Parade in New York City. Interested families have attended the parade, while other families take advantage of a spring day in the city with the kids.

Alternatives To a Jewish Museum

There is a variety of possible alternatives to, or variations on, the program if a large Jewish museum is not accessible. One possibility is to make use of the synagogue itself (including the gift shop) as the museum. Students will, of course, have many fewer objects from which to choose, but this in itself could lead to a valuable discussion of financial priorities for the institution. What Jewish ritual objects is the synagogue missing? Students should look through Judaica catalogs and determine how much it would cost for the synagogue to acquire those objects. What other programs or services might the synagogue have to give up in order to be able to afford those objects? Would it be worth it?

Another variation on this theme would be to invite the manager of the synagogue gift shop to explain to the group how he/she determines which items the shop will sell. Again, students might be invited to look through catalogs to make recommendations for merchandise the shop should carry. They should also be encouraged to think carefully about when certain items should be displayed in the shop. This is a good chance to remind students of the ritual objects needed for the cycle of the Jewish year. Would people buy *chanukiot* all year round? What about special order items, such as the *lulav* and *etrog*? Families could then create advertisements for items which the gift shop sells. Some advertisements might be in the form of posters which are hung throughout the synagogue and remain up all year. Others might be copy for pieces to run in the synagogue newsletter which advertises items needed for specific holidays or celebrations. (Be sure to research the newsletter guidelines so that these ads can in fact be used.)

DALED: MENTSCHLICHKEIT AND KEDUSHAH (Bayn Adam L'Chavero and Bayn Adam L'Makom)

Essential Questions

Following are the essential questions to be considered during this unit:

- What does it mean to be a good person and a good Jew?
- What does it mean to be a holy individual and a member of a holy people?
- How have the traditional texts of the Jewish people (Torah, Talmud, etc.) guided us in our quest for goodness and holiness?
- What are a Jew's responsibilities to his/her neighbors *(Bayn Adam L'Chavero)* and to God *(Bayn Adam L'Makom)*?

Family Education Program #1: Ushpizin

Adult Education Segment: Being Good and Being Holy

In this first meeting of the year, parents are introduced to the values of *Menschlichkeit* and *Kedushah* and the relationship between these values. Specifically, we focus on the twin concepts of *Bayn Adam L'Chavero* and *Bayn Adam L'Makom*. We start out the year's focus on *Menchlichkeit* by studying traditional conceptions of *Bayn Adam L'Chavero* from *Sefer HaAggadah* in *Book of Legends* by Hayim Nahman Bialik and Yehoshua Ravnitsky, translated by William Braude (Schocken Books, 1993), or from the selections from *Pirke Avot* found in Appendix B. (If time permits, parents might study these selections with their children, or the passages might serve as an at home assignment for families. These family discussion questions are a part of Appendix B as well.)

Family Education Segment: Honored Celestial Guests

This first Family Education program for *Dalet* is scheduled to coincide with Sukkot.

Jews achieve glory through their good deeds. This is one basis for deciding whom to invite to our *sukkah* as an honored guest (the tradition of *Ushpizin*). Families are divided into small groups (two to three families in each group). Each group "visits" five famous Jewish characters: Abraham, Jacob, Joseph, Sarah, and Moses. At Bnai Keshet we have updated some of our "guests" to include post-Torah and post-biblical personalities (and more women), such as King David, Esther, and Hannah Senesh.

Teachers and/or volunteers from the congregation often take the role of these people. This is a great opportunity to involve other members of the congregation in our family program. Each personality talks about the good deeds he/she performed in the course of his/her lifetime. Each character's job is to convince the group that he/she should be the honored guest in the family or congregational *sukkah* because of his/her performance of good deeds.

Families rotate and spend five minutes with each character. Afterward, they discuss with one another who they thought was indeed the best model of a Jewish *mitzvah* doer. The groups then rank their heroes in order from 1 to 5 on a ballot. The person voted best receives five points, number two receives four points, etc.

In the second activity of the day, each family chooses a new *Tzedakah* organization to sponsor for the year through their home *Tzedakah* collection. Short summaries of perhaps a dozen of the organizations described in Danny Siegel's books and his ZIV Newsletter are provided. Families talk with one another about which organization seems to do the most interesting *mitzvah* work and then make a decision.

Family Education Program #2: Kedushah and Menchlichkeit

Adult Education Segment: Ethical Wills

In preparation for this session, we compile a set of traditional and contemporary ethical wills. See *So That Your Values Live On* by Jack Riemer and Nathaniel Stampfer (Jewish Lights, 1991). We explain to parents the tradition of leaving in the form of a will a spiritual and moral (as well as a financial) legacy. This custom is at least 2000 years old, predating Talmudic times. Together, we read and discuss a few paragraphs from the ethical wills of Ibn Tibbon, Eliezer of Mayence, and Nachmanides. We then split into small groups to study other ethical wills. Each group receives two different wills to read and discuss. When we come back together, each group presents its impressions of the wills read. In the ensuing discussion, participants are asked to evaluate the tradition as a whole.

Parents are then asked to write a few key thoughts in response to the following question: What are the important values and lessons you want your child(ren) to learn from you? After a good pep talk about the Reconstructionist value of experimentation and finding new meaning in old traditions, participants are encouraged to write on their own and draw up a draft an ethical will. In class that week, their children are asked what they thought their parents might put in such a document. Parents and students share this information at the beginning of the Family Education program or at home.

Family Education Program #3: Tzedakah and Gemilut Chasadeem

This program focuses on understanding the relationship (similarities and differences) between *Tzedakah* and *Gemilut Chasadeem*. Parents and children study together the sources on *Tzedakah* and *Gemilut Chasadeem* (See Appendix C), filling in the information on the handout together. After 20 minutes, the groups come back together to share answers and new understandings of the difference between the two concepts. The entire group is then asked to brainstorm examples of *Gemilut Chasadeem* that they can perform in their everyday lives.

Students are asked to keep a journal for two months about acts of *Gemilut Chasadeem* on this list which they have performed. Each week in class, students share their journal at the beginning of the session. Some teachers have kept a chart on the wall of these acts. Such a chart is not meant to promote competition, but to serve as an incentive for the whole class to meet class goals for *Gemilut Chasadeem*. A celebration might even be held at the end of the two months or after reaching certain goals. More important than a numeric goal is the chance to reflect on the experience of *Gemilut Chasadeem*. Teachers provide time for this reflection during class, but parents are encouraged to have these discussions at home as well.

Family Education Program #4: Conceptions of God

Adult Education Segment: God Searching

In the second part of this year, we switch our attention from *Menschlichkeit* to *Kedushah*, keeping in mind the connection between the two. This first hour is an introduction to the idea of *Kedushah* and the beginning of a discussion about the nature of God that will continue with the children during the Family Education session. Each parent is given an index card with the beginnings of two sentences:

God is _____.

God is not _____.

Parents are asked to complete these sentences and to put the card (without their names on it) back into the pile. We then read through their answers and discuss each of them and their place in the larger historical Jewish discussion of the nature of God. This is all designed to help parents prepare for the second half of the morning, talking about God with their children. In the first few years of this program, the Rabbi led this discussion with parents. But we found parents somewhat reluctant to engage in honest theological dialogue in the presence of the Rabbi. When the Family Educator leads the discussion, parents seemed to be more open.

Family Education Segment: God's Vitae

Kedushah is a difficult concept for both children and adults. It is thus important for children and parents to see each other struggling to understand this concept — and God — in their own lives. This program allows families to open up this dialogue on the nature of God in a non-threatening way.

Participants are divided into family groups. Each family is given a large piece of paper and markers and a set of directions (see Appendix D). Families are asked to develop a job description for God and to write that job description on the paper. We then meet again as a whole group for a discussion and presentation of their ideas about the nature of God. Families are sent back to work on job descriptions for human beings. These are also presented to the whole group. Once back in the large group, we discuss what is expected from God and what is expected from ourselves. What are the similarities and differences in these expectations? How do we explain this overlap?

For the final part of the program, families are given "Applications for the Position of God" (see Appendix E). From this they decide which one best fits their job description. This is usually a good discussion to complete at home if there is not enough time. Students may bring their answers back to the class for the next week to continue the discussion. This segment of the program is adapted from *Shema Is for Real* by Joel Lurie Grishaver (Torah Aura Productions, 1970.)

Family Education Program #5: Kedushah Moments

Adult Education Segment: Shabbat, Heschel, and Kedushah

In preparation for this discussion on the nature of *Kedushah*, parents are asked to read in advance *The Sabbath* by Abraham Joshua Heschel (1966). The focus here is not simply on "the Sabbath," but what we learn about *Kedushah* from this example. The overall theme of this session should be helping the adults locate sacred moments in their own lives. A second focus can be helping them think through how they might create more *kodesh* moments in their own lives with the help of Jewish tradition.

We start this discussion by responding to the quote from Ralph Waldo Emerson: "Things are in the saddle and ride mankind." What did Emerson mean? What kind of things ride us in contemporary life?

Parents then share with the group a tradition (Jewish or non-Jewish) that is meaningful to each individual, and which is threatened by contemporary society. This leads to our discussion of Heschel's book. The group's attention is turned to passages that deserve a rereading and a response from the group as a whole.

Finally, we share with the group the Rabbinic insight that the family (and in particular the dining table) serves as the *mikdash ma'at*, a replica in miniature of the holiness contained in the ancient sanctuary. We then allow for open discussion of how family life might bring in more of this holiness.

Family Education Segment: Shoresh Hunting

Families are given the information related to the root *Kuf-Dalet-Shin* in *The Jewish Lexicon* by Edith Samuels (UAHC Press,1976). A game begins this program. We call out Hebrew-Aramaic words from the list and ask family members to call back the correct English translation. Families start seeing the linguistic connection between ideas like *Kedushah, Kiddush, Kaddish, Kiddushin*, etc. We then read the poem "Where Do We Find Holiness?" by Sidney Greenberg in *Moment of Transcendence* by Dov Peretz Elkins (Jason Aronson,1992), and assign each family the task of explaining what is holy about a particular word from the lexicon.

The main part of the program involves families going through a round robin learning session. Each family receives a "Kedushah Moments Album" (see Appendix F). One page in the album is devoted to each of the three stations in which they will either talk with a leader or perform some tasks related to *Kuf-Dalet-Shin*: *Kiddush* (sanctification of holidays and life), *Kaddish* (mourner's prayer), and *Kiddushin* (Jewish wedding ceremony). Here is a listing of the three stations:

Station 1 – Kiddush: Wine and a tablecloth are provided for recitation of *Kiddush*. Discussion focuses on the interweaving of the themes of the Exodus from Egypt and the creation of the world.

Station 2 – Kaddish: Families say *Kaddish* together and discuss the apparent anomaly that the prayer for the dead does not mention death.

Station 3 – Kiddushin: Here we show a wedding video to stimulate discussion about the element of

Kedushah in a wedding. Attention is focused on the root meaning of *Kuf-Dalet-Shin* in the context of marriage (i.e., how does marriage set two individuals aside as having an absolutely unique relationship?).

A constant theme that runs through all of our discussions about these events is making holy by making separate. The Sabbath is made separate. When a wife and husband circle one another at the beginning of the wedding ceremony, they are making a separate and holy space for themselves. And when we say *"Kaddish,"* we are making time (separating) to remember those who are no longer with us and to reaffirm our faith. Children and adults need to be reminded that none of the above happens without the conscious effort to separate the time and space so that *Kedushah* can emerge.

HEY: TZIONUT

Essential Questions

Here are the essential questions with which this unit is concerned:

• What are the sources of and motives for the Jewish attachment to the Land of Israel, and how has this attachment been expressed in classical Jewish texts such as the Tanach and the *Siddur*?

• What are the distinct meanings of such terms as *Eretz Yisrael*, *Medinat Yisrael*, *Am Yisrael*, and *Tzion*?

• How did the dream of Zion retain its force through the centuries of exile?

• How did the Jewish people return to the land of Israel after so many years of exile?

• How does a Jew living in North America today retain a vital and meaningful connection to Israel?

Family Education Program #1: Eretz Yisrael: The Dream of 3,000 Years

Adult Education Segment: Zionist Paradoxes

Before beginning our activity with families, parents are introduced to some of the important issues and challenges raised by *Tzionut* and the land challenges in the State of Israel. Undoubtedly, some parents have much to say about the current political situation in Israel or their recent trip there. But we start our discussion of *Tzionut* each year by looking

at a central question of this historic movement: For what purpose a Jewish state?

Parents are given two quotations to study in pairs (see Appendix G). These present two very different, but equally valid interpretations of the meaning of *Tzionut*. The Israeli author and peace activist A.B. Yehoshua presents us with a contemporary Herzlian understanding of Zionism — that the goal of *Tzionut* is for us to become a nation like all other nations. Martin Buber, on the other hand, rejects this basic nation-state argument in favor of giving the return of the Jewish people to the land of Israel a task beyond simply creating a nation-state: the task of Hebrew humanism. This ongoing debate over the significance and purpose of the State of Israel continues to frame many of the historic and contemporary issues surrounding *Tzionut*, Israel-Diaspora relations, the role of religion and religious pluralism in Israel, and the Arab-Israeli conflict. The discussion of these texts creates a framework for the discussion of these issues during this opening study session and throughout the year.

Family Education Segment: Israel and Zion through History

After our study with parents, the children join us for an exploration of the role that *Eretz Yisrael* has played throughout all of Jewish history. As families enter, they receive a passport marked "Zion" in Hebrew and English. Around the room are various personalities from Jewish history (teachers and/or members of the synagogue who have been drafted in advance and prepared for their tasks), such as Moses, Ezra, Yohanan Ben Zakkai, Yehudah HaLevi, Herzl, Hannah Senesh. It is important that the individuals who take the part of these personalities are well prepared, in costume, and ready to add a little *schmaltz* to their presentations. (See Appendix H for a chart of the personality and texts at each station.)

Before beginning their journey through Jewish history, the families receive an orientation about what Israel has meant to the Jewish people and what will happen at each station. We introduce a theme song (*"HaTikvah"* or *"Im Tirzu"* are both possibilities), which can be sung at the beginning and end of the program by the whole group. The same song might be sung and re-sung by smaller groups as they complete their visit to a particular station.

Participants move from station to station. At each, they learn a different text or tradition that highlights the centrality of *Eretz Yisrael* to the life of the Jewish people. The "personality" at each station presents his/her background and a favorite text spoken in the first person about the meaning of *Eretz Yisrael*. After listening to the speech, each family is given a task to complete that is pertinent to this personality or moment in history. After completing the task, the family's passport is stamped and they can move on to the next station. (Depending on the size of the group, it might be important to keep the whole group together or to stagger their journey through Jewish history.) The chart in Appendix H outlines the different personalities, time periods, texts, and tasks for each station.

As we reach 1948, the families are welcomed into the modern state of Israel. David Ben-Gurion proclaims the establishment of the state and the whole group sings "*HaTikvah.*" Here we have our celebration of Yom HaAtzma'ut, which might include food, singing, and dancing. During all of this, a message is read about the war that has broken out with the Arab neighbors. The celebration stops, and we move to the final station. There it is announced that after four wars and the loss of many lives on both sides, the search for peace still continues between Israel and her neighbors. Together we sing "*Oseh Shalom,*" a prayer for peace.

Family Education Program #2: The Rise of Modern Zionism

Adult Education Segment: The Impact of Theodor Herzl

During our first hour together, we study the founder of modern Zionism, Theodor Herzl – providing parents with the historical context in which Herzl's Zionist movement begins. This includes: an understanding of previous and contemporary efforts of the Jewish people to return to *Eretz Yisrael*; the world political situation; the Jewish condition in Eastern and Western Europe, as well as in the Arab countries, and in *Eretz Yisrael;* and a

background of Herzl's life with an emphasis on his reaction to the Dreyfus affair.

Depending on the group, the study of Herzl's writings might take two different directions. Some groups have been given the chapter on Herzl to read in *The Zionist Idea* by Arthur Hertzberg (Jewish Publication Society, 1977). Or, they may purchase this important source as a companion to their own children's ongoing study of *Tzionut*. This book gives an excellent background on Herzl and also includes his key writings. For other groups, a sheet of quotes from Herzl's writings is provided and we study these together. The discussions that have ensued from this close reading have been important and provocative. In fact, an hour in the morning might not be long enough for an honest discussion of Herzl and the broader issues of *Tzionut* and Jewish life in Diaspora. One year, we had this discussion at a parent's house on the Saturday night before this Family Education session. People enjoyed the opportunity to sit with members of their community, have refreshments, and discuss history, politics, philosophy, and Judaism late into the night.

Family Education Segment: A Simulation of the Sixth Zionist Congress

Note: For a more comprehensive introduction and explanation of this program, see *Creative Jewish Education*, Jeffrey Schein and Jacob J. Staub, editors (Rossel Books and Reconstructionist Press, 1984).

This program is adapted from "A Simulation of the Sixth Zionist Congress" by the Staff of Society Hill Synagogue's Ann Spal Thal School in *Creative Jewish Education*. During that Congress, a proposal was brought by Herzl in 1903 to accept Uganda in East Africa as a Jewish homeland. This situation served as a "test case for the intensity of Jewish feeling about *Eretz Yisrael*." On one hand, there was the need for a political solution for the growing suffering of Eastern European Jews. But there were also potent emotional feelings for a return of the Jewish people to their historical homeland. This simulation raises important issues for both parents and their children about the Jewish people's attachment to this particular piece of land, the nature of Jewish nationalism and nationalism in general, and the challenges of anti-Semitism in Europe. It also allows families to explore questions of idealism versus realism at an important moment in Jewish history.

Families walk into a room set up as the Sixth Zionist Congress with a large sign welcoming them to Basle, Switzerland. "Theodor Herzl" speaks to the group about the important decision facing them at this crucial moment. Efforts to establish a homeland for the Jewish people in Palestine have been unsuccessful, and the situation of Jews in Eastern Europe is continuing to deteriorate. Britain has offered to allow a Jewish colony in some of its territory in East Africa. The delegates of this convention must decide whether to take this offer at least as a temporary haven for the Jews suffering in Russia.

After the introductory comments, the participants are divided into three groups. One group, representing the delegates to the convention, is responsible for studying the proposal and preparing questions for advocates from both sides. The rest of the participants are divided into two groups representing the pro- and anti-Uganda forces. Each group is given a list of arguments for its side. They read and discuss the arguments and prepare a convincing presentation in support of their position. They also make posters to bring to the convention. (Directions and handouts are in Appendixes I, J, and K).

After 20 minutes of preparation, the convention is returned to session. Each side gives its passionate presentation and is then questioned by delegates. The floor is open to discussion, debate, and argument. By this time, most participants have become emotionally involved and we sometimes witness heated arguments. It is important that both parents and children have the opportunity to be involved. The tendency is for parents to sit back and watch their children play active historical roles. But we are looking for parents to share their own knowledge and abilities as well. The children learn a tremendous amount from their own parents' emotional involvement in this discussion of the Jewish people's future. At the end of the debate, delegates are asked to vote for or against this proposal and the results are announced to all.

Family Education Program #3: Israeli Elections

Adult Education Segment: Political Debate in Israel

In this program we explore the Israeli political system and key issues facing Israel today, such as religious pluralism and the peace process. During the Adult Education part of the morning, we study together the complicated Israeli political spectrum. This includes an understanding of coalition politics, the ideologies of Zionism, and past and present political alliances. Specifically, we take a look at the platforms of major parties in Israel. An update on each party's platform can be found by accessing the Web site of the Israel Foreign Ministry at www.israel-mfa.gov.il/mfa/go.asp. Parents have lots of questions concerning the current political situation in Israel and the Middle East. Especially in the case of an election year, this might even take the form of an extra long adult education program a week before the elections.

After studying the platforms of major parties, parents are prepared to become candidates in a mock Israeli debate preceding an election. Provide a handout that describes the political situation. Include issues related to peace and land, fear and reconciliation. Parents study their platforms in groups, prepare their speeches, and make signs for their parties. The candidates are encouraged to be animated and passionate about the pressing issues.

For elections to be most effective, the children begin preparation for this program weeks in advance. It is more important that they have some understanding of the issues than for them to be completely familiar with the workings of coalition politics in Israel. They also prepare questions in advance for our candidates' night. An interesting variation of this election program is the mock Knesset simulation developed by the New Israel Fund, which deals with issues of peace and pluralism. (Their address is P.O. Box 91588, Washington, DC 20077.)

Family Education Segment: Israel Election

When the children enter the room, parents have assumed their roles as candidates who are prepared for a debate. Candidates are introduced and each gives an opening speech. The moderator then allows candidates to ask questions of other candidates. We usually allow candidates to argue passionately for their positions. Finally, the floor is opened up to questions that have been prepared in advance. At the end, children meet separately with their teacher to discuss what they have learned. Before everyone leaves, a vote is taken and results announced. Children enjoy the roles their parents play as passionate public figures. It helps them become more involved in the issues.

VAV: TIKKUN OLAM

Essential Questions

Following are the essential questions related to this unit:

- What are the responsibilities of Jewish persons and of the Jewish people to improve the world?
- Do these responsibilities extend to non-Jews, and are they shared with non-Jews?
- In what ways have the dream of Zion and the establishment of the State of Israel contributed to these ideals?
- What aspects of the current state of the world demand *Tikkun* (correction)?

Family Education Program #1: Visions of the Messianic Age

Adult Education Segment: The Human and Divine Dimensions of Tikkun Olam

During the first hour, parents meet together with the Rabbi or Family Educator to be introduced to the concept of *Tikkun Olam*, social action, and messianism. The traditional and contemporary sources on the handout introduce ongoing Jewish concern for *Tikkun Olam*. These sources are studied as a group or in *hevruta*. (See Appendix L.)

Our perceptions of what needs *tikkun* is rooted in the imperatives presented earliest by the prophets. To begin a year focused on the repair of the world, families first need to come to a common understanding of what the world could look like at the end of the process: the messianic age. We human beings are part of the process of bringing it about through our work in the world. This activity follows these steps:

1. Imagining the messianic age from the prophets: Each family is given a set of prophetic texts that envision a messianic age (see Appendix M). Family groups read and discuss these texts. Families discuss the following questions: What would the world look like if these visions would come true? How would it be different from today? How would life be different for the Jewish people? After 15 to 20 minutes, families are brought back together to discuss these visions.

2. Imagining our own messianic visions: Families are asked to create the world the way they want it to look in the year 2050. (It is hoped that these visions will be inspired by the prophetic visions previously read.) They can do this through any form of art, as long as they are willing to share it with the rest of the families. Some might choose poetry, some song, and others crafts. Have available a variety of arts and crafts supplies (markers, paper, scissors, glue) and household odds and ends (pipe cleaners, buttons, tubes, etc.). The greater the variety, the better. Families use any of these supplies in their preparation. It is very important that the entire family, and not just the children, be involved in both planning and implementing this vision.

3. Display and presentations: All of the messianic visions are placed in the center of the room or presented to the group. Each family is asked to explain their vision and how it is similar to or different from the prophetic visions.

4. Next Steps: Each family is asked to make a list of ten things they can start doing right now to help make this vision a reality. These lists will be used to develop *Tikkun Olam* projects in the students' classes.

Family Education Program #2: Tikkun Olam Project

Adult Education Segment: Preparing for a Tikkun Olam Project

This morning is dedicated to introducing and planning the family *Tikkun Olam* project, which is the central element of the *Vav* Family Education program. In the beginning, we simply told families to find a *Tikkun Olam* need and then create a project to help meet that need. We had some wonderful projects, but there was a feeling that the experience lacked a connectedness to Jewish tradition. So we began to create a linkage between traditional Jewish values and the important work families do in the community.

Parents are first introduced to the upcoming Family *Tikkun Olam* project. We stress to them that this is not simply an opportunity to watch their chilren grow as they experience the power of taking concrete action in their communities. This is also a chance for the family to share in this endeavor and collectively to encounter the intellectual, emotional, and spiritual rewards of planning, implementing, and reflecting on their work. Guidelines for the ongoing project are explained to parents (see Appendix N). These include the fact that this is not a one-time action, but part of the ongoing work of *Tikkun Olam.* Work that affects the lives of others outside the family, work tied to Jewish values, documentation of *Tikkun Olam* work, and reflections are to be used in our final celebration (pictures, video, stories, posters, etc.).

Parents are then introduced to Jewish values that might inspire their *Tikkun Olam* work. These values are discussed and additional background is given by the educator on the origins and interpretations these values have taken. The values include:
Bal Tashcheet (protecting the environment)
Gemilut Chasadeem (acts of loving-kindness)
K'lal Yisrael (the unity of the Jewish people)
Tza'ar Ba'alay Chayim (taking care of animals)
Kibud Zekaynim (honoring the elderly)
(Our entire list of values can be found in Appendix O.) Finally, parents are given an opportunity to rank these values in their order of importance.

Family Education Segment: On What Three Things Does the World Stand?

In order to get students involved in commitments to some of the values of *Tikkun Olam,* we hold a Values Auction. Each family is given a list of the values we discussed in Adult Education (see Appendix O) and $1000 in cash (usually *Monopoly* money). One year, families had spent most of their money before the auction was over, so we allowed families to purchase additional *Monopoly* money at a rate

of $50 for $1 cash. This cash went into the class *Tzedakah* box.

Before the auction begins, families study and prioritize these values of *Tikkun Olam.* This allows children to become more familiar with these values and places parents in the role of the educator. During this animated auction, both parents and children become excited as they try to obtain the values most relevant to them. Families are constantly reevaluating the relative importance of these values. As each value is auctioned off, a certificate of ownership is given to the family.

After the auction is over and families own a few values each (with a large group, we might have two or three copies of each value to purchase), the *Tikkun Olam* project is introduced to the children. Their project must revolve around at least one of these values, but they are encouraged to incorporate as many as possible. Families then meet again separately to brainstorm ways of acting on these values in their communities. Finally, they are given action plans to complete at home (see Appendix P) and to mail back within a couple of weeks. This program usually takes place in November so that families have a few months to work on their projects.

At the end of the year, we invite families in for a celebration of their projects. Each family presents their work in stories, video, pictures, writings, etc. It is important that families feel the importance of their work. Certificates are given out to all families, and an article is placed in the synagogue newsletter describing all of the projects.

Family Education Program #3: Tu B'Shevat

Adult Education Segment: Nature, Tikkun Olam, and Jewish Mysticism

Tu B'Shevat offers an opportunity to draw meaningful connections between the Kabbalistic roots of *Tikkun Olam* and modern ideas about repair and protection of the physical world.

The morning begins with a study session about the concept of *Tikkun Olam* in *Kabbalah.* Most parents have little background in *Kabbalah,* so an introduction to it is necessary. Of course, it is difficult to acquaint parents with *Kabbalah* and *Tikkun Olam* in only one hour. Often, we invite the Rabbi to introduce these ideas and present some relevant texts. Still, parents leave this session with an understanding that the process of *Tikkun* is not simply a new word for social action. In a society skeptical about significant social change, parents explore the spiritual dimension their work in the world might reflect. For many parents, this introduction to *Kabbalah* and *Tikkun Olam* has fostered further interest in this area. Finally, a brief introduction is given of Tu B'Shevat, stressing its many levels of meaning. The *Seder* in which we participate with the children contains many of these levels, from the Kabbalistic to the environmental. While children might not be prepared for understanding on all of these levels, parents will have some of the conceptual knowledge to reflect on new meanings.

Family Education Segment: Family Tu B'Shevat Seder

Families gather together for a Tu B'Shevat *Seder*. A large table is set with two colors of grape juice, a variety of nuts and fruits, and a special Tu B'Shevat *Haggadah*. After an introduction to the holiday, we read through the *Haggadah* together, pausing to discuss and explain new rituals, drinking different concoctions of white and purple grape juice, eating our various fruits and nuts, saying blessings, and singing songs. There are quite a few Tu B'Shevat *Sedarim* now available (see Appendix Q for a list of these), including the *Trees, Earth and Torah: A Tu b'shvat Anthology* by Ari Elon and Naomi Mara Hyman (Jewish Publication Society, 1999).

ZAYIN: CHOCHMAH

Essential Questions

These are the essential questions with which this unit is concerned.

- What have the Jewish philosophers said about the nature of God, of humanity, and of the world?
- What is the relationship among the three?
- What can be known about God and about God's expectations of us? about the way God acts in the world?

- How can Jews come closer to God and achieve a spiritual life?

In this Bnai Mitzvah year, the focus of our Family Education is on unearthing the child's own *Chochmah* as it relates to the values we have explored over the five years in Family Education. Each child will prepare a *Brit*, a covenant or contract, as a complement to his/her Bar or Bat Mitzvah preparations. This *Brit* outlines a set of understandings the Bar/Bat Mitzvah child has regarding the Jewish values studied. It is handed out in written form to all the members of the community on the day of the Bar/Bat Mitzvah. The process of creating this document takes months, and is probably much more important than the final product. Parents are intrinsically involved in the process. The discussions (sometimes emotional and painful) between parents and children are essential as they get to know each other as adults and young adult Jews.

Family Education Program #1: An Introduction To Brit

Adult Education Segment: Choice and Coercion in Human Relationships

Before joining the children for the Family Education component of the morning, parents meet to discuss issues of coercion and choice in relationships. There are important concepts to explore before parents and children begin their own discussion later of the concept of *Brit*.

The discussion session focuses on *Aggadot* about the *Brit* made at Sinai. The Talmudic sources present a wide variety of understandings of the conditions under which this *Brit* was made. Before looking at these *Aggadot* (see Appendix R), the participants spend five minutes completing in writing these three sentences:
When God offered the Jewish people the Torah in the desert _____.
The reason the Jewish people accepted Torah was _____.
The reason God gave the Torah to the Jewish people was _____.

Together, we discuss our *midrashim* about the nature of this *Brit*. The discussion focuses on the extent to which choice existed in the formation of the *Brit*. One *midrash* suggests that Israel was the only people to choose to accept this offering, while another *midrash* tells of a God who holds Sinai above the heads of the people, forcing them to submit or be buried. A third *midrash* is the story of a God whose first word at Sinai was so strong that it killed the people. (For translations of these *midrashim*, see "*Matan Torah*/Giving of Torah" in *Book of Legends* by Bialik and Ravnitsky. And God must learn to soften and tailor these words so as to communicate effectively the message of Torah to Israel. All of these are interesting *midrashim* for parents engaged in learning to communicate commitment and understanding to their children, as an evolving covenant of family. In many ways, the dichotomy between choice and coercion found in the relationship between God and the Jewish people in these *Aggadot* mirrors the tensions between parents and their children. These texts then give insight and open up a rich discussion for parents of children moving into adolescence when "holding the mountain" over their children's heads might no longer be an effective means of communication. We therefore spend less time talking about the literal nature of the events of Sinai and more time exploring this "happening" as a metaphor for their relationships with their children.

Family Education Segment: Creating a Brit

As an introduction to *Brit*, parents and their children study together in *hevruta* three instances of *Brit* in Torah (see Appendix S): the *Brit* with Noah (Genesis 9), with Abraham (Genesis 17), and with Israel at Mt. Sinai (Exodus 19-20). For each *Brit* they are asked to answer the following questions:

• Who is this *Brit* between?
• What are the terms of this *Brit*?
• What obligations does God have in this *Brit*?
• What obligations does the other party have in this *Brit*?
• What sign is used to signify the existence of the *Brit*?
• Where do you see your place in this *Brit*?

After completing their study session, the whole group comes back together to discuss their findings. We specifically focus on the last question: Where do you see yourself in this *Brit*? At this point we introduce the *Brit* project to the families. The prospective Bnai Mitzvah are told that they will be preparing their own *Brit* with Judaism, to be presented to the community during their ceremony.

In the midst of frantic preparation for a Bar or Bat Mitzvah, the additional task of preparing a *Brit* is often not the first priority of families. The remaining Family Education programs are meant to facilitate this process as much as possible.

Adult Education Segment: Five Years of Family Learning — Parent Review

In the first two hours, we take parents on a journey back through the five years of Family Education programs. This is done via a copy of the essential questions from our six values, as well as a list of Hebrew and English values (not just these six, but also *Ivrit*, *Tzedakah*, and *Gemilut Chasadeem*). We reminisce about Family Education programs as parents try to remember the object they brought in for our Jewish family museum five years previous, the role they played in the Sixth Zionist Congress, and/or the *Tikkun Olam* project from last year. Parents need to remember these programs and these values so that they can interview their children about them later in the morning.

After remembering and reigniting thoughts and feelings about these values, we introduce the tools of oral history to parents. Parents have been asked to bring a tape recorder with them and a blank cassette. On this day, parents will be interviewing their children to help them reflect on what they have learned about these Jewish values and where they see these values in their lives today. However, getting children to talk about these topics is not easy, and some time and strategy have to be put into preparing interview questions which will engender meaningful responses. Parents receive a copy of a chapter on "What Questions to Ask?" from *Like It Was: A Guide to Writing Oral History* by Cynthia Stokes Brown (Teachers and Writers Collaborative, 1988). In this chapter, Brown gives us ideas of how to write questions. For instance, we are told to avoid simple yes/no questions or questions that might get us one word answers. Instead we are encouraged to ask questions that force the interviewee to describe an experience or feeling. Brown also talks about the importance of follow-up questions. Parents need to be listening during the interview (which is why a tape recorder is essential and pen and paper just won't work) so they can be finding those reflections to delve into in a deeper fashion.

Parents are then divided into small groups to develop questions around our values. These questions are designed to allow their children to remember and reflect on past experiences both in the program and in the home, and to discuss the way they see these values in their lives today. Parents will listen to these tapes and transcribe selections that articulate their children's understandings of these values. These selections will form the basis of the *Brit*. Developing these questions is no easy task. All of the groups come back together to share their best questions, and parents are encouraged to pick and choose from the questions they hear presented.

Family Education Segment #1: Five Years of Studying Jewish Values — A Family Reflection

After a brief introduction, parents and their interviewees spread out across the room with their tape recorders to conduct their interviews. Again, this may be difficult. In the past, these conversations have brought up important and sometimes painful dialogue. Parents are encouraged to allow their child to explore his/her own feelings. But this is often a struggle for parents as they find out new revelations about their child's thinking. We often meet with parents immediately after the interviews and find many parents surprised and sometimes frustrated by the process. Mostly, however, parents say that they really got to know their child better.

The next step is for parents to transcribe parts of the tape at home and to develop follow-up ques-

tions. We encourage parents to have at least one or two follow-up interviews over the next few weeks. In preparation for our next meeting, parents transcribe from these follow-up sessions as well.

Family Education Program #2: Completing the Brit

This final session is dedicated to writing, editing, and completing the *Brit*. Families sit together and review the transcripts of interviews. Children are asked to choose those passages that reflect their authentic reflections and understandings of these values (kids say lots of things in interviews that they won't commit to later on). Together, parents and child write an introduction to their *Brit*. Under the heading of each of the values studied (or other values they choose to include), they compile their reflections and understandings. These might take the form of anecdotes about the past, feelings about the present, and/or commitments to the future. Importantly, we stress that this is a snapshot in time. These feelings and attitudes will change over time, and it will be most revealing to look back at this document in the future. The end of the document includes a passage that parents write. This passage outlines their own commitment to helping their children as they continue to develop understandings of these values and as they work to live in the world according to their values.

The *Brit* is typed up and handed out at the respective Bar and Bat Mitzvah ceremonies.

CONCLUSION

"The Bnai Keshet Program" is rich in possibilities for families, adults, and children. It demonstrates that families are ready for Jewish learning on a high intellectual level. Further, a value-based program of this type can significantly influence the entire congregation.

APPENDIX A
HIDDUR MITZVAH

Commentary #1

Commentary #2

Place Polaroid here.

2: Simeon the Just was of the survivors of the Great Synagogue. He used to say: Upon three things the world stands: upon Torah, upon worship, and upon the showing of loving-kindness.

5: Jose ben Johanan of Jerusalem said: Let thy house be opened wide, and let the poor be thy household . . .

6: Jehosua ben Perahjah and Nittai the Arbelite received from them. Jehosua ben Perahjah said: Make thee a Master and get thee a companion, and judge every person by the scale of merit.

7: Nittai the Arbelite said: Keep far from the evil neighbor, and consort not with the wicked, and be not doubtful of retribution.

8: Jehudah ben Tabbai and Simeon ben Shetah received from them. Jehudah ben Tabbai said: Make not thyself as they that prepare the judges; and when the suitors are before thee, let them be as wrongdoers in thy sight; and when they have departed from before thee, let them be in they sight as innocent men, seeing they have accepted the sentence upon themselves.

10: Shemaiah and Abtolion received from them. Shemaiah said: Love work and hate mastery, and make not thyself known to the government.

Family Assignment:
1. As a family, read and discuss the meaning of the six *mishnayot* from *Pirke Avot* above.
2. Choose one *mishna* that your family thinks is the most beautiful, meaningful, or important to your family member's everyday lives.
3. Discuss ways that your family can incorporate this *mishna* into your lives. Make a list of these ways. Have the student bring them to class.

APPENDIX C
FAMILY EDUCATION PROGRAM #3:
TZEDAKAH AND GEMILUT CHASADEEM

Level: *Gimel*

Curriculum: *Kedushah* and *Menschlichkeit*

Tzedakah = righteousness

Gemilut Chasadeem = deeds of loving-kindness

Our Rabbis taught:

Gemilut Chasadeem is greater than *tzedakah* in three ways:

Tzedakah can be given only with one's money;

Gemilut Chasadeem can be given both by personal service and with money.

Tzedakah can only be given to the poor;

Gemilut Chasadeem can be given both to rich and poor.

Tzedakah can be given only to the living;

Gemilut Chasadeem can be given both to the living and dead. (*Sukkah* 49b)

Discuss the following questions:

• Which is more important — *Gemilut Chasadeem* or *Tzedakah*? Why?

• What would the rich need?

• How does one help the dead?

• What are some examples of *Gemilut Chasadeem* that you have performed in your life?

• Are you currently involved in any ongoing type of *Gemilut Chasadeem*?

Below is a list of activities. To which category do the belong — *Tzedakah* or *Gemilut Chasadeem*? Why?

Giving money to the poor

Visiting the sick

Burying the dead

Supporting a student through school

Respecting the elderly

Feeding the hungry

Helping to save captives

Showing hospitality to strangers/guests

Giving clothes to the poor

Giving a wedding to a bride who is poor

How would you explain *tzedakah* to someone who does not know what it is?

How would you explain *Gemilut Chasadeem* to someone who does not know what it is?

APPENDIX D
FAMILY EDUCATION PROGRAM #4: GOD'S VITAE

Level: *Dalet*

Curriculum: *Kedushah* and *Menschlichkeit*

Directions:

On a large piece of paper prepare a job description for the "position of human being." Include the following information in your description:

• Qualifications and background needed
• Description of responsibilities
• Hours of job
• Location of job
• Rewards of job

Prepare to share your work with the rest of the group.

APPENDIX E
FAMILY EDUCATION PROGRAM #4: CONCEPTIONS OF GOD

Level: *Dalet*
Curriculum: *Kedushah* and *Menschlichkeit*

APPLICATIONS FOR THE POSITION OF GOD

A Cricket (as in Jiminy Cricket) – God is our conscience, a small voice within us

A Plant or Flower – God is order, the laws of nature, scientific truth

A Marionette – God pulls our strings, controls our actions, determines the future, performs miracles

A Watchmaker – God puts the world together like a watch, winds it up, and then leaves it running.

A Clipboard – God takes notes on what we do, and eventually we will get rewarded or punished for our actions.

(Adapted from *Shema Is for Real* by Joel Lurie Grishaver, Torah Aura Productions, 1970)

Level: *Bet*
Curriculum: *Kedushah* and *Menschlichkeit*

KODESH MOMENTS ALBUM
Complete the following statements about each of
the *kodesh* moments you have seen:

Kaddish is a *kodesh* moment because . . .
Kiddush is a *kodesh* moment because . . .
Kiddushin is a *kodesh* moment because . . .

Record, draw, photograph a *kodesh* moment in
your family's life and place it in the frame below.
_____ is a *kodesh* moment because . . .

APPENDIX G
FAMILY EDUCATION PROGRAM #1: ZIONIST PARADOXES

Level: *Hey*
Curriculum: *Tzionut*

- I believe that the basic aim of Zionism has been fulfilled. I do not consider Zionism an all-embracing ideology, neither a way of life nor some kind of social philosophy, but first and foremost a historical act, the aim of which was to bring about a certain normalization of the Jewish problem by concentrating part of the Jewish people, territorially, in a State of their own. Had we not become involved as we did with the Arabs, Zionism would indeed have brought this normalization to the Jewish people, and its main task would be almost completely fulfilled. (A.B. Yehoshua)

- I am setting up Hebrew humanism in opposition to that Jewish nationalism which regards Israel as a nation like unto other nations and recognized no task for Israel save that of preserving and asserting itself. But no nation in the world has this as its only task, for just as an individual who wishes merely to preserve and assert himself leads an unjustified and meaningless existence, so a nation with no other aim deserves to pass away.

  By opposing Hebrew humanism to a nationalism which is nothing but empty self-assertion, I wish to indicate that, at this juncture, the Zionism movement must decide either for national egoism or national humanism. If it decided in favor of national egoism, it too will suffer the fate which will soon befall all shallow nationalism, i.e., nationalism which does not set the nation a true supernational task. If it decides in favor of Hebrew humanism, it will be strong and effective long after the shallow nationalism has lost all meaning and justification, for it will have something to say and to bring to mankind. (Martin Buber, "Hebrew Humanism" in *Israel and the World: Essays in a Time of Crisis*, Schocken Books, 1973)

APPENDIX H
PERSONALITIES/TEXTS/ TASKS FOR FAMILIES

Level: *Hey*
Curriculum: *Tzionut*

Station	Text and Personalities	Tasks for Families
Promised Land	**Moses** Deuteronomy, *Ki Tavo*	Make a list of 3 things they remembered about life in Egypt and 3 things they looked forward to in the Promised Land.
Longing for Jerusalem after the destruction of the First Temple	**Ezra** Psalm: "By the Waters of Babylon"	Illustrate "If I Forget Thee O' Jerusalem" by making a mural as a whole group.
Destruction of Second Temple	**Johanan Ben Zakkai** Account from Talmud of his escape from Jerusalem and meeting with Roman emperor	Create a list of 10 good reasons why prayer and Torah study can replace the Temple.
11th Century Spain	**Yehudah Halevi** Poem: "My Heart is in the East"	Write an acrostic poem using the letters in the word "Jerusalem."
19th/20th Century Basle Conference	**Theodore Herzl** Excerpt from essay on Herzl in *The Zionist Idea* (Hertzberg)	Make a list of 3 reasons we should vote for the creation of the State of Israel, 3 reasons we should vote against its creation.
Pre-State Period	Introduction to the life of **Hannah Senesh** and the struggle to save Jewish lives in Europe in the pre-State period	Learn and sing *"Eli, Eli"* by Hanna Senesh.
1948 Creation of the State	**David Ben-Gurion** Short excerpt from Israel Declaration of Independence	Sing *"Hatikvah"* . . . . announce that war has broken out with Arab neighbors.
Israel Today	Announce that after four wars and the loss of many lives on all sides, the search for peace still continues between Israel and her neighbors.	Sing *"Oseh Shalom."*

FAMILY EDUCATION PROGRAM #2: ZIONIST CONGRESS

Level: *Hey*
Curriculum: *Tzionut*
Title: Sixth Zionist Congress

Delegates

Directions:

1. Here are some of the things at stake in the Uganda proposal. Rank them in order of their importance for the Jewish people.

    _____ Freedom from physical danger for the Jewish people.

    _____ Working and living in a land in which Hebrew was originally spoken and where the Bible developed.

    _____ Having a country that will allow Jews to become productive farmers and provide a living for themselves.

    _____ Living in peace with the non-Jews in the country you will settle.

    _____ Living in the Jewish people's historic homeland.

2. Make a list of questions you would like answered about this little known territory that will help you know whether it is a suitable homeland for Jews.

    a.

    b.

    c.

    d.

    e.

    f.

3. Make a list of all of the pros and cons you can think of about the proposal to settle the Jewish people in Uganda.

    Pros   Cons

Level: *Hey*
Curriculum: *Tzionut*
Title: Sixth Zionist Congress

Pro-Uganda
List of Arguments:

- Uganda can help the Jews now when they need it. Palestine is still a dream.
- The soil of Uganda is much better suited to farming than Palestine. The climate is better suited to Europeans than is Palestine.
- The fact that Britain is offering the colony is important. It means that one of the world's major powers is saying that Zionism is good and legitimate. This will give Jews a lot more prestige in the eyes of non-Jews.
- Uganda now does not mean that Palestine could not come later. In fact, having a Jewish colony in Africa might convince the Turks that the Jews can govern their own country.
- When Jews were allowed to run their own affairs and were not discriminated against by the ruling governments, they were able to live fairly well outside of Israel. Being outside of Israel (Palestine) isn't automatically bad for the Jews.

- Herzl's address itself shows how difficult the Turkish government, which controls Palestine, can be. It's better to take an offer from the British. It will mean more because Britain is stronger and will keep its word.

Add more of your own arguments:

1.

2.

3.

4.

5.

6.

Further Directions:
- Read and discuss the arguments above.
- Prepare an interesting and convincing presentation in support of the Uganda proposal.
- Make a poster to display during your presentation to the delegates.

APPENDIX K
FAMILY EDUCATION PROGRAM #2: ZIONIST CONGRESS

Level: *Hey*
Curriculum: *Tzionut*

Anti-Uganda
- There are Jewish settlers already in Palestine. There are no such settlers in Uganda.
- Jews are emotionally attached to Palestine. They have prayed to return to it for two thousand years. They will work much harder to create a Jewish state in Palestine than anywhere else.
- While Herzl may not be able to get a charter from the Turkish government, there is a different way to build a Jewish settlement: to do it acre by acre, from the beginning. This doesn't seem as dramatic, but it's the best way in the long run to create a Jewish state.

- There's no guarantee that Britain will be able to keep her word about a colony for Jews.
- A homeland in Africa would be farther removed from Europe than one in Palestine. It would be less able to be part of the events affecting Jews in Europe.

Directions:
- Read and discuss the arguments above.
- Prepare an interesting and convincing presentation in opposition to the Uganda proposal.
- Make a poster to display during your presentation to the delegates.

APPENDIX L
ADULT EDUCATION PROGRAM #1: TIKKUN OLAN/SOCIAL ACTION SOURCES

Level: *Vav*
Curriculum: *Tikkun Olam*

If I am not for myself, who will be for me?
But if I am only for myself, what am I?
And if not now, when? (*Pirke Avot* 1:14)

Whoever is able to protest against the transgressions of his/her family and does not do so is punished for the transgressions of his/her family. Whoever is able to protest against the transgressions of the people of his/her community and does not do so is punished for the transgressions of his/her community. Whoever is able to protest against the transgressions of the entire world and does not do so is punished for the transgressions of the entire world. (*Shabbat* 54b)

If a person of learning participates in public affairs and serves as judge or arbiter, he/she gives stability to the land. But if he/she sits in his/her home and says to him/herself, "What have the affairs of society to do with me? Why should I trouble myself with the people's voices of protest? Let my soul dwell in peace!" If he/she does this, he/she overthrows the world. (*Tanchuma To Mishpatim*)

A man stood at the entrance to Sodom crying out against the injustice and evil in that city. Someone passed by and said to him, "For years you have been urging the people to repent, and yet no one has changed. Why do you continue?" He responded: "When I first came, I protested because I hope to change the people of Sodom. Now I continue to cry out, because if I don't, they will have changed me." (*Midrash*)

Woe to those who are at ease in Zion,
And to those who feel secure on the mountains of Samaria . . .
Woe to those who lie upon beds of ivory,
And stretch themselves upon their couches,
And eat lambs from the flock,
And calves from the midst of the stall;
Who sing idle songs to the sound of the harp . . .
Who drink wine in bowls,
And anoint themselves in the finest oils,
But are not grieved on the ruin of Joseph.
(Amos 6:1, 4-6)

In the hour when the Holy One created the first man, The Holy One took him and let him pass before all the trees of the Garden of Eden and said to him: "See my works, how fine and excellent they are! Now all that I have created, I created for your benefit. Think upon this and do not corrupt and destroy my world, for if you destroy it, there is no one to restore it after you. (*Ecclesiastes Rabbah* 7:28)

If your enemy is hungry, give him bread to eat. If your enemy is thirsty, give him water to drink. (Proverbs 25:21)

The world rests on three things: on justice, on truth, and on peace. And all three are one, for where there is justice, there is also truth, and there is peace. (*Pirke Avot* 1:18; *Ta'anit* 4:2)

Give of yourself, give as much as you can! And you can always, always give something even if it is only kindness! Give, give again and again, don't lose courage, keep it up and go on giving! No one has ever become poor from giving. (Anne Frank)

APPENDIX L, CONT.

It is not your obligation to complete the task. But neither are you free to desist from it. (*Pirke Avot* 2:21)

We came because we could not stand silently by our brothers' blood. We had done that too many times before. We had been vocal in our exhortation of others, but the idleness of our hands too often revealed our inner silence . . . . We came as Jews who remember the millions of faceless people who stood quietly, watching the smoke rise from Hitler's crematoria. We came because we know that second only to silence, the greatest danger to man is loss of faith in man's capacity to act.
(Group of Rabbis explaining why they came to St. Augustine, Florida, in 1964, to demonstrate against segregation in that community)

APPENDIX M
FAMILY EDUCATION PROGRAM #1: SOURCES OF MESSIANIC VISIONS

Level: *Vav*
Curriculum: *Tikkun Olam*

Isaiah: Chapter 2: 2-4
2. And it shall come to pass in the last days, that the mountain of *Adonai's* house shall be established on the top of the mountains, and shall be exalted above the hills; and all nations shall flow to it: 3. And many people shall go and say, Come, and let us go up to the mountain of *Adonai*, to the house of the God of Jacob; and God will teach us of God's ways, and we will walk in God's paths; for from Zion shall go forth Torah, and the word of *Adonai* from Jerusalem: 4. And God shall judge among the nations, and shall decide for many people; and they shall beat their swords into plowshares, and their spears into pruning hooks; nation shall not lift up sword against nation, nor shall they learn war any more.

Isaiah: Chapter 11:4-9
4. But with righteousness shall God judge the poor, and decide with equity for the humble of the earth; and God shall strike the earth with the rod of his mouth, and with the breath of his lips shall God slay the wicked: 5. And righteousness shall be the girdle of God's loins, and faithfulness the girdle of his reins: 6. The wolf also shall live with the lamb, and the leopard shall lie down with the kid; and the calf and the young lion and the fatling together; and a little child shall lead them: 7. And the cow and the bear shall feed; their young ones shall lie down together; and the lion shall eat straw like the ox: 8. And the sucking child shall play on the hole of the asp, and the weaned child shall put his hand in the viper's den: 9. They shall not hurt nor destroy in all my holy mountain; for the earth shall be full of the knowledge of *Adonai*, as the waters cover the sea.

Hosea: Chapter 2:20-24
20. And in that day I will make a covenant for them (Israel) with the beasts of the field, and with the birds of heaven, and with the creeping things of the ground; and I will break the bow and the sword and the battle out of the earth, and will make them lie down safely: 21. And I will betroth you to me forever; I will betroth you to me in righteousness, and in judgment, and in grace, and in mercies: 22. I will betroth you to me in faithfulness; and you shall know *Adonai*. 23. And it shall come to pass in that day, I will answer, says *Adonai*, I will answer the heavens, and they shall answer the earth: 24. And the earth shall answer the grain, and the wine, and the oil; and they shall answer Jezreel.

APPENDIX N
FAMILY EDUCATION PROGRAM #2: TIKKUN OLAM PROJECT REQUIREMENTS

Level: *Vav*
Curriculum: *Tikkun Olam*

Tikkun Olam Project Requirements
The project must include:
- Ongoing work of *Tikkun Olam* (not a one-time action)
- Work that affects the lives of others outside your family
- Family participation
- Work tied to Jewish values

- Ongoing reflection on the work by family members (journal, discussions, tape recording)
- Documentation of *Tikkun Olam* work and reflections for celebration (pictures, video, stories, posters, etc.)
- All work will be completed before _____. On that date, we will have our celebration.
- Students will not have completed the *Vav* class until this project is completed.
- All action plans will be submitted by _____.

APPENDIX O
FAMILY EDUCATION PROGRAM #2: LIST OF VALUES

Level: *Vav*
Curriculum: *Tikkun Olam*

Values of Tikkun Olam
"Bal Tashcheet" – Protecting the environment ('don't be wasteful")
Gemilut Chasideem – acts of loving-kindness
"K'lal Yisrael" – the unity of the Jewish people
Tza'ar Ba'alay Chayeem – taking care of animals
Kibud Zekaynim – honoring the elderly
Eretz Yisrael Yafah – the land of Israel is beautiful (we must preserve it)

V'ahavta Larayacha Kamocha – Love your neighbor as yourself
Mi Layv El Layev – from heart to heart/care and compassion (mutual responsibility)
Kal Hat-chalot Kashot – all beginnings are difficult/ assisting those who are beginning on all levels
Pikuach Nefesh – saving lives
Bikur Choleem – visiting the sick
Tzedakah – justice/charity
Kol Yisrael Aravim Zeh BaZeh – all Israel is responsible for one another
Shalom – seek peace and pursue it

APPENDIX P
FAMILY EDUCATION #2: ACTION PLAN

Level: *Vav*
Curriculum: *Tikkun Olam*

Action Plan

"It is not your obligation to complete the task, but neither are you free to desist from it" (*Pirke Avot* 2:21)

1. Important values for your *"Tikkun"* work:

    a. _____

    b. _____

    c. _____

2. Goals of your *"Tikkun"* work:

    a. _____

    b. _____

    c. _____

    d. _____

3. What actual work will your family do?
4. How does this work fit in with your values?
5. Specifics:
    a. When?
    b. Where?
    c. With Whom?
    d. How?

Student _____

Family _____

Address _____

Phone # _____

Level: *Vav*
Curriculum: *Tikkun Olam*

Resources for Tu B'Shevat Sedarim

Appelman, Harlene Winnick, and Jane Sherwin Shapiro. A *Seder for Tu B'Shvat*. Rockville, MD: Kar-Ben Copies, Inc., 1984.

Bialik, Hayim Nahman, and Yehoshua Hana Ravnitzky, eds. *The Book of Legends: Sefer Haagadah: Legends from the Talmud and Midrash*. New York: Schocken Books, 1992.

Gaster, Theodor H. *Festivals of the Jewish Year*. Magnolia, MD: Peter Smith, 1962, o.p.

Kaplan, Mordecai M, and Eugene Kohn, eds. *Sabbath Prayer Book*. New York: The Reconstructionist Foundation, 1965.

Seid, Judith. *We Rejoice in Our Heritage: Home Rituals for Secular and Humanistic Jews*. Ann Arbor, MI: Kopinvant Press, 1989.

Siegel, Richard; Michael Strassfeld; and Sharon Strassfeld, eds. *The First Jewish Catalog*. Philadelphia: Jewish Publication Society, 1973.

Gersh, Harry. *When a Jew Celebrates*. New York: Behrman House, Inc., 1971.

Level: *Zayin*
Curriculum: *Chochmah*

27. [As to the consequences of Israel's refusal to accept the Torah], Resh Lakish said: Why is it written, "And there was evening, and there was morning, the sixth day" (Genesis 1:31)? What is the significance of using the definite article? Singling out the "sixth day" by means of the definite article shows that the Holy One stipulated with the preceding works of creation, saying to them: "If Israel accepts the Torah [on the sixth day of Sivan], you will continue to exist; if not, I will return you to desolation and chaos."

29. "God came unto Sinai; after having [first] risen at Seir unto the people thereof, then having shined forth at Mount Paran, God came unto the myriads holy, at God's right hand a fiery law for them" (Deuteronomy 33:2). When God Who is everywhere revealed Himself to give the Torah to Israel, God revealed himself not only to Israel, but to all the other nations as well. At first, God went to the children of Esau. God asked them: Will you accept the Torah? They said right to God's face: What is written in it? He said: "Thou shalt not murder." They replied: Master of the universe, this goes against our grain. Our father, whose "hands are the hands of Esau" (Genesis 27:22), led us to rely only on the sword, because his father told him, "By thy sword shalt thou live" (Genesis. 27:40). We cannot accept the Torah.

Then God went to the children of Ammon and Moab, and asked them: Will you accept the Torah? They said right to God's face: What is written in it? God said: "Thou shalt not commit adultery." They replied: Master of the universe, our very origin is in adultery, for Scripture says, Thus were both the daughters of Lot with child

by their father" (Genesis 19:36). We cannot accept the Torah.

Then God went to the children of Ishmael. God asked them: Will you accept the Torah? They said right to God's face: What is written in it? God said: "Thou shalt not steal." They replied: Master of the universe, it is our very nature to live off only what is stolen and what is got by assault. Of our forebear Ishmael, it is written, "And he shall be a wild ass of a man: his hand shall be against every man, and every man's hand against him" (Genesis 16:12). We cannot accept the Torah.

There was not a single nation among the nations to whom God did not go, speak, and, as it were, knock on its doors asking whether it would be willing to accept the Torah.

At long last, God came to Israel. They said, "We will do and hearken" (Exodus 24:7). Of God's successive attempts to give the Torah, it is written, *Adonai* came unto Sinai; after having [first] risen at Seir unto the people thereof, then having shined forth at Mount Paran, God finally came unto the myriads holy, at God's right hand a fiery law for them" (Deuteronomy 33:2).

32. "And they stood under the mount" (Exodus 19:17). R. Avdimi bar Hama said: "The verse implies that the Holy One overturned the mountain upon them, like an inverted cask, and said to them: If you accept the Torah, it is well; if not, your grave will be right here."

35. "I am *Adonai* thy God." Because the Holy One appeared to them at the Reed Sea as a mighty man waging war, at Sinai as a pedagogue teaching Torah, in the days of Solomon as a young man, and in the days of Daniel as an aged man full of mercy, the Holy One said: "Because you see Me in many guises, do not imagine that

---

[1] All of these sources from *The Book of Legends: Sefer Ha-agadah: Legends from the Talmud and Midrash*, edited by Hayim Nahman Bialik and Yehoshua Hana Ravnitzky (New York: Shocken Books, 1992), pp. 78-81.

there are many gods — for I am the One Who was with you at the Reed Sea, I am the One Who was with you at Sinai, I am the same everywhere. I am *Adonai* thy God."

36. "His mouth is most sweet" (Song of Songs 5:16). It is said in the name of R. Yohanan: "The moment Israel at Sinai heard the word 'I,' their souls left them, as is written, 'My soul left me when He spoke' (Song of Songs 5:6). At once, the Word returned to the Holy One and said: 'Master of the universe, You are ever alive and enduring, the Torah is ever alive and enduring, yet You are sending me to the dead? They are all dead!' So, for Israel's sake, the Holy One went back and sweetened [made soft] the Word, as is said, 'The voice of *Adonai* is powerful, the voice of *Adonai* is stately' (Psalm 29:4), which, as R. Hama bar Hanina explained, means that the voice of *Adonai* was powerful for young men and had measured stateliness for the aged. [In agreement with R. Hama bar Hanina], R. Levi said: Had it been written, 'The voice of *Adonai* is in *Adonai's* strength,' the world could not have stood it. Hence Scripture says, 'The voice of *Adonai* is fitted to the strength' (Psalm 29:4), that is to say, to the strength of each and every person — the young, according to their strength, the aged, according to their strength; the little ones, according to their strength; the sucklings, according to their strength; the women, according to their strength."

R. Simeon ben Yohai, however, taught: "The Torah that the Holy One gave to Israel was the one who helped restore their souls to them. She pleaded before the Holy One for mercy on their behalf, saying, 'Is there a king who gives his daughter in marriage and stays the courtier whom she is to wed? The entire world rejoices for my sake, yet Your children [Israel, to whom I am being given], are dying!' At that, their souls returned. 'The Law of *Adonai* is perfect, it restores souls'" (Psalm 19:8).

Another exposition of "His mouth is most sweet" (Song of Songs 5:16): [The Holy One was] like a king who spoke so harshly to his son that the latter fell into a faint. When the king saw that he had fainted, he began to hug him, kiss him, and speak softly to him, saying, "What is it with you? Are you not my only son? Am I not your father?" So, too, as soon as the Holy One said, "I am *Adonai* thy God," then and there Israel's souls left them. When they died, the angels began to hug them and kiss them, saying to them, "What is it with you? Be not afraid; ye are children of *Adonai* your God" (Deuteronomy 14:1). At the same time, the Holy One repeated the Word softly for their sake, saying, "Are you not My children, even as I am *Adonai* your God? You are My people. You are beloved unto Me." God kept speaking gently to them until their souls returned.

41. At Sinai, when the Holy One gave the Torah to Israel, God manifested marvels upon marvels for Israel with God's voice. How so? As the Holy One spoke, the voice reverberated throughout the world. At first, Israel heard the voice coming to them from the south, so they ran to the south to meet the voice there. It shifted to the north, so they ran to the north. Then it shifted to the east, so they ran to the east; but from the east it shifted to the west, so they ran to the west. Next it shifted to heaven. But when they raised their eyes toward heaven, it seemed to rise out of the earth. Hence Israel asked one another, "But wisdom, when shall it be found? And where is the place of understanding?" (Job 28:12).

"And all the people perceived the thunderings" (Exodus 20.15). Since there was only one voice, why "thunderings" in the plural? Because God's voice mutated into seven voices, and the seven voices into 70 languages, so that all the nations might hear it.

APPENDIX S
FAMILY EDUCATION #1: CREATION

Level: *Zayin*
Curriculum: *Chochmah*

#1: Brit with Noah: Genesis 9

1. And God blessed Noah and his sons, and said to them, Be fruitful, and multiply, and replenish the earth. 2. And the fear of you and the dread of you shall be upon every beast of the earth, and upon every bird of the air, upon all that moves upon the earth, and upon all the fishes of the sea; to your hand are they delivered. 3. Every moving thing that lives shall be food for you; even as the green herb have I given you all things. 4. But flesh with its life, which is its blood, you shall not eat. 5. And surely your blood of your lives will I require; at the hand of every beast will I require it, and at the hand of man; at the hand of every man's brother will I require the life of man. 6. Whoever sheds man's blood, by man shall his blood be shed; for in the image of God He made man. 7. And you, be fruitful, and multiply; bring forth abundantly in the earth, and multiply in it. 8. And God spoke to Noah, and to his sons with him, saying: 9. And I, behold, I establish my covenant with you, and with your seed after you. 10. And with every living creature that is with you, of the bird, of the cattle, and of every beast of the earth with you; from all that go out of the ark, to every beast of the earth. 11. And I will establish my covenant with you; nor shall all flesh be cut off any more by the waters of a flood; nor shall there any more be a flood to destroy the earth. 12. And God said, This is the sign of the covenant which I make between me and you and every living creature that is with you, for everlasting generations. 13. I set my bow in the cloud, and it shall be for a sign of a covenant between me and the earth. 14. And it shall come to pass, when I bring a cloud over the earth, that the bow shall be seen in the cloud. 15. And I will remember my covenant, which is between me and you and every living creature of all flesh; and the waters shall no more become a flood to destroy all flesh. 16. And the bow shall be in the cloud; and I will look upon it, that I may remember the everlasting covenant between God and every living creature of all flesh that is upon the earth. 17. And God said to Noah, This is the sign of the covenant, which I have established between me and all flesh that is upon the earth.

#2: The Brit with Abraham: Genesis 17

1. And when Abram was 99 years old, *Adonai* appeared to Abram, and said to him, I am the Almighty God; walk before me, and be perfect. 2. And I will make my covenant between me and you, and will multiply you exceedingly. 3. And Abram fell on his face; and God talked with him, saying: 4. As for me, behold, my covenant is with you, and you shall be a father of many nations. 5. Neither shall your name any more be called Abram, but your name shall be Abraham; for a father of many nations have I made you. 6. And I will make you exceedingly fruitful, and I will make nations of you, and kings shall come out of you. 7. And I will establish my covenant between me and you and your seed after you in their generations for an everlasting covenant, to be a God to you, and to your seed after you. 8. And I will give to you, and to your seed after you, the land where you are a stranger, all the land of Canaan, for an everlasting possession; and I will be their God. 9. And God said to Abraham, You shall keep my covenant therefore, you, and your seed after you in their generations. 10. This is my covenant, which you shall keep, between me and you and your seed after you; every male child among you shall be circumcised. 11. And you shall circumcise the flesh of your foreskin; and it shall be a sign of the covenant between me and you. 12. And he who is eight days old shall be circumcised among you, every male child in your generations, he who is born in the house, or bought with money from any stranger, who is not of your seed. 13. He who is born in your house, and he who is bought with your money, must be circumcised; and my covenant shall be in your flesh for an everlasting covenant.

#3: Brit with Israel at Mt. Sinai: Exodus 19-20

(Chapter 19) 3. And Moses went up to God, and *Adonai* called to him from the mountain, saying, "Thus shall you say to the house of Jacob, and tell the people of Israel: 4. You have seen what I did to the Egyptians, and how I carried you on eagles' wings, and brought you to myself. 5. Now therefore, if you will obey my voice indeed, and keep my covenant, then you shall be my own treasure among all peoples; for all the earth is mine. 6. And you shall be to me a kingdom of priests, and a holy nation; these are the words which you shall speak to the people of Israel."

7. And Moses came and called for the elders of the people, and laid before their faces all these words which *Adonai* commanded him. 8. And all the people answered together, and said, All that *Adonai* has spoken we will do. And Moses returned the words of the people to *Adonai*.

(Chapter 20) 1. And God spoke all these words, saying: 2. I am *Adonai* your God, who brought you out of the land of Egypt, out of the house of slavery. 3. You shall have no other gods before me. 4. You shall not make for you any engraved image, or any likeness of any thing that is in heaven above, or that is in the earth beneath, or that is in the water under the earth. 5. You shall not bow yourself down to them, nor serve them; for I *Adonai* your God am a jealous God, visiting the iniquity of the fathers upon the children to the third and fourth generation of them that hate me. 6. And showing mercy to thousands of those who love me, and keep my commandments. 7. You shall not take the name of *Adonai* your God in vain; for *Adonai* will not hold him guiltless who takes his name in vain. 8. Remember the Sabbath day, to keep it holy. 9. Six days shall you labor, and do all your work. 10. But the seventh day is the Sabbath of *Adonai* your God; in it you shall not do any work, you, nor your son, nor your daughter, your manservant, nor your maidservant, nor your cattle, nor your stranger that is within your gates. 11. For in six days *Adonai* made heaven and earth, the sea, and all that is in them, and rested the seventh day; therefore *Adonai* blessed the Sabbath day, and made it holy. 12. Honor your father and your mother that your days may be long upon the land which *Adonai* your God gives you. 13. You shall not kill; You shall not commit adultery; You shall not steal; You shall not bear false witness against your neighbor. 14. You shall not covet your neighbor's house, you shall not covet your neighbor's wife, nor his manservant, nor his maidservant, nor his ox, nor his ass, nor any thing that is your neighbor's. 15. And all the people saw the thunderings, and the lightnings, and the sound of the *shofar*, and the mountain smoking; and when the people saw it, they were shaken, and stood far away. 16. And they said to Moses, Speak with us, and we will hear; but let not God speak with us, lest we die. 17. And Moses said to the people, Fear not; for God has come to test you, and that his fear may be before your faces, that you sin not.

CHAPTER 7

REFLECTIONS ON ADULTS IN THE BNAI KESHET PROGRAM

CONTRIBUTOR: RABBI DAN EHRENKRANTZ
ADDRESS: Bnai Keshet
99 South Fullerton Avenue
Montclair, NJ 07042
PHONE: (973) 746-4889
E-MAIL: dcehr@aol.com
TARGET: Parents

Note: This chapter expands on the relationship between adult and family learning implicit in Chapter 6, "The Bnai Keshet Program." In this chapter, Rabbi Dan Ehrenkrantz, a primary shaper of the program, responds to four questions put to him by the editors of this volume about family and adult learning.

1. *In what specific ways is the parent participating in family programs different from the "typical" adult learner participating in other synagogue programs?*

Family Education implies adult education. While a great deal of adult education can take place in the company of children, sometimes it is necessary to create a strictly adult learning environment. Adult education as part of a comprehensive Family Education program contains many challenges not typically found in other adult education settings.

The main difference between adult education undertaken in a Family Education context and other adult education programs is the motivation of the learner. In a Family Education context, persons entirely uninterested in Jewish learning may find

themselves studying Talmudic texts on a Sunday morning. Their motivation is to contribute to a family goal of educating their child.

In other adult education contexts, one can assume that the learners are interested in the topic being taught. This assumption can not be made in a Family Education setting. On the other hand, participants in a Family Education program are actively sharing a common life situation, namely, providing a Jewish education for their children. This commonality of life stage may make the participants more open to the community building and social benefits of studying with other adults.

Following are profiles of "typical" adult learners who have attended Family Education sponsored adult education programs:

Stan G. is an accomplished psychologist. He looks back on his own Jewish education with contempt and would prefer not to be a member of a synagogue. His wife, however, has won the family battle over synagogue affiliation and the children's religious education. Stan is a devoted father and he understands the mixed messages his children pick up about their religious education. In order to minimize this problem, Stan is willing to participate in the Family Education program sponsored by the synagogue. He participates, but is most engaged when he is able to find the lines of appropriate and acceptable ideas. If he finds such lines, he is quick to step over them in order to strengthen his belief that he doesn't belong.

Melissa W. is a devoted mother. She was brought up in an observant Protestant home and wants her children to have the benefits she believed she received from her religious upbringing. Melissa married a Jew and agreed to raise their children as Jews. Though she has never been interested in converting, she now finds herself learning about Judaism in order to help raise her children as Jews.

Sarah B. is a dedicated synagogue member. She has served on the congregation's Mutual Support Committee, providing help to congregants especially in times of family distress. She has also been active in the synagogue's Social Action Committee. Her Judaic background is not extensive and she is not particularly interested in learning more. She values education, but believes that we should spend more of our energies helping others. Her deep commitment to Jewish life is expressed socially and communally.

Herman W. works for an insurance company. Over the past five years, he has devoted much of his spare time to Jewish learning. He spent a few weeks in Israel, has been studying Hebrew, and has become quite observant. Herman is particularly interested in Jewish mysticism, and has taken advantage of educational programs offered by Chabad. He questions the philosophy of his Reconstructionist synagogue, and wonders if he is making the right choice for himself and his family. However, he has been a member of the synagogue for many years and still finds much that is compelling there. Herman looks forward to any Jewish learning and is pleased to participate in adult education programs. He is distressed, however, that others do not share his passion for Jewish learning.

A quick scan of the above profiles reveals that the only things the learners have in common is a willingness to attend a program of study as part of their commitment to their children. They may not be interested in the topic or even in their own learning, but they are willing to be present.

2. *How does one take into account such differences in thinking when planning lectures/discussions/activities?*

Not coincidentally, the mix of parental attitudes closely reflects the mixed attitudes of their children. Jewish educators have long struggled with students who are not motivated to be present and learn. A successful teacher is able to create a classroom environment in which learning and enthusiasm are present despite the initial reticence of some of the students. This same challenge is present when we teach adults.

Building on this common commitment to their children, we have found that a surefire method of engaging parents is to make their learning directly applicable to a family educational activity. Typically, this activity immediately follows the adult education session. Early on during the adult session, the tie-in to the upcoming program with their children is made explicit. No parent wants to appear unprepared or uneducated to his/her child. It is the goal of the adult session to make sure that all parents will have the necessary learning to be full participants in the family session.

In making parents co-teachers of a particular lesson, the school must be careful to make sure the goals of the lesson are shared by the parents. On the one hand, educational goals must be broad enough to allow the wide range of parents to find their place. On the other hand, goals must be clear enough to be compelling. An adult education session which is directly tied in to a following family session provides an opportunity to create consensus for particular goals. For example, coming into a class, Stan G., the aforementioned psychologist, believes that perpetuating a belief in God serves only to control people and to reduce their capacity for responsible action. If the goal of the family session is to have parents and children engage in discussion about God, Stan will need to be assured that his beliefs can be accommodated. He, like all the parents present, will also need to be convinced that there is a value in exploring beliefs other than their own. If this can be accomplished in the adult education session, the family session that follows is likely to contain a different kind of parent-child interaction than is usually present. On the surface, the adult session may be a discussion of different theological views. Just below the surface lies the goal of convincing the parents that theological views matter.

When I teach adult education classes in other contexts, I rely on the material to create interest in the topic at hand. In a Family Education context, I rely instead on the interest of parents to be teachers of Judaism to their children. If the material is weak, it will certainly undermine this interest. Judaism will appear to the parents as less important. But interesting material which can not be translated to their children or somehow integrated into the life of the family is typically not enough to engage an adult class in a Family Education context.

3. *How might we recognize a desire for more independent adult learning in parents?*

While there are added challenges to teaching adults in a Family Education context, there are also surprising benefits. Parents participate in the Religious School education of their children. Critiques of Religious School education on the part of the parents become more informed and more realistic. The quality of education becomes more important to parents because they are participants as both learners and teachers.

For many parents, participation in Family Education programs is the most exposure they have had to Judaism since they were children. For some, like Melissa W., it is the most exposure they have *ever* had. In many cases, this exposure leads to a new interest in learning. This interest is expressed in their enthusiastic participation in class sessions, and sometimes it leads to enrollment in other synagogue and community adult learning opportunities.

4. *How can we follow up on significant family learning and strengthen the adult learning component of these programs?*

Ideally, we should be able to take advantage of their enthusiasm by directing parents to more intensive classes on topics which have interested them. While it may not be realistic to have these classes running at all times, a rotating schedule of classes designed to further the learning that occurs in Family Education programs would enable us to channel parents' enthusiasm into continued learning. A program of this nature would almost force a congregation to create an adult education curriculum, one that would closely mirror the curriculum offered to the children in the Religious School.

Engaging in an intensive Family Education program within the Religious School may bring about many repercussions. For example:

• By bringing parents into the school, their expectations of the level of education offered in the school have been raised. While in the short term, this can cause some discomfort for the administrators, in the long term, it is a great benefit to the school. As co-teachers of their children, parents gain a more realistic sense of the challenges of educating their children. As a result, there is a better sense of collaboration between parents and children.

• Increased adult learning through Family Education can lead to a more organized and methodical adult education curriculum in the synagogue.

• If a family is giving mixed messages to their children concerning Judaism, Family Education sessions will frequently provide a forum to make these tensions explicit. While this is not the goal of these sessions, it is no surprise that it occurs. Consequently, Rabbis and educators should be prepared to work with families over tensions that arise which are connected to the family's religious life. Absent Family Education, these tensions are usually most clearly seen by Rabbis at the time of Bar or Bat Mitzvah. At that time, it is frequently too late to address the difficulties in a way that can bring resolution.

• By bringing a class and its families together on a regular basis over the course of a number of years, the school fosters a sense of community.

When we teach a regular synagogue adult education class, we hope that the learning will lead to increased social ties and reinvigorate the entire community with the excitement and knowledge the participants have gained from the class. In a Family Education context, we hope that the social ties and shared communal goal of educating their children will lead to an increased interest in Jewish life and learning.

CONCLUSION

Adult education in a Family Education context builds upon motivations different from those of a typical adult education class. We are wise to capitalize on these motivations rather than assume motivations that may not be present. We are used to seeing adult education influence the life of an individual, and through that individual, influence the life of a family. In Family Education, we begin with the life of the family. The growth and development we may see will run from the family to the individuals.

Adult education in the synagogue typically reaches only the interested elite. Adult education in a Family Education context reaches everyone. This presents both special challenges and special opportunities. If we are to take advantage of these opportunities, we must take into account the differences and adapt our teaching to match the different situation.

CHAPTER 8

A MINYAN OF TECHNIQUES FOR ENGAGING THE ADULT JEWISH LEARNER

CONTRIBUTOR: LOIS J. ZACHARY
ADDRESS: **3042 East Sierra Vista Drive**
Phoenix, AZ 85016
PHONE: **(602) 954-9934**
E-MAIL: leadservs@aol.com
TARGET: **Parents as Adult Learners**

Family Educators must be prepared to meet diverse learning needs of a wide variety of individuals simultaneously. Since there are more differences in learning among adults than between adults and children, the uniqueness of adult learners is a given. Malcolm Knowles, in *The Modern Practice of Adult Education: From Pedagogy To Andragogy* (Follett Publishing Co., 1980), has provided valuable insights about adult learners. In general, these individuals have (1) a deep ego involvement and strong self-concept, (2) a background of experience and expertise, (3) a readiness to learn based on their experience, and (4) a problem-centered orientation to their learning. Accordingly, appropriate assumptions inform good practice (see Table 1 below).

When adult learners come to Jewish education, the learning situation is compounded. In addition to the Jewish context, a lack of congruence between the level of academic knowledge and level of Jewish knowledge frequently exists. Experience, life stage, and desire to solve a problem are drivers, but ego needs often get in the way. Understandably, adults don't want to appear stupid or incompetent or diminished in front of their peers, so they are reluctant to participate, or do so minimally.

How, then, do we pay attention to the array of learning needs among diverse adults, and, at the same time, honor the integrity of Jewish content? This chapter presents ten learner-centered techniques to assist the Family Educator in developing a repertoire of learner-centered techniques that do just that. Why ten? Simply because a *minyan* is a good Jewish value!

Jewish educators need to be facile with many techniques to meet their students' needs. It is not a case of *either/or*, but of *both/and*. We must be flexible and able to provide "hooks" that evoke reflection on the wellspring of experience learners bring to their learning.

The techniques described below provide a menu of experiential (hands-on and interactive) and experience-focused options. Learner-centered adult education practice gets learners recounting

Principle	Assumption
Concept of Learner	Increasingly self directing, proactive
Role of Learner's Experience	A rich resource for learning by self and others
Readiness to Learn	Develops from life tasks, problems, transitions
Orientation To Learning	Task or problem centered

Table I
The Andragogical Conceptual Framework of Malcolm Knowles

their experiences, analyzing them (individually and/or collectively), and positions the learner to identify and act on the implications of what it is they learn from the analysis of their experiences. For more on this, see *Learning and Change in the Adult Years: A Developmental Perspective* by M. Tennant and P. Pogson (Jossey-Bass, Inc., 1995, p. 160). The word "experiential," on the other hand, is associated with David A. Kolb's learning cycle which involves moving through four stages (see *Learning Style Inventory Technical Manual* by David A. Kolb (McBer and Co., 1985). Learners create knowledge by (1) acquiring information through experience and (2) abstraction, and then transforming it through (3) reflection and (4) experimentation. Every learner has a preferred point of entry into that cycle. Educators of adults need to be savvy about how adults learn so that learning environments can be structured to support affective, perceptual, symbolic, and behavioral learning.

The following ten techniques can be combined, interspersed with lecture and demonstration, or used separately. They illustrate how content and process can be integrated to encourage students to maximize the different experiential modes.

1. JOURNALING

Journaling is one of my favorite techniques! It provides an anonymous venue for students to reflect on their experience and assists them in personalizing their learning. It can be a catalyst for student observation and self-understanding, and at the same time provide a vehicle to integrate learning and intensify focus on content matter.

For these reasons, I always begin class sessions with a journal activity. In the first session of a seminar, I give the student an overview handout describing the journal writing process, a journal cover, and some blank pages with a question at the top of each. Typically, I ask students questions such as the following:

• What are your personal goals/expectations for the seminar? That is, what do you want to get out of the seminar?

• How might this seminar help you in doing your job better?

• Identify some new learning or ways of seeing things (emphasis, perspectives, etc.) related to the topics in this course that may already have affected you and your job or that may influence you later.

I encourage students to journal on their own as they read course materials and prepare assignments. I make it clear that the journals are theirs, and there is never a point at which they need to feel their privacy is compromised. Still, there is some reflection I ask them to share with me. At the end of each class session, I hand out to each participant a two-ply NCR form (so that the teacher and learner can each keep a copy) with three or four questions and lots of blank space, asking the students to reflect on the session anonymously. Here are some questions I use:

• Identify three things you learned today.

• What stands out in your mind about your learnings today?

• What questions remain in your mind as the day ends?

The student separates the completed sheets of NCR paper, keeps a copy, and hands in a copy. Before the next class, all student responses are clustered into like response categories under each question. At the next class, I hand out a table containing these responses. Students are given time to read and reflect on the responses and comment in class. Usually I hear comments such as: "When I left last time I felt like I was all alone. Now I realize what I was feeling is normal." The exercise also reminds students about topics covered in the last class.

Once this exercise is complete, I again ask students to journal. I hand out question pages for students to add to their journal. I say that they should reflect on their previous entries and on what has happened in the last month. Some of these questions are:

• Where are you right now in relation to your answers to those questions?

• Do these answers still make sense to you?

• What, if anything, has changed?

Some of my students prefer more open-ended journal writing. I always give the option of answering my questions or their own for the in-class journal exercise. Some other stimuli you might use for journals are:

- How are you doing?
- How are you doing spiritually?
- What is the most memorable thing you have learned so far, and how are you applying it in your life?

At a Journal Workshop by Ira Progoff (Dialogue House, 1975) provides good triggers for stimulating student writing. He suggests tracing any phenomena in one's life through writing prompts, such as "at first," "and then," "and now."

2. FEEDBACK

Whether we intend to or not, we are always giving feedback. While most adult learners appreciate feedback in whatever form it is given, others just can't handle it or don't appreciate it. There is an art to giving feedback and to receiving it. Students and teachers need to learn to do both. Some advice I share with colleagues:

- Catch someone doing something right and let them know it immediately.
- Give feedback continuously, not just on special occasions.
- Help students know what kind of feedback you want.
- Be specific in the feedback you provide.
- Be honest.
- Be clear.
- Don't be overly helpful. Leave room for student discovery.
- Show empathy.
- Remember, feedback goes two ways.

The concept of *chevruta* is a classic example of a useful technique to encourage candor, communication, and feedback. When done well, it gives students an opportunity for input and reflection, as well as integration of what has been learned. Here are some ground rules I follow when giving feedback.

In giving feedback, we are sometimes not as helpful as we could be. I am stroking and praising, not providing useful feedback when I say something like, "Your group did a terrific job. You've obviously got the concept. You should feel pleased with a job

well done. We will look forward to next time you all get together."

In the following example, I am challenging and providing support, reinforcing, and praising: "I like your presentation because you took the information from class last week and applied it in some really unique and thoughtful ways. You've incorporated the concepts of *Tikkun Olam* and *Gemilut Chasadeem*, for example, when you _____. Next time, why don't you try to do _____. You might want to _____. You should feel proud of what you've accomplished in such a short time."

3. NETWORKING

It is not often that we think of networking as a classroom technique. However, networking is one of the best ways to create a learning community and to set the climate for collaborative learning. Networking plays to the reservoir of experience of adults, which is often unknown to the class. In order to encourage networking, I provide small and large group interaction, creating a community bulletin board as the focus for connection. Here's how to do it.

Community Bulletin Board

On a large wall, post butcher paper. On the paper, list headings, such as "Questions In Search of Answers," "Good Reads," "Help Wanted," etc. Include graphics and cartoons (the more colorful the better). Fill a baggie with push pins, post-it notes, writing material, etc. Post the baggie in a visible and accessible space near or on the butcher paper. Explain the concept to students and tell them, "It is your board." Encourage the students to respond to the topics listed on the butcher paper with questions and reflections.

Some classes take to this exercise more than others. I check in with students and scan the posted items, and I encourage students to do likewise. I bring materials myself to add to the board during the breaks.

Question Box

In some circumstances, using the community bulletin board concept just isn't appropriate. Since question posing is such an important outcome of adult education. I use a question box and invite students to write questions about the course or seminar topic and drop them in the box. For this, use an attractive box and display it prominently. Include 3" x 5" cards with your handout packet, and leave a stack near the box with pens and pencils nearby. If you can find a cute cartoon to stand near the box or paste on the box, so much the better. Stop several times during the session specifically to check the box and to respond to questions.

4. ASSUMPTION HUNTING

As educators, we must be aware of our assumptions and check them out frequently for their validity and accuracy. Immediate reaction is certainly not the basis for informed educational practice! Rather, we should be reflective and continuously aware that we each bring who we are to what we do. The following quotation is helpful when thinking about assumptions:

> In many ways, we are our assumptions. Assumptions give meaning and purpose to who we are and what we do. Becoming aware of the implicit assumptions that frame how we think and act is one of the most challenging intellectual puzzles we face in our lives. *Becoming a Critically Reflective Teacher* by Stephen D. Brookfield (Jossey-Bass, 1995).

Assumption hunting is difficult and challenging work. This means that we must make time to think about the beliefs we take for granted. We ought to engage in thoughtful reflection about why we do what we do. What do we say to ourselves (or to others) so as to justify our actions? Assumption hunting is vital to teaching, since assumptions determine how and what we think about our students in particular and the learning process in general. Assumptions guide our actions and are often self-reinforcing.

Beginning an internal dialogue of assumption hunting is not easy. One way to start the habit of assumption hunting might be to look at *what it is we do* in the classroom and then work backward and ask ourselves, "Why did I do that?" or "What are my assumptions about the adults in this class?" or "What are my assumptions about what will go on in this classroom?" Check out these assumptions for validity by seeking student feedback. I often ask students to reflect on their assumptions about an area of content or a concept.

For example, say you were beginning a discussion about the concept of *Tzedakah*. After discussion and explanation of the topic, you might ask students to write down their assumptions of *Tzedakah* for (1) themselves, (2) their children, and (3) their community. Each set of assumptions — 1, 2, and 3 — should be written on separate sheets of different colored paper. Gather these up and sort them by color. Then divide the class into three subgroups. Ask each subgroup to process a set of assumptions. Provide them with clear guidelines for proceding. Here are two examples:

• Select someone to read all responses in the group's assigned category without revealing the identity of any of the respondents. Everyone is to listen to all of the responses without comment.

• Discuss each of the following questions: What can be concluded about these assumptions? Is there consensus? If so, on what items? If there is not consensus, why do you think this is so? What are the implications of those conclusions?

5. CASE STUDIES

Case studies offer a powerful tool for helping adults reflect on their own experiences. They can be used effectively with students who are at different levels of understanding to stimulate in-depth reflection and learning of a real event, problem, or situation. The discussion which ensues generates excitement from students because they can easily enter discussion at the level of their experience. Designing case studies should not be taken lightly. They must be carefully constructed and relevant to the students for whom they are being created. When you design your own case studies, field test them first for understandability, clarity, and most of all relevance. The characters and dilemmas that are developed must in some fundamental way remind the students of themselves. A case study cannot be an exercise in nineteenth (or increasingly even twentieth) century history.

6. INTEGRATING LEARNING

For example, suppose you are teaching the class about *chagim* (holidays). You present a critical incident in a case study, and pose questions about a family in which the children know more than the parents. First, summarize the situation as it is presented, then ask questions such as the following to help them integrate their learning:

- What is going on here?
- What are the critical concerns facing this family at this time?
- Select a ritual, ceremony, or activity that we have discussed which might help make this family's celebration of the *chag* more meaningful. Why did you select it? Discuss the specifics of what you think this family should do to incorporate this ritual, ceremony, or activity. Ask: What steps do you need to take? How should you go about it?

7. ASSIGNMENTS

Class assignments are also a technique for meeting an array of adult learning needs. I use assignments to help students integrate and apply learning. I want to know if my students are grasping the concepts and making the necessary leaps to practice. I use an assignment as a calibration exercise and to get feedback to guide teaching. Just as in the case study, good design and construction are imperative. I strive to ask learners to integrate what it is they are learning so that they can apply it. I also include information about the criteria I will use to evaluate the assignment. This gives students clues as to how to structure response and apportion their time. When grading assignments, I provide feedback using those criteria. Here is an example of focused responses:

Instructions: You have 30 minutes to write your response to one of the two sets of questions below. Since you have only a limited amount of time, you will want to focus on the most important aspects of the questions. You may use notes or consult sources, but direct quotes or page references are not needed. If you have been doing your readings and integrating the information into your thinking, there should be little need to consult the readings or text. Use your time efficiently. You may find it helpful to develop an initial outline and then write your response to the question. The outline can be submitted along with the paper. Please do your best to write legibly. In evaluating your work, I will be looking for evidence of the following:

- Importance of the topic to your work
- Clarity of description
- Demonstration of conceptual understanding
- Applicability to work setting
- Integration of information, course material, and sources

I use "assignments" in situations in which grading is not part of the course requirements. Again, I provide guidelines to help adults focus and use their time and energy well, and I provide support for adults who require structure.

To help students make connections, you might hold a panel presentation on *Tzedakah*, featuring a Federation president, a Rabbi, and a foundation director. Afterward, say to the students: Today you heard a variety of presentations about *Tzedakah*. You also prepared for the class by gathering information from a variety of sources (handouts, texts, visits to community agencies, and your own individual reading). Here are some projects from which to choose:

a. Select one of the issues related to *Tzedakah* presented by today's panelists. It must be one which has relevance to you, your family, and/or the community. Describe this issue briefly and explain why you selected it. What key points strike you as particularly important? How does this issue relate to the material which you read in preparation for today's session? Do one of the following activities.

b. Select one of the readings you prepared for today's class. It must be one which has relevance to you, your family, and/or the community. Describe this article/book/resource briefly and explain why it "speaks to you." What points strike you as particularly important? How do they relate to key issues raised by today's panelists?

8. LEARNING CONTRACT

The learning contract is another technique for helping adults to be more or less self-directed in their learning. Adults are given the freedom to design, implement, and evaluate their own learning. This technique is attractive to both the learner and the teacher. Its flexibility makes it adaptable to most learning styles, since the learner defines the means and the ends. Adults who are less comfortable without teacher direction have the opportunity to build in as much support for learning as they need. While the parameters for the assignment (the subject matter) are prescribed, the adult remains in control of his/her own learning. For me, there is another more valuable aspect: the learner is learning a process of pursuing his/her own learning goals, whether it be mastery, acquisition of a body of knowledge, or specific application. Thus, I know that if an adult successfully completes a learning contract, he or she has internalized the tools for applying this technique to any subject matter. The learning contract technique is a disciplined approach which includes clarity about goals and outcomes of the learning, definition of objectives, selection of learning strategies and resources, evaluation of the learning, and specific time frames for accomplishment.

Developing and implementing a learning contract is one avenue to assist adults in completing assignments, while encouraging self-directed learning. In class I present the learning contract as a methodology for achieving specific objectives. Thus, I ask the adult to lay out the means and the ends (the goals) clearly: to define objectives, identify resources needed, explore learning processes to be employed, detail critical success factors, and set target dates (including a date for self-evaluation). In the ideal situation, I ask them to develop a rough draft of their contract and bring it to class. During class time, I do a group process exercise encouraging students to seek and receive feedback from class colleagues. The experience of exchanging contracts with another learner usually suggests alternative sources and modalities for accomplishing objectives. The draft with annotations gets turned in to me at the end of the class. I review each contract proposal and provide feedback before the final proposal is put in place.

I always provide a debriefing of the learning contract process so that adults can employ this methodology to learn on their own. In addition, I review the entire process from start to finish and, based on class input, provide a worksheet for adults to use as a model in the future.

9. NOMINAL GROUP PROCESS

The nominal group process is a productive technique to mine the expertise of group members and create an experiential situation. Using it assures that everyone gets heard, and results in prioritization of "issues" related to some common concern or problem. In this participatory exercise, the class members work individually, in small groups, and as a whole class. The process takes approximately two hours.

For example, so as to elicit all the possible ways a family can celebrate a Bar or Bat Mitzvah, I like to break the larger group into small groups of five to eight people. Although the process is designed to develop a dialogue among group members and share information about perceptions of the members (including the importance of the items to the individuals), the results of the process can be utilized as the background for developing a personal family action plan.

The process starts with the statement of the task or charge to the group members: Identify the most important things to include in planning a Bar/Bat Mitzvah. (This refers to "all of the possible things" or to the "big picture.")

After the task statement is described and understood, the steps to the process sequentially are as follows:
a. Idea generating focus
b. Silent brainstorming – members record their individual responses to question (15 min.)
c. Idea recording – round robin listing without comment (20 min.)

d. Idea clarification – discussion without value judgments (20 min.)

e. Priority setting

f. Ranking ideas – individuals rank most important ideas (15 min.)

g. Recording rankings – posting rankings by group members (10 min.)

h. Discussion – group discusses and explains why some items were ranked by various members while others were not (20 to 30 min.)

i. Scoring – individuals record revised rankings and/or ratings (10 to 15 min.)

10. SIMULATION

According to Gilley (see *Methods of Adult Education*, by Galbraith (Jossey-Bass, 1990), "Simulation is a technique which enables adult learners to obtain skills, competencies, knowledge, or behaviors by becoming involved in situations that are similar to those in real life." The most important part of any simulation is the debriefing that occurs after the simulation. About a decade ago, some colleagues and I presented a session at CAJE during which we simulated a teaching lesson on *Birkat HaMazon*. We started the class by having the students actually participate in a lecture on *Birkat HaMazon*. We constructed the simulation using technical language, talking down to students, acting disorganized, and talking around whatever questions were posed by students. Following the simulation, we debriefed the learners, asking them to describe what it was they experienced. We used emotions and reactions as a way of identifying the assumptions behind the teacher's lessons, and bridged to models and processes of three other models of teaching. We charged students with the task of creating a new simulation using the theoretical models as a basis, thereby providing a simulation experience for everyone else in the group.

For example, one could simulate the building of a *sukkah,* and in that simulation have an individual in the group give the orders, dismissing suggestions from others. Ask: How did it feel? What is missing?

Simulation can also be used as a demonstration of the ideal. A *Shabbaton* is an example of this type of simulation. One can surely see that the debriefing of a simulation is critical, because it is the link or connection for a good learning experience.

YOU

Learner-centered technique is not a template. It requires the sagacity and experience of the educator to bring it to life. While this chapter posits that educators must have many techniques at their command, we must remember that we are learners ourselves and never reduce teaching to mere technique. See "Good Teaching: A Matter of Living the Mystery" by Parker J. Palmer, *Change,* January/February 1990, 22(1), 11-16.

We need continuously to motivate, educate, and inspire the adults we teach by asking them what they want to know, checking out our assumptions and their assumptions, not relying on convention, making sure we support learning by creating a climate for stimulating questions and self-reflection, and pushing learning beyond the classroom.

Journal writing by the teacher is a discipline for continuous improvement. Build an extra half hour into your teaching session — 15 minutes before you come to class and 15 minutes at the end. Review your journal periodically. Add *Becoming a Critically Reflective Teacher* by Stephen Brookfield (Jossey-Bass, 1995) to your library.

Invite feedback, provide meaningful feedback to your students, and seek feedback on your feedback!

CONCLUSION

A *minyan* is often considered the minimal requirement for engaging in Jewish prayer and communal life. The same is true for adult and Family Educators. We should master a *minyan* of techniques. Use those that work for you in your setting. We are continuously creating communities of learners in our classrooms who are as disparate and varied as those we find in any *minyan*. The goal is to fashion a hospitable space and to create common ground through thoughtful reflection that honors how adults learn best.

RETREAT PROGRAMS

CONTRIBUTOR: ROB SPIRA
ADDRESS: The Pardes School
26500 Shaker Boulevard
Beachwood, OH 44122
PHONE: (216) 514-2244
E-MAIL: spira5@earthlink.net

As can be seen by the chapters in this section of *Growing Together,* there are many ways in which a retreat or *Shabbaton* can be envisioned and actualized.

A retreat, *Shabbaton,* or out-of-classroom learning environment allows both the educator and the participant to interact in a different, less formal way than is usual. In these programs we can sense that a relaxed environment makes people more responsive and engaged than they might be in a more formal program. In these programs time does not dictate. We are not rushed by bells. We have the luxury of allowing conversations and activities to develop naturally. We can revisit issues and ideas that have been dealt with fleetingly in other venues.

Retreats build a sense of cohesion and community among the participants. In a world in which we are members of multiple groups, this sense of community is often hard to come by. The three programs in this section offer the opportunity for congregants to come together and engage in Jewish learning in an exciting way.

While building and maintaining community are important components to any retreat or *Shabbaton,* this alone is not a sufficient goal for an educational program. Correctly, each of these programs has

used a content-driven focus as a unifying force for their programs. This theme or focus also allows for the integration of skills, language, and experiences with Jewish ritual, Jewish thought, Jewish history, and Jewish values.

Finally, these programs all allow for learning through a variety of styles. This kind of education allows for an idea to be explored from a variety of perspectives and with many different learning tools. From listening to doing, from praying to digging in the mud, this model of education allows for the involvement of the whole person: the physical, the emotional, the intellectual, and the spiritual.

This section of *Growing Together* begins with two chapters authored by me. In Chapter 9, "Considerations for Planning Retreats and Informal Education Programs," I discuss the benefits of extended time programs, and the challenges inherent in planning and implementing them. In Chapter 10, "Planning Methodology for Text-based Family Retreats," I suggest a five-point model for developing successful learning experiences. Risa Shatz Roth and Caren Shiloh, in Chapter 11, "Dorot — A Family Shabbaton Experience," describe a long-term program of successful *Shabbatonim* that are *Shomer Shabbat.* They include a detailed schedule for one such retreat.

The ambitious program offered by Jeffrey Sultar in Chapter 12, "Dor L'Dor: A Jewish History Shabbaton," attempts to familiarize participants with an overview of Jewish history through a variety of creative approaches. Prior to the retreat experience, participants learn about the topic during Family Education programming. This is a good example of a retreat experience that is integrated into a curriculum.

Despite the fact that the educational opportunities presented by extended time programs are limitless, many educators shy away from such a labor intensive undertaking. While this is understandable, it is clear that retreats are a sure way to engage and inspire both children and parents.

CHAPTER 9

CONSIDERATIONS FOR PLANNING RETREATS AND INFORMAL EDUCATION

CONTRIBUTOR: ROB SPIRA
ADDRESS: The Pardes School
         26500 Shaker Boulevard
         Beachwood, OH 44122
PHONE: (216) 514-2244
E-MAIL: spira5@earthlink.net

INTRODUCTION

Retreats, *Shabbatonim,* and other programs that go beyond the school or synagogue present us with rare opportunities to interact with families in settings that foster learning. Instead of a single program, these structures allow us to connect many forms of learning, individual programs, playing, eating, and praying into a comprehensive whole. In addition, the extended time utilized in these programs allows for interaction within families and between families that otherwise rarely takes place.

Retreats, or extended time programs, whether held in or out of a synagogue or institution, allow us to create a holistic, integrative approach to Jewish learning. Through such programs, we can blend the body, the emotions, the intellect, and the spirit, providing the opportunity to look at a single topic or theme as a whole person and as a family. Truly, retreats offer us the chance to provide a rich and potentially transformational experience for individuals, families, and communities.

While there are many attractive reasons for employing this style of programming, such programming also presents the educator with challenges. These range from logistics and administration to the actual educational planning and implementa-

tion. Finely crafted programming will not be what people remember if there is not enough food. Likewise, gourmet catering does not make for a successful program if some of the educational pieces fall below our normal standards. In addition, if the program costs more than families are willing to spend, there will be no participants, and if the setting is problematic, the program will be, as well. While the challenges are many and complex, a thorough planning process can address them in ways that result in a program rich in learning and meaningful experiences.

CONSIDERATIONS

There are important considerations to take into account when planning a retreat — some are obvious, while others may not be. Clearly, for a retreat to be successful, careful planning and attention to detail make the difference between an adequate program and a potentially transformational experience.

The first consideration should be the theme or topic. Care must be taken in clearly articulating the goals for choosing a particular theme. It is important to remember when making this decision that even though a retreat includes more contact hours with the participants, this doesn't mean that the topic can be overly broad. A retreat allows us to experience more depth and have a larger variety of learning strategies, rather than providing us with the opportunity to cover more material.

Another important early consideration is the site. Certain sites lend themselves to different topics.

A retreat about "Judaism and the Environment" might work better in a park or camp-like setting than at a hotel or synagogue. Also, when considering a site, we have to take into account the learning community with which we are working. If we are including grandparents or young children, can the site handle the special needs of these populations? Are the families going to be comfortable in a rustic camp setting? Will a retreat site cost more than families are willing to spend? Is there adequate breakout space for different groups and programs? How can issues of *kashrut* be addressed? These are just some of the questions to think about. It is essential to visit the retreat site early in the planning process, as the meeting space has great impact on shaping the program. While there is no perfect retreat site, the site can often be adapted and utilized to meet the retreat needs.

One of the often overlooked early pieces of planning is the recruitment process. Even before the hard-core educational planning begins, a strategy for getting the word out about the event is important. Families are very busy. Sometimes an educational program that is going to last a day, or even a weekend, is intimidating. As a result, the public relations must be carefully thought through so that the target population knows about the event early enough to make the proper calendar arrangements and also to address any questions and concerns from potential participants.

The next piece of work is the actual planning of the programs. This process can sometimes feel daunting. We are used to planning a program that lasts for two hours or perhaps an afternoon or morning, but all day, two days, a whole weekend — that's a lot of programming! At this point, it is often helpful to draft a working schedule, block out times for meals, for prayer, and for some unstructured time. This helps determine the time available for programs and how they can flow and connect into a whole experience.

When doing the actual educational programming, again there are many factors to think about, including the following:

- Who are the potential participants? Levels of experience, knowledge, and background vary, along with the age ranges of the younger participants. Some of the groups may be a cohesive learning community, while others may just be embarking on the learning journey.
- What kind of balance is desired between parallel learning and whole family learning?
- If the program is over the course of Shabbat, what types of activities will be acceptable to the congregation or institution?
- How will prayer and some unstructured time be built into the overall schedule?
- How will meal times and worship reflect the theme of the retreat?

It is also important to remember to make connections between the various segments of the program so that the participants can integrate the learning experience. Keep in mind that the introductions, transitions, and wrap-ups help to develop the flow of the retreat.

CONCLUSION

This chapter has spelled out in brief some of the necessary considerations when planning a retreat and when leading educational programming. If each of these considerations is addressed in a thoughtful, thorough manner, your retreat experiences will surely be successful.

CHAPTER 10

PLANNING METHODOLOGY FOR TEXT-BASED FAMILY RETREATS

CONTRIBUTOR: ROB SPIRA
ADDRESS: The Pardes School
26500 Shaker Boulevard
Beachwood, OH 44122
PHONE: (216) 514-2244
E-MAIL: spira5@earthlink.net
TARGET: Families, adults, and children of
all ages

As a retreat educator, I have found that in order to implement any successful program, all of the individuals involved in delivering the program must be part of a planning process. Included in this process should be intensive study of Jewish text(s) that relate to the theme or issue on which the program is focused. Often, in the pressure to come up with a program, educators bypass the important component of our own immersion in and exploring of the subject matter.

In order to deliver a Jewishly authentic and meaningful program or event, we as the implementors must have grappled with the issues in which we are asking participants to engage. This study and learning should be a part of every program that we implement. We read the same *parshiyot* year and in year out, yet we are always reviewing, refining, and finding new insights in the text. So, too, with the Family Education programs that we implement. Even if we have done a similar program in the past, it is necessary to engage in a study process before we begin to plan for our programs. This is necessary not only for the new insights we glean from revisiting the subject matter itself, but also for the renewed energy and collaboration of the retreat staff in planning and implementing the program. Text study can serve as a way for the staff to begin to work together, sharing ideas and ways to approach the material and engage the participants.

After going through a process of study, the educational planners then engage in a collaborative effort at translating the ideas gleaned from the text into a meaningful and doable program. In planning for Family Educational experiences, we must be conscious of providing for the needs of the whole family — children and adults. One of the most effective ways of doing this is to have our programs include whole family activities in addition to age segregated activities. This can be done by beginning the program with the entire family for an introduction to the ideas they will be exploring. This then flows into activities for the different age groups, and then concludes with the entire family or all of the families engaged in some type of summative experience.

A MODEL FOR DEVELOPING SUCCESSFUL LEARNING EXPERIENCES

Following is a five-point model for developing successful learning experiences.

1. **Choosing a Theme**

A theme or focus for the program can be chosen for various reasons, including a deeper exploration of something in a school's curriculum, Shabbat or holidays, or something chosen for its immediate relevance (Jerusalem 3000, or the Rabin assassination, for example). The theme is generally chosen by the Family Educator, Director of Education, or the Rabbi, although a group or committee could also do this. In addition, whoever chooses the theme should also choose an appropriate Jewish text(s) for study that contains this theme.

2. Exploring the Theme

After the theme and text(s) have been chosen, a planning committee made up of professional educators or a lay committee, or a combination of both, is selected. The initial meeting of this committee might consist of a brief introduction to the process of planning a program and an overview of the time frame and goals of the program. Also, this meeting begins the process of studying and exploring the theme through the use of the relevant text(s). The conclusion of this phase of the planning process occurs when the planners have articulated a particular approach to the selected theme that has been arrived at through a process of study, or when a text has been explored that sheds light on the chosen theme. Suppose, for example, that Shabbat is the initial theme for the program. Shabbat is a massive subject which can be approached from various angles. Through studying, this theme can then be narrowed to an exploration of the ideas *Zachor et Yom HaShabbat* (Remember the Sabbath) and *Shamor et Yom HaShabbat* (Observe the Sabbath).

3. Program Planning

This phase of the planning process consists of translating the results of studying the text and the program goals into actual learning experiences for the families involved in the program. Prior to designing the actual programs, some kind of flow for the general schedule should be discussed. The combination of a clearly articulated approach to the theme and the goals of the program and an understanding of the desired flow for the general schedule can greatly influence the type of programming planned. In addition, the type of meeting space must be considered, as it, too, impacts program design.

4. Implementation

As is obvious, the above process is time-consuming, but the rewards become clear in this phase of the process. All of the parties implementing the program have been involved since its inception. They are much more invested in the success of the program, but, further, they are a part of the big picture. The implementors aren't reading a script or working from a lesson plan, but are its designers and authors themselves. They know intricately the flow and content of the program and are able to be flexible, relaxed, and responsive with the participants.

5. Evaluation

It is very important that both the program itself and its planning process are included in the evaluation.

An Example

The following is a brief and oversimplified example of how the above process can work. Congregation X decides to do a Family Education program about Pesach. The obvious text to choose for studying Pesach is the *Haggadah*. Pesach and the *Haggadah* have many different aspects that can be used as a theme for a Family Education program. In addition, the *Haggadah* is a large piece of text and cannot adequately be studied in a few sessions. As a result, the primary planners must make a decision about how to narrow the focus and select the text(s). This might be done by brainstorming possible themes, such as the following:

- Liberation, both physical and spiritual
- Confinement, using the word *"mitzrayim"* as a starting point
- The Human-God relationship
- Why is Moshe not mentioned in the *Haggadah*, and what is this telling us?
- The Four Sons and their possible meaning/revelance
- Exploring the symbolism of the items on the *Seder* plate
- The meaning of *Chamaytz* and *matzah*, both on the literal level and on the level of allegory

- How to conduct a *Seder*
- Using the *Seder* as a model for developing pedagogy

These are just a few ideas. The insights that can be gleaned from the study of Pesach and the *Haggadah* are limited only by our ability to explore the different aspects of the text and the holiday. The same can be said for almost any Jewish text. The levels are endless. Some themes or ideas are easy to see, while others need clearly drawn connecting lines, but almost any piece of text has multiple levels of meaning and approaches that can be developed into effective and meaningful Family Education programs.

In the above example, the next step would then be for someone from Congregation X to identify the piece of text that most clearly relates to the particular theme chosen to focus on. If they decide to focus on the four sons and their meaning, they would then choose that section of the *Haggadah* and some commentaries that discuss that piece. After exploring these pieces of text — and only then — are the planners ready to begin planning the actual programs for the event.

CONCLUSION

One possible model for planning educational programs has been outlined in this chapter. As should be clear, this model emphasizes the need for educators to be engaged in a process of study — not only the process of studying pedagogy, but also the extreme importance of studying the content area to be taught. Our own comfort level, familiarity, and experience with engaging in a given subject ensure that the programs that we plan and implement will be meaningful experiences for both the educators and the participants.

APPENDIX A
PRESCHOOL FAMILIES RETREAT

OBJECTIVES
- To introduce or reacquaint young families with the rituals and spirit of Shabbat.
- To offer a model of how Shabbat can be experienced and celebrated with young children.
- To create a *chevrah* of young families to become active in ongoing Judaic learning through the sponsoring institution.

OVERVIEW OF THE PROGRAM
The retreat consisted of a combination of family programs, parallel study sessions, *tefilah*, Shabbat rituals, and play. Following is an outline of the program.

Friday
- Late afternoon arrival at Camp Wise
- Settling in
- Snacks and Name Tag Making – Participants enjoy a snack, and make name tags out of available arts and crafts supplies.
- Kabbalat Shabbat – A short Kabbalat Shabbat service takes place in the dining room, including a story and a brief introduction to several *tefilot* and the Shabbat dinner rituals.
- Dinner and *Zemirot*
- Games – A few short children's games are played, and parents are given a "Goodnight Packet" that includes a Shabbat story and a copy of the *Shema*.
- Children's Bedtime

- Adult Study – Babysitters are provided so parents can engage in a text study focused on *Shamor* and *Zachor et Yom HaShabbat*, and then socialize.

Shabbat
- Breakfast
- Family *Tefilah* – Elements of the Shacharit service take place at different stations all around camp. At the last station, the babysitters watch the children and the adults continue their text studies, focusing on the meaning of "rest."
- Free Time
- Lunch and *Zemirot*
- Free Time
- Family Torah Study – The *parashah* is explored as a family in a series of stations, including puppet shows, sand painting, and impermanent sculpture.
- Minchah – Adults and children worship separately.
- *Seudah Sh'leesheet*
- Children's *Havdalah* Program
- Bedtime for Children
- *Havdalah* and Campfire for Adults

Sunday
- Breakfast
- Parallel Study – Participants discuss what they have gained from the retreat, and if and how they will implement their learnings at home.

CHAPTER 11

DOROT – A FAMILY SHABBATON EXPERIENCE

CONTRIBUTOR: RISA SHATZ ROTH
ADDRESS: Congregation Shaarey Tikvah
26811 Fairmount Boulevard
Cleveland, OH 44122
PHONE: (216) 765-8300, ext. 103
E-MAIL: risa123@hotmail.com

CONTRIBUTOR: CAREN SHILOH
ADDRESS: 9165 Fairmount Road
Novelty, OH 44072
PHONE: (440) 338-1379
E-MAIL: e.shiloh@stratus.net
TARGET: Families with children from PK to
teenagers

BACKGOUND

Congregation Shaarey Tikvah is a Conservative synagogue of 320 families with a seven-year history of successful *Shabbatonim* that are *Shomer Shabbat*. These retreats are limited to 20 participating families plus *Shabbaton* staff (and sometimes staff families) for purposes of having a community of manageable size. The reputation of the *Shabbaton* is so strong that there has been a waiting list the last several years, and all spots are filled in the first week or two of open registration. There is a large number of returning families, as well as some new participants each year. A *Shabbaton* format was established a number of years ago, which the synagogue has continued to utilize, so as not to reinvent the wheel each year. The changes each year are in the choice of themes, art projects (completed before Shabbat), related songs, study, family activities,

and a *Tzedakah* component. Other themes in past years included, "Let My People Go" (Pesach), "Purim Unmasked," "Envisioning Israel: A Journey of Dreams" (Israel's 50th anniversary), "Leading the Way" (Jewish leaders), and "Sacred Circles."

GOALS

Following are the goals of the *"Dorot"* program:

Jewish
- To explore a wide variety of Jewish texts
- To experience a participatory style of *Tefilot*
- To celebrate a Shabbat experience as part of a synagogue community
- To make personal and meaningful connections to Jewish text, rituals, and traditions through an intense 28 hours in an informal setting

Family
- To leave homework and our preoccupation with jobs behind and escape to a Shabbat in time
- To socialize, learn, sing, and pray together as a family and as part of a supportive community
- To enjoy quality family time in a Jewish setting
- To enhance our understanding of family relationships within a Jewish context through study and discussion.

Educational
- To find the power in text because of its personal relevance to us
- To explore the secular parent/child relationship and compare and contrast the Jewish parent/child relationship using text

- To compare and contrast parent/child relationships in the Bible, in the Rabbinic period, and, later, in modern Jewish family relationships.

PROGRAM DESCRIPTION

The theme of this *Shabbaton* was "*Dorot:* Generations of Tradition and Innovation." The text and study materials were taken from the CAJE publication called *Dorot: Generations, A Study Guide for Chevruta* (one-to-one) *Learning on the Theme of Family Relationships.* It was developed in collaboration with Limmud UK, the British counterpart to CAJE. Two major questions were examined: "What do we owe our parents?" and "What do we owe our children?" We chose to use the first two sections of the book in their entirety. In addition to using the text pieces to examine these questions, we also introduced adult participants to *chevrutah*-style learning, working with trained lay facilitators. The above mentioned study guide spells out exactly how this type of program can be set up.

Our retreat program was developed to incorporate a balance and blend of learning for different age groups and intergenerational groups, rest and relaxation, prayer, and *ruach*. Our theme was woven into every program and aspect of the retreat, including meals, hospitality bags, pre-Shabbat art project, group mixers, prayer services, and room decor.

The retreat experience is crafted with a sense of flow and sequence. We typically begin with a pre-Shabbat art activity that involves many retreat participants. This group art creation remains on display throughout the retreat as a reminder of the theme of the retreat and as a reminder of our working together as a community. After Kabbalat Shabbat and Friday evening dinner, time is devoted to mixers and light activities to set both the mood and the theme for the retreat. Shabbat morning is a time for more focused learning. Shabbat afternoon allows free time for families to have recreational activities followed by an interactive family program, Minchah, *Seudah Shlisheet,* Ma'ariv, Havdalah, and wrap-up. (The schedule in Appendix A provides an overview of the *Shabbaton.*)

Pre-Shabbat family art activities this year consisted of sponge painting a huge "*Dorot*" wall hanging with figures of people and our logo, the tree with the encircling branches. The Friday night program consisted of a group mixer we now refer to as "Connections," a game with wood pieces, nuts and bolts in which individuals were dependent on each other to have the right pieces in the right order connecting approximately 20 pieces of wood into a huge circle. This was a get-to-know-you and community building game in which every piece was essential to building a complete connection. Next on the agenda was "Now Playing: Babies To Bubbes," a vaudeville-type show including comedy, song, and poetry for all ages, written and performed by both lay and staff members.

On Shabbat morning and afternoon, study groups consisted of adults and teens (Grade 8 and up) together for *chevrutah*-style study. Teens had their own facilitator. Younger children were divided into four learning groups by ages, each room led by a teacher. (Refer to Appendix B for specific children's study sessions and lesson plans.) Each group got a puzzle piece that was part of a big "*Dorot*" velcro puzzle that had their study topics written on it. This puzzle was an introduction for each children's group to what they would be studying. At the end of their study sessions, groups came back together, reassembled the puzzle, and shared what they had learned. Also included as part of the *Shabbaton* weekend was a *Tzedakah* component consisting of donating toys and art supplies to a local Jewish shelter for abused women and their children.

NUTS AND BOLTS

The secret to a successful *Shabbaton* is following a planning time line, having an active *Shabbaton* lay committee, hiring responsible *Shabbaton* staff, and having an enthusiastic synagogue population that continues to come back each year. Community funding is also an essential component. Congregation Sharrey Tikvah's retreats are supported programmatically, logistically, and financially by the Retreat Institute (R.I.) of the Jewish Education Center of Cleveland, which is in turn supported by the Fund for the Jewish Future of the Jewish Community Federation of Cleveland.

Lesson plans for the teachers also unified the children's study groups and the staff members appreciated being given copies of the children's books, selected ahead of time with the help of the lay committee. *"Derech Eretz"* letters were sent out two weeks before the retreat containing administrative information for *Shabbaton* participants (see Appendix C).

EVALUATION

Participant feedback on this retreat highlighted an appreciation for discovering *chevrutah*-style study by adults and teens. It was highly successful and very well received. Also, noted was the popularity of the study segments due to the relevance of the parent/child topic. As staff, we observed active participation and taking leadership roles by participants in areas of *Tefilot*, study, and *ruach*.

THE PLANNING PROCESS

The theme of the retreat, as well as general goals and homework, are developed in the spring of the previous school year in order to apply for community funding. We are often able to run several theme ideas by the committee to get feedback at this time, but the synagogue staff makes the final decision. We follow the recommended three-month retreat planning process of the R.I. (see Appendix D). The Family Educator from the synagogue works with a R.I. liaison to begin to map out the planning process and brainstorm programming ideas. Working in partnership with the R.I., and often in consultation with the Rabbi and Education Director, a first draft of the program is developed. The program begins to evolve with input from *Shabbaton* staff and synagogue lay members. Typically, three meetings are held with the full synagogue *Shabbaton* staff, and three meetings are also held with the lay committee. Sometimes, these meetings overlap. The lay committee consists of congregational members who volunteer to work on the retreat as well as partici-pate with their families in the actual *Shabbaton*. The meetings are facilitated by the synagogue Family Educator and by a member of the staff. The planning meetings with synagogue staff, retreat staff, and lay committee members deal with program ideas, logistics of the event, menus, and the educational components. Ideas are brought up and discussed with the committee. Lay members take on several specific jobs, such as manning the welcome table and the pre-Shabbat art project during the *Shabbaton*.

Programming

Over the years, both Congregation Shaarey Tikvah and the R.I. have approached the area of programming for this retreat with a very strong commitment to Jewish Family Education. Both the professional staff at Congregation Shaarey Tikvah, as well as the educators at the R.I., are believers in the invaluable benefits derived when families learn together. That is why we include family learning pieces along with the parallel (age appropriate) learning parts of the program. Family learning can be included in meals by using table cards which ask families to share stories related to the theme of the retreat, or which challenge them with ethical questions to discuss with the other families seated around the table. Family learning can also be encouraged in the mixers or icebreakers, which we design to complement the theme of the retreat. Family learning is also facilitated during the *Tefilah* on the retreat, when families are given pre-assigned *aliyot* together, or are asked to share a meaningful reading that they chose to bring with them to the *Shabbaton*.

In addition to the family programming pieces, we create parallel programming. This is an interesting process because we base our *Shabbaton* on traditional texts, and the same texts or textual concepts are used for the children's as well as the adults' programming. For instance, for the *"Dorot"* retreat, we explored the traditional Jewish texts related to what parents owe their children and what children owe their parents. While the adults were deeply involved in *chevruta* learning, using traditional Jewish sources, the children were exploring the same issues using children's secular picture books. Issues of respecting elders, educating children, parental obligations, rebellious children, etc., were all illustrated by the stories read in the children's groups. Then, the teachers incorporated the concepts contained in the traditional Jewish texts to the stories in informal and often lively dialogue. This is an exciting technique for demonstrating to children how one can apply Jewish learning to one's life outside of the synagogue and make important connections between Jewish texts and life experiences. The learning for the family is rich, because the parallel learning sessions on similar texts and themes enable families to discuss the issues they've learned about and share new insights with each other.

One of the most important aspects of programming for this retreat, and for all retreats in general, is to keep coming back to the theme. It is vitally important throughout the entire retreat to weave a consistent thread of meaning and content derived from the main theme. It is often helpful during the planning stage to "script" program introductions, transitions, and conclusions to reinforce the theme and specific concepts and to have staff members prepared for this role of "program announcer." Making connections between programs enables participants to see that their learning experiences are linked together and not separate, self-contained pieces; this enables them to leave feeling satisfied and nourished.

Professional Staff

Professional leadership at Congregation Shaarey Tikvah includes the Rabbi, Educational Director, and Family Educator. In addition to this staff, two to three teachers and two to three baby-sitters are hired by the synagogue, all of whom are typically recruited from within the congregation's Religious School or from qualified, experienced lay people within the congregation. Retreat staff, consisting of teachers who are staffing the retreat, and synagogue professional staff meet for three preparation sessions prior to the retreat during which we invite their input on the programming, review the schedule and structure of the retreat, and confirm roles and responsibilities. We also meet afterward to evaluate the retreat.

Lay Committee

In addition to the retreat staff process, we incorporate lay involvement. At Congregation Shaarey Tikvah, the annual congregational *Shabbaton* lay committee has become an invaluable partner in the planning and implementation of the retreat. It is involved with almost every aspect of the planning process, and we believe this is critical to the continued success of this retreat.

We have been extremely fortunate to have a knowledgeable and committed team of six to eight lay leaders (usually equal numbers of men and women) who are willing to devote approximately 12 to 15 hours of their time to the *Shabbaton* planning process. There has been remarkable consistency this committee, and one member has even been involved since the very first *Shabbaton* nearly a decade ago.

The lay leaders are asked to participate in three two-hour pre-retreat planning meetings and one two-hour post-retreat evaluation meeting. During the course of the meetings held during the two months preceding the retreat, these individuals are asked to assist the professional staff in a variety of ways. We discuss the theme of the retreat with the lay committee. The professional staff might brainstorm two or three programming ideas which we then present to the lay committee, soliciting additional ideas and input from them. Every year, the lay committee also works with professional staff to come up with a *Tzedakah* project that is tied in to the theme of the retreat. The *Shabbaton* on the theme of families included a *Tzedakah* piece in which retreat participants came to the *Shabbaton* with donations of toys, books, toiletries, etc., for the local Jewish shelter for women and children.

The lay committee's favorite task is deciding on the menu, which is always fun, and saved for the last agenda item of the last planning meeting before the *Shabbaton*. However, the lay committee is not responsible for working in the kitchen during the *Shabbaton,* since they are there to experience the retreat fully as participants, and not as staff. While they might be called upon to act as lay facilitators in the *chevruta* study sessions, they would not be asked to serve Shabbat dinner.

Retreat Site and Logistics

The challenges in planning for this retreat are numerous and complex. A key challenge is the retreat site itself and managing food and logistics. Since the Cleveland community currently does not have a Jewish retreat site, negotiations are necessary with local camps, parks, hotels, and conference centers to meet the needs of our various partner institutions. (These negotiations are done every year, with every site we use, to clarify contract details and specify needs.) Congregation Shaarey Tikvah's retreat is a very large one, and therefore requires a dining room that can comfortably hold up to 125 people, a sizeable room in which to hold services, approximately 30 sleeping rooms, and at least five breakout rooms for parallel learning sessions. These needs narrow our retreat site options considerably. The R.I. has established relationships with a few hotels within 30 to 40 minutes of the Cleveland suburbs, which have provided adequate and reasonable (although not always optimal) space for this retreat. These sites allow the R.I. to bring in kosher food and to *kasher* an area of the kitchen for kosher food preparation. In addition, the hotel allows the R.I. to have one or two retreat staff members work in the kitchen with their banquet staff to help supervise the preparation and serving of meals. The R.I. has been fortunate to have this level of flexibility, although it requires negotiating on budget. Some hotels charge additional fees on top of the actual food costs for the kosher meals that are brought.

The task of catering an overnight, *Shomer Shabbat*, kosher retreat for over 100 people held at a non-Jewish, non-kosher facility can be daunting. The R.I. has been fortunate in having established a working relationship with a wonderful local kosher restaurant which has designed a *Shabbaton* menu full of delicious choices for us. The R.I. has developed a menu planning guide based on these selections, to help streamline the meal planning process. In addition, the R.I. does some grocery shopping at a local supermarket for many "fill-in" items, such as snacks, fruit, beverages, and breakfast foods.

Because of the complexity of organizing this retreat, we need to be very thorough in our logistical planning and communications, specifying instructions and confirming agreements in writing. The R.I. typically drafts a logistics grid for hotel staff, noting time, activity, meeting space and room set-ups, and meal details for the entire retreat. This document allows the R.I. to communicate with and manage and supervise everyone involved in working on the retreat. It becomes, in effect, a "working Torah" for the site. Even then, some things inevitably fall through the cracks or unexpected crises arise, so there can be a bit of thinking on one's feet during the implementation of such a *Shabbaton*. Detailed communication with hotel staff can help avoid too many surprises.

An important item to consider is hotel check out time. Typically, hotels have a 4:00 p.m. check in and a noon check out time. It is critical to discuss check out time with the appropriate hotel staff, to negotiate extended check out fees and/or luggage storage issues if check out is later in the afternoon, but before the conclusion of the *Shabbaton*. (We don't check out of the hotel until after *Havdalah* on Saturday night.)

In addition to retreat site challenges there are congregational challenges as well. Finding a date for the *Shabbaton* that doesn't conflict with any other significant events on the congregational calendar, the Jewish community calendar, and the secular calendar can be a frustrating task at best. Gratefully, deciding on a text-based retreat theme has not been a difficult issue at Congregation Shaarey Tikvah. And we have also been particularly fortunate in the areas of participant recruitment, lay committee volunteers, and finding qualified teaching and baby-sitting staff.

Planning Time Line

A planning time line, developed at the very beginning of the planning process, serves to anchor the process and keep it on track. The planning process for a retreat of this size and complexity is three to five months long, and encompasses recruitment, program development, staff training, lay involvement, meals and logistics, participant communication, and retreat site coordination.

CONCLUSION

One can see that planning and executing a successful retreat is a process with many facets. We believe that the learning and growth that retreats offer participants are certainly worth the effort that we expend on them. In our opinion, a successful retreat process can be achieved by careful attention to organization, sufficient time and energy put into planning, and the giving and receiving of support by a motivated and caring team of individuals.

APPENDIX A
"DOROT — GENERATIONS OF TRADITION AND INNOVATION"
Shabbat Parah/Parashat Ki Tisa

FRIDAY

Arrival/Settling in/Welcome	Lobby	4:00-5:00 p.m.
Refreshments Available	Ballroom D	
Optional swimming (no lifeguard)		
Family Art Activities	Conference Lobby	4:00-5:00 p.m.
Choir	Ballroom A	4:30-5:00 p.m.
Preparation for Shabbat	Rooms	5:00-5:30 p.m.
Candlelighting	Ballroom D	6:00 p.m.
Welcome to the Program	Heartland	6:00-6:30 p.m.
Kabbalat Shabbat		
Shabbat *Seder* and Dinner	Ballroom D	6:30-7:45 p.m.
Family Mixer	Heartland	7:45-8:45 p.m.
Oneg Shabbat	Ballroom D	8:45-9:15 p.m.
"Ready for Bed" for preschool & under	Rooms	9:15-9:30 p.m.
Optional: Baby-sitting	Boardroom	9:30-10:30 p.m.
Now Playing: "Babies To Bubbes, Jewish Generations" (All ages)	Heartland	9:30-10:30 p.m.

Baby-sitting ends at 10:30 p.m.

SHABBAT

Breakfast	Ballroom D	7:30-8:30 a.m.
Preliminary Service	Heartland	8:30-8:45 a.m.
Shacharit Services		8:45-10:45 am
During Shacharit Services, baby-sitting is available in the Boardroom for children seven & under.		

Thanks for your cooperation!

Kiddush	Ballroom D	10:45-11:15 a.m.
Grouped study sessions for all ages: Adults and teens	Heartland I, II and III	11:15-12:45 p.m.
"Dorot" Puzzle – all children and teachers	Ballroom D	11:15-11:30 a.m.
5th/6th grades	Ballroom A	11:30-12:45 p.m.
4th/5th grades	Peninsula	11:30-12:45 p.m.
Kindergarten and 1st grades	Brecksville	11:30-12:45 p.m.
Baby-sitting	Boardroom	11:15-12:45 p.m.
Shabbat Lunch	Ballroom D	12:45-1:45 p.m.

Free Time
    Swimming (lifeguard on duty)
    Snacks available
Relocate luggage, if needed
	
	Ballroom D
		1:45-4:15 p.m.

Grouped study sessions for all ages:	Same as in the morning (see 11:15-12:45)	4:15-5:30 p.m.
"Dorot" Puzzle wrap-up – all children and teachers	Ballroom D	5:15-5:30 p.m.
Minchah	Heartland	5:45-6:30 p.m.
Seudah Shlisheet	Ballroom D	6:30-7:15 p.m.
Ma'ariv and Havdalah Services	Heartland	7:15-8:00 p.m.
Fill out Evaluations	Heartland	8:00-8:15 p.m.

APPENDIX B
CHILDREN'S STUDY SESSIONS AND LESSON PLANS

CHILDREN'S STUDY SESSIONS

Morning Sessions
Family – Grades K-1
Honor Your Father and Mother – Grades 2-3
Hand-Me-Down People – Grades 4-5
Names – Grades 5-6
(We divided up the 5th graders because we had such a large group.)

Afternoon Sessions
Honor Your Father and Mother – Grades K-1
Family – Grades 2-3
Names – Grades 4-5
Hand-Me-Down People – Grades 5-6
(We used a grid that showed the grades and sessions that flip-flopped from morning to afternoon. That way, preparing four study sessions was all that was needed for the eight study segments.)

TOPIC #1: HAND-ME-DOWN PEOPLE
Books/Stories:
Something from Nothing by Phoebe Gilman (Scholastic, 1993)
Song and Dance Man by Karen Ackerman (Alfred A. Knopf, 1992)
Doing Difficult Mitzvot Booklet; Three Generations story, p. 12

Text:
"Moses received the Torah on Sinai and handed it down to Joshua; Joshua to the elders; the elders to the prophets; and the prophets handed it down to the men of the Great Assembly." (*Pirke Avot* 1:1)

Focus:
• Love and respect one generation has for another
• Our commitment to an unbroken history, shared past and future
• Learning to love people younger and older than ourselves

• Values our parents hand down to us

Sharing:
Share a special Jewish item that has been passed down in your family, or chose an item you would like to pass down to your children. Bring the item if you can, or bring a picture drawn at home of the object, or tell about it.

Discussion Questions:
• What do we want to hand down to our children?
• How do things get passed down? Writing, telling, showing, etc.

Activities:
In a circle, pass around simultaneously for several minutes five spoons, each filled with a Ping-Pong ball. Then discuss whether it was easier to pass or to receive. Relate this to passing down our Jewish heritage. Play the game *Telephone*. What happens when things get passed down? What changes occur?

TOPIC #2: HONOR YOUR FATHER AND MOTHER
Books/Stories:
A Chair for My Mother by Vera B. Williams (Greenwillow, 1984)
Sophie by Mem Fox (Harcourt Brace, 1997)
"Honor Your Father," in *Stories from our Living Past* (Behrman House, 1974, o.p.)

Text:
"Honor your father and mother, so that your days be long upon the Land which the Lord your God gives you." (Exodus 20:12)

Focus:
The fifth commandment

Discussion Questions:
- What does it mean to honor your father and mother?
- What does "to honor" mean?
- What does it mean to honor your children? How do you like to be treated?
- Should we honor others like the elderly, e.g., our teachers, or just our friends?
- Does this commandment tell us how we should treat just our parents or all people?

Activities:
Building blocks for a family: Take one cardboard brick apiece and start to build a wall. Each child adds a brick as they tell one way they honor their parents (e.g., clean their room without being reminded, help set the table). The bricks alone seem small and not very important, but added together they make a family strong and able to withstand a lot, just like a real brick wall. This wall could be the foundation of a whole building.
Play *Ima B'vakashah* (the game *Mother May I?*).
Also play *Abba B'vakashah* (*Father May I?*).
Abba and *Ima* dress up clothes for role playing

TOPIC #3: NAMES — "WHAT'S IN A NAME?"
Books/Stories:
Chrysanthemum by Kevin Henkes (Mulberry Books, 1986)

Josephina Hates Her Name by Diana Engel (Consortium, 1999)

Texts:
"A good name is to be preferred over great riches." (Proverbs 22:1)
"Know from where you came . . . and where you are going." (*Pirke Avot*)

Focus:
- Our names and what they mean
- Biblical names and what they mean

Sharing:
Share the "Find Out Your Name History" questionnaires filled out at home.

Discussion questions:
- After whom are you named?
- What does it mean when we name our children after our ancestors?

Activities:
Bring in a regular baby naming book and a Jewish baby name book. What does your name mean? Play large scale *Concentration* game with two teams using biblical names and meanings.

Date

Welcome Shabbaton Friends,

The Congregational Shabbaton Planning Committee would like to extend to you a warm welcome to this year's *Shabbaton — "Dorot:* Generations of Tradition and Innovation." We have been working hard to assist our synagogue staff in developing an opportunity for fun, camaraderie, and spiritual growth. We are very excited to share this weekend with you. In order to make the flow of the *Shabbaton* more comfortable, there are a few "housekeeping details" to explain.

1. Arrival time: Arrival will be from 4:00-5:00 p.m on Friday. You will receive your *Shabbaton* folder at the welcome table in the lobby. You will also receive name tags. Please make sure that these are worn at all times in the hotel — especially by the children. Upon arrival, refreshments (hot soup!) will be available. Family art activities will be from 4:00-5:00 p.m., and choir with our song leader will take place from 4:30-5:00 p.m.

2. Shabbat observance: Candelighting is at 5:38 p.m., and dinner will be at 6:15 p.m. The committee would like to emphasize the Shabbat mood that will prevail:
   • Friday evening and Shabbat morning will have a festive "dress code." Suits and sports coats are not required, but T-shirts and jeans are discouraged. For women, slacks or a casual skirt are appropriate.
   • Shabbat afternoon dress tends to be less formal.

3. Baby-sitting: Baby-sitting will be provided for children seven years of age and younger during services, and four and younger during programs. Availability will be:
   • Friday 9:30-10:30 p.m.
   • Saturday 8:30 a.m.-12:45 p.m.
   • Saturday 4:15-5:30 p.m.

Parents are responsible for supervising their children's activities during the free time, which is scheduled Saturday from 1:45-4:15 p.m. All children are expected at all times to be either with their parents, in age appropriate supervised activity sessions, or in baby-sitting. We are utilizing a public building, and since the safety of our children is paramount, we cannot permit unattended children on hotel grounds.

4. Meals: Delicious (and plentiful!) kosher food and snacks will be provided from Friday night dinner through Saturday night. There is no need to bring your own food, as healthy snacks will be available at all times during the weekend.

5. What to bring:
   • For children in Grades K-3, please bring a family photo or a picture of your family (drawn at home) to share in your study sessions.
   • For children in Grades 4-6, bring the following two items for your study sessions: (1) the "Find Out Your Name History" questionnaire filled out at home, and (2) a special Jewish item that has been passed down in your family or an item that you would like to pass down to your children. Bring the actual item if you can, or bring a picture (drawn at home) of the object, or bring a photo.
   • Clothing and personal items for the weekend
   • Swimsuits, if you wish to enjoy the pool
   • *Tallit* and *kippah* and other religious items; *Siddurim* will be supplied
   • Any Shabbat appropriate games (no electronic or battery games, or toys that involve writing), favorite toys, puzzles, or books you may wish to share (labeled please)
   • Don't forget favorite dolls or stuffed animals — with labels
   • The desire to learn from and participate in a wonderful experience

- The willingness to get to know one another
- A camera to use before and after Shabbat
- Candlesticks will be provided, but feel free to bring personal candlesticks and candles from home.
- A *Tzedakah* donation for Project Chai — a new stuffed animal, art or school supplies

6. Hotel Accommodations: The staff members are doing the best they can to arrange for rooms that are close to each other.

7. Thank you for accepting the following *Tefillah* Honors.

_____

_____

_____

If you have any questions or special needs, please call Risa Roth at the synagogue. Again, we look forward to learning and sharing with all of you.

Sincerely,

The Congregational *Shabbaton* Planning Committee

APPENDIX D
RECOMMENDED THREE-MONTH RETREAT PLANNING PROCESS

Weeks 1-2
- Initial meeting with liaisons to establish or review: location, staff and/or lay committee, recruitment process, budget, staffing, planning calendar, text and derivative themes, program schedule, approach to *Tefilah* and observance, food, supplies, division of responsibilities. The study of relevant texts is also important early in the process.

Weeks 3-4
- Continue with above categories.
- Hold first committee meeting.
- Get well planned recruitment process underway: mailings, calls, ads, personal conversations.

Weeks 5-6
- Proactive recruitment from staff and committee.
- Liaisons and staff refine discussion on topics from weeks 1 and 2.

Weeks 7-8
- Proactive recruitment by school or congregational staff and committee.
- Hold second committee meeting.

- Final registration is due; determine whether numbers meet Retreat Institute guidelines for implementation.

Weeks 9-10
- Liaisons and staff refine discussion on topics from weeks 1 and 2. Adjust budget, program activities grouping, and make staff assignments based on registration.

Weeks 11-12
- Finalize space use.
- Finalize schedule and activities.
- Finalize menu.
- Gather and buy supplies.
- Send welcome and *Derech Eretz* to participants.
- Third meeting with committee.
- Final meeting with staff.

RETREAT IMPLEMENTATION
Post-Retreat
Evaluation with committee
Evaluation with staff
Financial summary and evaluation sent to Retreat Institute

CHAPTER 12

DOR L'DOR: A JEWISH HISTORY SHABBATON

CONTRIBUTOR: RABBI JEFFREY SULTAR
ADDRESS: 1006 Highland Road
Ithaca, NY 14850
PHONE: (607) 257-2683
E-MAIL: jsultar@yahoo.com
TARGET: Families with children ranging in age from Grades 1 to 6
TIME FRAME: 25-hour *Shabbaton*

The retreat described in this chapter was designed to give participants an overview of Jewish history, its flux and flow, its major turning points, so that they will have an understanding of how Judaism has evolved. A primary goal is to introduce participants to the major events in Jewish history, and also to give them a sense of the interrelationship between those events. Therefore, this retreat aims to provide participants with knowledge and understanding of the order in which different events occurred, and what led to what. This enables even those adults who knew many of the specific events of Jewish history to come to a deeper understanding of how Jewish history has unfolded.

OVERVIEW

This retreat was designed as part of the Family Education program at Congregation Am Haskalah, a Reconstructionist congregation in Allentown, Pennsylvania. As preparation for the retreat, the previous monthly Family Education program had taught/reviewed/recreated the earliest events in Jewish history, beginning with the Creation and

continuing through the selling of Joseph into slavery. (We left the program with a cliffhanger, Joseph bound and dragged off, with the lure of picking up during the upcoming retreat where the story left off.)

PURPOSE

This retreat was designed to provide an immersion experience in Jewish history. By experiencing so much of the history in such a short period of time, participants gained a better appreciation for the relationship between events, how one led to or affected another, something that might be lost in a course of study occurring over a more prolonged period of time. The retreat was scheduled in the late fall. By then, families had already had some time to get to know each other in earlier monthly Family Education programs. Yet, it was still early enough in the school year for the deep bonding that occurs on retreats to help form stronger relationships between families. It was our hope that the newfound appreciation for the course of Jewish history would serve as a solid foundation for the families' ongoing education and appreciation of Judaism. Finally, the purpose of this retreat was to learn in a manner that was experiential and fun!

PREPARATION

To replicate this retreat, a suitable site for the retreat must be located well in advance. A large common room with significant open space is needed. Getting out of the synagogue helps foster the feeling of shared adventure. It also helps make clear that Jewish education does not happen solely in the synagogue. We found a camp available off-season, near enough to all the families so that we could run the retreat on a commuter basis. If economics and logistics allow, the experience might be further deepened through a sleepover.

The Rabbi ran our retreat with significant support from the parents. Depending on your group's particular needs and financial resources, additional staff for preparing meals, running subgroups, and the like, could be helpful.

Brainstorm a list of what you consider to be the most significant events in Jewish history. The process of compiling this list is in itself an education. Many important events must be left off the list, and the criteria is: What are the fundamental turning points, the times at which Judaism took off in a new direction that cannot be understood without knowing about this event? Gathering some of the more Jewishly informed members of the congregation together and coming up with this list would make for quite an interesting adult education class! Here is the list we used:

Creation
Adam and Eve
Joseph
Slavery
Moses and the Burning Bush
Ten Plagues
Splitting of the Sea of Reeds
Mt. Sinai
Golden Calf
Spies
Wandering in the Desert for 40 years
Joshua
David
Solomon
Building of the Temple in Jerusalem
Prophets
Destruction of the Temple in Jerusalem
Building the Second Temple in Jerusalem
Maccabees
Second Destruction of the Temple in Jerusalem
Rabbi Yochanan ben Zakkai

Synagogue
Talmud
Spain
Hasidism
Haskalah
Zionism
Shoah
Israel
Our Own Congregation

After compiling this list, an activity must be figured out for each event. The criteria for these activities are that they should have as many of the following characteristics as possible: memorable, fun, participatory, related to previous events on the list, and/or tying into future events.

The nature of these activities will determine the preparation necessary before the retreat.

Finally, as mentioned above, we got a head start in the Family Education program held in the month preceding the retreat. During that session, we evoked the Creation; submitted Adam, Eve, and the snake to a grilling á la a TV talk show; introduced Abraham and Sarah acting out scenes from their life as depicted in *Sedra Scenes: Skits for Every Torah Portion* by Stan J. Beiner (A.R.E. Publishing, Inc., 1982); dressed Joseph (our Rabbi) in a multi-colored coat, tied him up with ropes, and left him bound as the program ended. This cliffhanger — "come see if or how Joseph gets out of this one!" — was used to connect the program to the upcoming retreat, and to help build anticipation.

COMMENTARY
(From Rob Spira)

The program "Dor L'Dor: A Jewish History Shabbaton" is both interesting and ambitious. Inherent in a program like this is the necessity to make difficult decisions about what to include and what not to include. How do we determine what events we are going to highlight and which we are going to ignore? Is our goal depth or breadth?

In this instance, the programmers made a choice to cover what they had determined to be the most important topics in Jewish history for their congregants. They chose to cover a great deal of material in an effort to draw out the connections and flow of Jewish history. The template for the above retreat provides a wonderful organizing tool no matter what lens is chosen through which to look at Jewish history. Here are a few other ideas for ways of accessing Jewish History.

- Concentrate on a smaller piece of Jewish history. This program focuses mostly on the biblical period of Jewish history. Even this focus may be a bit large to tackle at one event. Instead, one might choose to focus on a particular piece of the Tanach — for example, the Abraham narrative, the Joseph narrative, or the Exodus from Egypt.

- Choose a different perspective on Jewish history as the thread that holds the program together. For example, one may choose to focus on major personalities in Jewish history. Have Moses interact or explain things to Rashi or Nachmanides. Or, allow the programming to focus on one personality at a time. As learners, we are interested in people and can learn much about the history of our people by studying them, the times that they lived in, and what was going on in the Jewish world and in Jewish thinking when and where they lived. What were they dealing with as people? as Jews? To what were they responding? What is original in their thinking? their actions?

- Use historical events as a focus. Rather than using only the Tanach as a resource, explore Jewish history by identifying several turning points and focusing the programming on these events and their results.

Additional Commentary

1. Allow parents to "nominate" the events they consider the fundamental turning points in Jewish history as part of the pre-event preparation. (BDK)

2. Make sure that such significant post-Rabbinic events, people, and literature such as Kabbalah, Rashi, Maimonides, the Crusades, and the Jews coming to North America are not overlooked. (BDK)

3. Try a storytelling session with the Baal Shem Tov as one of the stops. (BDK)

4. Take these other events from the Jewish History *Shabbaton* and put them back into the Pesach *Seder* of that year. (SW)

5. The prose poem of Rabbi Abba Hillel Silver, "I Was with Abraham" in *Moments of Transcendence: Inspirational Readings for Rosh Hashanah*, edited by Dov Peretz Elkins (Jason Aronson Inc., 1992, p. 187), can serve as a wonderful advanced organizer for the *Shabbaton*. (EC)

6. A good visual overview of Jewish history (in just 28 minutes) comes from the film *Fleagle's Flight* (available from The Media Center of the Board of Jewish Education of Greater New York, 212-245-8200, ext. 316). (EC)

7. Divide this single *Shabbaton* into four *Shabbatonim*. Construct a time line as the closing event of each *Shabbaton* so participants can recreate Jewish chronology in a constructivist fashion. (EC)

8. Another important part of preparation might involve giving a playful multiple choice test. (EC)

COMMUNITY JFE PROGRAMS

CONTRIBUTOR: DR. JEFFREY SCHEIN
ADDRESS: Cleveland College of Jewish Studies
26500 Shaker Boulevard
Beachwood, OH 44122
PHONE: (216) 464-4050
E-MAIL: jschein@ccjs.edu

We are accustomed in Jewish Family Education to the financial support of our local Federation and central agency for Jewish Education. This support is no less powerful and appreciated when it is indirect — a grant to train Family Educators or partial funding for programs. The counterpoint in this symphony of Family Education programming comes when the community itself sponsors programs because they are too expensive or too sophisticated to be undertaken by one institution alone.

In Part IV, we highlight four such communal programs. Chapter 13, "Reclaiming Shabbat" by Elise Passy, describes the efforts of the Houston community to involve families in a city-wide program of Shabbat learning and celebration. The goal of "Reclaiming Shabbat" was to create not one but many opportunities to enhance a family's experience of Shabbat, and to have more Houston families celebrating Shabbat in their homes and synagogues.

In Chapter 14, "Sulam: Ladders To Literacy," Amy Grossblatt Pessah describes a program of the Baltimore Jewish community. The *"Sulam"* program demonstrates how a central agency can support family reading programs within its synagogues and JCCs. This grows out off the same programmatic soil as "The Parent Connection" (Whizin Institute,

1994), which Joan Kaye has chosen in Chapter 2, "Aytzahs and Chochmahs: Practical and Philosophical Advice from the Experts" as the Family Education program she believes is "guaranteed" to succeed. Sulam extends the age-range for Jewish family reading at home from the preschool to Grade 2 level up to Grade 5 level. It will be interesting to observe whether as children grow older — hence more social, busy, and independent — the same reading approach will encounter similar success.

Chapter 15, "The Adat Noar: Family Program" by Joan Kaye and Jay Lewis, reminds us that post B'nai Mitzvah, often the "stepchildren" of JFE, can be integrated into the Family Education enterprise when there is concerted cooperation among the synagogues and the central agency. In this chapter, the authors "confess" that they once believed that JFE was for anyone but Jewish teens (swallowing whole the conventional wisdom that as part of the development challenge of teens was to separate from parents). The reader will see that the successes of "Adat Noar" has led to a change of heart and mind on their part.

The final program in this section is Chapter 16, "It Takes a Garden to Grow a Community" by Ellen Abrahams Brosbe. What actually began as a synagogue program soon became a communal matrix of *Tikkun Olam*. Here we have an excellent illustration of how awareness of community resources can redeem a synagogue's JFE efforts from the parochialism that sometimes accompanies even our best attempts to be congregations of learners.

CHAPTER 13

RECLAIMING SHABBAT

CONTRIBUTOR: ELISE PASSY
ADDRESS: 5233 Dumfries
            Houston, TX 77096
PHONE: (713) 729-7000
E-MAIL: passy@houston.rr.com
TARGET : The entire Jewish community of
            Houston
TIME FRAME: Six months to a year of
            preparations; the program is
            ongoing

OVERALL PURPOSES OF THE PROGRAM

Concern for strengthening Jewish identity and continuity has become a unifying focus for every segment of the Jewish community. Religious, communal, and educational institutions represent the best hope for reaching Jews with a message that Judaism and Jewish involvement can add richness, meaning, and purpose to our lives. But, for communal institutions to succeed in today's environment, they must become more vigorous and must work together more effectively.

Two overarching principles are fundamental to the continuity planning process: (1) synagogues represent the central instrument for the transmission of Jewish identity, and as such, must be integrated as full partners into all facets of Jewish communal planning and program implementation; and (2) if the community is to pursue a broader vision for planning for Jewish identity and continuity, then that vision must focus on recovering the spiritual dimension of Judaism and creating a climate for a return to religious observance.

To these ends, the development and implementation of the program "Reclaiming Shabbat" served as model for future program planning and implementation. It was a factor in the development of a Jewish Continuity Coordinating Council, which now facilitates and coordinates program planning and fiscal resources for community and continuity initiatives. The program was the impetus for a community-wide program which targeted the many affiliated, but marginally involved, individuals in the community, encouraging their participation in a spiritual and religious activity that is also family building, and strengthens family affiliation with the synagogue of their choice.

The basic concept of the program was that the entire community would dedicate itself to the observance of the first Shabbat of each month through participation in both a family-based Shabbat dinner and a synagogue-based Shabbat service. Participation was encouraged by an extensive public relations program and by the personal example set by community and synagogue leaders. The synagogues strengthened their programming for these special Shabbat observances and developed a cadre of members who were willing to host in their homes families who were unfamiliar with Shabbat dinner rituals and traditions. The synagogues also developed special educational programs about Shabbat, while the community organized community-wide educational programs. Special population groups such as students, singles, single parent families, new Americans, and the elderly were targeted for special programming.

DESCRIPTION OF THE PROGRAM

For a program of this scope to work, everyone needed to take ownership of the program. Therefore, the following responsibilities were given to each institution. The Federation facilitated the community planning process, developed and organized the Continuity Coordinating Council (Commission on Jewish Continuity), and developed and provided fiscal resources. Synagogues were responsible for the development of special Shabbat programs for Friday night and/or Saturday morning, the implementation of special educational programs, and the organizing of a significant number of host families. Schools were utilized to encourage all families to participate and to strengthen their education about Shabbat. The local Hillel Foundation developed and implemented programs for students. The Jewish Community Center organized Shabbat dinners-to-go, and supported the efforts of the community. Seven Acres, our local geriatric facility, facilitated resident participation in family dinners and joined with a local Day School for programming. The Jewish Family Service was used to coordinate services to refugee populations and other special groups. Young Judea, BBYO, and other youth groups developed and implemented programs for teens. The Bureau of Jewish Education of the Jewish Federation of Greater Houston coordinated the entire operation and developed and disseminated educational support materials.

Initial funding for the project was $95,000 for 18 months. Of this, $30,000 was used to engage a part-time project director who would be responsible for the areas of Lay Leadership, Governance and Community Coordination, Program Development and Implementation, Resource Bank, Marketing and Public Relations, Special Population Group Programming, Project Evaluation, and Budget. Another $25,000 was spent on a public relations campaign, while $15,000 was spent to develop and distribute resources to the community at large. Finally, $25,000 was spent for programs for special populations and institutions unable to provide support.

The time table was as follows:

January 1994	The proposal was reviewed by synagogue leadership
February	The proposal was reviewed and funding approved by the Federation Board for Spring and Fiscal year 1994-95. A project coordinator was hired, an advisory council was assembled, and institutional liaisons were identified and given individual institutional responsibilities.
March-June	Detailed project planning began, along with a special grant process for special populations.
August-September	A large-scale public relations campaign began. Initial education programs were held in the community, and guests were assigned to their hosts.
October-December	The initial three months of the program began. Public relations materials and education continued.
January 1995	The Coordinating Council did the initial evaluation of the program and gave preliminary consideration to future plans.
Spring	As the project continued, special activities were designed to reinforce the project.
March	The evaluation of the program was completed, and final decisions were made about the future of the project. Expansion to other areas was considered.

This was the initial time table. Since March of 1995, "Reclaiming Shabbat" has held a community-wide Havdalah service with over 2000 individuals in attendance. The program has also been extremely successful in substantially increasing attendance at Friday night synagogue services. Moving into its third year, "Reclaiming Shabbat" has become a cornerstone in our community.

During the three and a half years of "Reclaiming Shabbat," various subsidiary programs were initiated. "LIGHTS" (Love Is Going Home To Shabbat) was a program that encouraged students to fulfill four *mitzvot* — the giving of *Tzedakah* before Shabbat, and saying the blessings over the candles, wine, and *challot*. Each child was required to document these *mitzvot* on a check list and return the completed form to the Bureau of Jewish Education at the end of each month. A student's name was drawn each month to be featured in the local Jewish paper and to receive a gift.

Another program was entitled "Catch the S.P.I.R.I.T. (Shabbat Provides Inspiration Rituals Identity and Traditions) Week of Learning." Local synagogues, congregational schools, Day Schools, preschools, Seven Acres, the Jewish Community Center, and youth groups opened their doors and provided a week devoted to study and learning about Shabbat. During this eight-day period, a variety of classes took place that appealed to all segments of the Jewish community.

After two and a half years, "Reclaiming Shabbat" became institutionalized, and the Coordinating Committee focused its efforts on enhancing what had already been created. The "Art of Shabbat" program provided each congregation a grant to pay for a program featuring a local Jewish artist. These programs included a storyteller, a song leader, creative dramatics, Israeli dancing, or a puppet show. The Bureau of Jewish Education provided the congregations with the names of local artists and worked with synagogues to arrange programs.

"Reclaiming Shabbat" began with an intense amount of publicity. Many mailings were sent to everyone on the Federation's mailing list. A booklet on how to celebrate Shabbat in the home (which included blessings in Hebrew, English, and transliteration) was mailed to the entire community. There was a mailing of coupons for Shabbat items from local merchants. A postcard was mailed monthly reminding people to rejoice in Shabbat by attending local synagogue services, and there were mailings that publicized the subsidiary programs mentioned above. Each participating synagogue and agency also sent publicity informing its constituency about what they were planning for "Reclaiming Shabbat." In addition, the *Jewish Herald Voice*, the local Jewish paper, was involved from the inception by donating a page to highlight what local congregations were doing for "Reclaiming Shabbat." In January of 1997, the Committee decided to reformat the page in the *Jewish Herald Voice*. The new focus would be on what was unique about each congregation's Shabbat experience or personal anecdotes on how Shabbat had made an impact on people's lives. Two congregations each month were featured, along with a listing of "Reclaiming Shabbat" activities for the month. Publicity and marketing were among the reasons this program was such a success.

NUTS AND BOLTS

"Reclaiming Shabbat" has been replicated in over 70 different communities around the world. Each community has created its own steering committee with representatives from each of the local congregations which developed its own unique way to teach people about Shabbat. In addition, each institution set up its own "Reclaiming Shabbat" Committee. Its focus was to determine how they would incorporate "Reclaiming Shabbat" into their programming. Some committees were more active than others, just as some institutions were more involved than others. The city-wide "Reclaiming Shabbat" Committee created a *How to Shabbat* booklet that was mailed to each congregation. Some synagogues created their own "Reclaiming Shabbat" worship services that were held at the first of the month. Packets for the L.I.G.H.T.S. program were developed to help encourage students and family to reclaim Shabbat in their own homes and were distributed by the individual schools. The beauty of "Reclaiming Shabbat" was that each institution could participate in a community program at their own location, on their own level, and with their own institutional flavor.

EVALUATION

"Reclaiming Shabbat" is an example of how a community can work together while celebrating separately. Since its inception, synagogues have seen an increase in attendance on all Friday nights, not just the first of the month. Some synagogues have instituted early six o'clock services as a result of "Reclaiming Shabbat." We don't know if the increase in synagogue affiliation is a direct result of "Reclaiming Shabbat," but we feel certain it was a contributing factor.

Not every aspect of the program was extremely successful. One of the areas that never achieved the same success was the Shabbat Mentor program. For some institutions, it was the overwhelming task of finding and matching mentors. For others, it was a shortage of families willing to participate. Some felt that what hindered the program was the word mentoring. Interestingly, the mentoring program was successful in the more traditional communities. Additionally, the "Catch the S.P.I.R.I.T. Week of Study" also found more success in some institutions than others.

As a by-product of the "Reclaiming Shabbat" program, the community is more unified. Everyone doing the same thing in their own way has proved to be a successful formula. As "Reclaiming Shabbat" entered its third year in Houston, the glitz and newness had worn off. The committee's original goal was to put itself out of business and in large measure this has happened.

CONCLUSION

One of the most challenging parts of the "Reclaiming Shabbat" program is how to keep communal energy and vision flowing through the program once it has become part of cosponsoring synagogue institutions. With all these challenges, it is helpful to remind ourselves that this program was the winner of the 1996 Council of Jewish Federations' Avi Chai Award, which recognizes excellence in community programming.

CHAPTER 14

SULAM: LADDERS TO LITERATURE

CONTRIBUTOR: AMY GROSSBLATT PESSAH
ADDRESS: 7675 Estrella Circle
Boca Raton, FL 33433
PHONE: (561) 218-1952
E-MAIL: pessah@earthlink.net
TARGET: Grades 3 and 4

The importance of books cannot be overstated. Reading gives us insights into the lives of others, allowing us to "experience and explore" another's realm of reality. Through books, we come to understand and appreciate diversity in ourselves and in others.

"Sulam: Ladders To Literature" is a reading program which affords Jewish families the opportunity to explore various aspects of Jewish culture and heritage. Geared for third and fourth graders and their families, "Sulam" (which means ladder) enables families to spend time together reading and discussing Jewish books and concepts.[1] Through such family interaction, children come to see their parents as Jewish teachers and role models.

GOALS

The following are the goals of the "Sulam: Ladders To Literature" program.
- To emphasize the value of Jewish learning through books.

---

[1] The present contact for information about Sulam is Marci Wiseman, the Pearlstone Family Educator at the Baltimore Community Foundation for Jewish Education, (410) 578-6955.

- To enable families to spend "Jewish time" together — discussing Jewish issues and materials with Jewish content.
- To encourage meaningful "family time."
- To help raise Jewish consciousness in the home.
- To allow children to see their parents as Jewish teachers and role models.

There is also a "Sulam: Ladders To Literature" program for fifth graders and their families. The premise of the program is the same; however, changes have been made to engage the expanding developmental capacities of the fifth graders. In the bibliography at the end of this chapter, you will find a list of books we have chosen for each age group. These constitute the "Sulam" library. In general, the "Sulam: Ladders To Literature" family reading program is modeled after the "Parent Connection" by Joan Kaye, a program published by the Greater Boston B.J.E. and reissued through the Whizin Institute.

PROGRAM DESCRIPTION

This program provides families with the tools and vocabulary needed to discuss issues of Jewish content. The activities encourage families to experience various aspects of Jewish life together. It is hoped that these activities and the reading selections will enable families "to view the world through Jewish eyes."

The program has now expanded to the upper elementary and B'nai Mitzvah ages, and is called "Sulam Salon: Family Book Talk for Teens."

Here is a *ta'am* (taste) of "Sulam" for 3rd to 4th graders. A family reads *A Day of Delight* by Maxine Rose Schur, which describes the celebration of Shabbat in Ethiopia among the Beta Yisrael. The family then receives the following discussion and activity prompts:

To Talk About:
Why is this book called *A Day of Delight?*
What do you think it would be like to be born a member of Beta Yisrael and have lived in Ethiopia (even if you later made *aliyah* to Israel)?
If Menelik were to visit you in your city, what is the first thing you would show him?

To Do:
Check out a book with photographs of Ethiopia from the library.
Sample some of the food mentioned in the book: chickpeas, honeycomb, yogurt.
Like the elders of the village, create a family chant, song or ritual for announcing that it is *Erev* Shabbat.

IMPLEMENTING THE PROGRAM

Within a school setting, "Sulam: Ladders To Literature" can be implemented in two ways:
1. The program can become an integral component of the curriculum, thereby enriching classroom experience with outside readings.
2. If the school is unable to integrate the program into its curriculum, the "Sulam" program may serve as an extracurricular activity that has minimal ties to the classroom. In this case, families participate in the program, but the classroom teacher does not incorporate "Sulam" books into the classroom. While this is an option, we highly recommend that "Sulam" be included in the existing class curriculum.

Of course, an overriding value of "Sulam" is that of exposing children and parents alike to fine Jewish literature. A sampling of the books included in the Sulam library include:

Selected Books (Grades 3-4)
Adler, David. *Our Golda.* New York: The Viking Press, 1984.
Berkow, Ira. *Hank Greenberg.* Philadelphia: Jewish Publication Society, 1991.
Cohen, Barbara. *Make a Wish, Molly.* New York: Delacorte Press, 1994.
———. *The Secret Grove.* New York: UAHC Press, 1985.
Cowan, Paul, *A Torah Is Written.* Philadelphia: The Jewish Publication Society, 1986.
Goldin, Barbara Diamond. *Cakes and Miracles.* New York: Penguin Books, 1991.
Lowry, Lois. *Number the Stars.* Boston: Houghton Mifflin Company, 1989.
Oberman, Sheldon. *The Always Prayer Shawl.* Honesdale, PA: Boyds Mill Press, 1994.
Sasso, Sandy Eisenberg. *God's Paintbrush.* Woodstock, VT: Jewish Lights Publishing, 1992.
Schur, Maxine Rose. *A Day of Delight.* New York: Penguin Books, 1994.
Schwartz, Howard, and Barbara Rush. *The Sabbath Lion.* USA: Harper Collins, 1992.
Wasburn, Hope R. and Hilda A. Hurwitz. *Dear Hope . . . Love Grandma.* Los Angeles: Alef Design Group, 1993.

Selected Books (Grade 5)
Jaffe, Nina, and Steve Zeitlin. *While Standing on One Foot.* New York: Henry Holt & Co, 1993.
Lasky, Kathryn. *The Night Journey.* New York: Frederick Warner, 1981.
Levitin, Sonia. *The Return.* New York: Atheneum, 1987.
Ransom, Candice. *So Young to Die: The Story of Hannah Senesh.* New York: Scholastic Inc., 1993.
Roseman, Kenneth. *The Tenth of Av.* New York: UAHC Press, 1988.
Schur, Maxine Rose. *The Circlemaker.* New York: Dial Books, 1994.
Schwartz, Howard. *Next Year in Jerusalem.* New York: Viking, 1996.
Singer, Isaac Bashevis. *Zlateh the Goat and Other Tales.* New York: Harper & Row, Publishers, 1966.
Speregen, Devra Newberger. *Yoni Netanyahu.* Philadelphia: Jewish Publication Society, 1995.
Yolen, Jane. *The Devil's Arithmetic.* New York: Viking Penguin, 1988.

SUGGESTED TIME FRAME

The Principal is responsible for the following tasks:

Spring (March/April)	Discuss the possibility of implementing "Sulam" with the appropriate lay and professional leaders.
Summer	Order books and other supplies.
August	Meet with teachers who will be implementing the "Sulam" program.
Early September	Begin publicity.
Late September	Hold a Parent Orientation meeting.
Early October	Begin "Sulam" program.
October-April	Implement "Sulam: Ladders To Literature" in school and homes.
November	Mark Jewish Book Month Celebration.
May	Hold Culminating Event.
June	Set in motion the overall evaluation process for Principal, teachers, and families.

NUTS AND BOLTS

Materials

- One set of "Sulam: Ladders To Literature" books per classroom (12 books for Grades 3-4; ten books for Grade 5)
- "Sulam" guide cards
- Index cards to keep track of books checked out
- Ladder or tree on which to mark how many books families have read
- Reading verification forms
- Prizes, including Family Participation Certificates

Getting Started

- The Director of Education should meet with lay leaders and other professionals who will be involved in the "Sulam" program.

- Hold a teacher orientation meeting for teachers of participating grades. At this time, the books and "Sulam" packets should be distributed.
- Teachers are responsible for setting up a "Sulam" section in their classroom, in addition to a book checkout system. There should also be a chart indicating the number of books read by each family. We suggest a ladder with 12 rungs, one for each book, but teachers can choose whatever method they prefer (i.e., bookworm, tree with leaves, etc.).
- The school should send a letter to parents explaining "Sulam," and should set a date for a Parent Orientation for participating grades.
- The guide cards that accompany each book should be photocopied as a packet of 12 and sent home with a letter explaining the details of "Sulam," as well as the Reading Suggestions for Parents.
- Each school should maintain a laminated set of guide cards for its own reference in case a set is misplaced by a family.
- Each teacher must submit to the Principal a list of all their "Sulam" families, noting the number of books completed. The school's administrative staff should be responsible for keeping track of the number of books "Sulam" families have read.
- The school's administrative staff should prepare entrance tickets and award certificates for the students and their families who have read the minimum five out of 12 books. In addition to entrance tickets and award certificates, the Principal should procure discount coupons from local Jewish merchants and other places frequented by participating families. If creating a coupon booklet is too difficult, find another exciting, worthwhile prize to distribute to the families at the culminating celebration.

Families that have read the minimum five out of 12 books will receive an entrance ticket to the culminating celebration and an award certificate. Families that have read ten out of 12 books will receive a Discount Coupon Book in addition to entrance tickets and award certificates.

The entrance tickets should be given to each teacher to distribute to his/her students. The certificates and coupon books should be awarded at a culminating celebration.

Implementation in the Classroom

Establish a special class time and place for "Sulam: Ladders To Literature." Decide what time would be best to do "Sulam" business (before the lesson begins, during the break, etc). Keep all "Sulam" materials (books, library cards, and guide cards) together in a designated area.

In order to keep up the momentum during the year, publish at least one newsletter midyear to keep all of the participating families informed of the program's progress.

Suggestions for the End of Year Program

Following are suggestions for the end of year program:

- Have each family prepare a display focusing on their favorite book. Set up displays in booth-like format and create a "Sulam Museum." Booths can be as simple as art projects (e.g., posters, paintings, or dioramas) or more complicated (e.g., music, cooking, or drama). Qualifying families that attend the celebration will be able to browse through the Museum to learn about each of the "Sulam" books.
- Hold an awards ceremony. Invite a special community person to serve as the emcee.
- Invite a storyteller.
- Do arts and crafts projects related to books. Some ideas include making bookmarks, bookends, or bookplates.
- Serve refreshments. You may want to include a cake, which reads "Mazal Tov, Sulam Families."
- Hand out a suggested summer family reading list.

EVALUATION

Overall, "Sulam: Ladders To Literature" is a solid Jewish Family Education program that helps to bring Jewish books into homes and encourages families to discuss Jewish topics. The schools that used and promoted the program experienced almost 90% family participation. It is safe to say that if the Principal makes "Sulam" a priority and shares his/her enthusiasm with the teachers, who also made "Sulam" a priority, then the program will be very well received by the families. For those schools that liked the idea of "Sulam," but were not willing to make its implementation a priority, the level of family involvement was considerably lower.

From speaking with Principals, the Grade 3-4 program seems to work better than the Grade 5 program. Many educators felt that fifth grade students are already bombarded with many other assignments from their secular or Day Schools. It was difficult for them to read additional books for Religious School. Nonetheless, from a philosophical perspective, offering such programs to fifth graders is important because of the message it sends to them. So often students complain that they learn the same thing each year in Religious School and that they are bored, which implies that what they are learning is not engaging enough for them. This perpetuates the myth that Judaism is a kids' religion. For this reason, it is valid and important to offer Jewish books with varying topics to older students. It is crucial that maturing students see that reading Jewish books is important, that these books have meaning and are relevant to their own lives, and that Jewish books bring up difficult and challenging issues that young Jews will need to discuss.

In their evaluations, many Principals shared that the students were excited to participate, but that oftentimes, their enthusiasm was not shared by their parents. The greatest challenge for "Sulam: Ladders To Literature" is assessing the level of parental involvement. It is sometimes impossible to know whether families actually discussed the book and completed the suggested projects together or whether the child read the book on his/her own and the parent simply provided the signature. The reading verification form asks the family to share their favorite part of the book and one lesson they learned. In addition, parent signatures are required. One adaptation I would make is the creation of some type of mechanism or feedback loop that would verify the family's use of the guide card, although I am uncertain as to how to do this. Since, in most schools, this is a voluntary program, I believe such a mechanism would be difficult to enforce.

At the Grade 3-4 culminating celebration, some of the feedback from the parents was heartwarming. One mother shared with me her daughter's utter dislike for reading until she was exposed to the "Sulam" books. Suddenly, her daughter became an avid reader, completing nearly all 12 books. She could not thank me enough not only for getting her daughter "hooked" on Jewish books, but also getting her "hooked" on reading in general.

CONCLUSION

It is no great *chidush* (insight) that those families and schools which got involved and participated

loved the program and felt that they benefited greatly. In my opinion, the most important factor in attaining success is the level of involvement and commitment of the both the Principal and the teachers. Their energy, excitement, and enthusiasm are carried over to the students and families with whom they work.

COMMENTARY

- Utilize the librarians, schoolteachers, and writers in your parent body to expand the range of books available for the program. Ask each of these to take a very recent and excellent Jewish book and create a guide card using the same format as the already existing books in the "Sulam" collection. This keeps your collection growing and current. (EC)

- By the time a family has participated in "The Parent Connection" and "Sulam," the child has grown older and is capable of more independent reading. Think about forming a junior Great Jewish Books Club for your 6th and 7th graders. (EC)
- End the year with a traditional *hadran* or *siyyum ha-sefer* celebrating all the Jewish books that have been started and completed as part of "Sulam." (EC)

CHAPTER 15

THE ADAT NOAR FAMILY PROGRAM

**CONTRIBUTORS: JOAN KAYE AND
JAY LEWIS**

ADDRESS: BJE

250 East Baker Street, Suite B

Costa Mesa, CA 92626

Phone: (714) 755-4000

PHONE: (714) 755-4000

E-MAIL: joankaye@bjeoc.org

jay@bjeoc.org

TARGET: **Ninth grade students and their
parents**

**TIME FRAME: Five sessions spread out from
October through April**

BACKGROUND AND RATIONALE

"Adat Noar" is a ninth grade program which
has been run for the Orange County and Long
Beach communities by the Bureau of Jewish Education for 22 years. It is co-sponsored by the 16
Reform, Conservative, and Reconstructionist synagogues in the two communities, and has an enrollment of 175 students. The ninth graders participate
in five mini-courses, each consisting of two three-
hour Sunday afternoon sessions followed by a weekend retreat at Brandeis-Bardin Institute. More
recently, a full-scale parent component was added.

Since its inception, for the first session of "Adat
Noar," parents were invited to a joint orientation,
followed by their own learning session. Historically,
over 90% of the parents attended. Several years ago,
a second parent experience was added, focusing on
the Jewish family (including issues of interdating,
intermarriage, and conversion). This session was

held toward the end of the year, and incorporated
an evaluation component of the student program.
This also had a high participation rate. What
emerged from this forum was that parents were
going through a difficult "stage." As their children
entered adolescence, many parents were becoming
anxious due to a feeling that they were "losing"
their children, that they were no longer a part of
their children's lives. Parents didn't know what their
children were learning, to whom they were talking,
what they were thinking. And, after years of close
and immediate involvement in their children's
activities, they were now feeling left out. They didn't
know how to reshape their involvement so as to
retain the connection they had throughout their
children's early years. Then they had participated in
all of their children's activities by coaching soccer,
bringing refreshments, running the book fair for
the PTA, etc. Hearing these feelings, we realized
that we had a wonderful opportunity to address at
least some of these concerns through a Family Education program that would offer parents ways to
connect Jewishly with their growing children.

GOALS

While we believe that the participation of the
parents enhances the experience of the teens, the
overriding goal for this program is strengthening
the Jewish connections between parent and child,
thereby strengthening the Jewish identity of both.
The Jewish content for parents is designed to provide information, background, and opportunities
for exploration and clarification so that they can

respond to the material their teens are studying (which itself is focused on the questions Jewish adolescents are likely to raise). For example, in the mini-course "My American Jewish Self," parents study ten different essays on "Why be Jewish?" in order to formulate their own answers to this question. Parents and students then meet together (in non-family groupings) to create an advertisement for an unaffiliated teen on the subject: "Why be Jewish?" When they return home after the session, both parents and teens are stimulated by what they have been discussing, and it is easy to share experiences. Parents can respond to their adolescents' questions, and are better prepared to guide them as they seek answers in this area.

Exploring personal Jewish issues is the core Jewish goal. Each *"Adat Noar"* mini-course is structured to explore its topic on three progressive levels: personal, peer, and communal or global. Parents, participating in the first sessions of the mini-courses, focus on the first two of these, giving them sufficient experience to engage their teens as they progress through all three levels. In addition to providing a setting in which parents can explore their own Jewish issues and concerns so as to be able to respond to those of their children, this program also offers opportunities for parents and teens to share Jewish learning experiences. Finally, we hope that through their participation in this program our parents will come to see Jewish educational settings as venues in which to find support for their Jewish parenting needs.

Adolescence is a time of particular stress for any family, but even more so for Jewish families. Layered onto the common adolescent issues of communication (or lack thereof) and the push-pull of the individuation process is that of interdating. The *"Adat Noar"* family program provides parents with a safe place in which to explore and reveal concerns. In our experience, parenting programs targeted to parents of teens (unlike those at the preschool level) are not successful. It is our hunch that this is because parents of adolescents are uncomfortable admitting their parental struggles. Whereas not knowing how to deal with the challenges of parenthood is acceptable for new moms and dads, there

is a sense that after 13 years or so, one should know what to do. Furthermore, it is one thing to admit that your child doesn't sleep through the night; it is another to say that he or she has, for all intents and purposes, stopped talking to you. The former is developmental; the latter may imply failure on the part of parents, thus exposing them to being judged by others. Parents of new babies spend a lot of time talking about their children; parents of teens rarely do.

Yet, there is no stigma to attending a Jewish education program with one's teen. Once there, parents readily begin to open up about their concerns. They are usually astounded and relieved to discover that their concerns are shared by just about every other parent in the room. The program, therefore, provides a support group for parents who heretofore have been dealing with these issues in isolation. It allows them to discuss and get feedback from other parents going through the same or similar "traumas." The opportunity to deal with parenting issues becomes a major component of the program.

Our final goal is that of communication: the *"Adat Noar"* family program is designed to foster increased communication between parent and teen, providing a safe forum in which they can dialogue on issues of importance to both. And communication is the key to success for this program (as it is in most Family Education programs). In order to achieve our goals, we deal with parents' feelings of being left out of their teens' lives. This is done by providing every possible type of information about the *"Adat Noar"* program and what their youngsters do during it. We are aware that we need to do this again and again.

DESCRIPTION OF THE PROGRAM

Our parent program really starts with the precursor to *"Adat Noar,"* an orientation weekend retreat for eighth graders held the previous spring. After the youngsters board the bus, the parents remain to go over, in detail, the schedule for the retreat. They are given specific information about activities and reassured about the Bureau's unswerving commitment to both physical and psychological safety. Finally, they are given suggestions for questions to ask their children when they return, questions designed to elicit something other than monosyllabic answers. To allay parental concerns, a message is left on a voice mailbox at the BJE office once the buses have reached the campsite (a practice which continues throughout the following year) so that those parents who wish to be reassured can call in and know that their children have arrived safely. This mailbox also serves the purpose of letting parents know if there is any delay in the returning of the buses on Sunday.

The expectations set for extensive communication are met throughout the ninth grade year. In addition to the normal logistics information, each mini-course is preceded by an information packet and followed by a newsletter containing highlights of the weekend so that parents know what their children have studied and experienced. "The Adat Noar Family Program" is composed of five large group programs. Parents attend the first session of each *"Adat Noar"* mini-course, spending three hours on a Sunday afternoon approximately once every six weeks between October and April. Topics for the courses are decided during the eighth grade orientation weekend, at which time students choose five from the following ten subjects: God and Spirituality; Jewish Ethics: Why be Good?; My Jewish Self; Holocaust and Anti-Semitism; Discover Israel; Dilemmas and Adaptations; American Jewish Experience; Relationships; Jewish Art and Expression; Who are the People in Your Neighborhood?; and My Jewish Family. Each three-hour program includes some time together for parents and teens, a content component, a parenting component, social time around a coffee break, and evaluation.

A variety of formats are used during the three hours. Frontal presentations are mainly done as set inductions with skits or panel discussions designed to evoke conversation. Once during the year, the program will center around a talk given by an engaging speaker who can involve both teens and adults. The adults will also have one lecture, usually on some aspect of Jewish history related to a topic under discussion. The most frequent format for parents is small group discussion.[1] Parents and teens come together for as short a time as 20 minutes during the session or as long as the full three-hour session. Decisions are made on the basis of type of topic under discussion. For example, we have found that parents tend to preach and youngsters tend to stop talking entirely if parents are in the room for a discussion on interdating. While parents and their children can attend a panel presentation on interdating or conversion together, the discussions generated by the presentations are much more productive when held separately. This sets the stage for follow-up conversations at home.

For topics that lend themselves to joint discussions, we use three different "sets" of discussion groups: (1) mixed groups of parents and students (in which parents are never placed with their own children); (2) groups of parents only and groups of students only, which come together at the end to share results; (3) initial groups of just parents and groups of just students, followed by new groups of parents and students who come together at the end. One interesting technique which is particularly effective with the second alternative (but works with any of these sets) is to ask parents and teens to write on an index card "One thing I wish my parent (teen) understood about (me/this issue)." For any of these formats, our ultimate goal remains to promote conversations at home (or in the car) which have been stimulated by the discussions during the program.

PARENT FACILITATORS

The final element of the program is the parent facilitators. Each year, all parents are invited to be part of a corps of parent facilitators. We look especially for any parents with teaching or psychology backgrounds. After checking with synagogue edu-

---

[1] Students, in their separate sessions, have a wider variety of formats that are beyond the scope of this chapter.

cators where possible, we follow up the general invitations with calls to those we have identified. From a list of 25 or so, 15 people usually express interest. Of these, ten to 12 start out with us and six to eight are consistently available. These parents attend a two-hour training session so that they are prepared to lead the small parent discussion groups. Prior to each session, they receive highly detailed lesson plans explaining their roles in the program. Serving in an advisory capacity and, in a sense, being our ears into the community of parents, they also meet with the parent program coordinator and the Director of Youth Programs several times during the year. We have found these parents to be particularly effective for the parenting discussions, as parents feel more comfortable with a peer than with an "expert."

WHY DIDN'T WE DO THIS SOONER?

On reflection, because it has been received so well, the major question has been, "Why didn't we do this sooner?" We believe we were caught up in the conventional wisdom that says teens need their own "space." The last thing they need or want is to have parents intruding on that space. As a Bureau whose initial *raison d'etre* was teen programming, our focus had been on recruiting more teens and strengthening the existing program. We made the mistake of defining these teens as ninth graders only, rather than ninth graders who are members of families. Knowing that teens are in the process of moving away from parental influence and values, we forgot that they are also looking for opportunities to hold on. In fact, what they may need most as they struggle to define themselves as adult Jews are ways to connect with their parents. Where our emphasis in staffing was finding young people to serve as wonderful adult Jewish role models, we lost sight of the fact that these teens lived with adults who had the potential for functioning in that role. We began to see our role as facilitating the "Jewish" connection and providing ways for parents to function as role models and teachers to their youngsters. We wanted to help parents learn what they needed

in order to serve in that capacity, not only by giving them opportunities to clarify, refine, and sometimes even discover their own ideas, but also by helping them learn to deal with their teens on a different level. Once parents are able to articulate their beliefs and understand that their adolescents have a "right" to struggle with their own beliefs, the parents are on the way to becoming the support the teens need as they engage in their own search for Jewish identity.

TIMING IS EVERYTHING

If the three essential words in real estate are "location, location, location," for Family Education they are "timing, timing, timing." And timing has two different meanings in this context. In the first instance, timing refers to time of life, to reaching out to people when they are at crucial or difficult life stages. We spoke above about the needs of teenagers, but, as Family Educators, we must also be concerned with the needs of the parents. Offering a Family Education component to *"Adat Noar"* at a crucial time in parent-teen relationships is a sure way to bring parents in, and also to say to them that the Jewish community cares, that it can offer comfort, support, and even, occasionally, provide some answers. The other sense in which timing is used refers to time of day, to holding programs when parents are likely to come. Our parents drive up to 45 minutes to bring their students to *"Adat Noar."* For many, it is just as easy to stay as to leave and return three hours later. This makes it particularly convenient for them to participate.

ATTENDANCE

As with many adult education or any "voluntary" programs (which most teen programs are), attendance tends to decrease as the year goes on. We generally have over 100 parents at our first program. By the fifth program, however, we may see as few as 30. And we find comments on the final evaluations such as, "I wish I had come to more of these sessions!" Despite its convenience (and the quality of the program), for many overcommitted parents, Jewish education is still a non-essential activity, one that takes time away from all the other things they have to do, and it requires an effort to attend. Our favorite comment on this comes from one mother who said, "It's like getting up at 5:00 a.m. to go skiing. You hate doing it, but once you get there, you really enjoy it." Jewish education, for most of the adults with whom we work, is not a habit; it is something that takes them out of their ordinary lives. As meaningful or as "painless" as we make it, it will still be a struggle to move parent programs such as these to the top of their priority lists.

FUTURE DIRECTIONS FOR THE PROGRAM

Our newest addition is a teen/parent weekend. There seemed to be two groups of parents requesting this: those who remember wonderful camping experiences from their youth, and those who have never been to camp, but are enticed by what their teens feel about their experiences. Our weekend retreat offered parents a chance to experience a retreat with its attendant freedom from everyday tensions and worries.

While two *Adat Noar* families took advantage of the program, it really attracted more families from our "T.A.L.I.T." program (see below). After two to four years of retreats, the teens were willing, and, in some cases, even eager, to share their camp world with their parents. The weekend was designed to provide a variety of joint family experiences and separate opportunities for parents and teens to interact. Younger siblings were invited and had separate programming for all but meals and worship services. Unlike the in-town programming we do, in which parents and teens are rarely if ever in family groups during joint programs, families are kept together in almost all the weekend programming.

Once we have parents in the door, we want to take advantage of the positive experiences they have had, the bonds they have formed with one another, and the trust they have in our staff by introducing them to a wide variety of paths to ongoing Jewish learning. We now have two sets of parents who are accustomed to meeting together — those from "Adat Noar," and those who have been part of our TIES program (see Chapter 40, "Connecting Parents To the Teen Israel Experience"). Because they have become accustomed to sharing their experiences, we believed that parents would now be open to classes specifically for them, which are offered through "T.A.L.I.T.," our 10th through 12th grade leadership training program. In addition, we target these parents as possible students for our adult education offerings. A few years ago, "T.A.L.I.T." went from a monthly leadership training program to a full-scale, albeit unusually structured,[2] community high school. Built into this structure are many opportunities for parents and students to learn together, including two "extravaganzas" each year, a mini-course on Jewish ethics for parents and children together, and a Jewish leadership series for teen community leaders.

TAKING THE PROGRAM TO OTHER AUDIENCES

"The Adat Noar Family Program" model consists of taking an established teen program and adding a parent component. Where these programs exist in synagogues or centers, parents can also be invited to participate. Clearly, the programs would have to be taking place at a time when parents are available (not weekday afternoons). In a synagogue, numbers would probably be smaller, but that could have advantages as well as disadvantages. On the plus side, there is more opportunity to form deeper relationships both among the parents and the families; on the negative side, there is less anonymity when talking personally with fellow synagogue members than there is in a community-wide group.

---

[2] While students will continue to come together monthly, this new program is designed to meet a wide variety of needs, offering everything from weekly classes for which college credit is available to social service projects, advanced leadership training, etc. This is a "school without walls," as classes and programs are held at different sites throughout the community (e.g., synagogues and private homes).

Further, if attendance lags, the number could become too small to be workable. We would suggest beginning with one or two programs on topics that are almost "guaranteed" to draw parents, such as interdating or anti-Semitism and building from there. Parent facilitators may or may not be necessary, depending on the numbers. If they are used, there is the advantage of knowing the population and being able to target the most appropriate people.

CHALLENGES

There are many challenges in such an ambitious program. Two of the major ones are outlined here.

Our most exciting challenge is working with the parent facilitators. Because we do not personally know most of the people (although we do rely on the synagogue educators as advisors), we wind up with facilitators who have an enormous range of ability and experience, from Rabbis and educators for whom no training is necessary, to others who will never be able to lead a discussion no matter how much training we could provide. (Regardless of their abilities, these are people who are interested and committed. We don't want to turn them away, so we try to have enough facilitators that they can work in pairs, asking the weaker to "assist" the stronger.) While the less experienced need help with the process of facilitation, the most experienced need to be convinced to read the detailed materials we send them (ten days in advance) prior to walking into the parent session. We have found that, with a few exceptions, primarily among the professional Jewish educators and Rabbis who turn up as parents each year, our facilitators do not have the sophisticated skills necessary for handling mixed groups of parents and teens. Since few of our "Adat Noar" teen staff have that capacity either, doing this type of program is the most difficult for us. We handle it by having some mixed groups and some single population groups, having the teen director and parent program director function as discussion leaders while facilitators deal with administrative functions, and by using this format later in the year when attendance is lower.

Our second most challenging aspect is that parents will not R.S.V.P., so we never know whether we will have over 100 or under 50 parents in attendance. We considered insisting on responses by refusing entrance to those who did not respond, with the idea that they would learn from that experience, but we decided that they would most likely learn never to come back! We decided to work with the situation, rather than try to control it. This means preparing for 100 in terms of handouts, seating, and facilitators, and readjusting as necessary. It also means we never predetermine discussion groups. Round tables are set up, discussion leaders are seated, and then parents fill in as they desire. When we do mixed groups, the students are assigned in advance and seated; parents are then asked to choose a group that does not contain their own child.

PARTICIPANT FEEDBACK

Our teens rarely express enthusiasm for this program; as long as we give them enough time alone, they tend to be neutral in their formal responses. Watching them, and listening to anecdotal reports from parents, however, it is clear that they are having conversations that would never otherwise take place. They are seeing their parents give up their time for Jewish education, and that has to have an impact. Despite their unwillingness to state it, we have no doubt that they are benefiting from the experience.

In terms of parent feedback, there have been practically no comments on the topics of study, and parents varied widely on their feelings about formats. Some wanted more interaction with the students, some less. Some wanted more discussion, others more lectures. Parents were, however, uniformly enthusiastic about the opportunity to exchange views with other parents. One parent explained, "I learned about the concerns and needs of other parents, that we have a need to talk to each other about shared issues. There are plenty of support groups for parents of babies or toddlers, but this is what parents of adolescents need." Another felt the program "helped us as parents to redefine our goals with other parents, to validate ourselves and our beliefs." One parent felt strongly that his participation sent an important message: "I enjoyed the sessions. But most particularly I came *with* my son, which showed him how important I felt they were." Finally, parents clearly felt that the programs really did help them make those Jewish connections with their children. As one frustrated father put it, "I think by formally involving parents in the course of study you have given an opening for discussion on Jewish issues with a teen whose normal speech consists of grunts!"

COMMENTARY

- It is often easier to begin discussing sensitive issues from a third person perspective. For this reason, movie, TV, and video clips are often exceptionally effective triggers for discussions with teens and between parents and teens. This also models to parents an approach they might use to open other discussions with their teens. (LI)
- In our own experience, the technique of assigning parents and their own children to separate discussion groups is most effective. (LI, RI)
- Jewish texts can be a critical part of this program. This can be empowering to both teens and parents because it is so very important to teach families that Jewish tradition does have something valid and important to teach about contemporary issues. (RI)
- Use Jewish texts on various (sometimes conflicting) aspects of parent/child relationships, the nature of the family, etc. Put giant post-it notes on the walls, and have parents and teens write commentary around the quotes which are most meaningful to them. Discuss the commentary within each group, then have groups share with the entire community. (RI)
- These parents are also modeling something important just by being part of the *"Adat Noar"* experience. Through their participation in the Jewish community program, they are sending a message that Judaism is not just for kids, and that the Jewish community provides resources for their continued Jewish learning. (BDK)
- As parents and teens carpool to the *"Adat Noar"* session, provide a tape that will raise for discussion in the car one of the issues to be discussed at the program. (EC)
- Every once in a while, stop the product/dialogue orientation of the program. Give adults a chance to comment on the learning processes of their teens — what surprises and puzzles them about teen participation in these programs. (EC)
- Have a reunion for returning college students and/or a special "advanced" *"Adat Noar"* seminar for *"Adat Noar"* alumni and their parents. (EC)

CHAPTER 16

IT TAKES A GARDEN TO GROW A COMMUNITY

CONTRIBUTOR: ELLEN ABRAHAMS BROSBE
ADDRESS: Congregation Beth Ami
          4676 Mayette Avenue
          Santa Rosa, CA 95405
PHONE: (707) 545-4334
E-MAIL: Ellenbsr05@aol.com
TARGET AUDIENCE: Congregational
          members, Religious School and
          Nursery School families
TIME FRAME: Gardens are by definition
          seasonal and geographic. In
          California, April to October was
          our most critical programming time.

INTRODUCTION

The congregational garden of Congregation Beth Ami in Santa Rosa, California, was located on a small plot of garden space (25' x 75') on the grounds of the synagogue. The location offered convenient access to water and to the parking lot.

The idea for the garden was suggested by a congregant, and received the enthusiastic support of the Rabbi, Family Educator, and members of the congregation. An application for a grant for the program was submitted to the Jewish Family Education Project of San Francisco (which is funded by the Jewish Community Endowment). The grant was received, and was supplemented by donations to the Family Education Fund of the congregation and by in-kind support from businesses in Santa Rosa. (Additional grants might have been available through local gardening clubs, Rotary Club, and national organizations. However, the research and application process related to such grants take a great deal of time, and these were not pursued.)

The Family Educator, the Garden Coordinator, the Family Education Committee, and the Garden Committee coordinated all programs. Teachers and parents ran parts of the programs.

Unfortunately, the Garden Coordinator and Family Educator are no longer working at the congregation, and this garden no longer exists. There is hope that it may be revitalized in the future.

Here is a listing of the programs related to the garden that took place in the first and second years:

Year One Programs:
- Kick-off to Sukkot at synagogue open house in September
- Havdalah/star-gazing (two hours) in November
- "Celebrate Creation" extravaganza during Religious School
- Zucchini bread baking for the food bank
- Classroom opportunities and connections between the nursery school and the garden
- Delivery of flowers and *challah* to homebound elders or congregants who are ill

Year Two Programs
- A Garden of Family Stories – theme for Family Education 1997-1998
- Fund-raiser – artist painted a garden portrait, T-shirts and aprons sold
- Raffle of a composter
- Donations made to the Family Education program

PURPOSES OF THE PROGRAM

The goal of the Congregation Beth Ami garden was to create a visible, ongoing, Family Education project that could involve families and individual members in Judaism and ecology. The placement of the garden adjacent to the synagogue parking lot enhanced the beauty of the synagogue while attracting attention and pride for the project. The program goals included combining projects in the garden with activities in the school and congregation. Thus, a Havdalah spice garden was planned and grown, and the herbs were used at a Havdalah stargazing event. A larger, Religious School-wide event was held in January near Tu B'Shevat, which combined garden themes, studying creation, and exploring Jewish creative arts.

Our diverse team, made up of nursery school, social action, Religious School, administration, and Family Education, we made a *Gemilut Chasadeem* commitment during year one of the program to donate all the food to a local AIDS food bank or food pantry and to bring flowers to homebound or isolated elders. We were pleased with our 400 pound yield the first year and the 500 pounds in our second year.

In addition to Jewish learning and social action, goals such as gardening enabled a wider cross section of congregants and families to take part in synagogue life in varied and different ways. The garden crew met one Sunday morning adjacent to the room used for the weekday *minyan*. The Rabbi's grandmother was visiting for her great-grandson's Bar Mitzvah. As she pinched basil and identified other herbs, she exclaimed "This is my *davening*!"

As a congregation involved in Family Education for nearly eight years, the garden project enabled us to think about and advance to a higher level in Jewish Family Education. How can a congregation think beyond programs in the nursery or Religious School and think across committee, generation, and curricular lines? Just as the tomatoes sprouted in our garden, new ideas for programs and content flourished. We found that just as in Jewish learning, some garden volunteers were intimidated by garden tasks and by garden experts. How could we provide all levels of involvement?

DESCRIPTION OF THE PROGRAM

The goal of the program was to create a small vegetable garden that would provide fresh vegetables to families in need, both in the congregation and in the general community. The Garden Coordinator used a method called French intensive gardening. This enabled us to produce a large quantity of organic vegetables on a small plot of land. Basic vegetables were chosen to offer a variety of eating and cooking choices, including cucumbers, tomatoes, green beans, squash, and corn. Gourds were grown to use for Sukkot. Flowers were grown for Shabbat, and herbs for Havdalah. As the garden flourished, other ideas emerged and were acted upon, such as making tomato sauce, baking zucchini bread, and drying lavender.

Groups of Religious School children helped in the garden. In addition, congregational workdays were held during Religious School hours, and families were recruited as summer volunteers.

The following is a description of the planning, creation, and sustaining of the congregational garden. The Family Education programs, such as the Havdalah/stargazing and "Celebrate Creation" events, were planned and carried out along the basic guidelines of many existing Family Education programs.

These programs were made possible with grants offered by the Family Education Project of the Bureau of Jewish Education of San Francisco. This grant process was also the incentive and catalyst for the project.

Fall of Year One:

For such a project to succeed, institutional support from the various departments and committees of the synagogue is essential. Therefore, representatives from all of these were included in the initial meetings, and all issues related to the garden were discussed. There were issues of design (e.g., whether or not the garden would look ugly and whether or not it would make the synagogue look run down). And there were also practical issues (such as keeping out deer).

- Create a multi-department team to discuss the Family Education goal of creating a congregational garden. The original garden idea was adapted from existing community and congregational gardens. The idea "seed" was planted by a congregant.

- Meet to brainstorm the garden idea. The Family Education Project team included Rabbi, Family Educator, board representatives, social action committee, senior group, Religious School, Nursery School, synagogue administrator, and garden experts.

Site Selection: A site was chosen during the next few months. The garden experts in the group discussed sites with the synagogue board person in charge of buildings and grounds. The long-range plan of the synagogue included expansion in one of the proposed sites. This garden "mini-team" looked at light, soil, water access, possibility of vandalism, size of space, and other uses of the space (proximity to play areas for the camp, Nursery School, or Religious School).

Community Resources: The Family Educator checked with public school and community garden resource people. Each contact provided additional help and suggestions. We then contacted nurseries, home improvement stores, a compost business, and other potential donors. In mid-March, we applied for a $2,000 grant from the Jewish Family Education Project of the Bureau of Jewish Education of San Francisco, the Peninsula, Marin and Sonoma Counties with funding from the Jewish Community endowment fund. This required a matching grant of $1,000 from the congregation. The money would be used for the garden, programs, Family Education assistant hours, and some Family Educator salary. We checked the National Gardening Association and Community Garden organizations for other resources. We received a merchandise credit from the locally owned home improvement center and some donated flowers from nurseries. Congregants donated some plants and vegetables.

A Garden Committee was formed of those congregants (including teens) interested in the garden itself. Ideas flowed and enthusiasm was high. The site had been selected and work parties planned. Between March and April, the garden was planned, graphed, and organic seeds and plants ordered or purchased.

NUTS AND BOLTS

While the Family Educator met with the education planning team, the garden experts planned the garden. Consultation with the B.J.E.'s Jewish Family Education project director, Vicky Kelman, had yielded great ideas for Judaic content, including the Havdalah herb/spice garden, bilingual signs in Hebrew and English, a monthly garden column in the synagogue newsletter, and the major Family Education programs for the year. The garden theme was also linked to other Family Education programs in the design of the publicity. "Think Garden" was our mantra for the year.

Garden workdays were advertised, and balloons and signs posted. We worked during Religious School, which attracted a crew of parents and teaching assistants. Basic garden preparation books outline the schedule we followed. A job board included 3" x 5" index cards which volunteers could select to sign up for a simple or complex job. Our season ran from approximately March to October. A cold climate garden can also succeed with wise adaptation.

Tasks

These are a few of the tasks that workers in the garden accomplished:

- Clean up of site and plant and shrub removal
- Tree cutting and stump removal
- Delivery of compost
- Building of fence
- Installation of drip irrigation and timer
- Recruitment of volunteers

Planning, Scheduling, and PR

Program ideas are as unlimited as the suggestions for what to grow in the garden. But, at the root of any good program is what the Jewish Family Education Project of the Bureau of Jewish Education in San Francisco calls "The Big Jewish Idea." Our programmatic links related to the cycle of the Jewish year, the cycle of the growing season, and the realities of the school schedule.

Here is a list of the main planning, scheduling, and PR tasks:

- Make sure all events related to the garden are on the master synagogue calendar.
- Review the upcoming garden events at meetings of synagogue staff, Religious School staff, and the Family Education Committee.
- Clarify goals for the year for the garden, the school, and the congregation.
- Be sure the garden is featured at the annual congregational open house.
- Publicize the garden during High Holy Day services.
- Write regular articles about the garden for the Religious School newsletter, synagogue bulletin, Federation newspaper, and local paper.
- Create a garden T-shirt and apron. Include a logo, a slogan, and the name of the synagogue and the funder(s).

LOOKING BACK/LOOKING AHEAD

Following are some of my reflections, second thoughts, and ideas for the future. It is hoped that these will be helpful to groups considering a similar garden project.

Reflections: In preparation for the garden project, the Family Educator toured several local gardens at Jewish Community Centers, senior centers, and schools. Just as with Family Education programming, our question was building the capacity to sustain the project in the event funding and staffing changed. Funding has decreased in our second year, but the cost of the garden itself is less after the initial expense. We estimated the cost of the actual garden to be less than $1000.

Second Thoughts: Having a strong Family Education program in place in the congregation strengthens projects such as these. A part-time or full-time Family Educator is ideal. It is not necessary to have many garden experts, but it is vital to have a small team of them. Regular meetings with synagogue board, Religious School Director, and Nursery School Director increases the potential for involvement and support.

Future Directions: Some ideas for future directions include: using the synagogue grounds for additional eco-Jewish projects (planting some of the seven species), creating links to Neot Kedumim (the biblical garden in Israel), consistent efforts to work with other Judaism and ecology groups, making a congregational commitment to energy saving, ecological planning.

It was found to be very difficult to continue this venture without the key staff. Hiring a landscaping company is just not the same as having congregants dedicated to growing food to feed the hungry. Simply installing ornamental bushes and attractive benches is different from inviting people to sit in a memorial garden and read Jewish texts to comfort the soul. If the garden is a priority of the board, staff, and members, it can continue. However, it takes a huge amount of time and energy on the part of one or two dedicated individuals.

Garden resources abound in print and online. Check your community and newspaper regularly for potential partners and support. Innovative fundraising ideas can bring energy to a project.

Regular review and evaluation is very effective. An evaluation form can be used and should yield a 20% or more return. (However, we did not have great success with such a form.)

Perhaps your congregation or Jewish institution does not have space for such a garden. In this instance, you might be able to think outside the box by remembering:
- Congregation Emanu El in San Francisco uses unused cemetery land to grow produce and flowers.
- Peninsula Temple Sholom in Burlingame, California has a flourishing garden program.
- Congregation Shomrei Torah partners with Christ Methodist Church in Santa Rosa in a huge "harvest for the hungry" garden.
- Community garden plots can be rented and tended by congregants.
- Congregant/gardeners may be able to raise and donate produce from home gardens.
- The San Francisco League of Urban Gardeners (SLUG) assured me that watermelon could be grown in window boxes!

BIBLIOGRAPHY/RESOURCES

Bernstein, Ellen, and Dan Fink. *Let the Earth Teach You Torah*. Wyncote, PA: Shomrei Adamah, 1992.

Elon, Ari; Naomi Mara Hyman; and Arthur Waskow. *Trees, Earth and Torah: A Tu B'shevat Anthology*. Philadelphia: Jewish Publication Society, 1999.

Hareuveni, Nogah. *Tree and Shrub in Our Biblical Heritage*. Lod, Israel: Neot Kedumim Ltd., 1984.

Stein, A. David. *Garden of Choice Fruit: 200 Classic Jewish Quotes on Human Beings and the Environment*. Wyncote, PA: Shomrei Adamah, 1991.

Publications

Organic Gardening
www.organicgardening.com

Sunset Magazine
www.sunset.com

Organizations

American Horticultural Therapy Association
362 A Christopher Ave.
Gaithersburg, MD 20879
(800) 634-1603
http://www.ahtp.org

Coalition on the Environment and Jewish Life (COEJL)
433 Park Ave. South, 11th Floor
New York, NY 10016-7322
(212) 684-6950, ext. 210

National Gardening Association
180 Flynn Ave.
Burlington, VT 05401
(800) 863-1308
www.garden.org

Neot Kedumim
P.O. Box 1007
Lod 71100
Israel
http://www.neot-kedumim.org.il

COMMENTARY

- To me this is an exemplar of Jewish Family Education reaching its potential in a myriad of ways. (LI)
- A more focused concept might be a biblical garden with Hebrew names and biblical verses for the various plants, flowers, and vegetables. Material for this is available from Neot Kedumim in Israel (see address above). (LI)
- Bring the first fruits from the garden to the *bimah* as part of Shavuot. (LI)
- Focus on the concepts of *leket*, *shichechah*, and *peah* as found in Leviticus 19:9-10. Discuss how these biblical *mitzvot* can be carried out in a different form today. (RI)
- As you walk into the garden around Tu B'Shevat, recapture the Rabbinic meaning of the holiday. Decide how much of the garden's produce to tax for *tzedakah*. (RI)
- Plant parsley in the garden that can be used at *Sedarim*. (EC)
- Think of doing this garden in a more ecumenical fashion — either with the whole Jewish community or with cooperating Christian and Muslim groups. Think in the latter context about creating a spice garden, since spices play a role in the ritual of all three traditions. (EC)

DAY SCHOOL JFE PROGRAMS

CONTRIBUTOR: MARK DAVIDSON
ADDRESS: **The Agnon School**
               26500 Shaker Boulevard
               Beachwood, OH 44122
PHONE: **(216) 464-4055, ext. 124**
E-MAIL: mdavidson@agnon.org

Are there any essential differences between Family Education at a Day School and Family Education in a supplementary Religious School? Indeed, an excellent program can succeed in either setting, and Jewish Family Education programming at a Day School is often indistinguishable from that at a synagogue. Conventional wisdom holds that Day School parents are more committed, knowledgeable, active Jews than supplementary school parents. And while this may be partially true, Day School personnel are aware that they, too, work with many ambivalent, questioning, Judaically uneducated parents. Hence, many of the difficulties facing supplementary school educators are present in the Day School as well.

Family Education programs often function as gateways for parents to increase their affiliation with a synagogue community. Some say that Day Schools have an exclusive mission to educate children, and that any programming aimed at parents should exist primarily to build parental support for the curriculum and values of the school and to enhance a child's engagement with that curriculum. But my experience indicates that while Day School parents are deeply committed to supporting their child's learning, they are also eager to learn for their own

sakes. They look to the school community as one of the places in which they can engage in Jewish learning and enhance Jewish life.

I have found three unique aspects of Day School-based Family Education. The first is the ability of a Day School to integrate elements of general and Judaic studies into a single program. The faculty expertise and resources available in fields as disparate as studio art, biology, Tanach, and music can be combined in a low cost manner to create very innovative programs that speak to both the Jewish and the secular identities facets of the contemporary American Jewish family.

Second, a profound diversity in population lies below the surface of any Day School both in terms of individual family home practice and wider communal affiliations. Day Schools are thus an excellent venue for which to develop pluralistic programming, encouraging families from a wide variety of backgrounds to explore traditional practices or to experiment in ways they haven't tried before.

Finally, the range of Judaic studies at a Day School — from Hebrew to Israeli history to Tanach — are core subjects of the curriculum, and students are expected to perform as well in these areas as they do in algebra or spelling. Day School parents have an interest, at minimum, in making sure that their child's academic record reflects achievement in all subjects. At best, they hope that their child will integrate knowledge from both general and Judaic studies and truly excel at both. Nonetheless, many parents are deficient in the skills necessary to help their child with Hebrew or Bible homework. Day Schools have a unique opportunity to address this need by offering parallel courses to parents that help them understand what their child is studying. Along the way, parents discover the joy of Jewish learning.

In this section, we first provide snapshots of Family Education at two schools in two different communities. Both Chapter 17, "Jewish Texts at the Center" by Sara Lynn Newberger, and Chapter 18, "A Portrait of JFE at the Abraham Joshua Heschel Day School" by Barbara Harris Klaristenfeld, address the three challenges as part of the functioning of their school communities.

We then turn to chapters that address at least one, if not all three of these processes. Chapter 19, "Havdalah, Diamonds, and Toothpicks: A New Curricular Approach" by Jill Jarecki Mainzer and Barbara Ellison Rosenblit is a fine example of a program that integrates content and activities from academic disciplines as disparate as literature, Rabbinics, science, and Tanach. But just as important is the description of the planning process undertaken in creating this program. As you will see, developing an integrated curriculum takes time and effort, but the results are worth it.

Chapter 20, "Shabbat at Sunset," describes a program I developed that not only allows a pluralistic group of families to study together, but creates a context for post-denominational observance and celebration of Shabbat, again within a Day School setting. And by showcasing a variety of Torah study techniques used by the Agnon faculty, the program not only gives parents tools for home-based study, but also conveys core practices and values of our school's Tanach curriculum.

Selma R. Roffman and Ellen R. Tilman have created a series of adult Hebrew and Torah study classes. These are described in Chapter 21, "Jewish Day School Adult Learning Programs." Originally designed to help parents with little Judaic background acquire skills to assist their children in their studies, the classes have produced a cohort of parents who now enjoy learning "for its own sake." These programs show how a group of adults from a wide range of backgrounds can create a learning community in a Day School setting.

CHALLENGES

Day School teachers and administrators will also have to meet two challenges that synagogue educators have wrestled with for years: (1) how to craft programs and create learning environments that are not threatening, but are nonetheless intellectually stimulating for adults, and (2) how to provide tools, resources, and support for continued learning and ritual observance in the home. As you will discover, each of the programs in this chapter has a component that attempts to engage adults as mature, capable learners, and each hopes to influence the Jewish dimension of family life beyond the school. These goals have only recently been placed on the Day School's agenda.

While Day Schools have always been interested in teaching parents to understand and support the educational goals and values of the school, they have spent little time helping parents learn how to be lifelong Jewish learners or how to create a Jewish home. While these goals may seem at first glance to be beyond the mission of the Day School, educators at those institutions will increasingly be asked to meet them. Because many parents will choose not to affiliate, or will participate marginally in the life of a synagogue, Day Schools may need to take on some of the tasks currently filled by the synagogue.

And if Day School leaders hope for a parent body that supports a demanding Judaic curriculum, they will need parents who understand the content and values of a serious program of Jewish studies. Most parents do not need to be convinced of the importance of English literature. Even if they spend little of their own time reading "serious" works, they understand its significance and can assist their child in making sense of the material. But if we hope to have support for Torah study, Hebrew, and *Tefilah*, we will need to work with parents to help them understand the significance of our Jewish cultural heritage. If we do our work well, and parents are willing to meet us halfway, we can convince them of the importance of Jewish living and learning. At a minimum, they will understand its significance in the curriculum. Ideally, they will find personal meaning in the tradition, allowing it to transform their own lives and the lives of their children.

LOOKING TO THE FUTURE

Many of the comments above could be seen as problematic for both Day School and synagogue leaders. If Day Schools take on increased responsibility for life cycle events and adult education, it could be seen as "invading the turf" of Rabbis and synagogue educators. And Day School administrators and staff, already overwhelmed by the demands placed upon them and with little formal background in Family Education, may not feel up to the task. Nonetheless, Jewish families who choose Day Schools will spend perhaps seven to 15 or more years of their lives affiliated with such an institution. The possibilities for Day Schools doing important educational and spiritual work with all members of a family (not just their "students") are significant. The creativity of the process ought to buoy our educational spirits.

Imagine some new features of Day School Family Education a decade from now. What would it be like if Day Schools explored the tensions, contradictions, and confluences between general and Judaic studies with parents at their schools. What if, for example:

• Schools crafted educational experiences that ask parents to wrestle with differences between the scientific and biblical descriptions of the creation of the universe. They already do this kind of work with children on a daily basis (in schools that aim for integration of subject matter). Day Schools could play a key role in helping adults and children navigate personal meaning in an era in which people no longer have "blind faith" in religion or science.

• A program such as the one just described could be taken off-site to a science or natural history museum.

• General and Judaic studies faculty might collaborate on such a project. Consider how it might be if parents, board member, or area professional were asked to help plan programs that explore Jewish issues from both secular and religious perspectives.

• And what if Day Schools admitted the diversity that lies beneath the surface of school policies and *minhagim*? We live in an era when divisions between Jews are growing, in which many Jews have little understanding of the Jewish world beyond their own family's tradition and that of their synagogue. Can the Day School provide a context, a meeting place, where people from a variety of backgrounds and affiliations can come together to discuss honestly their differences and search for common ground?

• Think about the possibilities inherent in a "lunch and learn" series during which Rabbis from different synagogues and denominations study together with the parents and children of other synagogues, as well as their own.

• Suppose parents were asked to bring melodies, *minhagim*, and rituals from their synagogue and share them at school and during *Tefilah*.

• At a time when divisiveness among Jews prevails, a neutral arena for discussion and debate could provide an extremely valuable service. Ultimately, the Day School may come to be seen as one of numerous venues in which Jewish children, parents, teachers, and community leaders learn, explore, and live out their Jewish lives.

CHAPTER 17

JEWISH TEXTS AT THE CENTER

CONTRIBUTOR: SARA LYNN NEWBERGER
ADDRESS: **Talmud Torah of St. Paul**
768 Hamlin Avenue, South
St. Paul, MN 55116
PHONE: **(651) 698-8807**
E-MAIL: newlev@ix.netcom.com
TARGET: **Grades K-8 in Day Schools**

A child receives her first complete Hebrew *Siddur*. For the child it is a big event, a rite of passage, a real book instead of a book of photocopies. For the school it indicates a certain level of competence in prayer skills and in Hebrew reading, and it opens up possibilities for additional learning and exploration. For parents, if they are brought into the event, it is a moment for celebration of and reflection on their child's growth. It is a moment rich with possibility and opportunity for involving parents in the Jewish life of this child. What follows are some examples of how we at the Talmud Torah of St. Paul have used some of these moments to give families the opportunity to study Jewish texts together.

BACKGROUND AND PHILOSOPHY

Text study is a central part of what we do in the school. We take very seriously the task of teaching children to value, analyze, and see themselves in Jewish texts. We celebrate stages in children's learning and progress by marking some of the transition moments. We use these important milestone events in the lives of children as an opportunity to inform parents about what their children are doing in school, and to give the parents a chance to engage with the texts, to get a taste of how their children study.

We also realize that while as a Day School we have the optimal time for teaching kids, we also have the worst time for bringing parents in when school is in session, since most of the parents work during the day. After many poorly attended evening parent study sessions, we found some creative ways to bring parents and children together during the day.

At first, we attempted to find opportunities for parents to have an in-depth experience with the material that their children were learning. We scheduled parent study sessions in the evening. The few people who came found them very worthwhile, but the attendance was usually less than 20%. We also tried linking the study to a parent art night when they made book covers for their children's new books. While attendance at that was very high, combining art and study made for a very long evening. We tried one program, the fourth grade *Siyyum* described below, for which we invited patents to study with their children. This was so successful that we tried to create a version of this program in each grade.

The principles that we try to keep in mind for these programs are:
• Curriculum linkage – Almost all of these programs are tied to some regular unit of study. As a result, they fit naturally into the life of the child and the school. Many are "milestone" events that already carry some amount of excitement for both children and parents.

- Real study – These parts of the program are not "children report on what they have learned and parents watch." These are real opportunities for parents, or children and parents together, to study Jewish texts.
- All participate – Parents are not asked to facilitate children's study, but to study with their child.
- All are learners and we, as a community, value learning – Students and parents share the opportunity to see parents as learners.
- *Dor L'Dor* – We make sure to note, where appropriate, the passing on of tradition that is part of each of these events. The presence of at least a few grandparents at these programs further highlights this value.
- Advance notice – Since we are asking parents to take off of work to attend some of these events, we try to give as much advance notice as possible so that, if necessary, they can change their schedules. And, if we are asking parents to come during the day, we try to make the program at drop off time so that we can save parents a trip.

As we did more of these programs, we realized that an additional benefit was that they were wonderful publicity for the school. Parents walk away very impressed by their children's level of thinking, and sometimes they even wish they could enroll in the school themselves!

GOALS

As Jewish Family Education Programs, these events address each of those elements — Jewish, family, and education.

Jewish

These programs are centrally Jewish. They focus on Jewish texts which are studied with a clearly Jewish bent. The programs frequently contain Jewish ritual: programs in the morning begin with Shacharit, others may include the *brachah* "*La'asoke b'divray Torah,*" which we say before studying. Most contain "*Shehecheyanu*" to mark the specialness of the event and the fact that it is a milestone for parents as well as for students. And, of course, in such a Jewish context, Jewish concepts and values form a central part of all discussions.

Family

Some of these text-based programs provide a wonderful opportunity for families to come together for real conversation, for sharing ideas, for listening to one another, and for seeing one another in different roles. Students see parents as learners and parents see students as growing thinkers and teachers. These programs provide the opportunity for families to interact around centrally Jewish activities. Since these are milestone celebration events, grandparents sometimes attend, further underlining the aspect of *dor l'dor* — from generation to generation. In addition, whenever children are presented with a new book, parents have the chance to create art (cover or bookplate) for that book and to write a dedication to their child that is placed in the book, thereby highlighting the significance of the moment.

Educational

These are opportunities to study a Jewish text together. The goal is not only to convey the information in the text, but to give parents practice in approaching texts and seeing them as accessible. Our hope is that the experience of text study will move families one small step on their Jewish journeys.

A SAMPLING OF OUR PROGRAMS

Kindergarten – Kabbalat Shabbat

As the kindergarteners study about Shabbat, they learn the basics of the Friday night ritual, discover Shabbat through the senses (Shabbat looks like_____, feels like_____, etc.), and make a basic set of ritual items for Friday night (candlesticks, *challah* cover, *Kiddush* cup). The students also learn short Shabbat songs and a dance as they prepare to perform at and lead the school's Kabbalat Shabbat program. We had always invited parents to attend this program, which they did in large numbers as this was their child's first school performance. In looking for an opportunity to add a family and a learning component to this program, we decided to invite parents to come to school one evening in the week prior to the Kabbalat Shabbat service. Children and their parent(s) braid *challah* together. Students then go to the art room and make a bag to hold all their ritual items while parents remain together in the kindergarten room and study a text about Shabbat. (Instructors choose the text, one that will generate discussion.) After the study session, children and their parents come back together to brush egg on the *challot*. Parents and kids go home and one parent stays to bake and bag the *challot*. Then, on Friday, after Kabbalat Shabbat, the children take home their ritual items and *challah* to share with their families.

Second Grade – Brachot

As part of a unit, students study the *brachot* for food and some of the blessings said over sights, sounds, and smells. For the last many years, as a culminating activity, we have had a "*Brachot* Dinner" for children and their families. Students select the menu, making sure that there are foods from each of the *brachah* categories. After dinner, the students perform a music and creative movement piece highlighting the blessings in God's world. Also on display that evening are the watercolor and ink *brachot* books that the students make in their art classes. To apply and extend the learning, each family at the end of the evening receives a packet of information and "do together" activities about *brachot* to apply and extend the learning.

For several years, we invited parents to an evening study session about *brachot* so that they could be introduced to the concepts underlying the blessings which their children were studying. These sessions were very poorly attended. We then decided to do something on the night of the *Brachot* Dinner. Now children come one hour before the dinner for a final rehearsal and parents are invited to study at that time. Some parents end up needing to set up the room and finish cooking, but about 60%-70% of the parents are able to attend the study session. In this case, parents are not studying with their child, but rather, getting a summary at an adult level of the material their child has studied. Our hope is that this information, and the packet that we send home, will encourage discussion on and the saying of *brachot* by families at home.

Third Grade – Siddur and Parashat HaShavua

Our third graders receive their own hard covered *Siddur* to use each morning for Shacharit services for third through sixth grades. Several years ago, we began to have parents make beautiful book covers for the *Siddurim*. While they were at the school, we added a study session on a prayer. Attendance was very high, but the program was very long. So, we unlinked the parts. Parents still come to make covers for their child's book. At that time, the classroom teacher teaches "*Shma B'nee*," a great old song about children learning the teachings of their parents. Parents have the opportunity to write a book dedication, taking a moment to reflect, as parents, on their child's milestone.

For the day of the program, we invite all the parents to come to school in the morning. (We frequently have grandparents and even older siblings who attend the school come for the program.) We do a few of the prayers up to "*Barchu*" and stop. Families then gather into small groups (one to three families, depending on the number of people present) and study a passage from the *Siddur*. Each group is provided with copies of the prayers in Hebrew and English and some guide questions. After studying for about 20 minutes, the groups each present something they have learned in the discussion. The new *Siddurim* are handed out and parents get to take a moment with their child to look at the cover and the dedication. At this point, parents also sing the "*Shma B'nee*" song to their children. Shacharit is concluded using the new *Siddurim* and snacks are served. Some years, we have collected the group notes from discussions, typed them up, and sent home a packet with all of the prayers that were looked at, the discussion questions, and the notes. Our hope was that families might study additional prayers together.

A second Jewish Family Education program for the third grade is a weekly interactive homework assignment on the weekly *parashah*. Each week students receive a quote from the *parashah* to read in Hebrew, as well as questions on the *parashah*. The questions require both comprehension and higher level thinking. They also require the parents' help to complete them due to the complexity of the language of the Torah text (even in English) and the questions.

Fourth Grade – Siyyum Sefer Beresheet

In our school, students receive their first *Chumash*, a JPS English translation of the Torah, in first grade. They spend Grades 1 to 3 studying the narratives of the book of Genesis. There are usually a few chapters of Genesis left for the beginning of fourth grade. When students start Exodus, they begin to study the text in Hebrew. So, early in the year, as we celebrate completing the book of Genesis, we invite parents to come for Shacharit and to pray with the class. (Grandparents and older siblings who attend the school also come for the program.) After Shacharit, families gather in small groups (one to three families, depending on the number of people present) to study the last 12 verses of Genesis. Groups are provided with a copy of the text in English and some guide questions. (Alternatively, we study the story of Cain and Abel, a story that always seems to get less attention than it deserves in the course of a child's Bible study.) After the groups have had a chance to discuss the texts, we do a summary discussion with the whole group based on the small group discussions. We then read the last verse of Genesis together and read a simplified version of the *Hadran* (the prayer traditionally said upon completion of a tractate of Talmud). We pass out Hershey's Kisses (these are less messy than honey), to symbolize our hope that students' learning will be sweet. Everyone studies the first verse of Exodus in Hebrew and we say "*Shehecheyanu*." Snacks are served.

Fifth Grade – Mishnah

As part of their study of Mishnah, students prepare to be on the school's justice committee, or *Va'ad Din*. They study the Four Categories of Damages from *Nizikin* and look at modern applications. We invite parents to join us one evening. The Mishnah teacher quickly reviews the text and students present short skits they have prepared explaining each of the four categories. The teacher presents a case dealing with damages and the students

and their families (one to three families, depending on the number of people present) break into small groups to discuss the case. After the discussion, there is a chance for groups to report their conclusions to the whole group.

EVALUATION

We have no formal evaluations of these programs. We have the impression, based on comments from parents during and after the programs, that they have enjoyed the experience, and are impressed by their children and the school. So we have assumed that the programs are successful because they appear that way.

We have also never followed up on the packets that we have sent home after the Grades 2 and 3 programs, so we have no idea if they have been used, enjoyed, or just tossed.

With the exception of the third grade *Parashah* Program, these are all one-time programs. They do give parents a window into the school, they do give children and parents a chance to interact around something Jewish, and they do mark events in a significant way. We don't know if they do more than that. Do they make a difference in the lives of families, or can they even be expected to impact families to want to make changes in their Jewish lives is at present unmeasured? We need to find out.

NEXT STEPS

It is our intention to begin a systematic evaluation of these programs. We need to know what they accomplish and how we might modify them to accomplish even more. We also want to investigate whether or not the take-home packets are being used. If they are, we might try to add these to more programs. We also hope to develop a similar program for Grade 6. It is an important year in the lives of families, and we are seeking more continuity in our JFE program.

We are a Day School rich in programming; some parents might say we are over-programmed. Yet, if we are to expand our JFE program it will most likely be in programs such as the interactive homework described Chapter 39, "TIPS: Interactive Homework in a Jewish Context," as this allows families more flexibility in implementation.

CONCLUSION

The JFE programs we have begun to develop reflect the centrality of text study and, for the duration of each program, create a community of learners. As we expand the scope of our programming, our goal is to become a community of learning families.

CHAPTER 18

A PORTRAIT OF JFE AT THE ABRAHAM JOSHUA HESCHEL DAY SCHOOL

CONTRIBUTOR: BARBARA HARRIS KLARISTENFELD

ADDRESS: 7524 Sedgewick Court
West Hills, CA 91304

PHONE: (818) 704-1274

E-MAIL: chesed48@aol.com

TARGET: Transitional Kindergarten-Grade 8

I have been affiliated with the Abraham Joshua Heschel Day School, a community Day School in the San Fernando Valley of Southern California, for 24 of its 29 years. For 21 of those years, as the parent of four sons who attended the school, I experienced a variety of activities and programs that were provided for the parents and families. Then several years ago, Luisa Latham, the Judaic architect of this school, offered me the opportunity to be the Family Education Coordinator. Together we pulled these seemingly disparate pieces into a cohesive unit and began to grow and enrich this Family Education program. With foresight and vision, Luisa had mapped out the direction of this program from the start. It was time for it to take flight! And that is exactly what has happened over the past several years as we continue to learn and adjust this program to the needs of our ever-growing and ever-changing community.

What are the goals of this Heschel Day School? Shirley Levine, our Principal, states that it "is dedicated to providing an integrated secular and Judaic educational program which develops competent, independent, and resourceful students who will possess a strong sense of self and a lifelong commitment to learning and to Judaism." Only through living Judaism in the home, school, synagogue, and community will we bind one generation to the next, thereby transmitting our religious and cultural traditions.

Our school philosophy and program validate the belief that each individual can be empowered to make a difference in the world. Rabbi Abraham Joshua Heschel, for whom our school is named, said, "To be is to stand for." Could we offer or expect any less for our parents than we do for our students?

Who are the parents who have chosen this setting and these educational goals for their children? They run the gamut from Jewishly well educated to having little if any Jewish education. Some have had a Day School education and/or are Jewish educators, Rabbis, or Cantors. Some come from traditional backgrounds, and some do not come from a Jewish background at all. Parents are from all over the United States, Israel, Iran, Russia, South America, and Canada. In some families both parents work to support their chosen lifestyle, which includes Jewish Day School education. Many are professionals: doctors, lawyers, accountants, while others are business people. Some are self-employed.

Our families live primarily in the San Fernando Valley. They carpool to school anywhere from five to 45 minutes. This is not a neighborhood school, although some children walk or ride the bus or their bicycles to school. For the many who come from long distances to school, it takes great effort to bring them back to the school for an evening activity or class.

The majority of our families are members of the Conservative, Reform, Orthodox, and Renewal synagogues, and the Jewish Community Centers of greater Los Angeles. Approximately one-third are unaffiliated. There are two parent and single parent families. Some families have one child, while others have four or five children. Our parents are very busy people who nonetheless take time to be involved in their children's school. They do everything from helping out in the classroom and library to working on projects with our very active Parent Organization and Board of Directors. Their children are clearly a major priority in their lives.

GOALS OF THE PARENT AND FAMILY EDUCATION PROGRAM

Rabbi Abraham Joshua Heschel said that when " . . . a fellowship of spiritual experience is established, the parent connects to the child's soul." One of the beauties of the human spirit, Heschel went on, is that we appreciate what we share. Friendship/affection comes about when two people share a significant moment — have an experience in common. We hope to empower our parents by providing the tools, skills, and information for them to become partners with the school in the Jewish education of their children. By making them Jewish role models for their children, we hope to engender in them and their children a lifelong commitment to Jewish learning. We see ourselves as "lighting and fanning the fire." We don't have to provide the fuel, as we are fortunate to have great teachers and many wonderful learning opportunities outside of our school in the greater Los Angeles area.

"Opportunities" is a key word in our Family Education Program. We see ourselves as providing opportunities for parents (as adults and as families) to learn about and try on new rituals and behaviors in the safety of their own home. As families make these rituals their own, they are more likely to take on additional Jewish observances. Through some activities, we hope to empower the parents to become teachers of new skills for their child or their family. We see ourselves as the resource, the "prompter" behind the scenes.

SOME JFE PROGRAMS

Here are some examples of our JFE programs and activities at the Heschel School.

During Sukkot, we make *lulav* and *etrog* sets available to our parents — reasonably priced and easily accessible. We *schlep* across the Valley to get these sets, and then our parents can pick them up at school with a Family Limud Booklet page of explanation that answers the questions, "What do I do with this?" and "How?"

At our annual Sukkot Workshop, families come to make decorations for their *sukkah* or the school's. They learn how to build a *sukkah* and what to do with the *lulav* and *etrog*. This Sukkot Workshop is one of the best attended of our yearly offerings. Parents enjoy walking from station to station, trying out craft ideas with their children and by themselves. It is gratifying to walk around the room and watch parents get totally engrossed in a project. They leave with grins of satisfaction and a bag of decorations to hang in a *sukkah*. For some, this becomes the impetus to build a *sukkah*. (You have to have somewhere to hang all these goodies!) Sometimes, we "plant the seed." Families may spend time decorating an *etrog* box and when they see another parent pick up a pre-ordered *lulav* and *etrog* set, the thought of owning one themselves becomes that much more intriguing. (I always buy extra for those who forgot to pre-order and/or those who decide that this will be the year to "try on" this ritual.)

We have in the past structured this workshop with a formal learning component for the adults even though the majority do not want to leave their children and the noisy, creative "playroom." Now, when our Rabbi invites parents to help him build the school *sukkah*, a dozen or so people join in. He uses the moment to teach about the *sukkah* from both a practical (PVC pipes, tarps, etc.) and *halachic* (what makes a *sukkah* kosher) standpoint. This informal learning seems to work much better for those who avail themselves of the opportunity. We also have information sheets to go in the Family Limud Booklet (more on that later), which they take home for their own reading and reference.

This year, we tried to expand this informal teaching aspect by having the parent-in-charge at each station learn the connection between their project and the holiday so that they could be the teachers. For example, the "Rain Cloud" (white fabric cut in the shape of a cloud, stuffed with cotton and glued together with shiny "rain" falling down) pertains to the insertion between Shemini Atzeret and Pesach of the sentence in the "*Amidah*": "*Masheev ha'ruach u'moreed hagashem*" — acknowledging God as the One who causes the wind to blow and the rain to fall. Many of the workshop projects are in the category of *Hiddur Mitzvah* — enhancing and/or beautifying the particular *mitzvah*. Families network and invite each other to their *sukkah* celebrations. They share (or overhear) how *sukkot* are built and decorated.

Our Family Education Program is multifaceted. At many school programs (such as Back-to-School Night), there is a table set up with a variety of Judaic books for parents to peruse. This serves to heighten an awareness of what is available. At the Pesach Workshop, a table full of *Haggadot* and children's Pesach books are presented (some from our school library and some from the local Jewish bookstore), again expanding our parents' frame of reference and repertoire.

There are special classes for the adult learner, such as a Hebrew Reading Marathon, Basic Judaism, Jewish History, Hebrew Conversation, *Challah* Baking, and Synagogue Skills. Some classes are related to the subject matter of a given grade level. For example, the seventh and eighth grade classes learn Mishnaic principles related to "*Bayn Adam L'Chavero*" (interpersonal relations) and "*Bayn Adam L'Makom*" (between ourselves and our Creator). The parents have two sessions that explain these concepts, providing more in-depth learning than the students receive. Although every parent and grandparent in the school is invited to attend these classes, the "buy-in" is especially strong for the parents whose children are currently studying the same material.

Some classes relate to a life cycle event. For example, we invite the parents of our fifth and sixth grade students to a Bar/Bat Mitzvah Orientation Meeting to discuss ways to incorporate the values we espouse and teach in our school into the Bar/Bat Mitzvah experience and celebration. We hand out a Family Limud Booklet that we have prepared about the history and vocabulary of the Bar/Bat Mitzvah and a list of *Tzedakah* projects and community services which they and their child may wish to do. A great deal of sharing goes on among these parents who are at different levels of experience (for some this is their eldest child; for others it is their second, third, etc.) with respect to planning and scheduling for their child's Bar/Bat Mitzvah.

There are workshops for the entire family related to specific holidays. These are focused around Sukkot (described earlier), Chanukah, and Pesach. They include a learning element for the adult (formal or informal), as well as an arts and crafts element, song, dance, and, of course, refreshments and socializing for the entire family. They are very well attended. Parents seem to feel that if they are going to leave the house, they would much prefer to do it with their children, interacting with them in a structured activity.

There are also activities that stress our school community and its place in the greater Los Angeles Jewish community, as well as the community at large. For example, every fall, the Community Relations Council of the Jewish Federation sponsors a city-wide Mitzvah Day. We offer our parents and children many possible ways to participate in this event, such as planting trees in the park (under the auspices of Tree People); cooking and delivering food for AIDS patients (Project Chicken Soup); collecting, sorting, and distributing clothing and household items to those less fortunate (in connection with Social Services); making "Have a Good Day" cards for children in the hospital; creating "Happy Hats" for children with terminal illnesses; and participating in a Blood Drive at the school. Participants feel a wonderful sense of accomplishment when giving to the Jewish community and to the community at large.

For Thanksgiving, each classroom (TK-8) puts together a very full, beautifully decorated, box or basket to which we add frozen turkeys. Parents deliver these to the Family Violence Project. On a student-to-student basis, at the end of the school year, the students are invited to "Unpack their

Backpack" and donate school supplies they no longer need to less fortunate students. This form of recycling teaches them to give away rather than to throw away items that still have value for others. Some of the activities that work to build the Heschel community include "exchanges" when families who have a few extra seats at their *Seder,* their Shabbat table, or in their *sukkah,* invite other families to come join them for the experience, the camaraderie, and for the learning. (When requested, we send along background information and suggest activities to enrich the celebration.)

One of the goals of the school's Judaic program is for children over the course of their years in the school to have experiences which will give them the skills to function as a Jewish adult. Many of these experiences are shared together as a family. For example, Grade 2 classes have a Friday night service and dinner with their families at the school. The children learn the Friday Night service for the Shabbat table and the synagogue. Then they and their parents together experience Shabbat, complete with *zemirot* (songs), stories, and the Blessing of the Children. Each family receives a *zemirot* booklet with all of the blessings and songs — a "how to" of Shabbat that increases their knowledge, raises their comfort level, and empowers them to do this in their own homes on Friday evening. We remove the mystery and leave the magic!

An especially successful innovation is our Blue Limud Resource Booklet. Luisa had begun sending home resource packets on many of the holidays with a variety of information (knowing the diversity of our parent body in terms of Jewish knowledge and background). Building on that concept, we have expanded the booklets (adding information every year on a three-year cycle). Every new family entering the school receives the packet and a blue binder in which to keep it. This allows parents to learn in the comfort of their own home without feeling that someone is somehow measuring their knowledge. Year after year, they continue to add information, activities, bibliography, recipes for the holidays, life cycle events, and Jewish concepts. There are also packets on grade level and school-related activities as they occur over the year.

Mitzvah Day, for example, brings a page about *mitzvot.* *Sukkah* visits include a page on the *brachot* one says over all different kinds of foods. When picking up a pre-ordered *lulav* and *etrog* set, there is a page about *lulav* and *etrog:* how to use it, what it symbolizes, and what *brachot* to say. When the fifth grade has its Sephardic Havdalah ceremony and the students learn the service with special Sephardic melodies and songs, they create a *besamim* (spice) box, and also receive a resource packet about Havdalah along with a Havdalah candle. The entire family then has the tools and information to add this ritual to their Jewish repertoire. Of course, we are always open to suggestions from parents for additional topics.

WHAT DOES SUCCESS LOOK LIKE?

How does one assess such a program? in terms of programs presented? materials produced? the number of people who availed themselves of the opportunities presented? There are individuals – parents, students, families, and staff whom I have met and served by "networking." There have been interactions on a one-to-one basis, helping people feel more "at home" in the school community and in their "Jewish skin." Over the years there have been comments shared, messages left on my answering machine, or notes received, which reflect the impact of our Family Education Program on individuals and families. That impact, long or short term, cannot be measured. Parents have thanked me for the resource packet that helped them answer a question for their child or for themselves. One parent, responding to the Pesach Exchange, said that this year her family was invited to her father's home in Florida, but next year they would very much like to take advantage of such an experience, for they have no family locally to be with on the holidays. So the fact that only a few called to take advantage of the opportunity isn't as important as the clear need for the opportunity to be presented. This program is assessed one person at a time.

How does one "quantify" or assess parents sitting with their children reading a book of Jewish concepts and values? Is a program successful when several families get together to share dinner in the *sukkah* or around the Shabbat or Pesach table? Have we reached our goal when families discuss *Parashat HaShavua* around their Shabbat table . . . or sign up for a class at their own synagogue . . . or decide that this will be the year to learn to read Hebrew, have an adult Bar/Bat Mitzvah, or read a Jewish book?

Being seen as an "available resource" seems to me to be a sign of success. Last year a parent approached me with the idea of beginning a Judaic Book Club. I put out an interest sheet at Board Meetings and Back-to-School Nights, resulting in a list of over 30 interested adults. We have arranged for a discount at a major bookstore in the area and have been meeting for over a year. It is especially gratifying to respond to a request from our parents.

We have developed an end of the year survey (see Appendix A) and evaluation forms for activities and programs (see Appendix B for one on Passover University). We ask for input, suggestions, constructive criticism — what worked, what needs improvement, and anything else that someone wants to share. We have responded by reevaluating our programs from year to year. Our population has changed gradually over the years, and we have tried to respond in our programming. It would be a mistake to operate under the assumption that what was will continue to be.

WHERE DO WE GO FROM HERE?

We are pleased with the progress of our Family Education Program as we respond to the needs of our community. We are constantly looking for and developing new programs in response to parent requests (e.g., *Challah* Baking class and the Judaic Book Club) and in response to our school curriculum. We borrow from tried and true aspects of other Family Education Programs and customize these for our school population.

We are hoping to offer more classes for those who want to continue to grow beyond their already "more-than-basic" background. While those parents do take classes in other settings, we would like to offer a series of one or two sessions each on topics that would appeal to this population.

This is an exciting time to be in this growing field of JFE. The sky is the limit, and the only boundaries are one's creativity and willingness to try. I feel constantly enriched as we offer opportunities for our families to continue to explore and share their Judaism. As it says in *Tehilim* (Psalms 119:99) "*Mikol m'lamdei hiskalti*" (From all those I have learned with, I have grown wiser.)

APPENDIX A
FAMILY EDUCATION SURVEY

The great sage Hillel said, "He who does not increase his knowledge, decreases it."

Please help us in planning our program for the coming year. If these courses were offered, for which might you register? (Please feel free to add any suggestions of your own, for courses and/or teachers.)

___ Hebrew Reading Marathon

___ Basics and Blessings

___ Hebrew Conversation

___ Shabbat Morning/Synagogue Skills

___ Basic Judaism

___ Jewish History Overview

___ Introduction to Rabbinic Literature

___ Israeli Dancing (Level) _____

___ Introduction to Kabbalah

___ Introduction to Mishnah

___ Ongoing Mishnah Class

___ Jewish Feminism

___ Jewish Cooking

___ Torah Trop/Cantillation

___ Jewish Ethics and Values

___ Israeli Politics/Current Events

___ Forum – once a month with different speakers on one, OR several topics

_____

Suggestions for topics? _____

___ Hebrew Language Family Fun Nights (a family opportunity to play together in Hebrew.) All language levels, all ages are welcome.

___ Family Friday Nights – one per grade level

___ Family Weekend Retreats

___ Family Picnic

✡ ✡ ✡ ✡ ✡

APPENDIX A, CONT.

With regard to time and format, which works best for you?

___ Monday	___ 8:15-12:00
___ Tuesday	___ 12:00-3:15
___ Wednesday	___ Evenings 7:30-9:00 p.m.
___ Thursday	___ Would be helpful if we offered dinner?
___ Friday	
___ Sunday ___ (i.e., Bagel Breakfast) _____	

Is any time of year more or less workable for you? _____

_____

✡ ✡ ✡ ✡ ✡

Can you help with:

___ Brainstorming/Planning Activities

___ Breezeway Bulletin Board (with art and/or ideas)

___ Reading Torah (with Trop)

___ Reading Haftarah (with Trop)

We would appreciate any other ideas or suggestions _____

_____

_____

_____

Todah rabah, thank you for your input.

Parent's Name _____ Phone No. _____

APPENDIX B
PASSOVER UNIVERSITY SURVEY

Which classes did you attend, and how would you rate them?

Class/Instructor	Great	Very Good	Good	OK	Disappointing
Period 1 _____	☐	☐	☐	☐	☐
Period 2 _____	☐	☐	☐	☐	☐
Period 3 _____	☐	☐	☐	☐	☐

What other classes would you have liked to attend?

_____

_____

What other presenters would you have liked to hear?

_____

_____

Any other comments:

_____

_____

Thank you! Chag Samayach! Happy Pesach!

CHAPTER 19

HAVDALAH, DIAMONDS, AND TOOTHPICKS: A NEW CURRICULAR APPROACH

CONTRIBUTORS: JILL JARECKI MAINZER
and BARBARA ELLISON
ROSENBLIT
ADDRESS: New Atlanta Jewish Community
High School
2012 Womack Road
Dunwoody, GA 30338
PHONE: (770) 352-0018
E-MAIL: jljberry@aol.com
brosenblit@najchs.org
TARGET: Day School Families and Sixth
Grade Students

INTRODUCTION

We describe here a new, non-traditional approach to creating curriculum for Day School family programs. Using Havdalah as an example of the potential of this approach, we are aiming to change the process of designing curriculum from the traditional, static top-down model to a vibrant organic process. Such a model fully and systematically integrates all areas of learning, culminating in an interactive Family Education program. This model provides a method for developing curriculum with a diverse faculty of varying talents and backgrounds. Using a core theme connected to a holiday as its focus, this method develops curriculum around the combined contributions, talents, and abilities of those who will implement it. In this way, an unusual approach develops which yields an unusual product: a celebration of the complexity of learning rather than an attempt to simplify it, an approach to learning and understanding that gives equal attention to the needs of the teacher, as well as to those of the learner. This chapter does not provide a static plan to follow; this organic approach will, by design, change with each group that adopts it.

GOALS

Following are the goals of "Havdalah, Diamonds, and Toothpicks."

Jewish
- Participants will see, experience, and participate in the ceremony of Havdalah.
- Participants will take home a copy of the ceremony, a written explanation, a Havdalah candle, and a spice box made by the child.
- Participants will gain a new understanding of the underlying concepts, symbols, and metaphors of Havdalah, enabling them to continue the ceremony at home.
- Parents will be role models for children as they engage in study sessions together.
- Participants will be inspired to explore other familiar and unfamiliar Jewish rituals and ceremonies.

Family
- To provide an interactive format that adapts to the interests and needs of individual families.
- To create an entry point for active Jewish involvement that is safe, non-threatening, and friendly.
- To build a community around a shared Jewish ceremony.

- To structure an active evening that keeps families together, yet enables them to follow their own interests at their own educational level.
- To demonstrate the skills of Havdalah, and give parents a chance to be proud of their children's competence and performance.
- To make clear the deeper themes and concepts of Havdalah through participation at interactive learning booths.
- To foster appreciation of one another as families and as individuals in a new setting.

Educational

For the Teacher:
- Teachers will develop a curriculum based around a Jewish theme or ritual.
- Teachers will use their talents and interests to move outside the traditional boundaries of their subjects.
- Teachers will create a teaching community based on a new appreciation of each other's talents and work, while at the same time combating the loneliness and isolation inherent in teaching.
- Teachers will reexamine a familiar topic with fresh eyes to expand their own repertoire.
- Teachers will discover the hidden gifts of their colleagues.

For the Learner:
- Students will perform *Havdalah*.
- Students will explain the symbols and the ceremony itself.
- Students will design a booth to teach parents/visitors about their learning.
- Students will engage in activities that span the spectrum of the multiple intelligences, including projects and activities for the child as bridge builder, as songwriter, as poet, as scientist.
- Students will view Havdalah, like other Jewish rituals and holidays, as amazingly complex and rich and worthy of exploration.

A FACULTY-DESIGNED PROGRAM

The process described here will produce a two-week fully integrated Judaic/secular curriculum.

The unifying center of the curriculum is a single universal theme attached to a Jewish holiday, concluding with a family celebratory event. This curriculum is unlike any other, because it depends on the individual talents and interests of each participant, and because it must, by its very nature, be redesigned every year. This may seem like the ultimate in inefficiency — after all, who has time or energy to recreate the wheel every year, especially when attached to something as constant as the holiday cycle? In fact, though, the approach we offer will never get boring or tiresome as most holiday curricula do. The process can be applied to every grade and any holiday. It does not change. What does change is the product, and because the process is respectful and encouraging, what also changes is the energy and commitment of the faculty, the buy-in of the students, and the interest of the parent body, which becomes involved in the last step of the process.

How Does It Work?

We begin with three curriculum development sessions. It is important that enough time be allotted to yield the result that makes this process work. The first session is at least one half day of uninterrupted planning. The key participants at these meetings must include all general and Judaic teachers at a given grade level, and must include the Jewish Family Educator as well; the media specialists; and the art, music, and drama teachers. The key to success lies in the involvement of the broadest possible group of people in the school, connected not by interest or subject, but by the students whom they have in common. An often overlooked disappointment in teaching is the isolation and loneliness that teachers feel as a byproduct of the familiar structure in schools: separate classrooms and individual curricula. We aim to disassemble this traditional structure by creating a curriculum which is a collaborative effort, each participant sharing equally in its design and equally in its implementation. Talents and interests of individual teachers become central to the creation.

These curriculum development sessions have three goals:

1. To agree on a general universal theme that underpins a Jewish holiday or Jewish ceremony. In the program described here, Havdalah was chosen for its theme of separation/demarcation. Sixth graders are especially aware of impending demarcation in their Jewish lives as they approach their B'nai Mitzvah year. We used this life cycle moment to explore a theme connected to a time of transition, but other holidays lend themselves to other explorations. For example, at Chanukah, we explore the theme of light; for Shavuot, free will; for Purim, masks and deception; for Rosh HaShanah, introspection and self-reliance. Each unit is designed to be complex and rich and surprising, filled with opportunities for engagement by learners of all strengths. Some units have strong music and art components, others more of a social science direction. All share a sense of new-found energy, ownership, and commitment by the faculty, and the sense of surprise and interest by the students and their families.

2. To brainstorm an overarching and universal theme which the holiday reflects, along with projects and activities that teachers might pursue. This step is critical to the process. To brainstorm properly, there must be enough time, as well as a skilled facilitator who does not express a predetermined outcome. We explored the theme first as adults, uncovering its many nuances, and then as teachers who can design units around this topic. We worked in cross-disciplinary groups. By including teachers and art, media and technology people, and of course the Jewish Family Educator, the conversations build on the synergistic energy and interests of the group. It is important that each teacher leave the session knowing how he or she will integrate the agreed upon theme into his or her subject matter. At the celebratory evening, each teacher presents the product — or process — of their class's work, and so each should also be thinking about how they will display and share the work at the final event. The role of the facilitator is also to use the group energy to help each teacher with ideas about implementation of the theme into their classrooms, as well as the development of an interactive booth.

3. To calendar the time frame for the completion of projects and lessons, to envision a finished product including how the celebratory evening will work, and to agree on how all of the pieces will fit together. This calendaring comes in the last of the work sessions.

AN EXAMPLE OF HAVDALAH WITH SIXTH GRADE

The Havdalah unit described here was designed by an energetic and invested faculty. Other groups would, ideally, produce a different set of curricular outcomes. Each curriculum piece has an accompanying interactive booth displayed at the family night celebration/ceremony. Note that the key to the success of this sort of inventive work lies in providing sufficient time for adults to discuss and interpret the theme selected in adult terms so that all the rich associations and complexities connected with it can be explored. Only then will the faculty be engaged and energized; only then will the resulting curriculum be rich and complex.

Below are the subject area activities on which teachers chose to focus for the two weeks of the unit:

Overarching Theme: Demarcation/Separation
- Literature: "The Tunnel" by Doris Lessing, a story of a young boy's rite of passage into adulthood; short stories by Tom Bodette about growing up; writing diamond-shaped poems, which are poems that use grammatical forms to connect two opposing concepts. Interactive booth: There were two booths, one providing instruction sheets for writing diamond poems so that students and parents could create them together (and illustrate them if they wanted). In this booth were displays of their diamond poems written in class, as well as illustrations from their reading in "The Tunnel."
- Science: Pairs of students were challenged to build suspension bridges out of toothpicks which

could support certain weights. These bridges were entered in the Georgia Engineering Competition sponsored by Georgia Tech. When asked to connect their science study with this unit, students wrote in their daily journals some variations on the notion that bridges connect two disparate shores just as Havdalah bridges Shabbat and the weekdays. Interactive booth: A display of all the bridges created, with students stationed in rotating shifts to answer any questions about bridge engineering.

- Hebrew: Students learned the prayers of the Havdalah service and their meanings. Then they selected a verse or two and created micrographic designs with the Hebrew letters of the prayer woven into the shape of ceremonial objects. Micrography is an art form in which a picture is composed entirely of a text or prayer written in tiny, calligraphed letters. Interactive booth: The display booth was of the micrographic artwork. Materials to create micrography designs were also provided so that families could create their own designs.
- Bible: Students studied the history of the 39 *malachot* (work prohibited on Shabbat) and pairs of students chose one *malachah* to illustrate on a quilt square. Some included the modern equivalent in their illustrations. The 39 squares were joined together to form a wall-size quilt that was hung the night of the celebration. Interactive booth: Students created *Jeopardy*-style games with questions and answers about Havdalah to play with their parents.
- Art: Students made spice boxes in art class from clay. This artwork took two sessions, one to design the boxes, and one to glaze the boxes before firing. Teachers were given their own workshop by the art teacher, and each produced a box for herself. This enabled teachers to help students with their work.

Prepared by the art teacher, students also chose and illustrated key scenes from "The Tunnel." They also illustrated their diamond poems by dividing the paper into two parts and illustrating the opposite concepts they had linked in the diamond poems. These creative pieces were displayed in the literature booth, and the opportunity to create diamond poems and illustrate them was available there. Booth: exhibition of spice boxes, set up in "art exhibit" fashion.

- Writing: Students made daily journal entries in which they were asked to respond to the work they were doing and how it related to the theme of demarcation and separation.
- Rabbinics: Ceremony proficiency and songs. Interactive booth: *Chevruta* study was facilitated by a teacher. The texts selected were related to the theme of Havdalah, but purposely new for both parents and students.

Each faculty member came up with an idea for an interactive booth based upon their aspect of the curriculum. Here the help of the Jewish Family Educator became critical in designing these interactive stations, since teachers often think in terms of static displays, not necessarily ones that are sensitive to multi-generational interactions.

NUTS AND BOLTS

The following is the schedule for the evening:

The room is set up in advance. Name tags are made up for each family. Before the program begins, participants walk around looking at displays of student work, art, ceramic spice boxes. They eat and socialize. Everyone comes together for a welcome, explanation of the flow of the evening, and then the Havdalah service itself. (All of this should take about 15 minutes, including the service.)

Make sure there are enough copies of the Havdalah service in English, Hebrew, and transliteration, complete with explanations of the symbols and when and how the service goes.

Provide candles, wine, cups, spices for the spice boxes, matches, cloths for the tables, signs for each booth and their accompanying materials (e.g., pen and paper for the diamond poem writing, chromatography paper for the spectrum/paper chromatography booth). Each booth needs a sign and written instructions and explanations of what is being displayed and how to interact with the materials. Teachers arrived about 15 minutes early to be sure everything was in order. Food set up was on the side.

When the formal evening began, families were gathered, introduced to Havdalah as both a ceremony and a theme, and to the process, timetable, and integrated curricular approach leading up to this Havdalah evening program. The format of the evening was explained.

The students performed the service, standing in an inner circle surrounded by their parents who made up the outer circle. After one year's experience having each student hold his or her own Havdalah candle, we switched in the second year to having one candle per family held by a parent. Also, in the second year, we rehearsed the service in its entirety in the auditorium several times before the evening service to make sure everyone was comfortable with the structure of the evening, where to go, and what to do.

After the service, families adjourned to visit the booths. Families were told to structure their own evening and spend as much time as they chose at as many booths as they wanted. We were aiming for an evening with many choices and with little pressure to "move along" or "see everything." The booths, staffed by teachers whose classes had developed them, were designed to appeal to different family needs and interests. We did not have a closing activity. Families visited the booths, chatted a bit, ate some more, and went on their way.

EVALUATION

We did not ask for formal evaluations from the parents, but in anecdotal form we received more positive feedback from this program than other middle school programs held either during school hours or on school nights. We would suggest written evaluations to be filled out and collected the evening of the program for the purposes of future planning.

The most challenging aspect of doing this program is creating a new rich curriculum across all areas of study based on teacher interest and then creating interactive booths that can reflect these areas of study. This program was praised directly by faculty and administrators. It was also a big hit with families because it was meaningful, connected to the curriculum, interactive, and had no dead time (i.e., long speeches). Teachers had a chance to get to know each other in new ways; what might be competitive for children and teachers in other settings here created alliances. Students were proud of their work, their newfound skills, and the accomplishments that they were able to demonstrate for their parents in the interactive booths. Everybody wins.

Parents should be involved in all parts of the process, including meetings on curricular design, booth design, the structure of the evening, publicity, and the development of the evaluation. This key feature of parent inclusion would broaden the impact of the event

The process and structure of this technique can be adapted for any age or theme, including afternoon Hebrew schools. All you need is willing teachers whose ideas are valued, a facilitator without a preset notion of the outcome, and a Jewish Family Educator with vision who can pull it all together for family learning.

CONCLUSION

This approach works. No question that it seems daunting — it is far from the canned and static programs on the market that seem so easy to replicate. And, typically, innovation requires the constant testing of new processes. But here, the *process* remains exactly the same, while the *product* adapts to the personalities, talents, and individuality of the group designing it. Because of this, the outcome is constantly renewed with energy and inspiration.

Find a skillful facilitator and a talented Family Educator, and try this unique approach. You'll like it!

COMMENTARY

- Consider the value of introducing here the notion of boundaries/*havdalot* from the life cycle: the division between childhood and adolesence, adolescence and young adulthood. (SW)
- Think about returning to this program as a child approaches Bar/Bat Mitzvah. Consider how they can incorporate the Havdalah ceremony into their Saturday evening party in a meaningful, religious way. (RI)
- This program might include a "family life cycle booth" in which all the various transitions in the life cycle might be explored. (SW)

- Also see the section on Havdalah in Chapter 53, "Around the Family Table" by Jeffrey Schein. (EC)
- Consider a panel presentation by various people who can talk about boundaries and rhythms in other parts of our lives (scientists, psychologists, etc.). (EC)
- Invite parents who are creative scientists or science teachers to join with the Day School staff in designing the program. (EC)
- Send a Havdalah study packet home to parents several weeks in advance of the program. (EC)

CHAPTER 20

SHABBAT AT SUNSET

CONTRIBUTOR: MARK DAVIDSON
ADDRESS: The Agnon School
               26500 Shaker Boulevard
               Beachwood, OH 44122
PHONE: (216) 464-4055, ext. 124
E-MAIL: mdavidson@agnon.org
TARGET: Families with children in grades
               Kindergarten-Third
TIME FRAME: From three hours before to the
               end of Shabbat, three Saturday
               afternoons in the winter

INTRODUCTION

The "Shabbat at Sunset" program introduces families to the whole range of traditional Shabbat afternoon and early evening practices, including Minchah *Tefilah*, study of the following week's *parashah*, *Seudah Shlisheet*, *zemirot*, and Havdalah. The program was developed for families already engaged in basic practices, such as Friday night dinner and synagogue attendance, who were interested in extending their observance/participation into Saturday afternoon and evening. This is an aspect of Shabbat practice that even "committed" families have trouble with, particularly those with young children. While a majority of families attracted to the program were active, educated Jews, we also drew a significant number of families looking for a "way in" to Shabbat practice.

Indeed, most families were looking for a meaningful, family-oriented Shabbat experience, regardless of their initial level of knowledge or observance. Accordingly, the program was designed to maximize the time families spent together. *Tefilah*, text study, dinner, and Havdalah were all large group, multi-generational experiences. But some time was reserved for adults to meet separately with faculty in order to debrief the text study process.

These debriefing sessions were some of the most memorable moments of "Shabbat at Sunset." Faculty was able to share techniques for making sense of obscure or difficult texts. Parents were able to share their success and difficulties in studying Torah with their children. Moreover, parents and faculty were able to share difficulties and success concerning the fundamental challenge of passing on Jewish values to the next generation.

Educationally, we attempted to replicate Torah study methods that we use in the classroom with our students. Primarily, this meant encouraging people to imagine themselves in the role of a character and in the setting in which the character finds him/herself. We also had participants focus on gaps in the text, asking them to use contextual clues and their imagination to fill those gaps. Both of these methods work well with kids and adults alike, regardless of background or knowledge. We chose clear, modern, English translations of the Torah, and established a non-judgmental atmosphere that invited numerous interpretations. Finally, we provided articles to take home that gave concrete suggestions for home-based Torah study.

Regarding *Tefilah* and Havdalah, we consciously chose excerpts from numerous *Siddurim* from a variety of denominational movements to show parents the varieties of interpretations and language used by Jews to engage in ritual and prayer. We also included *kavanot* and imagery offered by our students on many pages of our *Siddurim*, and often read these throughout the service to help people focus their concentration during prayer. We also left large blank spaces between the beginning and ending of a prayer, and encouraged families to create collaborative artwork at home that reflected their understanding of that prayer. Finally, we created games that helped families assemble their own take-home Havdalah kit.

Given the wide range of denominational affiliations and different levels of *halachic* observance at our community Day School, we were wary of doing Shabbat programming with our families for fear of offending sensibilities. At the same time, we knew we had a large and growing number of families who were observing some aspects of Shabbat, and who were interested in spiritual development for themselves and their children. The Jewish Education Center of Cleveland (the central coordinating agency) sent out a request for proposals to fund programs such as ours for "non-beginners," and we decided to jump at the opportunity. Since the grant ended, the program has been funded by a combination of funds from the school's budget and the participant fees.

OVERALL GOALS

The main goals of "Shabbat at Sunset" are:

• To provide families with the opportunity to celebrate Shabbat afternoon within the context of a post-denominational, pluralistic Day School community.

• To provide parents with skills to engage in Havdalah and home-based Torah study with their children.

DESCRIPTION OF THE PROGRAM

Following is a schedule and description of the program.

Shabbat Afternoon 3:00-6:00 p.m.
Introductory Games and Singing (25 minutes)

Games and singing at the start of the program serve to occupy early arriving families while waiting for late arrivals. This is an important consideration when there are many young children in a room. It also serves as a fun, easy, non-threatening way to ease people into the program. Examples include a *Scavenger Hunt* for Havdalah objects, 20 questions on biblical characters or holidays, assembling a Havdalah kit, or singing simple Shabbat songs in rounds. We keep these going until all or nearly all of the participants have arrived.

Minchah Service (30 minutes)

We streamline the already brief Minchah service (although all essential *tefilot* were included). This was done for the sake of the attention span of elementary-age children. We provided them with opportunities to lead certain prayers and invited them up to observe the reading of the Torah. As mentioned before, *kavanot* developed by children in class, and artwork done by families, are shared during portions of the service.

Text Study (30 minutes)

In a large group, we begin to introduce the major themes of the *parashah* and to provide a set induction for the specific issue we will be addressing. We then break into smaller groups of two to four families, each with a faculty member, to study a portion of the text in more depth. Finally, we reconvene to allow families to share insights learned in each of the small groups.

Text Study Debriefing (30 minutes)

At this point, the kids go off to the gym with the babysitters to burn off some energy. The faculty then meets with the parents to unpack the learning that just took place. We begin by describing the experience we had as adult readers of a text (what appealed to us, what disturbed us, questions that the text left unanswered, emotional responses to characters or plot developments, etc.). We then describe the lesson plan and education goals we developed and the rationale for studying the text in the way we did. We reflect on how we thought the study session went, and ask parents if the methods we are using could be applied in their homes.

Inevitably, these discussions go in the direction that parents want to take them. Sometimes they want to continue discussing the *parashah* at a deeper level, which is wonderful, of course. But usually they want to understand how we make sense of texts, how we develop engaging questions, and most importantly, how they can take insights gleaned from the text and use them to make a better Jewish life for their families. One of the major benefits of this process is that faculty and parents come to see that they share common goals for children, and that school and home can truly function as a partnership to educate children and to improve family and school life.

Seudah Shlisheet, Zemirot, Birkat HaMazon (1 hour)

We are blessed with a Food Service Director who will come in on a Saturday afternoon to cook food for special programs. If you don't have such a person, make the food ahead of time and have it served by a combination of faculty and parent volunteers. In the latter case, it is best to keep the menu fairly simple. Baby-sitters usually help us serve and clean up. The time devoted to *zemirot* and *Birkat HaMazon* can be compressed or expanded depending on your schedule and/or how antsy the little kids are getting. Be sure to leave enough time for parents to get to know one another and relax.

Havdalah (15 minutes)

Havdalah was taught/performed in an educational progression. At the first session, we simply handed out copies of the blessings and the appropriate candles and spices and did the ritual. Then we realized that some families may need more guidance and background. The second session was more choreographed with brief explanations and instructions given before each blessing. The final session ended before sunset, so we spent a majority of the text study and debriefing time discussing the symbolism and deeper meanings of the Havdalah ritual. Families then assembled their own Havdalah baskets and were encouraged to do Havdalah at home that evening.

PREPARATION/PLANNING

Start promoting the event six weeks ahead of time by including a flyer in the school's newsletter with a tear-off registration sheet. (Also, put the program on the school calendar at the beginning of the year.) Follow up two weeks later with more flyers taken home by students in the specific grades you are targeting for attendance. Put reminder notices in all later additions of the newsletter. You may want to send home a letter to each registered family letting them know a little bit about what to expect, or you can make phone calls. Be sure to post flyers around the school building.

Start meeting with faculty at least one month in advance. The text study piece will probably take the most time to think through. Do you want to look at the *Parashat HaShavua* each time, or do you want a thematic approach? Perhaps you want to look at one story in detail. Make sure that you understand the methodology and goals you have for studying the text and that you can articulate these goals for non-professionals.

The games you play, the songs you sing, and the opportunities you establish for family participation in *Tefilah* and all aspects of the program are also critical to the success of the program. Think through each aspect of the program from the perspective of the youngest students in the room and the least educated adult in the room. At the same time, make sure that more skilled participants are not going to be bored. Plan staff meetings way in advance, given that it is often difficult to meet during school hours with faculty from different divisions.

NUTS AND BOLTS

Attention to logistical details is absolutely necessary and, in fact, will make or break the program. Decide far in advance which *Siddurim*, *Benschers*, song sheets, and texts you want to use, and make sure you have more than enough copies for everyone. Plan menus that young children will enjoy (pizza, dessert, and soda in abundance!). Because the program takes place on a weekend, make sure that rooms are unlocked, the building is heated, and the parking lot lights are on. You want the program to end when three stars appear so time the program to start approximately three hours before then.

Because you are working with families with young children who need to get to bed early, the best time of year to do this is between November and March, when the days are shorter.

The right setting for each aspect of the program is important as well. We begin with games and singing in an informal, central meeting space, near the front doors and the coat racks. We move into our sanctuary for *Tefilah*, the beginning of the text study, and the debriefing. Small groups break out into smaller common areas or classrooms. Kids playtime is in the gym or out on the playground. The dinner is not held in the cafeteria, but rather in a space in which we hold formal dinners and special programs. Havdalah takes place back in the sanctuary, or if you live in a warmer climate, you may want to consider going outdoors to look for three stars. It is important to have different rooms for each phase of the program, not only to set the proper tone and atmosphere for each segment, but to give people a chance to stretch and unwind periodically.

EVALUATION

The success of this program exceeded our expectations insofar as it provided families with a meaningful Shabbat afternoon experience, and gave them concrete tools and suggestions for replicating these experiences in the home. Families that wouldn't normally have the opportunity to meet each other did so, and faculty, students, and parents from a wide range of backgrounds were able to learn, pray, and celebrate together. Overall, the experience was so enjoyable and valuable that we have decided to organize a family retreat for the first time.

Possible changes to consider could include using improvisation and dramatization to explore texts. If *halachic* concerns are not an issue, you could include an arts component. You might also consider inviting skilled parents to lead aspects of the program, or invite congregational Rabbis and Cantors to get involved in *Tefilah* or song leading.

The most fundamental challenge of the program is coordinating all of the programmatic and logistical details among a fairly large staff. But each program became easier to implement as we went along. We learned when to compress some things and when to expand others. Keeping on schedule is very important the day of the event, or the program could easily last for more than four hours. Enough time has to be allocated to allow meaning to develop in each segment, while realizing that kids and adults have different, yet limited attention spans.

Feedback from participants was overwhelmingly positive. Parents loved the opportunity to spend quality time with their children in a Jewish context, away from the hassles and errands that often fill a weekend. Children participated enthusiastically in text discussions and loved having the opportunity to hold candles and spice boxes during Havdalah. Faculty and families alike enjoyed the opportunity to engage in new Jewish experiences in a familiar, nurturing environment. Finally, many parents said they felt empowered to begin studying Torah at home, or to make Havdalah with their children. And many children went home carrying their Havdalah baskets, eager to gaze again at the flames rising from their braided candle.

COMMENTARY

- Adults will find it extremely rewarding being able to use insights gleaned from this experience to enrich their family Jewish celebration. (BDK)

- The key to this program is to help families feel comfortable with Shabbat afternoon study and activities when they are not organized by the school or synagogue. Consider forming family *chevrutot* or *havurot*, and have these families create their own Shabbat experiences. (SW)

- Day schools might consider cosponsoring such programs with synagogues. (EC)
- Many Shabbat programs have "beginning kits" (candles, *Kiddush* cup, etc.). Think of this as an opportunity to create an "advanced kit": Minchah-Ma'ariv service, *zemirot*, *Seudah Shlisheet* stories, etc. (EC)

- Try moving this program from an "exposure" to a "mastery" plane. Interview each family. Get feedback about what part of this expanded Shabbat tapestry will work for them. Give them resources and support to become independent in the aspect of expanded Shabbat celebration/observance. (EC)

CHAPTER 21

JEWISH DAY SCHOOL ADULT LEARNING PROGRAMS

CONTRIBUTOR: SELMA R. ROFFMAN
ADDRESS: 216 Waring Road
Elkins Park, PA 19027
PHONE: (215) 635-6239
E-MAIL: hamorah@home.com

CONTRIBUTOR: ELLEN R. TILMAN
ADDRESS: 1096 Sparrow Road
Jenkintown, PA 19046
PHONE: (215) 886-1297
E-MAIL: ERTilman@aol.com
TARGET: Parents of our students
TIME FRAME: 1½ hours a week for 10 weeks

PURPOSE OF THE PROGRAM

Helping our parents to acquire the tools to study text, which is a part of the school's curriculum and which will make them more knowledgeable Jews, is at the core of our program. The purpose of our adult education is to expose our parents to and give them a working knowledge of Hebrew and Torah texts, which are major areas of study in our school. These classes are designed to allow parents to grow Jewishly along with their children. Our hope is to promote conversation within the family and among peers about the text and about being a family as well. Participants in our study sessions have a better understanding of the values and goals of the school and are thus better able to support their children's interests and educational development.

GOALS

The following are the goals of the adult learning programs at the Perelman Jewish Day School:

• To promote a common knowledge base for parents and students.
• To structure an opportunity for parents to increase their own Jewish knowledge in a non-threatening environment.
• To bring parents into the school to increase their sense of belonging.
• To expose adults to Hebrew and Torah study and create a better understanding of the lessons and traditions of our people.
• To create family dialogue in general, and in particular on subjects relating to Judaism and families.

DESCRIPTION OF THE PROGRAM

Our program is modeled after the open university adult learning models found most frequently in communal venues for adult learning. The goal is to offer an array of classes drawing on the talents and teaching resources (professional and lay) within the Schechter community. Lots of choice, lots of focus, and enthusiastic teaching is the formula we use.

At our Open University, we also try to create opportunities parallel to the child's curriculum. A few examples:

The *"Tal Am"* curriculum from Montreal is the oral-aural Hebrew language program being used in our schools. In our parallel adult education Hebrew language class the same texts are used. The classes usually meet on a weekday evening from 7:30 to 9:00 p.m. in a classroom with the curriculum charts prominently displayed. The teacher creates a "Hebrew" atmosphere in the room by using mostly spoken Hebrew and songs and poems, which are also used by our younger students during the school day.

In our Torah study sessions, participants are asked to bring their own Torah text, but extra *Chumashim* are available for use by all participants. No Hebrew knowledge is needed for the Torah discussions, but comparison of translations of text is often a catalyst for heated debate over intended meanings. The staff uses a variety of Torah texts with different commentaries. A popular one among the students is the new Jewish Publication Society Torah volumes, which present several commentaries. The study sessions take place on Friday mornings from 8:20 to 9:30 a.m., immediately after dropping off the children at school. These sessions are held in our Head of School's office. Chairs are set up in the round so as to create an informal and friendly atmosphere.

NUTS AND BOLTS

Here are the things that need to be done in late September before the program takes place.

- Arrange for faculty to teach the courses. It is helpful to use staff members who are thoroughly versed in the school's values and goals and are also familiar with the curriculum. Our Head of School, Principal, teachers of parallel grades, and parents have all served as teachers in our programs.
- Circulate flyers advertising the adult education classes. We offer alternative days for the classes in our flyers in order to determine when most people are able to participate.
- Arrange starting dates and times for the classes.
- Send letters to participants to tell them about location and time of each class. Include information in the letter about supplies needed for the class, e.g., a *Chumash* and a notebook.

- Order textbooks and prepare materials for the classes.
- Reserve room space in the building.
- Arrange for coffee, bagels, light snacks, etc.

These programs usually attract 12 to 15 participants. Those who attend on a regular basis are highly motivated and come consistently. The adults who participate in these programs report heightened interaction with their children. The children take pleasure in seeing their parents doing "Torah" or Hebrew homework. Parents have reported sitting together with their children and preparing the *parashah* each week for their classes.

The participants in the programs are professionals in a multitude of fields — lawyers, doctors, psychologists, business people, and educators. Some are novices in the study of Jewish subjects, while others are fluent in Hebrew and are comfortable reading Rashi and other commentaries. The training and educational background of this latter group bolsters class discussions. Yet each participant brings from his/her own background and adds new dimensions and layers to any exploration of the deeper meaning of the text.

To prepare for the *Parashat HaShavua* class, the students read the weekly Torah portion at home. Some look on the Internet for the latest commentaries and the highlights of the portion. For the first ten weeks, the facilitators for the discussions were our Head of School, Mr. Jay Leberman, and Mrs. Sora Landes, former Principal. When the group asked that the program be continued, parents and other educators affiliated with our school took on the responsibility of leading the group, while our Head of School and Principal continued their participation as guiding forces.

EVALUATION

Our adult students tell us that the greatest challenge is finding time to prepare for these courses. However, they also report that they get so much more out of the class when they are prepared. They also tell us that they have made new friendships through the programs, and have built bonds with the faculty and administrators who lead the sessions. Study of Hebrew and the *parashah* has strengthened their knowledge of Jewish customs and ceremonies. This has ranged from learning more about the origins and reasons for *tefillin* to how to observe Pesach. Life cycle events (*Brit Milah,* etc.) and their origins are also explored in the Torah text, which heightens observance and deepens meaning for those studying in the program. By connecting the sources of our Jewish observances, participants report a better comprehension of why we Jews do some of the things that we do.

Another positive benefit of the Torah study class is that since each person uses his/her own text, students become familiar with so many commentaries. Discussion is open and limited only by the creativity and imagination of the participants. Some of our adults say the class is the highlight of their week. Others report that they go to their synagogues on Shabbat and are able to participate more actively in Torah discussions there, or are able to follow the reading with a greater understanding of the words on the page. The class is also a catalyst for family discussions around the table on Shabbat.

Parents become role models for their children. They become resources and partners in Jewish studies. At one time, we had hoped to have the children sitting in and studying with their parents.

Perhaps in the future this type of program will also take place in our Day School. However, we feel that it is beneficial that parents are not inhibited by their children, and that the format allows them to do something for their own edification.

At the time of this writing, our Torah Study discussion group is now in its fifth continuous year of existence. The group regularly welcomes new members. Participants strengthen existing skills as they develop new abilities and confidence to analyze text. The group has also studied several related texts, such as the Book of Joshua and *Pirke Avot (Ethics of the Fathers)* during the summer months. We move forward from week to week in anticipation that the words of Torah will continue to be sweet and enticing to our adult learners.

EVALUATION

While no formal evaluation of our adult Family Education programs has taken place, anecdotal information and the groups' longevity attest to their success. Hebrew classes often appeal to new parents in the school. At the Torah study group, 12 to 14 parents join in lively discussions weekly, with veteran participants taking on leadership roles more and more frequently. Some participants feel that there is more discussion when a group member leads the discussion, rather than an outside expert.

COMMENTARY

- See Chapters 38 and 39 on family-school partnerships and examples of interactive homework. Perhaps the adult students in the Jewish university can be given such an expanded, more

sophisticated role in their children's homework. (EC)

- As adults finish segments of Torah study, perhaps they can lead small discussion groups of students in exploring the big ideas in a portion students are studying. (EC)

JEWISH IDENTITY AND HERITAGE

CONTRIBUTOR: JULIE JASLOW AUERBACH
ADDRESS: Solomon Schechter Day School
19910 Malvern Road
Shaker Heights, OH 44122
PHONE: (216) 751-6100
E-MAIL: julirene@aol.com

CONTRIBUTOR: DR. JEFFREY SCHEIN
ADDRESS: Cleveland College of Jewish Studies
26500 Shaker Boulevard
Beachwood, OH 44122
PHONE: (216) 464-4050
E-MAIL: jschein@ccjs.edu
TARGET: Rabbis, Cantors, Principals, and
Family Educators

Programs in Jewish identity and heritage have a number of unique features. From an educational point of view, it is significant that the "content" of these programs is the lived experience of the family. Often family experience is the subject matter content, as well as the learning configuration for the program.

These facts frame the challenges of the family educator for this kind of program. Making explicit what is implicit in life experience, drawing from a deep but sometimes hidden well of family memory are essential modalities here. To paraphrase the book of Deuteronomy, the subject matter is neither in the heavens nor across the sea, but within the learners. The potential for the family becoming real partners in developing such programs is great. It is not surprising then that a community Jewish Day School recently won the Prentice Hall/National

Middle School Association "Team that Makes a Difference Award" because its program in Jewish family history created an "outstanding student/parent/educator partnership."

The chapters in this section mirror these dynamics. In Chapter 22, "Parent-Child Ivrit," Mona Senkfor and Orna S. Schafer remind us of the power of acquiring the "keys to the kingdom" (Hebrew literacy) as a family. The pedagogic challenges of parents and children learning together when the learning is for several years of ongoing classes are particularly fascinating.

Chapter 23, "*Yom Elijah*" by Jeffrey Schein, reminds us of how much family folk memory can be enriched by formal study. Everyone knows Elijah. The prophet visits us every Passover. But why Elijah? The program guides families deep into the stories of Tanach in which Elijah's character is formed. It also provides a broader Jewish context for understanding why Elijah visits Jewish families in apparent defiance of human laws of time and gravity.

Chapter 24, "Indiana Ike and the House of Jewish Treasure" by Eve Joan Zucker, and Chapter 25, "Creating an Intergenerational Cookbook" by Heidi Eichaker, retrieve resources from the Jewish home and make them central to a JFE program. For the Jewish version of Indiana Jones, the adventure is recovering the space and place of ritual objects in our home. Jewish objects, family photographs, and most of all traditional Jewish recipes mark the spots along Heidi Eichaker's yearlong family roots and history project.

Chapter 26, "Shema: Anthem for the Ages" by Julie Jaslow Auerbach and Ben Zion Kogen, deepens our understanding of a familiar Jewish tradition, that of reciting the "*Shema*."

CHAPTER 22

PARENT-CHILD IVRIT

CONTRIBUTORS: MONA SENKFOR and
ORNA S. SCHAFER
ADDRESS: Temple Emanu El
2200 S. Green Road
Cleveland, OH 44121
PHONE: (215) 635-6239
E-MAIL: Msenkfor@aol.com
TARGET: Parents and Students in Grades 3-7

GOALS

Temple Emanu El in Cleveland has a tradition of Family Education going back almost three decades. The "Parent-Child Ivrit" program grew out of this culture some 20 years ago. A group of parents, including Rabbi Daniel A. Roberts, wanted to be an intrinsic part of their children's Jewish education, and were willing to invest their time and energy. They understood the value of connecting generations through study. What better way than through the study of *Ivrit!*

While the program has evolved over the years, the overall goals for participating families have remained the same. Broadly, we think of them in two clusters: Jewish identity and academic Hebrew.

Goals for Jewish Identity
- To develop positive shared Jewish memories from learning and studying together
- To strengthen Jewish identity through the usage and understanding of Hebrew
- To build supportive parent/child relationships centered on Jewish issues
- To share quality time together in an educational environment.

- To develop a *Havurah*-like feeling among participants.

Goals for Hebrew
We are using the Jewish Education Center of Cleveland liturgy curriculum developed by Project Curriculum Renewal 5757 (1997). Temple Emanu El's goals include *Siddur* reading with fluency and comprehension. The curriculum utilizes a thematic overview of prayers and progresses from *Shabbat Shalom* and general prayers to the Torah service, including *Kedushah* and *Brachot* and talking with God.

PROGRAM DESCRIPTION

As with most supplemental Religious Schools, our students begin their *Ivrit* studies in the primary grades. Using prayers as our texts, we begin teaching at the first stage through auditory and visual modalities — letter and word recognition is the goal. In the second stage, when a student enters the third grade, there are two options for learning *Ivrit*. Option one, "Midweek Ivrit," consists of classes one afternoon per week for 1¾ hours. On the weekend (either Saturday or Sunday, depending on the grade), the students have classes for three hours, including one 45-minute class of *Ivrit*, bringing the total number of hours of *Ivrit* per week to two and a half hours for 33 weeks.

Option two, "Parent-Child Ivrit," calls for parents and children to study *Ivrit* together for one hour per week. On the weekend (either Saturday or Sunday morning), instead of attending *Ivrit*, they attend "enrichment" class. Enrichment topics include Grade 3 - Israel, Grade 4 – *Mitzvot*, Grade 5 – *Pirke Avot*, and Grades 6 and 7 – *Parashat HaShavua*. Each class has a Hebrew component. The Parent/Child school year is also 33 sessions. The requirement is that one parent must be willing to attend class with his/her child on a regular basis. If, on a particular week, a parent cannot attend, either the other parent or a significant other adult relative (grandparent, aunt, uncle) must attend. On the very rare occasion when a parent or significant relative is unable to attend with the child, other adult members of the class will fill in by studying with the absent parent's child.

The curriculum is the same for "Midweek Ivrit" and "Parent-Child Ivrit." This is possible because even though the latter class consists of fewer hours, the class stays focused and is high achieving. Families are also required to study a minimum of one hour at home during the week. This shared learning experience includes reading for fluency and comprehension.

In *Mishle* 22:6, we are advised, "*Chanoch lo lana'ar al pea darko*" (teach the young child according to his way). Thus, the teacher guides parents to be sensitive and responsible to the child's learning style (e.g., for a visual learner, families make flash cards at home; for the auditory learner, the teacher makes tapes). As one parent said, "I get to see her attention span and learning style — very different from what I thought." One positive outcome of the program is that the teacher has more time to devote to effective teaching because parents handle discipline issues as they arise. A negative is that while the "Midweek Ivrit" program offers some music, art and craft projects, along with extensive holiday programs, inevitably the Parent/Child schedule must limit these activities because of time.

CRITICAL ISSUES

As we all know, the teacher is central to the success of any program. Obviously, the teacher must possess a strong background in prayer and language. In addition, the teacher must enjoy and have experience in working with several generations at once. In addition, he/she must be a self-starter, must be willing to take ownership and provide strong leadership of the class. The teacher must be able to recognize that each class takes on a life of its own and then adapt to the uniqueness of each class.

Given the unusual features of parent-child Hebrew, we made a deliberate decision that a teacher would continue with his/her class throughout the five years of study. We chose this for continuity purposes and for the sake of the leadership role in building a *Havurah*. The downside to this decision is that because the teacher is there for five years, section(s) of the curriculum may be minimized due to the teacher's natural strengths or weaknesses. In addition, a student may be "labeled" by the teacher early in his/her studies and not be able to escape this image. Also, the personality of a student/parent might not connect with the teacher. Occasionally, a teacher might have to leave the class before the five years are over. When this happens, families experience a sense of loss, and the class must build a relationship with another teacher. Fortunately, this problem has not proven to be unmanageable.

The responsibility of the Educational Director is to oversee the program with a light touch, particularly focusing on classroom issues such as:

- Attendance: Making certain that families come on a regular basis to ensure continuity and to uphold the philosophy of the program.
- Curriculum: Making certain that the goals are met. The teachers need to stay focused on the more demanding curriculum (e.g., cursive writing with the participants).
- Relationship of parent and child: Making certain that the teacher understands the various parenting styles that will show up in the classroom. It should be noted that some parents stay focused and support the child, while others want to socialize instead of guiding their children. Additionally, some parents become impatient or angry when the child does not understand or is distracted. Some parents compete with the child or with other parents/children, and some can be self-

absorbed and do not pay attention to the needs of the child. Thus, the Education Director will need to encourage the teacher to include the teaching of parenting skills, so that parent(s) will focus adequate attention on their child.

- Who is the teacher teaching? We have struggled to define a target population. We found that when we teach the parent, the child gets lost. When the teaching was directed to the "family unit," it became more difficult for individuals to feel responsible for their own learning. When the learning was directed to the parent, the learning became too sophisticated and kids got lost. Ultimately, we decided that we were most successful when we directed the teaching toward the child. The end result in our most successful classes has been that the parent/child roles stayed in place and the parent acted as support to the child while both learned. Although we believe that much mischief enters Jewish life when a parent's sole motivation for engaging in Jewish living and learning is *"fur der kinder"* (for the children), here we have relearned the pedagogic power of parenting at the beginning of the learning process.

To understand more fully the cross dynamics going on, look at Diagram A. It shows that the teacher deals with at least three units and they, in turn, interact with him/her in some manner.

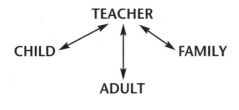

Diagram A

Diagram A is descriptive of a traditional teacher-centered classroom in which the students in the class are both parents as well as children. Alternatively, as illustrated in Diagram B, we have illustrated a more child and family centered dynamic.

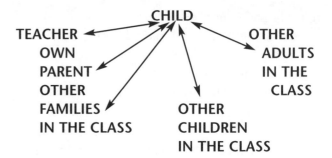

Diagram B

NUTS AND BOLTS

In the spring, we hold an orientation meeting for the current second grade parents to describe the curriculum and the goals of the two Hebrew tracks. The faculty (including the Rabbi) does most of the talking and also answers questions. We also invite some of the Parent/Child members to share their experiences along with "Midweek Ivrit" members. We encourage parents (and possibly children) to visit classes and suggest they examine each program carefully.

Families that chose the "Parent-Child Ivrit" program are required to pay a stipend of several hundred dollars. The class operates only if there is a minimum of six families, all of which must agree upon a time to meet. This decision is usually based upon the availability of a particular teacher and his/her schedule. Classes are held Saturday through Thursday. Those classes that meet immediately after Religious School begin with lunch and a simple exercise or game before getting into the curriculum. No food is necessary for those classes that meet at 6:00 or 7:00 p.m., because children have had a chance to go home after their secular school and do their homework, relax, and have dinner. The evening class does, however, end with a snack, because sharing food helps the group to bond. For bonding purposes as well as assessing comprehension, we ask that both the parents and the students take all of the tests. However, only students receive a "report card" grade.

One of the enormous challenges a teacher has is that the parents come with different backgrounds ranging from no Hebrew to an extensive education.

No matter when a child's Bar/Bat Mitzvah is scheduled during the year, our families are told that they are expected to continue Hebrew studies through the end of the seventh grade. As a result, we have an excellent retention rate (around 90%). One of the major reasons for this retention is the dedication and commitment of our families, along with our use of celebratory benchmarks, such as the Bar/Bat Mitzvah itself which the groups share. In addition, we have a Seventh Grade *Siyyum* which includes both midweek children and children from the Parent/Child program.

As in any ongoing group, there are moments of tension in the classroom and these need to be monitored. Humor is a very useful technique in alleviating tension. Because of the varied teaching skills, the intensity of the class, and the amount of preparation, teachers are paid at the highest level of our pay scale.

EVALUATION

Parent and Child Perspective

In assessing how we have met the overall goals outlined earlier in this chapter, we have asked both parents and children to evaluate the program.

Following is a brief sampling of these responses.

Developing positive and shared Jewish memories:
- For my dad and me to study together is really fun. He helps me a lot. When I can't think of the answer, he says a sentence in Hebrew and it helps me.
- Because they help you.
- We talk about Jewish stuff.
- It is somewhat easier, because if you have questions and you can't talk to the teacher at that moment, your parent is there for you to ask questions.
- It gives the students a chance to work with a parent and so the parents can see how to help their child at home.
- It strengthens our commitment to learning and to maintaining the cycle of Jewish life.
- It stimulates a heightened awareness of Jewish tradition.

- It improves our knowledge of the various prayers, the service, and various traditions so we are better able to share new ideas and concepts.
  It is great to learn with your child what they are learning in Hebrew School.

Building a supportive parent/child relationship around Jewish issues:
- It is easier to study and write answers and you have back-up if you make a mistake.
- It is nice to have your parents learn and know what you know.
- They see it as important because we take the time with them.

Professional Perspective

We believe that we must offer two different tracks for the study of *Ivrit*. Although we are proud of our regular Hebrew program, the "Parent-Child Ivrit" program is really the "jewel" of our school. For the families that elect the program, it is extremely successful. Occasionally, a family will move from the Parent/Child track to the Midweek track if they find it difficult to get along socially with other parents or children.

This program is only for certain families. Parents must be able and willing to devote the regular time to ongoing class study. They must understand their child's learning style. They must have the kind of parent-child relationship to be able to study and work together successfully at home and in the class. And there must be positive chemistry within the family in order for the teacher to create a positive learning environment for the class as a whole.

Some people have objected that this an elitist program because there is an extra fee. For some of our families who are on reduced dues, there is a feeling among the laity that they should not be eligible for the program because such dollars should go to paying their congregational obligations.

We have discovered that "Parent-Child Ivrit" families, individually and as a group, generally are more actively involved in the synagogue. They are always willing to help out. In addition, many of the adults have continued their studies through community adult programs such as *Midrashah* (adult community study program) and *Me'ah* (two-year community study program).

Rabbi Roberts points out that when he meets with the parents and children in "Parent-Child Ivrit" for Bar/Bat Mitzvah preparation, he is impressed that so many parents and children are comfortable with the material (especially when it comes to sight reading) compared to those in Midweek Ivrit. He finds that there is a higher percentage of children who are at the upper skills level than in the Midweek track. These superior students are therefore able to take on longer Torah portions.

Our teacher, Orna S. Schafer, comments, "This program builds *Havurah* spirit and *Ivrit* skills in the most positive way." For her, this type of teaching has stimulated personal growth, as well as academic and Judaic awareness.

There are some unresolved issues that need to be addressed. We are looking for funding to underwrite this program so that it will be available to all who want to participate. While we bring the students to closure with our *Siyyum*, we also need to find a way for the parents to continue their studies. We have a *Lilmod B'Yachad* program (for families to study together beginning in pre-kindergarten through tenth grade), but we are seeking an ongoing way for the "Parent-Child Ivrit" families to continue their involvement together beyond seventh grade. Also, we need to find better evaluative tools, despite the rich parent and student insight shared earlier in this chapter.

If, in summary, we were asked to provide an "on one foot" evaluation of the program, it would be this. We believe this program enables parents to model lifelong learning, as well as to teach their child — a blessing in itself. We believe the program produces positive experiences by studying *Ivrit* together. We believe the program builds connections between the generations and sets the foundation so that these children will do likewise with their children. Can we ask for more?

We recognize that this is simply a formative evaluation. It certainly would be desirable to put into effect a summative evaluation that would assess the program's impact more accurately.

COMMENTARY

- As editors, we were particulary delighted to include this program in this anthology. Hebrew — so critical to an overall goal of Jewish learning and living — has not been a usual subject for JFE programming. (EC)

- The families with elementary students who participated in this "Parent-Child Ivrit" program may constitute a wonderful core of high school families who engage in a program similar to "The Adat Noar Family Program," which is described in Chapter 15. (EC)

CHAPTER 23

YOM ELIJAH

CONTRIBUTOR: DR. JEFFREY SCHEIN
ADDRESS: Cleveland College of Jewish Studies
26500 Shaker Boulevard
Beachwood, OH 44122
PHONE: (216) 464-4050, ext. 123
E-MAIL: jschein@ccjs.edu
TARGET: Families with children ages 6 to 15
(program can be adapted "up" or
"down" depending on the demo-
graphic center of the group)
TIME FRAME: 2 to 3 hours

INTRODUCTION

This *"Yom Elijah"* program began as a community Family Education day sponsored by the
Cleveland Fellows Program. The Masters students
in the Cleveland Fellows program and I were interested in creating a Family Education program with
greater Jewish depth and complexity than we had
commonly encountered. The program has now
been adapted in a number of cities across North
America (Milwaukee, Columbus, and Philadelphia).

GOALS OF THE PROGRAM

Following are the Jewish, Family, and Educational goals of *"Yom Elijah."*

Jewish
- To deepen knowledge of the biblical narrative of
Elijah.

- To create a deeper sense of expectancy around
the figure of Elijah at the Pesach *Seder.*
- To develop a deeper appreciation for the
dynamism of Jewish tradition through the multi-
dimensional figure of Elijah.

Family
- To help ready the family for Pesach.
- To provide for a family dialogue around the
famous lines from Elijah that the "parents hearts
will be turned to their children, and children's
to their parents."
- To utilize role play and theater as ways of making
accessible the otherwise ethereal Elijah.
- To reorganize knowledge of Elijah into a more
coherent and integrated whole.

Educational
- To encounter big Jewish ideas through a theater
format.
- To engage all the major learning styles of the
group.

PROGRAM DESCRIPTION

Hour One: The Biblical Elijah

The program begins by guiding participants
through the biblical narrative of Elijah (I Kings
17-21; II Kings 1-2). I have used *The Torah for Family
Reading* by Joseph Gaer (Jason Aronson Inc., 1986)
or *The Story Bible* by Pearl Buck (Bartholomew
House, 1971) as the most readable English texts.

Whatever the text, this story is too long for the
audience (particularly with younger children) to
listen to passively. Instead, we first:

Unscramble the Story of Elijah

Below are ten critical events from the Elijah story. Blow the caption up on 11" x 17" paper and place one sheet in random order on a wall. For ease of reference, these events are outlined below in the order that they appear in the Hebrew Bible.

1. Elijah Proclaims: No Rain Or Dew for Israel (I Kings 17:1-8)
2. Elijah Revives the Child of the Widow Who Has Fed Him (I Kings 17:10-24)
3. Elijah Reunites with Obadiah and Other Prophets of Adonai (I Kings 18:1-16)
4. Elijah Battles the Prophets of Baal on Mount Carmel (I Kings 18:20-40)
5. Drought Ended (I Kings 18:41-46)
6. Ahab and Jezebel Plot against and Pursue Elijah (I Kings 19:1-2)
7. Elijah Gives Up and Heads To Wilderness (I Kings 19:3-4)
8. Elijah Encounters the "Thin, Quivering" Voice of God (I Kings 19:10-16)
9. Elijah Passes on Prophetic Cloak To Elisha (II Kings 2:1-10)
10. Elijah Ascends Upward toward Heaven in a fiery Chariot (II Kings 2:11-17)

The facilitator has two options now. He/she can become the storyteller who recreates the narrative thread as he/she unscrambles and puts in correct order the events in the Elijah story. Alternatively, he/she can make this a group exercise with everyone contributing to "getting it right" by putting the events in the right order.

Dramatic Reenactment of the Biblical Story

The facilitator then distributes the text for one of the top ten events in Elijah's life to a cluster of two to four families. When time is short or the group is small, I choose to focus on events 1, 4, 6-8, and 9-10 (combining the latter two). Family clusters are given approximately 25 minutes to read the text and develop a short skit about this aspect of the story to present back to the whole group. The group then recounts the Elijah story through their skits, with the facilitator filling in any gaps.

Hour Two: Elijah in Transition

Hour two is also divided into two different activities. The first is to discover when Elijah reappears in the Bible after his mysterious exit (the last chapter of the book of Malachi). This is the first appearance of Elijah as the Messianic harbinger of hope and, tellingly, this is the Haftarah reading for Shabbat HaGadol (the Sabbath preceding Pesach). It is here that we are promised an "awesome day" in which the "hearts of the children will be turned to the parents, and the parents back to the children." It is helpful here if participants return to the same family clusters used for their biblical readings. The Malachi text is read together, and then several questions are explored in the clusters:

- What turns parents and children away from one another? fights? arguments? misunderstandings?
- The Bible tells us only that Elijah will return us to one another. How does Elijah get us to get over grudges and anger? This isn't an easy thing.
- If you look closely at the text, what does the Bible hint might happen if children and parents are not willing to be turned by Elijah or themselves back to one another?

A note about Elijah's character development: Especially when the children are a bit older (nine and up), I will take a few minutes to process the development of the Elijah character before going to the next activity, "To Tell the Truth." Elijah in the Bible was severe and demanding. Is the Elijah of Malachi similarly severe and demanding? In the Talmud and Hasidic literature, there is reference to Elijah's *Tikkun* (self-improvement) over time. When Elijah bursts into Ahab's court, he is filled with a fierce demand for *Din* (judgment). Elijah himself needs to gain more psychic balance through developing his capacity for *Rachamim* (mercy). He will be allowed to minister only to infants, and will have the honor of *Kisay Elijah* (Elijah's chair) at a *Brit Milah* when his tenderness exceeds his anger.

To Tell the Truth

The focus now is on the multi-dimensional character of the Elijah of Rabbinic lore. This is evoked through the format of the TV show of the 1950s and '60s, "To Tell the Truth." Following this format, three characters (teachers or parents whom you have briefed in advanced) will each claim to be the real Eliyahu HaNavi. The short scripts for each is below. The claimants first make their presentation. The facilitator encourages the group to ask questions. Each "Elijah" can also play off the other two, discrediting their claims. In the end, the moderator asks the real Eliyah HaNavi to stand up. After each claimant rises halfway, all three rise simultaneously. This last gesture validates what a rich, multi-dimensional character Elijah does indeed become in Rabbinic folklore. Here are the scripts to give each Elijah.

Elijah #1

I am Elijah the Prophet. As mysteriously as I disappeared — whisked up to heaven in a chariot — so I reappear whenever I find worthy Jews in physical or spiritual need. I guide them. I clothe them. I challenge them. But beware, I am likely to disappear as quickly as I appear. I want people to focus not on me, but on the *mitzvah* I perform. To promote the mystery of such good deeds, I am full of surprises and disguises. You are as likely to see me as a poor beggar as in any other guise.

Elijah #2

I hate to be immodest, but I am really smart and knowledgeable beyond all belief. I know the Talmud by heart, and I understand the ways in which arguments among Rabbis emerge and need to be resolved. In fact, whenever our best scholars, in the heat of passionate argument, cannot find the way to resolve an issue of debate about *halachah*, they call me. From the academies of Babylon and Palestine, you will hear them urge me to come forward. They yell, *"Tayku."* This word comes from taking the first letter of four different words: *"Hatishbi* (that's me Elijah the Tishbite) *yitaraytz kushiyot u'avayot* (will decide the hard cases)." This means Elijah will come and decide the tough problems of *halachah*. That's how smart I am!

Elijah #3

The prophet Malachi really had it right. That's my real character. I come right before the Messiah to get people ready for a Messianic age. I do turn the hearts of children and parents to one another.

I bring back hope and faith when people are doubting. I bind up the wounds of a poor beggar who people couldn't recognize as the Messiah. You may even forget that you speak (or perhaps more correctly sing) of me in *Birkat HaMazon* when you say, "*HaRahaman*, send us Elijah the prophet, the one who will bring a message of salvation."

Hour Three: The Elijah of Folktales and the Future

Since I most often do the program "Yom Elijah" before Pesach, I usually choose to refocus on Elijah's role in the Pesach celebration. My favorite story in this regard is Uri Shulevitz's adaptation of the Yiddish story "The Magician" by I.L. Peretz (sadly, out of print). Other versions of this story and many other Elijah stories can be found in *Tales of the Prophet Elijah* by Peninnah Schram (Jason Aronson Inc., 1991).

Especially with younger children, I will have asked each family to bring some old clothes with them (shirts, oversized pants, suits, old dresses). I insist that everyone needs to be in some sort of Elijah disguise for the telling of this story. From the pool of used clothes, all participants should draw at least something that disguises their true identity. Parents and older kids will do this modestly, usually taking a hat or pair of old sunglasses. Younger children will dress to the hilt.

When everyone is properly disguised, I tell the story of "The Magician." I often give younger children the opportunity to show off their disguises and to show themselves as the magician at appropriate times in the story.

The final activity for the day points to our upcoming *Sedarim*. With the help of a teen or someone who is both more hip and a better singer than I, we teach the "Elijah Rap" (see Appendix A). This is sung to the rap of the television show "Fresh Prince of Bel Air." We then conclude by having families fill out the "Elijah Wishes" sheet found in Appendix B and (of course) sing *"Eliyahu HaNavi."*

EVALUATION

In large part, I enjoy doing this program because it is so Jewishly rich. I think the "Jewish" in Jewish Family Education is what comes through here. People are surprised that there is so much to the character of Elijah, and this helps release participants from oft held notion that Elijah is a Jewish Santa Claus. (How *does* he visit so many *Sedarim* in one evening?) As "Family" and "Education," *"Yom Elijah"* is solid and well grounded, although these elements are not as richly developed as the Jewish element of the program.

The program certainly could be enriched through more adult study. There are wonderful sections of the Talmud in which the Rabbis — even though they knew nothing of the television show "To Tell the Truth" — actually debate the question, "Who is the true Elijah?" (Or, perhaps more accurately, what is the most important function of Elijah the prophet?)

When the average age of the children in the group is around ages 10 to 12, I can imagine an activity that links Elijah to Piaget's concept of the transition between concrete and formal cognitive operations (Piaget) through which these children are going. I would challenge the group to design an experiment that could prove one way or another whether Elijah actually visited their *Seder* and drank from Elijah's cup. This might also be a way to help kids and adults understand the difference between empirical fact (a scientific view of Elijah) and faith and hopefulness (we know Elijah has visited us when our hearts are turned).

Finally, I believe the same Rabbis who so loved to make Jewish life thick, rich, and contradictory might still say of this program, "*Tafasta merubah, lo tafasta*" (If you reach for too much you get nothing). There is in most of my programs the educational equivalent of "death by chocolate." People adapting this program might do well to scale it back by a third in whatever way they find sensible.

COMMENTARY

• One can also imagine this program as an "Elijah Fair" for the whole school and synagogue community, as well as a grade level program. (EC)

• Think about adding a feminist twist: Miriam the prophetess as part of this study. In *Shirim U'vrachot*, edited by David Teutsch (Reconstructionist Press, 1991), one can find verses about Elijah the prophet that include Miriam. (EC)

APPENDIX A
ELIJAH WISHES

You who have tirelessly accompanied the Jewish people on our endless journeys, may you _____ at our *Seder*.

You who are known as the "messenger of the covenant," may you remind us this Pesach of _____.

You who have sipped from the bitter cup of slavery and oppression, may you come to our *Seder* and _____.

You who have known the pain of hunger, may you encourage us to _____.

You who have known both despair and hope, help us work for a world in which _____.

APPENDIX B
ELIJAH RAP
(Recited to the rap tune of "Fresh Prince of Bel Air")

This is a story all about how
Elijah became a prophet of a people called Israel.
I'd like to take a minute; just sit right there
And this is how I became the person of the air.

In West Gilliad, born and raised,
At the Temple where I spent most of my days;
Chillin' out nights and relaxin' all cool,
I was challenging prophets to a big duel.
With a couple of cows who were up to no good
Started bar-b-queing in the neighborhood.
Baal's cow didn't burn, but my cow did
So I ran to the desert and that's where I hid.

I whistled for a chariot and written very clear
The license plate said, "The End of Your Days Is Very Near."

If anything, I could say this chariot was flaming high . . .
But I thought, "Man, forget it. Yo' home to the sky."

I . . . was . . . up to heaven about seven or eight
And I yelled to Elisha, "Yo, home. See ya later!"
I looked at my life and I know I didn't fail
I was a prophet of Yisrael.

(By Enid Lader and Students at the Agnon Community Jewish Day School)

CHAPTER 24

INDIANA IKE AND THE HOUSE OF JEWISH TREASURE

CONTRIBUTOR: Eve Joan Zucker
ADDRESS: 4856 North Bartlett Avenue
Milwaukee, WI 53217
PHONE: (414) 332-8445
E-MAIL: evejz@aol.com
TARGET AUDIENCE: Families with children in
Grades 3-5
TIME FRAME: 2-3 hours

PURPOSE AND GOAL

"Indiana Ike and the House of Jewish Treasure" is a program designed to help families understand the meaning of the Jewish objects and Jewish values that inform their lives. The featured activities begin to connect the families to the sources for many of the familiar ritual objects, and emphasize some of the values inherent in our Jewish lives. Each family has the opportunity to examine its own relationship to its Jewish manner of living, and begins to define what is important to them. Every family member is given an opportunity to express his/her individual feelings. By exploring their backgrounds through various methods, individuals and families can focus on the rich heritage they bring to their lives today. Through this exploration, they will become aware of the importance of their heritage and its potential to enrich their future. In recording the Jewish objects in their homes, families become aware of special heirlooms — family pictures that go back several generations, Jewish books, pieces of art, etc., to which they may previously have paid little attention.

DESCRIPTION OF THE PROGRAM

Families are asked ahead of time to walk through their homes and list all their Jewish objects and to bring one favorite with them to the program.

Following is a schedule for the program. The actual treasure hunt is keyed into the 13 Jewish sources listed in Appendix A.

00:00-00:20: Our Jewish Home
Participants introduce themselves. Facilitator asks families to pair up with another family to tell why the Jewish object they have brought with them is special to their family, and to talk about the other Jewish objects on their list of treasures.

00:20-00:50: Searching the Sources — A Treasure Hunt
Each family receives a "Searching the Sources" sheet (see Appendix A). A table with all of the Jewish objects is placed in the center of the room. Family members circle the table looking for the correct objects to match the sources on the sheet. A child from each family holds the sheet and records the answers.

00:50-01:20: Our Treasured Jewish Community
Participants are instructed to pretend that they are leaving to start a brand new community in a faraway place. From the Jewish items on the table, each individual participant chooses the five things that they would take with them to make that community Jewish. They record those items on a card. Then each family group negotiates until it can agree on

the same five items. These items are recorded on a large piece of newsprint. Families then share with the group why they have chosen the items they did. The facilitator processes the information as each family presents.

01:20-01:35: Edible Treasures
A snack break with samples of treasured family recipes brought by participants.

01:35-01:55: Bringing the Treasures Home
Each family creates an art piece or picture that relates to the five Jewish objects they chose in the previous activity. They use the technique of handmade *midrash* (with torn paper and glue only) described by Jo Milgrom in *Handmade Midrash* (Jewish Publication Society, 1992).

01:55-02:00: Closure

NUTS AND BOLTS

This is an easy program to plan and requires very little staff. In fact, one teacher/facilitator can handle the entire program with a group of up to 15 families. Remind families of the event if it has been scheduled on the yearly calendar. A notice should be sent at least three to four weeks ahead, with follow-up notices and/or phone calls closer to the program.

MATERIALS REQUIRED

Following are the necessary materials for each component of the program.

For "Search for the Source": Include Shabbat candlesticks, *mezuzah*, *Tzedakah* box, copy of Talmud or other Jewish texts, empty chicken soup can and yogurt container, *tallit*, *Kiddush* cup, *chanukiah*, *matzah*, and/or *Haggadah*, two *challot*, *Birkat HaMazon* sheets, Havdalah set.

For "Our Treasured Community": Add items such as: *kipah*, miniature Torah, Hebrew dictionary, *menorah*, book of *Midrash*, Tanach, Israeli flag, Star of David, *Siddur*, *Machzor*, etc.

For "Bringing the Treasure Home": You will need colored construction paper and glue sticks.

SET-UP

This program requires either a home in which objects are placed or a synagogue space with tables to display the objects. There should also be a comfortable space for sitting around and discussing, and a place where each family can sit together for the family discussions.

The other activities all lend themselves to any setting. "Indiana Ike" has been held on Saturday afternoon as a Havdalah Happening and on Sunday morning during regular school time.

EVALUATION

Participant feedback has been exceptionally positive for this program. Sometimes the students will challenge the parents to a race as they match the appropriate objects to the sources. All in attendance are always impressed by the fact that there are specific sources for the objects we use and for the values by which we live. Families love the opportunity to discuss their Jewish lives in a safe and comfortable environment, and always tell us that the conversations continue after they leave the event. They also say that they are motivated to begin to use some of the objects.

CONCLUSION

This program has been done successfully many times in a variety of settings. For some groups it has been done with participants reading the quotations and choosing the correct treasures. For others, copies of the Tanach were provided and participants had to search for the citations before deciding what the treasures were. The latter is a richer, more involved program, and more adaptable to older age children. All participants enjoy the excitement of making the connection between the text and the objects, which they have ordinarily taken for granted as part of their inheritance. Asking participants to choose five things that are important enough to take to their new community challenges each of them, even the youngest among them, to pay attention to which objects have become special for them. This exercise creates opportunities for families to have a meaningful discussion together and to begin to focus on their own family values.

BIBLIOGRAPHY

Danan, Julie Hilton. *The Jewish Parents' Almanac.* Northvale, NJ: Jason Aronson Inc., 1993.

Frankel, Ellen, and Betsy Teutsch, *The Encyclopedia of Jewish Symbols,* Northvale, NJ: Jason Aronson Inc., 1992.

Grishaver, Joel Lurie. *Jewish Parents.* Los Angeles, CA: Torah Aura Productions, 1997.

Holtz, Barry. *Back To the Sources.* New York: Simon & Schuster, 1984.

Kelman, Vicky. *Family Room.* Los Angeles, CA: University of Judaism, 1995.

Reisman, Bernard. *The Jewish Experiential Book.* New York: KTAV, 1979.

Tanakh, The Holy Scriptures. Philadelphia, PA: Jewish Publication Society, 1985.

Telushkin, Joseph. *Jewish Literacy.* New York: William Morrow and Company, Inc., 1991.

COMMENTARY

- See Chapter 6, "Integrating Family, Adult, and Children's Learning: The Bnai Keshet Program," for some additional ideas for enriching this program. (EC)
- Extend the search for Jewish objects into the homes of congregants or members of the community who have Judaica collections. Collectors will feel honored to be asked to show off their Judaica, and families participating in the Family Education program will be delighted to see these objects. (EC)

1. Remember the Sabbath Day and keep it holy. (Exodus 20:8)

2. Take to heart these instructions with which I charge you this day. Impress them upon your children. Recite them when you stay at home and when you are away, when you lie down and when you get up. Bind them as a sign on your hand and let them serve as a symbol on your forehead; inscribe them on the doorposts of your house and on your gates. (Deuteronomy 6:6-9)

3. And when you reap the harvest of your land, you shall not reap all the way to the edges of your field, or gather the gleanings of your harvest; you shall leave them for the poor and the stranger: I the Lord am your God. (Leviticus 23:22)

4. Study is equal to all the other *mitzvot*. (*Mishnah Peah* 1:1)

5. You shall not seethe a calf in its mother's milk. (Exodus 23: 19)

6. And the Lord spoke unto Moses, saying: "Speak unto the children of Israel, and bid them that they make them throughout their generations fringes in the corners of their garments and that they put with the fringe of each corner a thread of blue." (Numbers 15:37-38)

7. Observe the Sabbath day and keep it holy. (Deuteronomy 5:12)

8. Blessed are you, God, Sovereign of the Universe, who has sanctified us by Your commandments and commanded us to kindle the Chanukah lights. (Shabbat 23a)

9. In the first month, from the fourteenth day of the month at evening, you shall eat unleavened bread, until the twenty-first day of the month at evening. (Exodus 12:18)

10. So they gathered it (manna) every morning, each as much as he needed to eat; for when the sun grew hot, it would melt. On the sixth day they gathered double the amount of food. (Exodus 16:21-22)

11. We praise You, our eternal God, who has ordained the separation between Sabbath and weekday. (*Pesachim* 103b)

12. You shall eat, be satisfied, and praise Adonai your God for the good land given unto you. (Deuteronomy 8:10)

BONUS: When in your war against a city you have to besiege it a long time in order to capture it, you must not destroy its trees, wielding the ax against them. You may eat of them, but you must not cut them down. Are trees of the field human to withdraw before you into the besieged city? Only trees which you know do not yield food may be destroyed; you may cut them down for constructing siegeworks against the city that is waging war on you, until it has been reduced. (Deuteronomy 20:19-20)

1. Shabbat candles
2. *Mezuzah*
3. *Tzedakah* box
4. Jewish text/Torah
5. Chicken soup and yogurt
6. *Tallit*
7. *Kiddush* Cup
8. *Chanukiah*
9. *Matzah/Haggadah*
10. Two *challot*
11. Havdalah set
12. *Birkat HaMazon*
Bonus – Recycling bin

CHAPTER 25

CREATING AN INTERGENERATIONAL COOKBOOK

CONTRIBUTOR: HEIDI EICHAKER
ADDRESS: 17213 Hillcrest Ridge Drive
       St. Louis, MO 63005
PHONE: (636) 530-1811 (home)
E-MAIL: hlbeich@aol.com
TARGET AUDIENCE: Families with children
       in Grades 3-9 (can be adapted "up"
       or "down," depending on the
       group)
TIME FRAME: 3 hours

INTRODUCTION

This program was originally created for the Family Involvement Time Jewish Education Program when Heidi Eichaker was a Family Educator in Milwaukee, Wisconsin.

OVERALL PURPOSE

The overall purpose of this intergenerational program is to discuss, experience, record, create, and emphasize traditions as a vehicle for transmitting the Jewish heritage to future generations.

GOALS

Family
- To provide an atmosphere of togetherness with one's family, other families, and synagogue staff.
- To create a sense of heightened awareness about the importance of continuing Jewish traditions at home after the program.

Jewish
- To increase awareness for children and parents about the importance of the intergenerational Jewish link, which is vital for Jewish continuity.

Educational
- To define and then explore traditions and heritage through experiences and the senses of taste, sight, and hearing.
- To gain knowledge about the importance of tradition and family heritage, as well as to learn more about how traditions add meaning to our lives.
- To examine, learn more about, and share individual family traditions, recipes, and symbols.
- To create a new "heirloom" — a *mezuzah* case — and to learn about the tradition of *mezuzah*.

DESCRIPTION OF THE PROGRAM

This program, which at our synagogue we call "Dor L'Dor Intergenerational Program," emphasizes that it is through traditions that we pass on the Jewish heritage. Families spend time together sharing traditions using food, family stories, and heirlooms, and then create an heirloom to take home. The program is built around the creation of a group/community cookbook that reflects the Jewish traditions of the participants that are related to food.

Cookbooks containing the recipes that were contributed in advance by the participating families should be ready to distribute. Tables are set up for the display of samples of different dishes, which are organized by category: appetizers, main dishes, side dishes, desserts, etc. Other tables are available where families may eat and socialize.

Each family brings to the program an example of a family heirloom. When families arrive, they write a description of their item on a 5" x 8" index card, along with their family name. These heirlooms are then displayed in a safe display case for viewing. Families are also asked to bring a blank videotape. (If desired, they may also bring a video camera, or they can use the one at the program.)

MATERIALS AND LOGISTICS

Preparation and timing are critical in order for this program to be successful. Following is a list of the necessary preparations and a projected schedule to accomplish them.

Four Months before the Program:
1. Send a letter describing the program.
2. Include in the letter a sheet to fill out with the name of the dish, the name of the person submitting the recipe, and the recipe itself. Give a deadline to hand in this sheet. The recipes must be typed, collated, and made into a cookbook by the Family Educator or a team of parents.
3. Arrange for one large room and three smaller rooms for the day of the program.
4. Arrange for items needed for the program to be available (e.g., video camera on a tripod, microphone, etc.).

Four Weeks before the Program:
1. Send a letter to families further describing the program, and announcing what each family must bring to participate.
2. Participants need advance notice that the program requires:
   a. an older adult to accompany the child
   b. a prepared sample of the recipe that they submitted for the cookbook. There should be enough for all of the other families to taste.
   c. a family heirloom with a story behind it.
   d. a blank videotape and, if possible, a video camera.
3. Make or order a *mezuzah* case for each family.
4. Order books and prepare handouts.

One Week Prior to the Program:
1. Type the recipes and bind them into the cookbooks.
2. Purchase decoupage, paints, and other craft items.

The Day of the Program:
1. Set up the tables for the samples of dishes made from the recipes.
2. Set up the tables for the families.
3. Be sure all needed supplies are on hand.

THE ACTUAL PROGRAM

Here is an overview of the actual program:

Station 1: Arrival and Sampling of Recipes (45 minutes)

As each family arrives, they receive a nametag, a folder that contains an outline of the various program segments, the room numbers of the stations their family will attend, and the order of the stations. In the folder there is also a cookbook and an extra copy of their special recipe page. Each family then places the sample of their special recipe on the food table, along with the copy of their special recipe page. This enables everyone to know at a glance which family made each food item and what each is called so that they can refer to it in their cookbook. While waiting for all the families to arrive with their food, early arrivals can look through their cookbooks.

When most of the families have arrived, everyone takes plates, samples the foods, and talks to other families about their special recipes.

Station 2: Sharing Heirlooms and Videotaping (45 minutes)

Each family shares the family heirloom and explains its special story. The adult may be the most "qualified" to share the story of the special item. Each presentation is videotaped, thus forming the first part of a special tape to record memories in the future. The importance of such recording in written, oral, or video form is emphasized to participants.

After the presentations, a copy of *My Generations: A Course in Jewish Family History* by Arthur Kurzweil is given to each family so that they can continue to examine and record their family history after the workshop.

Station 3: Painting the Mezuzah Case (45 minutes)

Each family together paints a ceramic *mezuzah* case — a new "heirloom," which they can take home. The Rabbi or Cantor provides information about the *mezuzah* and the procedure for affixing it. If the participants wish, they may sign up to have the Rabbi or Cantor come to their home to affix the *mezuzah*.

The Agency for Jewish Education in Southfield, Michigan publishes a wonderful handout entitled *Inside a Jewish Home* (see the bibliography below), which provides the blessing and information on how to affix the *mezuzah*.

Station 4: Family Shield or Collage (45 minutes)

Each family meets and works together to create a Family Shield or Family Collage. They find words, existing pictures, or they draw their own illustrations to share concretely what things define each person in the family, as well as the family as a whole. After creating the Shield or Collage, they mount it on wood with decoupage material to take home.

EVALUATION

A Participant Survey was distributed at the end of the program. Participants were asked which aspect of the program they felt was most valuable. They were also asked to explain (1) how the program experience affected their behavior in the present, and (2) how they felt it would affect their behavior in the future.

Six months after the program, questionnaires were redistributed to determine whether and how participants continued to emphasize traditions and heritage in their family and/or in their synagogue. It was interesting to find that behaviors that emphasized traditions positively affected attitudes.

The "Dor L'Dor Intergenerational Program" is successful on many levels. First, it dispels some of the myths about "tradition" that many of our families had before preparing for the program. Many did not previously focus on the idea that tradition

was being established in their homes every day on a conscious or unconscious level. The program helped define and identify tradition in each family's home through recipes, family heirloom items, intergenerational stories, and the thought and presentations of family members during the workshop. Second, the program fostered an awareness of the importance of remembering and recording old traditions, as well as creating new ones. Each of these connects and adds meaning to participants lives as Jewish individuals and as Jewish families.

CONCLUSION

This program can easily be adapted to a full year of study for Grades 4, 5, and above and their families. By working with the Religious School teacher, the program can take on more depth and branch out to incorporate other areas of study. If this is the case, the program described here can be the culminating event.

The most challenging aspect of this program is the time commitment needed by the organizers and by the participants. Tradition and heritage are complex subjects for both students and adults. This program brings the idea of passing down family traditions into focus. It enables participants to use senses, mind, and body. It propounds the idea that traditions are continuously in the making, and stresses that we are all vital links in the process. Participants come away feeling a strong link to and sense of connection with their past, and are more knowledgeable about how they might continue the process of expressing our traditions and heritage both in the present and the future.

BIBLIOGRAPHY

Kurzweil, Arthur. *My Generations: A Course in Jewish Family History*. West Orange, NJ: Behrman House, Inc., 1983.

Inside a Jewish Home. Southfield, MI: Agency for Jewish Education in cooperation with the Neighborhood Project, 1997. (Available from Jewish Experiences for Families, 21550 W. Twelve Mile Rd., Southfield, MI 48076)

CHAPTER 26

SHEMA: ANTHEM FOR THE AGES

CONTRIBUTOR: BEN ZION KOGEN
ADDRESS: Kellman Academy
2901 W. Chapel Avenue
Cherry Hill, NJ 08002
PHONE: (856) 667-1302
E-MAIL: kellman@camnet.org

CONTRIBUTOR: JULIE JASLOW AUERBACH
ADDRESS: 19910 Malvern Road
Shaker Heights, OH 44122
E-MAIL: julirene@aol.com
TARGET: Teens and their parents
TIME FRAME: 2-3 hours

BACKGROUND AND RATIONALE

The *"Shema"* is an affirmation of faith and of Jewish identity. It touches different generations in different ways. Kids and parents often don't understand the *"Shema"* in the same way, nor do either tend to reflect on its meaning or explore its origins. We know it's the "watchword of our faith," but what does that really mean? Are there also messages hidden within the *"Shema"* regarding communication and faith? First and foremost, the *"Shema"* is about listening — listening to God, listening to past generations, listening to Jewish *"echoes."*

Long before John Gardner presented his theory of Multiple Intelligences, educators knew that the use of the arts — music, dance, storytelling, graphic arts, etc. — are important teaching modalities. Through the arts, many students can best process and synthesize complex issues and tasks. Schools that can integrate the arts with traditional Jewish texts provide the greatest possibility for students to absorb material intellectually as well as emotionally.

In most communities, there are excellent teachers of texts, as well as talented musicians, storytellers, actors and actresses. How we combine the different teaching modalities can make the difference between an ordinary lesson or program and real interest in the discussion of texts. Parents of teens have the same needs for engagement with Jewish texts through the arts.

"Shema: Anthem for the Ages" is based on a CAJE workshop developed and presented by Ben Zion Kogen, Doug Cotler, and Julie Auerbach. This program tapped into the talents of each of these educators and featured music, *Midrash*, *Tefilah* texts, practical applications, and discussion. The following is a description of the Jewish Family Education program held at Adat Ari El, a branch of Los Angeles Hebrew High School, in North Hollywood, California.

PROGRAM SUMMARY

This JFE program was presented to students in Grades 8 to 12 and their parents. It was the opening program for the year. Fifty students and 40 to 50 parents attended.

Musician/composer Doug Cotler began the program with several warm-up songs and with his introduction of the "traditional" melody for the *"Shema."* An exercise involving the combination of the sounds of "sh" – "mmm" – "ah," together with hand motions followed, and was designed to make participants think about what they were saying, doing, and feeling.

Benzy Kogen shared a *midrash* from *Genesis Rabbah* in which Jacob, on his deathbed, describes the abundance enjoyed in Egypt and expresses concern with his sons' future relationship with God and the Covenant. His sons reply, *"Shema Yisrael . . . "* Jacob, heaving a sigh of relief, gasps, *"Baruch Shem Kavod . . . "* A discussion on Jewish continuity as seen in Jacob's time and in ours developed from the *midrash*.

As modern expressions of age-old themes, Doug Cotler introduced the songs *"Shema Beni"* by Doug Cotler and Craig Taubman, Doug's "Listen," and Craig's "Master of All Things." (These songs can be found on the audiocassettes of both Doug Cotler and Craig Taubman. Music for all three songs is also available in their songbooks.)

Benzy returned the group's interest to the "traditional" melody of the *"Shema,"* and guided a group "Question and Answer" session on other melodies, such as *Musaf Kedushah*, High Holy Day Processional, and rock and roll.

The group was then divided into two sections for 20 to 25 minutes each. Doug worked with parents and teens to write a "new *Shema*" that met the needs of the group. Benzy spent the time sharing early *Shema* memories. The groups switched at the end of the time, and then came back together to share and close the evening.

EVALUATION

This program guided teens and their parents through an exploration of the *"Shema"* and its significance as an anthem for the ages. Different connections with concepts of believing, belonging, and behaving emerged from the meaningful discussion in which all the generations partcipated. Soul touching memories were shared. "Shema: Anthem for the Ages" could be revised to suit any age group.

A well-known talent can be the drawing card needed to get parents to commit to an evening with their teens. As for funding, grants are usually available for such creative endeavors. But, whether you choose to bring in a well-known Jewish personality or use someone from your own community, the variety of styles presented by different personalities with different approaches can greatly enhance a JFE program. Using the artist or specialist in a safe setting can inspire families in your school to play with a subject or with texts in ways they had never thought of before.

COMMENTARY

In keeping with the metaphor of *Growing Together* as a gourmet cookbook (see the introduction), the editorial committee suggests some programmatic "spices" that could make this a very powerful program for teens and parents without depending on the Jewish arts to carry the program. These ideas are drawn from the volume *Connecting Prayer and Spirituality* (Jewish Reconstructionist Federation, 1996).

• Spice #1: God and Evil
If God is the source of all in Jewish life, do we attribute the bad as well as the good to God? We certainly bless God as the source of darkness as well as the source of light in the *"Yotzer Or"* prayer of the Shacharit service. This verse in its biblical context (the Book of Isaiah) proclaims God as "the creator of good and evil."

If we believe that God is one how does that affect our attitude toward evil?

• Spice #2: Radical Monotheism
The Protestant theologian Paul Tillich argues that "God" is whatever we ascribe ultimate value to in life. With this perspective, no one can be an atheist. In what ways do people replace God as an ultimate value with money, culture, possessions, power, popularity, television. While each of these can be valuable and important, when they become the center of our living, they are idolatrous.

Given this perspective, in what ways does the *"Shema"* call upon us to fight idolatry? How do we make God the center of our lives?

• Spice #3: The Shema and the Torah*

Explain that the chain of *brachot* from the *"Barchu"* through the *"Shema"* and the *"Mi Chamocha"* are called *"Shema u'virkotecha."* Therefore, this unit will focus on the *"Shema,"* the other blessings, and on core themes that run through them. Open the Torah scroll to *"Shema"* (Deuteronomy 6:4ff). Ask students to study the section and identify what is different about it.

What is changed here? What stands out? (*Ayin* in *Shema* and *Dalet* in *Ehad*) Why do you think the scribe made these letters stand out?

Give the participants the following explanations:

Explanation #1: There was a Rabbi who lived in the fourteenth century named Abudraham. He had an explanation about why these two letters were highlighted. The two letters *Ayin* and *Dalet* form the word *"ayd"* (a witness). By saying the *"Shema,"* every Jew testifies (bears witness) that God is One. (Adapted from *Shema and Company* by Joel Lurie Grishaver, Torah Aura Productions, 1985.)

What does it mean to testify? Why was/is it important for Jews to testify that God is one? (to affirm God's monotheism to the Jewish people and to people who worship many gods or different conceptions of God)

Explanation #2: Maimonides was a great Rabbi who lived in the thirteenth century, before Abudraham. He had a different explanation. When reading the *"Shema,"* one should be very careful to pronounce each word exactly. One should be careful to say *Shemá* (emphasizing the *Ayin*) and not *shéh-ma* (with an *Alef*). *Shéh-ma* means "perhaps" or "lest."

One should emphasize the *Dalet* in *ehad* to show that God is one and no other is the Sovereign both in heaven and on earth. *Dalet* also represents the number 4, hence, we affirm that God exists everywhere — in the four directions that a compass points.

What is the connection between the letter *Dalet* and the "four directions that a compass points?" (*Dalet* has the numeric value of 4.) According to Maimonides, what lesson is taught by the large *Dalet*? (the omnipresence of God) What lesson is taught by the large *Ayin*? (affirmation rather than an opening for doubt)

Explanation #3: If we mispronounce the word, we are changing the meaning. A small mistake, such as reading the last letter as a *Resh* instead of a *Dalet*, can make a big difference. Since *Ayin* and *Alef* sound alike (silent letters), a change from a *Dalet* to a *Resh* makes the word read *"ahar"* or *"ahayr"* instead of *"ehad."* *Ahayr* means "other," and *ahar* means "after."

What would it mean to misread the word *Ehad* in the *Shema*? What would these mistakes mean in our prayers? How would these mistakes change the meaning of the *"Shema"*?

• Spice #4: The Shema and the Prayer Service

The *"Shema"* is not an independent unit of prayer. The Rabbis understood the *"Shema"* as *"Shema u'virkotecha"* (the *"Shema"* and her blessings). This means that the *"Shema"* and *"Ve'ahavta"* become the center of prayers that begin with the *"Barchu"* and continue beyond *"Mi Chamocha."* From this perspective, Jewish philosophers have noted that the *"Shema u'virkotecha"* contain the three great themes of creation (*"Yotzer Or"*), revelation (the *"Shema"* itself), and redemption (*Birkat Ge'ulah"* and *"Mi Chamocha"*).

Below are contemporary poems that emphasize the chain of *brachot* that give the *"Shema"* its formal structure in the prayer service. Following the poems is an activity for helping families learn this structure.

Poems

Barchu
Of this chain of blessings, I do start
That's one of the ways I play my part
When there is a *minyan*, I call all to pray
I have a different tune when the Torah blessing we say

Yotzer
God in nature, I do explore
Creator, maker, fashioner, and more
The many names of God I do praise
Like "Maker of peace" and "Creator of days"
Officially, I'm the first *brachah* when we say the morning prayer
Though I come in second to the *"Barchu"* when a *minyan* is there.

Ahavah Rabbah

God loves us, and loves us without cease
Is the main theme of this third piece
Because of this love a great gift did God give
Teachings and laws by which we can live.

Shema

The core
The point
I am the central thought
The prayer that at a young age Jews are taught
I follow love and precede redemption
Of the *tallit, tefillin,* and *mezuzah* I make mention.

Ge'ulah

Last, but not least, I wrap up the chain
God is our champion and redeemer I claim
I quote from great moments in our history
Like when the people stood with Moses and
Miriam at the Reed Sea.

Activity

Reproduce enough copies of these rhymes so
that students can work in *chevrutah* or small groups.
First, read through the poems with the whole group.
Then give each small group key phrases from the
actual prayers. Have them link these to the appropriate verse(s).

EARLY CHILDHOOD JFE PROGRAMS

CONTRIBUTOR: JUDITH S. SCHILLER
ADDRESS: Retreat Institute of the Jewish
Education Center of Cleveland
26001 South Woodland Road
Beachwood, OH 44122
PHONE: (216) 831-0700, ext. 372
E-MAIL: torahmom@aol.com
jschillerri@aol.com

CONTRIBUTOR: JULIE JASLOW AUERBACH
ADDRESS: Solomon Schechter Day School
19910 Malvern Road
Shaker Heights, OH 44122
PHONE: (216) 751-6100
E-MAIL: julirene@aol.com

Many rich opportunities for Jewish Family Education are inherent in Jewish preschool environments. A Jewish preschool can begin to develop connections with young and growing families and help guide them as they take their first steps toward building Jewish life in their homes. In this section, we explore some examples of the range of opportunities for accomplishing this.

The chapters in this section represent examples of programs and activities that reflect creative strategies for reaching busy parents and engaging families in special and enriching Jewish experiences. From the classroom to the home, to programming that cultivates bonds among young families within schools, synagogues, and communities, the approaches presented here are warm and inviting in tone, and can easily be replicated.

In Chapter 27, "Building Home-School Connections through Surveys," Deborah Schein explains the benefits of sending surveys home to parents on the occasion of each holiday. Such surveys affirm the many different ways that families celebrate, and encourage students to share and learn from each other. In Chapter 28, "Shabbat in a Backpack," Ellie Rosenberg describes a "take home" activity in the form of a backpack filled with many special Shabbat items. The backpack is circulated among families and guides them in the celebration of Shabbat in a delightful way. In Chapter 29, Deborah Schein tells of an unusual "Tu'B'Shevat Breakfast." This program, the culmination of an integrated unit encompassing math and science, art, life skills, Jewish values, and spirituality, involves students and their parents in exploring Tu B'Shevat through a number of different lenses. In Chapter 30, "Jewish Discovery Zone," Treasure Cohen and Sheri Gropper describe programs that take place in various locations throughout the MetroWest area in New Jersey. These programs, which are offered to a geographically broad community, enable families to learn through a variety of modalities. Through art, hiking, nature, and games, Mark Davidson and Deborah Schein teach families about the three pilgrimage festivals in Chapter 31, "Shalosh Regalim: Jewish Holidays on Foot." Wrapping up this section is Chapter 32, "Shoresh: Planting Roots for the Future." Here, Ellen Chenchinsky Deutsch and Loree Bloomfield Resnik describe a series of connected programs they developed which enable families to explore how Jewish ritual can impact their families and home. A Rabbinic Commentary is provided by the Rabbi of Suburban Temple Kol-Ami, Michael Oppenheimer.

Experiences during the early childhood years represent the first threads in a family's evolving "tapestry of Jewish life." Thus, each JFE program has much potential for enriching family life. Parents are most likely to do things with and for their children during their early years. And it is during these years that parents are most receptive to Judaic information for themselves. At this time, parents are in the process of building their family culture. Each program of the kind included in this section provides young families with needed resources, and gives them a set time in which to try out new ideas.

CHAPTER 27

BUILDING HOME-SCHOOL CONNECTIONS THROUGH SURVEYS

CONTRIBUTOR: DEBORAH SCHEIN

ADDRESS: The Agnon School
26500 Shaker Boulevard
Beachwood, Ohio 44122

PHONE: (216) 464-4055

E-MAIL: deb749@aol.com

TIME FRAME: Any Jewish Holiday, Family Education, Early Childhood Education

TARGET: Pre-kindergarten children and their parents

Before many of the Jewish holidays, the prekindergarten teachers at The Agnon School in Cleveland, Ohio, send out a questionnaire asking families questions that help define how holidays will be celebrated in their household. Parents answer the questions in writing and send them back to the school. Children are invited to answer these questions by dictating words and/or drawing pictures. At school, the answers are shared during group time, and later posted or graphed for parents to see. The children and their parents are thus able to make a variety of interesting comparisons, seeing both similarities and differences among family celebrations. The final graphs are often left up during the year for families to look at. Revisiting these surveys offers families an opportunity to chart their own Jewish growth as they remember holidays that have passed.

Most families are comfortable participating in our surveys. Nonetheless, if a family is uncomfortable or too pressed for time and the survey is not completed, there is no stigma attached. By the

time Pesach comes around, we have built up such a trusting relationship that almost all respond. We celebrate all similarities and differences. We have had many families from a variety of homelands. Teaching tolerance is one of the main goals of our school, and sharing these surveys helps to accomplish this.

The questionnaires vary in their complexity, depending on the holiday and the time of year in which the holiday occurs. The Rosh HaShanah survey is short, given that the holiday takes place at the beginning of the school year when the classroom community is still new, and teachers, children, and parents, are just getting to know each other. These questionnaires help families learn each other's names and about each other's backgrounds. By Pesach, the survey is more detailed (see Appendix A for a sample Pesach questionnaire).

OVERALL PURPOSES OF THE SURVEYS

The overall purposes of the surveys are:
- To provide families with the opportunity to share their home holiday observance with their child's teachers prior to the celebration of any holiday. (This promotes continuity between home and school, a necessary component for sound early childhood education.)
- To offer families an opportunity to reflect on their practices and observances, and share their thoughts on these within their own family, thus increasing their own Jewish awareness.
- To attempt to create continuity and support between the home and school as holidays are explored by the children and celebrated at school.

- To provide reinforcement for Jewish identity in our young children (e.g., most people eat apples and honey during Rosh HaShanah, and so do we; most people help to plant trees in Israel for Tu B'Shevat, and so do we).
- To help create a developmentally appropriate approach to learning that begins with what one already knows. (The survey helps to communicate to both parents and teachers where families stand on a spectrum of observance.)
- To teach acceptance and tolerance of differences. Any unusual tradition serves to teach an appreciation for diversity and offers new ideas for growth.
- To offer some non-threatening guidelines to families who are just beginning their Jewish journeys.

NUTS AND BOLTS

When preparing the surveys, careful attention is given to the tone of each and to how questions are asked. The questions should be non-threatening, open-ended, and should not convey the feeling that a "right answer" is required. Parents should be told ahead of time that results will be posted so that no one is offended or made to feel uncomfortable. It is most important that both children and their parents come away with the desire to continue to grow Jewishly.

CONCLUSION

We have used surveys successfully prior to celebrating Rosh HaShanah, Chanukah, Shabbat, and Pesach. There is no reason not to use them for other holidays or to find out about other Jewish practices (e.g., synagogue practices, customs and observances surrounding births, death, B'nai Mitzvah). Such surveys can be tailored to fit any curriculum.

APPENDIX A
PESACH QUESTIONNAIRE

Name:

Since Pesach is a time for asking questions, we have created a Pesach questionnaire for you and your Pre-kindergarten child to answer together. Please return this questionnaire as soon as possible.

1. What do you buy for Pesach and where do you go to shop?

2. What other activities do you do to get ready for Pesach?

3. Who will lead the *Seders* and who will be there?

4. What special foods do you cook and/or eat for the *Seder*? Will your child help with the preparation?

5. Do you have a treasured *Seder* plate, *Kiddush* cup, *matzah* holder, etc., that you use for Pesach? If so, please tell about it.

6. What is your procedure for hunting for the *Afikoman*?

7. Who will recite the Four Questions at your *Seders*?

8. Do you have any other special Passover customs?

APPENDIX B
LETTER TO PARENTS

Dear Pre-K Students and Parents,

To help save your Rosh HaShanah memories, please take a few minutes together over the long weekend to talk about how you celebrated Rosh HaShanah. (Parents, you can jot down information that may help us evoke memories at school next week.) It would be terrific if your child could draw a picture of something he/she remembers about the Rosh HaShanah celebration. We will take dictation about the picture at school next Monday. (And, if your child doesn't want to draw at home, we will do it at school.)

Name: _____

This is how my family celebrated Rosh HaShanah: (You may want to talk about synagogue, family dinners, with whom you celebrated, what special foods you ate, or ceremonial objects you used. Anything is fine!

Ask your child to articulate some memories, and to jot them down below. Then ask your child to draw a picture. More than one picture is also welcome. Use all the spaces or other pages as needed.)

Here is a picture of what I liked and remember about Rosh HaShanah.

CHAPTER 28

SHABBAT IN A BACKPACK

CONTRIBUTOR: ELLIE ROSENBERG
ADDRESS: **Peninsula Jewish Community**
Center Preschool
2440 Carlmont Drive
Belmont, CA 94002
PHONE: **(650) 591-4438**
E-MAIL: elmoro1@aol.com
TARGET AUDIENCE: Preschool Families

RATIONALE AND PURPOSE

Jewish educators face numerous challenges when trying to educate today's children and their families. What better way to help families connect with Judaism than to find a way to bring it into their homes where it can be enjoyed in a relaxed and non-threatening environment! At the Peninsula Jewish Community Center Preschool in Belmont, California, we achieve this by sending home a backpack each Friday that is filled with all the ingredients for learning about and celebrating Shabbat. This backpack contains ritual objects, as well as projects that will appeal to all family members. The activities we choose allow for choice as well as creativity. We also include in the backpack a set of simple instructions for the adults(s). (For a list of what we include in our backpack, see Appendix A.)

GOALS OF THE PROGRAM

Following are the goals of the Shabbat Backpack program:
• To expand our Family Education Program by reaching out to include all interested families

with children between the ages of three and five years of age.
• To help families learn about and celebrate Shabbat in their homes in a relaxed and informal way.
• To reach approximately 150 preschool families by providing each class with a complete backpack and a sign-up sheet so that interested families can take turns using the backpack.
• To allow choices and creativity in the activities provided.
• To learn about and understand our families' needs through an evaluation sheet.
• To enhance this program by providing ongoing programs relating to Shabbat, such as Shabbat and Havdalah Family Dinners, speakers at parent meetings, articles in the monthly preschool bulletin, etc.

DESCRIPTION OF PROGRAM

Considerable thought was given as to the least threatening way to allow parents to bring this Shabbat backpack into their homes. After many discussions, it was decided to post a sign-up sheet with Friday dates. It is hoped that this method of dissemination doesn't pressure non-Jewish families or those who do not wish to take the backpack home for the weekend. It also gives families a chance to choose a convenient weekend.

The Shabbat Backpack program is introduced at the beginning of the school year during our first Parent Meeting. I show the contents of the backpack at the meeting and explain how the program works. We then send home a letter to parents explaining the backpack and inviting the parents to participate. Many of the classes have a weekly "Shabbat Family" that takes the backpack home on a designated Friday.

Parents feel comfortable using the contents because it is user friendly (everything is explained in a binder), and the contents are non-threatening. Families may choose a Shabbat project, such as designing *challah* covers or *Kiddush* cups. They may read a Shabbat story or play a Shabbat game, braid and bake *challah* with the dough provided, or simply listen to a Shabbat tape that includes many of the songs sung in our school. The blessings are included in the binder as well. There is nothing that a family *has* to do, but rather there is much here that they can *choose* to do. A Shabbat Manual is provided, and families may keep it for future use.

Families have the opportunity to document how they celebrated Shabbat for a class Journal by using a disposable camera, which is also provided (these photographs will later be placed in the Class Binder and displayed at the school picnic on the last day of school). A Family Sheet is also given to each family in which to write or draw how their family chose to celebrate Shabbat. This sheet is also included in the Binder and follows a story about how some families celebrate Shabbat.

We market the Shabbat backpack at our Open House and monthly Parent Meetings, as well as at our weekly Teachers' Meetings and annual Book Fair. It is highlighted in our monthly parent's bulletin, *Chai Lights*. I visit each classroom with a puppet named "Yad" to show the children what surprises are contained in the backpack. We hope to infuse a lot of excitement and also stimulate much anticipation.

By providing ten Shabbat backpacks for our three and four-year-old classes in all three of our preschool sites, we can bring Shabbat into as many as 150 homes each year, thus expanding the number of families that we reach. This "informal" and "relaxed" way of teaching families will, we hope, encourage families to continue learning and celebrating Shabbat. This program is reinforced by inviting speakers and holding holiday workshops for parents, as well as a "Hands On" section in *Chai Lights*, which includes Shabbat recipes, games, songs, and short stories for children.

EVALUATION

Originally, we used baskets rather than backpacks. However, families did not take baskets home because they were very large and awkward to handle. Backpacks with "PJCC Preschool" printed on them were much less cumbersome and more popular. Because we include a questionnaire with the backpack, we know how our families react to this project. The response has been very positive, and as a result, there is really nothing else that I would change.

I am absolutely delighted with this project. It has been very gratifying to receive feedback from our families (see below for some of their comments). Many of these families would not have spent Friday nights playing games, baking *challah* for dinner, making a family *challah* cover or *Kiddush* cup, or just listening to Shabbat music. It is fun to have the photos developed and see the "proof" of the success of this program. In future, it might be of interest to include some simple Shabbat recipes that a family could cook together. I also hope to create and send home a backpack for each holiday.

Excerpts from Parent Evaluations

Following are a few of the comments received from parents.

- It kept us all together for a longer period of time on Shabbat. We had more activities to share together.

- We have rarely celebrated Shabbat in such a fun way before. All of it was great, from the game, the book, the *challah* cover, and the blessings. We really got a lot out of it.

- The backpack helped enhance our Shabbat experience by reminding us to incorporate all the traditions and add some fun new ones.

- The backpack drew us together as a family. It created a special activity.

- It ensured that all of us participated together. Even our 20-month-old participated by putting stickers on the *challah* cover.

- The main thing that we enjoyed was being together as a family (one of those rare moments in our busy lives, especially with our work schedules). The backpack provided us with a specific reason to take the time to be together.

- We enjoyed using the items in the backpack, some of which we had not experienced before (e.g., the Shabbat music tape, the Shabbat manual). The explanation about Shabbat [in the manual] was great for both the adults and children). Also, the *challah* making was a fun experience, as we have never made it before.

CONCLUSION

Although there is some preparation in connection with sending the Shabbat Backpack home each week, the effort is minimal and quite worthwhile. It does help, however, to have some of the projects organized in advance so that the Backpack can be assembled quickly each Friday.

The opportunities to expand this program are numerous. We already have plans to include a Havdalah insert in each Shabbat Backpack to enable families to enjoy a closure to Shabbat. Included will be a brief Havdalah ceremony, as well as directions for making a family spice box and Havdalah candle. Similar backpacks could be designed for each Jewish holiday.

The many positive responses we have received have reinforced our conviction that the Shabbat Backpack provides an excellent opportunity to reach out to young families and enhance their family celebrations.

- A set of candlesticks
- Two Shabbat candles
- One silver *Kiddush* cup
- A small (individual size) can of grape juice
- One white cotton handkerchief to be decorated as a *challah* cover
- One set of fabric crayons to decorate the *challah* cover
- A lump of raw bread dough in a Ziplock bag for families to bake at home as *challah*. Directions for baking the dough are attached to the plastic bag.
- One disposable camera for each family to use to document their Shabbat experience.
- A story entitled "This Is the Way Some Families Celebrate Shabbat." This story is illustrated by one of our artistic teachers and contains ways that the backpack can be used (some families like to bake *challah*; some families like to read books; some families play Shabbat games; some families say the blessings over the candles, wine, and *challah*; some families go to synagogue, etc.). Following the story, a blank page simply says: This is the way our family celebrates this Shabbat.
- One "Hands On" Binder. Following the story entitled "This Is the Way Some Families Celebrate Shabbat," a page is provided for each family to write or draw what they wish about their Shabbat experience. Photographs taken by families will also be placed in this binder. Directions are included as to how to enjoy the backpack, along with an evaluation sheet for the adult(s). Class Binders are displayed at our family picnic at the end of the school year.

- A *Tzedakah* box.
- A Shabbat Manual, which contains the blessings as well as Shabbat songs. Each family will keep this guide. (We use one shared by Fran Cohn from the Palo Alto JCC and give her and the JCC credit.)
- One Shabbat book which relates to the theme of the backpack, such as a creation/celebration theme or knowing Noah theme.
- A Shabbat surprise, such as stickers.
- One board game such as *Kosherland, Jewish Match-It,* or *Noah's Ark Animal Match.*
- A Shabbat tape that contains many of the songs we sing in school.
- Later in the school, year after the children learn about Havdalah, A Havdalah candle and spice box is included in the backpack. (A Havdalah family dinner follows this unit.)

Each week, the following items need to be replaced in each backpack:
- Two candles
- Small grape juice
- Dough for *challah*
- Stickers
- Copy of Shabbat Manual
- One handkerchief for *challah* cover. (After the backpack circulates through the class, another project will be added, such as a *Kiddush* cup to decorate or clay to make candlesticks.)
- Camera in a box

CHAPTER 29

TU B'SHEVAT BREAKFAST

CONTRIBUTOR: DEBORAH SCHEIN
ADDRESS: The Agnon School
26500 Shaker Boulevard
Beachwood, OH 44122
PHONE: (216) 464-4055, ext. 175
E-MAIL: deb749@aol.com

TARGET AUDIENCE: Families with young children attending a Jewish Early Childhood Education Program; can be adapted for families with young children attending a weekend program.

TIME FRAME: An hour and a half, first thing in the morning, either on or close to the day of Tu B'Shevat.

OVERALL GOAL OF THE PROGRAM

The goal of this program is to involve parents and children in the study of the holiday of Tu B'Shevat using various learning modalities. Children will discover what comes from trees (science). They will visit a supermarket and actually do some research about the foods they eat. They will "purchase" goods and then sort them in a variety of ways (math). Foods will be cooked and then shared with parents (math, science). Finally, tree pictures will be created by the children (art and fine motor activities) to be sold to parents at the breakfast so as to raise money to buy trees for Israel (mitzvot).

PROGRAM DESCRIPTION

The "Tu B'Shevat Breakfast" is the culmination of many learning activities and discoveries. The program takes place on the morning of (or close to) Tu B'Shevat, and lasts about 1½ hours. Parents join their children for the opportunity to see their tree artwork (which is part of a fund-raising effort), do an interactive food sorting activity, share in saying blessings, and enjoy tasting many different foods.

After parents and children arrive, parents are given stickers to indicate how much they will pay for their child's tree picture (a $1.00 minimum is set). After looking at the Gallery of Tree Pictures, the family is then given a set of instructions for sorting the different foods, and a plate for the food they will select to eat. A second plate with sections is also given to each family, along with a drawing of the sectional plate. The families then sort their food according to different criteria — color, texture, size, peel, and pit — onto the sectional plates, and the children draw a picture of the plate of sorted fruit. (These pictures allow for reflection after parents leave.) Before eating, a *brachah* is said, and the families spend the rest of the time socializing and visiting with one another. The children are in their classroom, so they eventually leave their parents and begin their school day with activities such as tree puzzles, blocks made from trees, etc. Before the parents leave, we gather together to sing *"Shehecheyanu."*

PREPARATION AND PLANNING

This event is placed on the school calendar early in August so that parents can make their plans to attend. The classroom preparations begin about four weeks before Tu B'Shevat in the midst of snow and cold in Cleveland. Books with pictures of trees are placed in the classroom for children to look at. Tree books are read during reading time, and walks are taken to look at trees that are still leafless, but beginning to bud. The children are also introduced to the idea that in Israel almond trees are ready to blossom.

Each child is encouraged to find a picture of a tree that interests him or her and to learn its name (science and pre-reading). Next, each child draws a draft picture of his/her tree (perceptual development). Colored paper is then torn (good fine motor exercise) and sorted by color (math). Then the "collaging" begins. The children work long and hard on creating their tree collages, and the results have always been spectacular.

The next stage of preparation happens a few weeks before the breakfast. One parent, one teacher, and four to five children visit a supermarket to research foods that come from trees. This is repeated until many parents have been involved and all the children have gone to the supermarket. Last year, each group came away with at least 50 or more items. Some unusual items included cough medicine, pine cleaner, diapers, and ugli fruit. Other items were things that may be served at a breakfast. Some items raised questions. Do pineapples and bananas come from trees or bushes? What about chocolate? Back at school these questions were researched, and each shopping group shared what they discovered. The children chose what they would like to serve their parents. The only rule was that it must come from trees and should be something that can be eaten for breakfast. One year, we had lots of fruit, cereal made with chocolate, and hot cereal with maple syrup. Last year, along with a variety of fruits, we baked an assortment of breads: apple bread, orange chocolate chip loaf, nut breads. For drinks we had orange juice, apple juice, and coffee — all from trees. Finally, foods from Israel were available — olives, dates, figs, an assortment of nuts, etc.

Prior to the breakfast, the class discusses ways to sort the foods. Children sorted by color, by texture and by size. With a little guiding, the children were introduced to the idea of sorting them by how the food is eaten: those you can eat all of, those you must peel, those with pits. (This sorting often parallels a Tu B'Shevat *Seder*, and frequently captures the imagination of the parents.) Through much practice in sorting, the children are prepared to help their parents in the food sorting activity during the actual breakfast.

The breads were made ahead of time during school and frozen. The foods were purchased by teachers a couple of days before the breakfast to allow the children to familiarize themselves with the items and to practice sorting. The teachers did most of the last minute food preparations and setup.

EVALUATION

We have received both positive and negative verbal feedback from parents after this event. Generally, parents find the program to be educational, interactive, and integrated, as well as social. Problems arise because younger siblings are not invited. It is our intent to have the parents spend some focused time with their kindergarten child. I'm not sure if I would change this. I would, though, recommend a more formal type of evaluation so that we might make productive changes as needed.

CONCLUSION

This has always been an easy and fun program to do, and it provides a lot of learning both about Tu B'Shevat and about the foods we eat. The parents enjoy observing their children integrate their learning, and they appreciate having unplanned time in their child's classroom to visit with other parents.

By the way, the seeds and pits are saved, and lead our curriculum right into spring when we grow things from seeds!

CHAPTER 30

JEWISH DISCOVERY ZONE

CONTRIBUTOR: TREASURE COHEN
ADDRESS: Jewish Education Association of
MetroWest, NJ
Route 901 Route 10 East
Whippany, NJ 07981
PHONE: (973) 428-7400
E-MAIL: tcohen@ujfmetrowest.org

CONTRIBUTOR: SHERI GROPPER
ADDRESS: 28762 Peach Blossom
Mission Viejo, CA 92692
PHONE: (949) 454-0979
E-MAIL: gropperfam@aol.com
TARGET: **Affiliated and non-affiliated families
with children 3 to 5 years old**
**TIME FRAME: Two or three times a month in
different synagogues throughout the
MetroWest, NJ area, from 12:45-
2:45 p.m. on weekday afternoons.**

OVERALL PURPOSES OF THE PROGRAM

"Jewish Discovery Zone" is a community-based Family Education series for preschool families, based each month on a different Jewish holiday or theme. Each session is partnered with different synagogues, so that we are able to bring "Jewish Discovery Zone" to approximately 20 synagogues, representing all denominations and geographic locations, each year. The overarching goals are to provide:

- high quality Jewish hands-on activities and experiences for young children.
- shared parent-child activities, so that parents are involved and invested as their children's Jewish teachers.

- synagogue partnerships, supporting and offering a model for high quality programming for young families.
- outreach to the unaffiliated, giving families the opportunity to learn about different community synagogues while attending each program.
- regional sites for programming, so that programs are geographically accessible to families throughout the community.
- take-home materials and information for bringing Jewish living into the family home.

GOALS

Jewish Family

"Jewish Discovery Zone" gives parents and/or grandparents and their three to five-year-old children an opportunity to celebrate, create, and enjoy Jewish learning together. Parents/grandparents become involved and invested as their children's teachers. The take-home activities are an important aspect of each program. This "goody bag" of assorted craft projects and enrichment materials helps families add to their own home traditions and holiday celebrations, and provides parents with extra resources to nurture their role as a Jewish family teacher.

Educational

- To provide an enriching and continuing Jewish family experience that will attract a diverse group of young families throughout the MetroWest community.

- To offer educational opportunities for all family participants.
- To encourage the creation of family "heirlooms" by having the generations work together to make a "masterpiece."
- To familiarize families with Jewish holiday vocabulary, customs, and rituals.
- To provide materials and motivation so that family leaders can apply what they learn at home.
- To introduce young families to the wide variety of community programs available to them by promoting local synagogues and the Jewish Education Association of MetroWest.

DESCRIPTION OF THE PROGRAM

Every two-hour session is Jewish holiday or theme centered, and involves music, stories, hands-on learning projects, celebrations, and the distribution of valuable take-home materials. Each program is held in the early afternoon — after many preschool programs and before school pick-up and afternoon/evening Religious School. Programs are offered two or three times a month at geographically diverse synagogue sites throughout the MetroWest community. In an effort to ensure a smooth running, well organized, accessible program, we limit each site to 20 families. The cost is $10 per child, $18 for two children in a family, and families must register in advance. Last year, there were 27 "Jewish Discovery Zone" programs at 20 different sites.

The planning staff consists of a coordinator, a project assistant, and secretarial support as needed. On the day of the program, a coordinator and three assistants are sufficient.

NUTS AND BOLTS

Advance Planning

At the beginning of summer, a mailing is sent to synagogue educators (with a copy to the Rabbi and Administrator) to alert them of the opportunity to partner a "Jewish Discovery Zone" site for the coming year. A follow-up is made by phone to schedule the programs, then confirmation is sent with specific program description, time, and room needs. A reminder letter is sent to key contact people in the synagogue two months before their program, along with a flier for them to copy and distribute to their members and school population.

Promotion

In September, a brochure is sent to potential families and to all synagogue sites. The programs are publicized in Jewish newspapers and other local community "family" papers. It is important to seek creative ways to "get the word out" to families who are not connected to synagogues, JCCs, or other Jewish agencies. Each synagogue also sends out publicity to their members and especially to their early childhood population.

Set-Up and Overview of Program:

Each program is developed around the following framework:

12:45-1:15 p.m.	Greeting, Snack Bar, and Welcome Stations
1:15-1:30 p.m.	Parent/Child Opening Circle
1:30-2:15 p.m.	3 to 4 Activity Stations
2:15-2:35 p.m.	Stories in the Sanctuary
2:35-2:45 p.m.	Closing celebration (with food)

The room set-up and materials include the following:
- Greeting Table: A small table with chair, registration list, name tags, pens
- "Jewish Discovery Zone" banner and signs posted around the room
- Camera
- "Goody Bag" Table contains: white paper gift bags with handles identified with a J.E.F.F. (Jewish Experiences for Families) sticker stapled to the front. Each bag contains a schedule of the day's program outline, markers for labeling bags, educational hand-outs for parents related to program theme, flyers for next JDZ program, handouts for other synagogue and community events.
- Snack Bar: Mini apple juice boxes; containers of pretzels and Cheerios; mini-cups in which chil-

dren can carry their snacks, sliced bread, assorted mini jam/peanut butter cups, plastic knives, small plates, plus various other foods and containers that match the theme of the day. (Many families do not have time to eat lunch between preschool and "Jewish Discovery Zone," and they depend on this snack to tide them over.)

- Two Welcome Stations: The goal of these stations is to engage families right away in doing a simple craft together to introduce the theme, and to give them an opportunity to meet and socialize with the other participants. The craft enables families arriving at different times to have an easy entry point into the program without having to wait around for a formal beginning.

- Reading/Puzzle Center: A variety of Jewish preschool books, puzzles, and plenty of chairs, so those families that finish early will have another table to explore.

- Shalom Family Circle: Chairs in a semi-circle, one chair per parent (children sit on the floor in front of their parents). A small table and chair is set up in front of the semi-circle with a guitar and "Magic Box" on top of the table. This box, about the size of a cardboard file box, is decorated with Jewish wrapping paper and a bow. It contains Jewish symbols related to the theme of the day, as well as sample craft items to make. The contents are "introduced" through puppets, stories, and songs. The Magic Box also includes the popular "Magic Shin." When this is held up in front of a noisy group of people, they immediately make the "Shhhh" *(shin)* sound and quickly become very quiet.

- Three to four Activity Stations: Families are introduced to the activity stations during the opening circle. They are given a starting point, and then asked to rotate through the remainder of stations, pacing themselves as necessary. In addition to the supplies for the specific activities, colorful standing file folders are placed on each station table with directions stapled to each. Each station takes approximately the same amount of time. Because parents are working with their children, more meaningful crafts that require a wider variety of materials can be offered to the children. Typical station activities involve crafts and cooking. Families are encouraged to create "keepers" (i.e., "family heirlooms") that will be valued and used in their family celebrations.

- Stories in the Sanctuary: Using the sanctuary for story time helps connect families to the awe and beauty of the synagogue setting, and provides a peaceful listening space following the activity stations. It also provides an opportunity to identify the ritual symbols and artifacts in each synagogue.

- Closing Celebration Tables: Programs end with a joyful celebration of the topic with food. Tables are set up with festive plates, napkins, juice boxes, decorative blessing tents, and food relating to the topic. Often, the food item is something participants have made during their time together. Of course, families say appropriate blessings before eating. Thank-yous and closings follow. A sample program may be found in Appendix A.

EVALUATION

At this writing, we are in the fifth year of "Jewish Discovery Zone" programming. During these years, the staff has had ample opportunity to "listen to" our families and revise as necessary. At the end of every year, evaluation forms are sent out to participants. A good percentage of these are returned and they contain much useful feedback.

Greatest successes: Originally, we had conceived of this as one-shot programs for synagogues in different neighborhoods. As it turned out, a high percentage of participants attend every program and continue year after year. Many families report that "Jewish Discovery Zone" has enriched their Jewish life through the activities, Jewish heirlooms, and resources that are sent home. Word of mouth recommendations keep creating new demands and markets, and the program is continually expanding. Initially, we had to convince synagogues to "partner"; now they come to us and ask for this programming. The "Jewish Discovery Zone" serves a great cross-section of the community by moving programming into the neighborhoods. Families love the opportunity to visit a variety of synagogues. (That is an education in itself.)

Surprises: We did not expect that many grand-parents (some non-Jewish) would attend with their grandchildren (some interfaith). Also, many parents who are not Jewish enjoy attending these programs. The fact that families keep coming back year after year makes it necessary to keep varying the program. Preschool parents are very enthusiastic about participating and learning. Many take off from work to attend. Some have even sent nannies. There is a clear need for ongoing Family Education in preschools.

Changes: As the program evolved, we provided a light lunch. We began to meet earlier so that the program finished before the school bus arrived home with older children. We also offered additional programs to meet greater demands, such as "Shema PJ Parties" and "Shabbat Specials" (Friday afternoon *challah*-making, story time, and crafts to get ready for Shabbat).

Challenges: "Jewish Discovery Zone" presents many challenges. It is very labor intensive (it takes almost two hours to set up an entire learning environment in a synagogue for a two-hour program). Although we recommend that people don't bring babies or toddlers to the program, many cannot make other arrangements for these children. This puts stress on the attending parent and on the planning and programming processes. Further, it is difficult to plan for both returning families and first time families. How much of the program should change and how much remain the same?

Bringing the program to another level: Several options are available for expanding the program. One way is to help synagogues set up their own monthly "Jewish Discovery Zone," perhaps providing them with the format and activities, and training their teachers. Another is to offer parent education for those who wish to learn about how to enrich their family's Jewish lives.

CONCLUSION

After five years of "Jewish Discovery Zone," we have watched families grow into and out of the program, and have welcomed younger siblings who have waited eagerly to be old enough to attend. We now have a "following" of families that choose to sign up on an annual basis in order to be assured of a space at all of our programs throughout the year. The bittersweet consequences of this are that our programs often fill up before we can reach out to the unaffiliated and disconnected. We are now looking for ways to expand and pass on these programs and program concepts, while continuing to maintain quality.

One of the special benefits of a community-sponsored program such as ours is the opportunity to visit Jewish institutions, meet Jewish professionals, and learn about other activities and programs in our community. Families and staff alike enjoy gaining exposure and insight into the variety of synagogues and other Jewish institutions in our area. They also enjoy the new friendships with other young families.

A particularly joyful outcome for us as "Jewish Discovery Zone" teachers is the feedback from families that have brought our program "home." They talk about the stories they share, the songs they sing, and the keepsakes that have become heirlooms and that are used year after year. Those who have "graduated" are now requesting similar programs geared to families with older children. Based on such enthusiastic responses of participants, we believe that "Jewish Discovery Zone" has created Jewish experiences that are and will continue to be a significant part of the Jewish memory bank of these families.

APPENDIX A
SAMPLE JEWISH DISCOVERY ZONE PROGRAM

Theme: "Making Shabbat Magic"

1. Welcome Activity
   - Kiddush Cup Puzzle – Pre-cut out of foam board and decorated by child
   - "Challah Baby" Baking Pan – Extra large loaf pan to be decorated with stickers and Sharpee markers

2. Parent/Child Opening Circle
   - Welcome songs
     "Jewish Discovery Zone" theme song (*"Hinay Mah Tov Togetherness"* song)
     "Shalom Chaverim" with sign language gestures
     "Shabbat Shalom"
   - "Magic Box" – contains actual Shabbat ritual objects, as well as the corresponding craft that families will make in activity stations
     Candles: actual candles and felt board candles
     Kiddush cup: actual cup and decorated puzzle version
     Challah: real bread and a *challah* baby with *challah* cover

3. Activity Stations
   - *Challah* Babies (made out of three knee-hi stockings, stuffed and braided)
   - *Challah* Cover (made out of felt square with adhesive backed felt decorations)
   - *Challah* Baking (each family braids and bakes a *challah* for Shabbat)
   - (For those who finish early) Shabbat puzzles, books, games, activity sheets from *Let's Celebrate: Shabbat* (Behrman House, 1994)

4. Storytime: Families gather in the sanctuary where they are introduced to a small Torah and a picture Torah scroll. They are told the story of creation using the picture Torah scroll.

5. Shabbat Celebration: Every child receives a miniature felt board with felt Shabbat candlesticks, candles they can kindle, and a copy of the blessing over the candles.

   After welcoming Shabbat with candles, wine, and *challah*, children enjoy a Shabbat treat and *"oneg,"* and are given their *challah* (bagged) to take home for Shabbat

6. Closing Shabbat Celebration
   - Say blessings over candles, wine, and *challah*. Make sure celebration table is set with doily, juice boxes, cookies, a small *Kiddush* cup half filled with grape juice, and pre-cut pieces of *challah*.
   - Feast at the *oneg*

7. Take Home Materials
   - Shabbat candle felt board
   - *Kiddush* Puzzle
   - Song sheets
   - Baked *challah*
   - Recipes and instructions for making *challah*
   - *Challah* baby and cover and pan
   - "Making Shabbat Special" booklet (adult resource)
   - Laminated blessings

CHAPTER 31

SHALOSH REGALIM: JEWISH HOLIDAYS ON FOOT

**CONTRIBUTORS: MARK DAVIDSON and
DEBORAH SCHEIN**
ADDRESS: The Agnon School
26500 Shaker Boulevard
Beachwood, OH 44122
PHONE: (216) 464-4055
E-MAIL: mdavidson@agnon.org
deb749@aol.com
TARGET: Families with children ages 3 to 6
TIME FRAME: Sunday mornings

OVERALL PURPOSES OF THE PROGRAM

The overall purposes of this program are two-fold:
• To enable families to celebrate the Pilgrimage Festivals of Pesach, Shavuot, and Sukkot.
• To teach families the connection between the seasons of the year, the cycles of nature, and the Jewish calendar.

GOALS

Following are the Jewish, Family, and Educational goals of *"Shalosh Regalim."*

Jewish

This program derived from our desire to teach some of the original practices and concepts of the *Shalosh Regalim* as they were celebrated and observed in biblical and Talmudic times. We also hoped to convey corresponding spiritual themes that accompany each holiday, such as the anticipation of new growth and rebirth found at the beginning of the

harvest season (Pesach), and the celebration of human accomplishment and God's blessings found at the end of the harvest season (Sukkot).

These agricultural themes are relatively inaccessible to contemporary Jews, given that few of us are engaged in farming and that most of us live in urban areas. Nonetheless, our lives are connected to and ultimately dependent on the cycles of nature. The Pilgrimage Festivals offer a wonderful opportunity to teach families about God's presence in the natural order of things, and to enable them to see Jewish holidays as events that can enable them to orient themselves to the cycles of nature and the rhythms of the Jewish calendar.

Various *brachot* for each holiday are taught, as well as *brachot* for encounters with nature. Materials that help parents celebrate holidays at home are also distributed, such as a packet on enhancing children's participation in a *Seder* or inexpensive designs for building a *sukkah*.

Family

Families spend the bulk of the program together playing games, making art, hiking through nature, and eating. These are easy activities in which they can engage together away from school. All of these activities can be enjoyed regardless of age level. But a parallel learning session is also built into each program that allows parents to encounter themes in greater depth and/or share ideas for home-based celebration. During this portion of the program, children usually engage in art projects. Our goal is for each family to learn at least one blessing which relates to the holiday, and for them to create one piece of art together as a family at each program.

Educational

Families are guided toward further learning by introducing them to elements of their surrounding environment that are not instantly recognizable. Ideally, they will learn how to observe nature closely, identify plants and living creatures they haven't seen before, and gain a deeper appreciation of how disparate elements of an ecosystem interact with each other and change throughout the seasons of the year. The program then links scientific concepts such as birth, growth, and fruition of plants to corresponding themes of "birth" of the Jewish people at the Reed Sea and Mt. Sinai and their "growth" as a nation as they journey through the wilderness.

The program also affords an opportunity for families to meet nature educators and visit environmental education centers and parks which they may not have considered visiting before. Again, materials are distributed that can be used by families regardless of level of knowledge or observance, thereby providing a bridge from the school to the home.

PROGRAM DESCRIPTION

This program was originally offered as a three-part series, although it can be adapted as individual, one-time programs, or for a specific holiday. The following Sukkot program will serve as an example. The themes we focused on were "harvest" and "temporary shelters" — two core ideas associated with this holiday. We have held this program on Sunday morning in a natural setting, although schedules are flexible, depending on your institution. (A naturalist is very helpful in developing the educational program.)

9:30-10:00 a.m.: Breakfast, Art Activity, Welcome

A simple Continental breakfast is provided, including bagels, juice, and coffee, as participants arrive. Thematically, we made sure to include fruits that are harvested in the fall in our part of the country, such as apples and Concord grapes. Although they might like to arrive on time, it is difficult for young families to do so. Therefore, we plan an art activity that is simple to explain and which can expand or shrink given the time available.

Each family received a large piece of colored poster board, a sheet of paper, a gluestick, and some markers. They were asked to list on the paper at least one major accomplishment that each member of the family enjoyed in the past year. If they had more time, they could list additional accomplishments. They then glued the sheet to the poster board and gave their poster a title, such as "Weinstein Family Harvest, 2000." The idea was to have each family look back on a year of growth and then "harvest and store" in their memories those things of which they were most proud. Ideally, the poster was to be brought home and hung in the family *sukkah* or in a room where the family regularly gathers.

10:00-10:45 a.m.: Nature Walk

After introducing ourselves and especially our nature educator, we headed out on a trail in search of two things: (1) items we can "harvest," such as berries, leaves, acorns, and seeds that have fallen to the ground, and (2) as many examples of temporary shelters as we could find.

Parents and children alike were amazed at the number of temporary shelters we found. For example, some worms barely $\frac{1}{16}$ of an inch long attach themselves to the bark of a tree and encase themselves in a white covering. At first glance, the worms appeared to be merely a part of the bark. We also found holes in the ground and mounds of leaves, sticks, and mud, all examples of temporary homes built by mammals. We finally found another mammalian built structure — a small lean-to made out of sticks and tree trunks built by a group of students earlier in the summer. Did the original *sukkah* look like this 3,000 years ago?

At first, our nature educator would point out examples of temporary, natural homes. But after a few stops, families were finding their own examples and excitedly pointing them out to each other. When encountering a new shelter, we would teach the blessing *"Baruch Atah . . . Layshayv BaSukkah."* After repeating it about five times, everyone knew it.

10:45-11:15 a.m.: Parallel Learning

For Children

At this point, the children went off with the early childhood educators and assistants to an outdoor shelter to complete their family harvest poster. They glued what they had harvested on the nature walk around the sheet listing family accomplishments. The teachers and assistants also wrote down other accomplishments the children remembered.

This important activity really helped our young children internalize an understanding of their own growth in the past year. The poster provided visual, tactile, and emotional cues that triggered feelings of pride. We encouraged families to do this project on an annual basis. Comparing a previous year's poster to the current one also helps young children gain an understanding of the passage of time.

Whatever time was left was devoted to sharing completed works and eating what was left of the breakfast. We also had puzzles related to the holiday and puppets with which the children could act out stories from the holiday. If time allows, the group could also sing some songs or play some games at this point.

For Parents

Parents were brought to a peaceful, secluded area of the nature center — a wooden observation deck surrounded by a sea of five foot high cattails gently swaying in the wind. The Family Educator then led a debriefing on the educational components of the day's events. He briefly explained how, in biblical times, Sukkot celebrated the final, bountiful harvest of the year, and how agricultural workers would dwell in temporary structures out in the fields. He then linked these ideas to the program activities of "harvesting" accomplishments and items from nature and learning about the construction and use of temporary dwellings in the natural world.

Participants then discussed: "Why is it that a holiday that celebrates harvest, plenty, accomplishments, and security is commemorated by dwelling in fragile, temporary structures that expose us to the elements of nature?" We weren't looking for any one answer here, but hoped people would share with others whatever personal, spiritual meaning they assign to dwelling in a *sukkah* — and they did. We finished with a brief excerpt from an article that discussed how rich people will be humbled and poor people will be consoled by living for a while in a *sukkah*.

Parents then joined their children to see the completed posters, and everyone had a last bite to eat before heading home. An article on basic themes of Sukkot, *halachot* of *sukkah* construction, and an easy design for a homemade *sukkah* were handed out as people left.

Preparation

It is important to start publicizing this event well in advance. Because it was a three-part series, many families registered for this Sukkot program weeks before Pesach. Nonetheless, anyone who wanted to participate in one program only was allowed to do so. Flyers should go out at least two weeks in advance, and it's a good idea to include written notices in as many places and as many times as you can. If registration is lagging, you can always call (or better yet, have other parents call) parents at home to extend a personal invitation.

It is very important to meet early with your nature educator, and to make sure that he/she has experience teaching young children. He/she may or may not be Jewish or know much about the Pilgrimage Festivals. The job of the Jewish educator is to convey to the nature guide how these holidays originally commemorated birth, growth, and harvest in the agricultural world. Their job is to find parallel examples of birth, growth, and fruition in the ecosystem surrounding you. The possibilities for integrating knowledge and insights from the distinct fields of natural science and religious studies are endless and fascinating. You'll be pleased at how much you learn from each other.

Be sure to visit the hiking trail at least once before the event so you have an idea of what you will encounter. Also, make sure families know that the hike will take place "rain or shine" and that they should bring appropriate clothing and footwear.

NUTS AND BOLTS

Materials Required

Following is a list of materials needed for the program.

- Poster boards in fall colors
- Markers
- Copies of text for discussion
- Food and plates, napkins, etc., for Continental breakfast
- 8½" x 14" sheets of paper
- Glue sticks and glue
- Fruits in season

Set-Up and Logistics

The program requires a nature center or a public access park with trails and two shelters or meeting spaces for parallel programming. The program starts with everyone together in one large space (a shelter in or next to the woods is ideal). The nature walk, of course, takes place on the trail. The art activity needs a covered or even an enclosed space, especially if you live in an unpredictable climate.

As much of the program as possible should take place outdoors, taking into account the fact that it is hard to have a meaningful discussion in a downpour. Rain is one thing — you can still hike in it, but thunder and lighting threaten life. It's important to have props, books, and/or slides to share if it's impossible to venture outdoors. A map and directions to the site should be sent out prior to the event.

EVALUATION

There was no formal evaluation with participants of *"Shalosh Regalim."* However, staff met to evaluate program content and design and to evaluate the working relationship with the nature center and educator.

RESOURCES

Aspects of how the Pilgrimage Festivals were originally celebrated can be found in the Tanach or in any one of the many guides to Jewish holiday observance available. Holiday guides and the *Shulchan Aruch* can be consulted for contemporary and traditional practices associated with each holiday. If the park or nature center you use has field guides, trail maps, or reference books corresponding to their site, you may consider purchasing them as gifts for participants, or at least making them available for purchase.

CONCLUSION

We thoroughly enjoyed developing and implementing this program, and learned a lot along the way. Participants were amazed at how much life and how many species surrounded them in an area not very far from their backyards. Basic practices and rituals for each holiday were transmitted, and many participants said that they would be implementing these at home with their children. The children themselves brought what they learned back to the classroom — they now clearly link the idea of temporary shelter to their understanding of Sukkot, and they can identify the shelters of animals when participating in nature programs. We also established a strong relationship with an excellent nature educator and a wonderful nature education center.

The program succeeded at integrating themes and insights from science and Judaic studies, a primary goal of our school. Our Early Childhood Coordinator learned about the environment surrounding our campus and was able to share this information with other faculty. *"Shalosh Regalim"* was our first attempt at producing programs that attract families from across grade levels in our early childhood program. We had no idea how many families would respond or whether it would be possible to work with kids from different age levels and parents from a wide variety of denominational backgrounds and levels of observance. But by the final Sukkot program, we had almost three times as many participants as at the first, and people were saying how much they were looking forward to a Pesach nature walk.

COMMENTARY

- Taking families into nature is one of the most powerful ways to engage them in the contemplation of our place in the universe. But this program is both powerful and difficult at the same time. The challenge is crafting conceptually honest and developmentally appropriate ways of teaching "rest" as part of God and nature's rhythm. (LI)

- This is a great place to teach *brachot* to children. If there is parallel adult learning, Abraham Joshua Heschel's concepts of "radical amazement" and Shabbat as a "palace in time" can be introduced. (LI)

- A similar program can be developed for Tu B'Shevat, focusing on rebirth and renewal in the midst of winter, or for Chanukah, focusing on light in the midst of darkness. (EC)

- Teach some "marches" as part of the theme of the *Shalosh Regalim* — the time for maching up to Jerusalem. You might also teach one of the Psalms of Ascent as part of moving through nature on foot. (EC)

- Create a collective journal for the group reflecting on the changes the families have seen as they visited plants, flowers, lakes, etc., on Sukkot, Pesach, and Shavuot. (EC)

- On each of the days, gather different leaves and flowers that can be turned into a *besamim* (spice) blend for families to use at Havdalah. (EC)

- The same kind of program could be scheduled during Elul or during the *Yamim Nora'im* (High Holy Days). Such a program could focus on environmental degradation and the need to do *teshuvah* for harming God's creation. (EC)

- This program could be done just as easily at a farm or pick-your-own fruit orchard. The educational emphasis could change to focus on the relationship between human effort and divine providence in agriculture. This would be an interesting way to teach the second paragraph of the *"Shema"* or the *mitzvot* of not harvesting the corners of the fields and tithing to the poor. (EC)

CHAPTER 32

SHORESH: PLANTING ROOTS FOR THE FUTURE

CONTRIBUTORS:
    ELLEN CHENCHINSKY DEUTSCH
    and LOREE BLOOMFIELD RESNIK
    Rabbinic Commentary by Rabbi Michael
    Oppenheimer
ADDRESS: Suburban Temple-Kol Ami
            22401 Chagrin Boulevard
            Beachwood, OH 44122
PHONE: (216) 991-0700
E-MAIL: ecdeutsch@aol.com
           lbrtst@aol.com
TARGET: Families with preschool children;
          families in interfaith marriages and
          unaffiliated families with preschool
          children
TIME FRAME: Yearlong

INTRODUCTION

Suburban Temple Kol-Ami is a 50-year-old Reform congregation in the greater Cleveland, Ohio area. It is a mid-sized congregation of approximately 540 households. It is served by one Rabbi, who has been with the congregation for 25 years.

The program "Shoresh: Planting Roots for the Future" was made possible through a grant from the Jewish Education Center of Cleveland. As that two-year grant came to a close, a synagogue family with a strong commitment to Jewish education agreed to fund the program through its family foundation. Additional funding came from the Suburban Temple-Kol Ami Women's Committee. A member of the board of the Women's Committee serves as a lay chairperson of this program. The

current chairperson is a preschool parent, herself a program participant, who is invested in the planning and implementation of the program through interaction with the Family Educator. Other participants also serve in volunteer roles in the implementation.

This particular program also meets the goals of Outreach to intermarried families as structured by the Reform movement's Union of American Hebrew Congregations, and received a Belin Outreach Award of $1,000, which will also be used for the program. This program is published in its entirety in *New Ideas 1999*, which can be obtained from the Outreach Department of the UAHC, 633 Third Avenue, New York, NY 10017.

GOALS

More than 50% of the young families of our congregation are intermarried. Rather than look at this as a problem, we choose to view it as an opportunity. Because it deals with children five and under, this program gives us a chance to help these families understand what is involved in making Jewish choices. Many of the non-Jewish partners come from other faith communities in which ritual has played an important part. These individuals understand the value of ritual — how it plays a significant role in building family memories that are such an important part of the development of identity. Our program helps intermarried families explore how Jewish ritual can impact the families they have created.

Additionally, it is our goal to help the Jewish spouse access Jewish information so as to become more comfortable with his/her heritage. The facilitator understands the issues with which these couples are grappling. Thus, material is presented in such a way that one who doesn't know can learn, and one who might have known can review without embarrassment.

Next, we examine the more general goals of our project. *The Targilon: Charting a Course in Jewish Family Education* is a workbook by Leora Isaacs and Jeffrey Schein (JESNA and JRF, 1996). This workbook outlines three components that define a Jewish Family Education program: a Jewish component, a family component, and an educational component. In setting the goals for "Shoresh," all of these components are present.

Within the framework of the Jewish component, information regarding customs, traditions, history and practice are presented to parents and children in a Reform context. Traditional observances are often presented to adults, followed by discussion on how they could adapt these practices to their lives. Because holiday celebrations and Shabbat represented the core of the curriculum, these areas were covered extensively. The goal of building early Jewish literacy for the preschoolers is met through an integrated multiple intelligence approach using music, dance, arts and crafts, and literature. While trying to stay within the one-hour time frame, the information presented to adults is extensive — often enhanced by their eager questions.

To meet the family component, we have clearly stated goals. The intergenerational activities themselves are directed at the developmental level of the preschool child, but the parents learn concurrently the origins of the traditions and how to use them at home. Our plan is to give parents the opportunity to discuss the process of making informed choices regarding the role these traditions and how this information might play in their own families. Because the program is specifically for preschoolers, it is not necessary to design age appropriate activities for other children in the family. While cognizant of the differing developmental levels of toddlers and kindergarteners, we did not face the added challenge of having preteens or adolescents in the mix. All the children could create a *Kiddush* cup at some artistic development level and none would be "bored" by the activity.

The book *The Targilon*, mentioned above, emphasizes some integral goals regarding the educational component (the actual learning process). Our goal was to invest children (and their parents) in Family Education in their early formative years. Rabbi Eric Yoffie, President of the Union of American Hebrew Congregations, targeted children from birth to age five as central to his goal of achieving a Jewish population that is literate. Sharing this view, we sought to foster the value of continuing education with this group of learning families through the school age years. We wanted to establish a parent-congregation partnership years before the parents might begin to view Family Education as a parent-school partnership. It is part of our congregational mission that families understand lifelong learning and that the synagogue is a strong "family place to be" (an oft-stated slogan used in our congregation.) The parents would have exposure to Jewish learning through discussion and print materials, which would "whet their appetite" for more learning. Hence, the synagogue would be seen not solely as a Religious School for children, but as a learning center for adults as well.

DESCRIPTION OF THE PROGRAM

"Shoresh: Planting Roots for the Future" consists of a series of monthly programs for preschoolers, their parents, and their grandparents that follows the Jewish holiday cycle and includes child-centered activities, parent learning sessions, print material, and suggestions for bringing Judaism into the home and inculcating Jewish values during the formative years. The following descriptions of programs pertain to the planning of the various events that are integral to the yearlong *"Shoresh"* program. Each year, the series begins with a "Prayer and Share Shabbat" dinner or picnic and concludes with a "Prayer and Share." All of the components in the series provide families with something to take home. Each program features discussion topics, activities, and rituals which may be used at home. The Sukkot and Purim programs existed as intergenerational events. Specific preschool activities were added to the events to make them friendly to our youngest members. While all families are encouraged to attend all programs in the series, some are unable to do so. It is important for families to feel it's okay to do as much as they are able to do within the limits of their individual situations. Families may choose which of the programs to attend.

This program began with four events and, due to requests from both parents and youngsters, has expanded. One three-year-old called his grandmother and said, "Nanna, when can I go to Temple again?" A parent of a two-year-old reported that his child woke up each Saturday morning and asked, "Is it Temple day today?" This is exactly the response we had desired. These anecdotal comments, along with written evaluations. let us know that we are attaining the overarching goals of the program. Multi-generations are celebrating Judaism together, often including gentile parents and grandparents. Families are taking home child-created ritual objects which, they report, they continue to use at home. Through the photographs we take at events and the books the children create, the parents are empowered to provide positive memories of childhood celebrations for their children both at home and in the synagogue. Many of the families live in Jewishly isolated areas of the Cleveland metropolitan area; these programs have provided them with a welcoming community of people in similar circumstances. In addition, these events provided our Rabbi with an opportunity to foster warm and trusting relationships with these young families in an informal setting. Such relationships provide the children with a comfortable entry into the Religious School, which is directed by our Rabbi.

Structure

Each of the programs in the series is one hour in length. The first 30 minutes consists of a series of craft or cooking activities which children and adults do together. During the activities, the Family Educator or trained lay person is able to interact one-on-one with the families, sharing various ways of using the ritual objects which are being created. During the next 15 minutes, parents and children move to separate areas of the multi-purpose room. The children sing songs and listen to stories about the holiday from a teacher, Family Educator. or trained lay person, while parents engage in a discussion with the Family Educator and/or the Rabbi. The facilitator often uses storytelling to share a personal journey or family experience. This discussion provides a safe time and place for parents to share their feelings and concerns. It encourages parents to support each other as they raise their Jewish children. During the last 15 minutes, the parents and children join together for a shared snack that relates to the holiday (this could be something the children have prepared during the first activity period).

NUTS AND BOLTS

Programmatic Links

The early childhood events are coordinated with the synagogue and Religious School calendars. This is done as a combined effort of the Rabbi, Executive Director, Religious School Principal, and the Family Educator.

Public Relations

At the beginning of the Jewish calendar year, the congregation identifies families and grandparents with children from 18 months to five years old. Prospective members are added to this list as they are identified. Each family is sent a calendar of the preschool events for the upcoming year. Exciting invitations (see Appendix A) are sent to each preschool family three weeks prior to the specific event. An article in the synagogue bulletin describes the forthcoming events. Public service announcements are also placed in local papers and the *Cleveland Jewish News.*

Program Setup

Activities take place in a multipurpose room set up with child size tables, etc. The educator coordinates the purchase of materials, printing of informational handouts, facility set up, implementation of the plans, and follows up with participants when necessary. The lay chairperson helps with these tasks. Lay leaders play an active role in all aspects of planning and implementing each event.

Lesson Plans

The following lesson plans have been used over the past few years. These will provide specific how-tos to carry out a variety of early childhood Family Education programs.

EVENT: PRAYER AND SHARE SHABBAT

Date: August and June
Time: 6:00 p.m.
Place: Family Education Center

Goals

- To provide an opportunity for multi-generations to celebrate Judaism together.
- To connect the activities and parent discussions of the year.
- To experience a worship service appropriate to multi-generations in a small community of those new to Judaism and those discovering their own Judaism.
- To further the connectedness between Rabbi and participant in creating meaningful prayer experiences.
- To reinforce *Tikkun Olam.*
- To provide a model for Friday evening Shabbat celebration, both in the home and in the synagogue.
- To increase the comfort level of participants with Shabbat blessings and ritual.

Overview

A main course, *challah,* grape juice, wine, and beverages are provided for a nominal fee. Each family brings a side dish or dessert. Families are invited to bring *challah* covers, candlesticks, *Kiddush* cups, and other objects they use at home on Shabbat. (These could be the objects the children made at programs during the year.)

A brief Kabbalat Shabbat service is held prior to dinner. To set the mood for Shabbat, appropriate music is played. Families contribute canned goods as *Tzedakah.* Parents bless and say special words to

their children. Before eating, the candles will be blessed, the *Kiddush* said, and the *Motzi* recited.

After dinner, a brief service that has been planned by the Rabbi, the families, and the Early Childhood Educator is held. After services, everyone enjoys dessert and says good-bye.

Note: This event marks the end of the program year. This plan, with different activities, may be used for a number of other Shabbat experiences.

EVENT: MAKE IT AND TAKE IT SHABBAT

Date: November and April
Time: 9:45 a.m.
Place: Family Education Center

Goals

- To provide an opportunity for multi-generations to celebrate Judaism together.
- To convey the way to adapt rituals from childhood experiences to current family situations.
- To teach the linkage of Jewish values to rituals.
- To bring the tastes, smells, and all the senses connected with Shabbat into the home for all the generations.
- To begin the formation of a Jewish library in the home.

Craft Stations

The following four stations will be set up, and, during the first half-hour, children will rotate through the four. Pictures will be taken at each station and mailed to families after the event to be placed in personalized Tot Shabbat book.
- Bake *challah.* Children braid *challah* and take it home to bake.
- Create a *Kiddush* cup using clear plastic wineglasses decorated with glitter and permanent marker.
- Create candlesticks using clay, which may be baked at home.
- Create a *challah* cover using fabric markers. Glue felt cutouts onto the cover.

Alternative Crafts

- Make *Tzedakah* boxes out of milk cartons or the small, individual-size cereal boxes.

- Make *challah* plates by inserting glitter, paper cutouts or drawings between two clear plastic plates that are glued together.
- Create centerpieces. Make the flowers out of egg cartons, and paint them, or make them out of tissue paper.
- Make candy using candy molds of Jewish symbols.

Large Group Time

The parents meet with the Family Educator or facilitator, while the children listen to a story and have a music activity.

Parents/grandparents discuss the following: What rituals do they remember of their own Sabbath or Sunday celebrations? Were these positive experiences? What Jewish values do they wish to transmit to their children?

The facilitator shares memories through storytelling, and talks about creating new rituals that meet the needs of the family.

While this discussion is taking place, the Rabbi or other adult reads a book to the children. Some suggestions of books: *Tot Shabbat* by Camille Kress (UAHC Press, 1996), *Sammy Spider's First Shabbat* by Sylvia A. Rouss (Kar-Ben Copies, 1997), *A Holiday with Noah* by Susan Remick Topek (Kar-Ben Copies, 1990). Children also sing songs and engage in finger plays.

Whole Group Closing Activity

Everyone gathers around a table set with Shabbat ritual objects. The prayer over the candles is said, the *Kiddush* (grape juice is provided) and the *Motzi* are recited. The children and parents share a snack of *challah*, juice, and cookies. Each child is given a book to take home and a blank personal copy to be filled in with photographs.

Materials Needed

The activities selected will determine the materials that are needed.

Staff

The staff consists of the Early Childhood Educator or facilitator, Rabbi, Executive Director, lay committee chairperson, and committee members.

EVENT: HERE COMES CHANUKAH

Date: Sunday before Chanukah
Time: 10:45 a.m.
Place: Family Education Center

Goals

- To provide an opportunity for multi-generations to celebrate Judaism together.
- To expose parents to a Reform perspective of the meaning and values inherent in the Chanukah story.
- To begin to establish home rituals for newly formed families.
- To empower parents to reinvent memories of positive childhood celebrations in terms of Jewish values and traditions.

Craft Stations

The following four stations will be set up. Children rotate through the stations during the first half-hour.

- Grate potatoes for *latkes*. (These will be fried by an adult away from the children.)
- Make and decorate Chanukah cards using cutouts, glitter, and old greeting cards.
- Make Chanukah decorations. Cut out three-dimensional *dreidels* and decorate them.
- Make cookies in the shape of *dreidels* and Jewish stars. Decorate with frosting and various toppings.

Large Group Time

The parents meet with the Family Educator or facilitator, while the children hear a story and have a music activity. The parents focus on the two Jewish values inherent in Chanukah: (1) freedom, and (2) a small number of people can make a difference in the world. Discuss: What rituals both reinforce these values and are comfortable and meaningful for your family?

Pass out handouts with the Chanukah blessings for the participants to take home.

While this discussion is taking place, children listen to the story of Chanukah and sing traditional Chanukah songs.

Whole Group Closing Activity

Each child brings something for a gift exchange. The Rabbi passes out a gift to each child — a bag with Chanukah *gelt,* a Chanukah pencil, a *dreidel* and a box of Chanukah candles. Children, parents, and grandparents recite the blessings, light the *chanukiah,* and share a snack of *latkes,* cookies, and juice.

Materials

Materials needed for this program: paper, glue, crayons, scissors, string, various decorations, cookies, frosting, toppings, plastic knives, plastic bags, frying pan, spatula, paper towels, juice, cups, plates, napkins, etc.

Staff

The staff consists of the Early Childhood Family Educator or facilitator; a music leader/storyteller; Rabbi, lay leadership.

EVENT: BIRTHDAY FOR THE TREES

Date: Sunday near Tu B'Shevat
Time: 9:45 a.m.
Place: Family Education Center

Goals

- To provide an opportunity for multi-generations to celebrate Judaism together.
- To introduce to parents the Jewish value of *Tikkun Olam* .
- To take Judaism outside of the synagogue walls and into the daily lives of participants.

Reference

The following references are useful for this program:

Deuteronomy 20:19: Tu B'Shevat reminds us that all of nature was made by God and belongs to God. People were created to enjoy the beauty of the world and to take care of it — all of it, including the trees, lakes, air, and animals. We are commanded not to destroy in the *mitzvah* of *Bal Tashcheet* (do not destroy). When we throw litter in litter baskets and put out campfires so they cannot cause forest fires, we are observing this *mitzvah*. When we recycle paper and glass, water plants, and weed gardens, we are also taking care of the world and protecting it against harm.

Genesis 1:28: Human beings were created with the express purpose of having dominion over the rest of the earth.

Ecclesiastes Rabbah 7:13: "The Holy One lead Adam through the Garden of Eden and said, 'I created all My beautiful and glorious works for your sake. Take heed not to corrupt and destroy My world. For if you destroy it, there is no one to make it right after you.'"

Deuteronomy 14: "You shall set aside a tenth part of the yield so that the stranger, the fatherless and the widow shall come to eat their fill, and you may learn to revere your God forever."

Nehemiah 8:10: "We may 'eat choice foods and drink sweet drinks,' but we should 'send portions to those for whom nothing is prepared.'"

Leviticus Rabbah 25:3: "From the very beginning of the creation of the world, the Holy One has been occupied with planting, so when you enter the land, you shall occupy yourself with planting."

Craft Stations

Children will rotate through the following four stations during the first half-hour:
- Plant paperwhite bulbs in stones to be taken home.
- Decorate a cake baked in the shape of a tree with frosting, M&M's, toppings, etc.
- Make a fruit salad. Each child brings one or two fruits, and participants cut up the fruit for the salad.
- Make fruit prints. Cut apples, star fruit, lemons, or any other fruit with an interesting texture or shape, and make prints using thick tempura paint.

Alternative Project

Each family brings recycled objects and creates an instrument or art object using these items.

Large Group Time

The parents will meet with the Family Educator or facilitator, while the children hear a story and have a music activity. The parents focus on the value of *Tikkun Olam* and the Jewish value of "repairing the world." Discuss: What meaningful things can each family do to help repair the world? Relate *Tikkun Olam* to the texts on Tu B'Shevat and ecology chosen by the Family Educator and handed out to parents. While this discussion is taking place, children have a song session with the music professional.

Whole Group Closing Activity

Everyone gathers to say a prayer and share the fruit salad, cake and juice.

Materials Needed

Materials needed for this program include: plastic knives and plates, napkins, cups, juice, interesting fruits, frosting and toppings, stones, bulbs, clear plastic cups for planting, paper, paint or stamp pads.

Staff

The staff for this program is made up of the Early Childhood Family Educator or facilitator, Rabbi, music leader, and lay leadership.

EVENT: PASSOVER PARTY

Date: Sunday before Passover
Time: 10:45 a.m.
Place: Family Education Center

Goals

- To provide an opportunity for multi-generations to celebrate Judaism together.
- To begin the formation of a Jewish library in the home to promote the value of Jews as "people of the book."
- To provide ideas for creating a child friendly *Seder*.
- To bring into the home the actual objects to be used at the *Seder*.
- To create ritual objects which will become the heirlooms of the future.
- To reinforce the message of our partnership with God in making the world a better and safer place.

- To come up with ways families can separate the eight days of Passover from the rest of the year in a meaningful way.

Craft Stations

Children rotate through the following four stations during the first half-hour:
- Make chocolate covered *matzah*. Children dip *matzah* in melted chocolate and let it harden on waxed paper.
- Make *charoset*. Parents supervise the chopping of apples and nuts. Add cinnamon and a little grape juice.
- Create *afikoman* covers. Fold squares of felt in half and punch holes all around. The children put yarn through the holes and glue felt cutouts onto one side. Write "Afikoman" on the back of each cover.
- Make small pillows by having children decorate a store bought pillow. Children can use these to recline on at their *Seder*.

Large Group Time

Parents meet with the Family Educator or facilitator, while the children hear a story and engage in a music activity. The parents share memories of past *Sedarim*. Discuss: What rituals do they want to pass on to their children? In the discussion, stress the value of freedom. How can we all make the world a better place? Share suggestions on creating a child friendly *Seder*.

While this discussion is taking place, a staff member reads aloud *Hooray! It's Passover* by Leslie Kimmelman (Harperfestival, 2000). The song leaders sing Passover songs with the children.

Whole Group Closing Activity

Before the program began, a piece of *"Afikoman"* is hidden for each child. When a child finds a piece, he or she receives as a prize a copy of the Kimmelman book. Parents and children have a snack of chocolate covered *matzah*, as well as *charoset*, macaroons, and juice.

Materials

Materials needed for this program include: *matzah*, melting chocolate, large bowl, microwave to melt coating chocolate, small pillows, felt, felt cutouts, yarn, fabric markers, apples, nuts, cinnamon, grape juice, chopping bowl, chopper, paper plates, etc.

Staff

The staff for this program is comprised of the Early Childhood Family Educator or facilitator, song leader, Rabbi, and lay leadership.

EVALUATION

Our evaluation process includes many stakeholders — funders, parents, children, our Women's Committee Board, and the synagogue Board of Trustees. Among the many positive benefits of receiving a grant is that it requires a program evaluation.

"Shoresh" was evaluated in several ways, all of which we think were effective. First, anecdotal records were collected. Comments made by parents, by children, and by grandparents during the program became a part of the evaluation file. These comments were made to both of us, to our Rabbi, to our lay chairperson, and to others of our lay leadership who might have been in attendance. These were the important stakeholders in our project, and all comments were valued, whether shared immediately after the program at the synagogue or later in the parking lot, a supermarket, or a local restaurant.

In addition, at each program, each adult participant is given an evaluation questionnaire (see Appendix A for sample of this). This instrument was designed with much thought, and allowed the participants to comment on the various aspects of the program. We built evaluation time into the end of the program and were certain to collect forms before participants departed. This enabled us to receive responses from approximately 90 percent of the adults. We made certain that the children

continued to be engaged, either completing a craft or having a snack, so that the adults could give some real thought to the completion of these forms.

With responses from parents in hand, we move to the next phase of our evaluation, the staff session that follows each program. There we share what we have learned. How well are we doing? Continued attendance at the programs is one positive sign. Sign-in sheets enable us to know who attends regularly and who invited friends to become a part of the group. Yet, attendance is only one indicator. Was the program successful for those who *did* come? Goals are not staff driven, but rather are reflective of goals and strategies expressed by our own congregants in the synagogue's Strategic Plan.

As a final step, evaluation does go back to those goals. Do our instruments measure success based on those stated goals, or are they totally unrelated? If a child described a wonderful time because it was fun to eat the M&M's with which he or she decorated the birthday cake at Tu B'Shevat, that, too, may meet a goal. Some might consider the M&M's to be irrelevant to the Jewish informational component. However, one of our stated goals is that the child and parents consider the synagogue a "family place to be." Who knows, the M&M's may encourage the preschooler to come back to the synagogue regularly!

Evaluation is a complex process essential to the continuing success of any program. Positive responses encourage teachers and planners to continue, and helpful suggestions drive the tinkering and changes that need to take place. Negative comments can mean the end of a program that is not working and/or not meeting its goals. Our funder was certainly pleased with what he saw and continued to underwrite the program. But to assure him that his own "gut feeling" is correct, we will watch for the continued involvement of these families as their children enter Religious School. That, perhaps, will be the strongest evaluation of all.

COMMENTARY

By Rabbi Michael Oppenheimer

The "Shoresh" program provides me as a Rabbi with the unique opportunity to interact with families from marriage on. I officiated at the wedding of most of the parents participating in the program, and have tried to maintain a strong relationship with these parents as they move into the early years of child rearing. My direct participation in a program involving children and parents together strengthens Rabbinic-parental-family bonding. I thereby become more naturally accessible to families as they find allies and friends in the congregation, explore new options of Jewishness, and seek advice in problem solving. I am able to play a critical role both in the deepening of Jewish values for them as adults and in their process of translating those values into their children's lives. As well as sharing in their life cycle events as their Rabbi, I can help these families connect to other worthwhile Jewish activities offered by the congregation.

Because of my ongoing presence in their lives, their continued affiliation with the synagogue after the wedding is nurtured and supported. They have come to see the Rabbi and the synagogue as important for the health and well-being of their family.

Because I have expertise in curriculum design and developmentally appropriate Religious School practices, I also serve as Educational Director of the synagogue school. As such, I join with my Principal and Family Educator in overseeing the flow of our education programs (family and general) in Grades K-3, and also in "Shoresh." One of my tasks is to make sure that any repetition has new, developmentally challenging elements built into it (after all, how often should one make a "paper plate and lima bean *gragger*"?). Because "Shoresh" is open to preschool children of all ages, many families participate in the program over a several year period. Thus, while the basic curriculum remains somewhat constant, we build into the program a variety of activities, crafts, and stories which change from year to year.

Perhaps most critically, since I am ultimately the *Moreh d'atra*, the spiritual guide of the congregation, it is my job to clarify synagogue policy for everyone interacting in the "Shoresh" program. The Board of Trustees and I created guidelines regarding personal status and the participation of a non-Jew in synagogue activities. Prior to beginning this preschool programming, these policies are communicated to everyone involved so as to mitigate against hurtful or unfortunate experiences. Questions most likely to arise concern the Jewishness of the child, what non-Jewish parents may and may not do regarding rituals, and synagogue policy concerning intermarriage.

The editors have also asked me to share a thought about the Rabbinic role in Jewish Family Education. A Rabbi's involvement in the congregation's educational program is more or less a matter of choice. I personally believe that such involvement is vital. Most Rabbis are actively involved in teaching adults or high school students and adolescents. While this is important and reflects an authentic Rabbinic role, it represents only one small portion of what the Rabbi can give to individuals and families across generations.

The genius of Jewish Family Education is its embrace of multigenerational education, and such education necessitates a variety of techniques both cognitive and experiential. When it is the Rabbi who uses these creative methods, there is an especially significant impact on members. The Rabbi can lend perspective on the relevance of Judaism for the modern Jew. From insights into Tanach to an understanding of family dynamics, from questions of theology to concerns about death, from a deeper sense of rootedness to an expanded understanding of *mitzvot* and *Tikkun Olam* — all this and more the Rabbi can share with members of all ages.

When the Rabbi is involved in the many dimensions of the congregation's educational program, the relationship between Rabbi and members is both broadened and deepened. Children especially come to view the Rabbi not just as an authority figure and a source of values and ideas, but also as a person with whom contact is enjoyable and meaningful, someone accessible, someone real, someone who is a part of their lives.

Finally, a Rabbinic presence in Jewish Family Education is important not only for the parents and children, but also for the congregation's entire educational team — the Director of Education, the teachers, and all those involved in Family Education. Our presence is essential as leaders and role models in all levels of our educational and family programming.

APPENDIX A
EVALUATION: MAKE IT AND TAKE IT SHABBAT

We are interested in your opinion on this morning's program. Please take a few minutes to respond. Thank you very much.

What ages are your children? _____ _____ _____ _____ _____ _____

How did you hear about this program?

Were the activities well organized? Did your child actively participate?

What understandings have you gained about Shabbat that you wish to transmit to your children?

Are you interested in using, at home, any of the Shabbat ritual objects which your child created?

What did you take away from the parent discussion?

Do you have any suggestions for other types of early childhood programs?

Please feel free to add your comments on the program.

FAMILY TORAH STUDY

CONTRIBUTOR: JUDITH S. SCHILLER
ADDRESS: Retreat Institute of the Jewish
Education Center of Cleveland
26001 South Woodland Road
Beachwood, OH 44122
PHONE: (216) 831-0700
E-MAIL: torahmom@aol.com
jschillerri@aol.com

"And the study of Torah is equal to them all [the *mitzvot*]." (*Shabbat* 127a)

Inviting families to study Torah together creates rich opportunities for learning and growth. After all, Torah is our primary source, our central text; it has the potential to engage learners of all ages on a variety of levels. Torah informs us in a myriad of ways about things past and present. Once we dive in, we discover its relevance to our lives. Once the text is familiar to us, it can become part of our normal, everyday conversation.

But what if the text is unfamiliar and intimidating? How do we encourage families of varying levels of experience with Torah, from the uninitiated to the serious student, to engage in Torah study? How do we encourage dialogue between parents and children about a text that some may feel is remote and inaccessible? How do we incorporate Torah into our programs so that it feels lively and active?

While teaching families to study Torah together can be challenging, educators have addressed these challenges with creativity and insight. In this section, we present approaches and perspectives from five educators who have been successful in bringing parents, children, and Torah together in meaningful ways. Each program has its own particular structure and ideas that can be adapted for different audiences and settings. By putting in place essential scaffolding and cultivating a welcoming environment, each demonstrates how to make Torah study accessible to families.

In all of the programs included in this section, Torah is studied and explored as a living, guiding text containing important values that relate to current issues. All of these programs aim at making connections between the struggles we face today and how the Torah speaks to these issues. Torah serves as an anchoring text for families, and with different supports and approaches, it becomes the basis for discussing and understanding Jewish ethics and values. Implicit in these programs is a fundamental assumption that by engaging parents and their children in Torah study together, we create meaningful learning experiences that impact a family on a deep level. The more a family is immersed in the study, the more the Torah text becomes a natural and integrated part of family conversations.

An important aspect reflected in these programs is the empowering of parents to be teachers of their children and role models of Jewish learning. As Sharon Halper states, "children see parents in active Jewish learning." Rabbi Joy Levitt adds, "It is more important for children to see their parents doing Jewish things than for parents to see their children do Jewish things." A key part of the empowerment process is often adult education and coaching parents in their role as Jewish educators. Family

Educators who are considering any kind of family Torah study program need to concentrate on the parents' educational needs both as adult learners and as parent/teachers of their children.

In this section, we have two distinct programmatic venues. *"Torah B'Yachad"* and the "Family D'var Torah Project" are done primarily in the home. "Sharing Shabbat," *"Mi'Dor L'Dor,"* and *"Yom Iyun L'Mishpachah"* focus on developing a learning community of families. The community-oriented programs encompass learning opportunities, such as worship services and celebrations in addition to the Torah study. This broader scope may provide more "built in" support for families, whereas the home-based programs often require one-on-one mentoring from the Family Educator. The Family Educator may need to establish ways to communicate with families via phone, e-mail, or occasional meetings. This communication can create a network of families. It is essential to maintain a system to keep families involved in their Torah study efforts.

All these programs contain their own unique challenges encompassing logistics, appropriate program content, facilitation, initial and ongoing communication, program structure, and balance of parallel and interactive learning. Several educators note that chief among these challenges is implementing parent-child interactive pieces, especially when it involves whole families with children of different ages, as well as families at varying levels of experience with Torah study.

The ideas and program concepts presented here can be adapted and combined in any number of ways. Perhaps "Sharing Shabbat" could potentially evolve to include a "Family D'var Torah Project." In addition, there is much potential for community building. Sally Weber suggests incorporating a Shabbat lunch with "Sharing Shabbat," or pairing families once a month for potluck Shabbat lunch at each other's homes or at a park. For *"Torah B'Yachad,"* families could help coach and train other families and/or possibly form *chevrutas* of mentor families with families embarking on Torah study.

All these programs could be enriched and maintained with ongoing weekly or monthly com-munication (e.g., study guides for the *parashah,* bulletin articles with contributions from families, bulletin boards in the synagogue and school high-lighting families studying Torah, and messages on the Internet). And, to add a little extra fun into the mix, a synagogue could have "Torah study contests" on a monthly basis during which families respond to questions relating to recent *parshiyot.* Questions on all different levels could be developed, including a "family *midrash* question." These questions could be included in a synagogue bulletin, school-home communication, or posted on a bulletin board with a pocket for "Questions about the *parashah.*" Perhaps families could contribute their own questions regarding their study for "responsa" from other families.

Chapter 33, *"Torah B'Yachad,"* describes a three-session workshop with coaching, designed to provide skills and resources to families for their own home study. This program was originated by Dr. Jeffrey Schein and adapted by me. It has been implemented in many congregations over the last ten years.

Chapter 34, "Yom Iyun L'Mishpachah: Family Torah Study Day," is a grade level parent-child program for students in Grades 3 to 6. Each grade level invites parents once during the school year to study Torah in parallel and together sessions. This program was developed by Education Director Susan Wyner and her staff.

Chapter 35, "Sharing Shabbat," is a family and school program which offers a weekly ritual of worship and *parashah* study. Education Director Sharon Halper developed this program as an alternative to the regular Religious School program.

Chapter 36, "Mi'dor L'Dor: Family Torah Study in Havurot" by Tricia Berke Vinson, describes an ongoing, bimonthly Shabbat afternoon program for families with children in Grades K to 4. This program incorporates text study, children's literature, drama, games, and art projects as ways to explore Torah and bring its message to the participants.

In Chapter 37, Joy Levitt describes the "Family D'var Torah Project," which she developed when she served as a congregational Rabbi at the Recon-structionist Synagogue in Manhasset, N.Y. This project presents a divergent approach, focusing on

Family Torah study within the context of B'nai Mitzvah. The Bar/Bat Mitzvah experience provides a unique opportunity for a family to become engaged in the child's Torah portion, and to develop a creative presentation of their family *D'var Torah*.

CHAPTER 33

TORAH B'YACHAD

CONTRIBUTOR: JUDITH S. SCHILLER
ADDRESS: Retreat Institute of the Jewish
Education Center of Cleveland
26001 South Woodland Road
Beachwood, OH 44122
PHONE: (216) 831-0700, ext. 372
E-MAIL: torahmom@aol.com
jschillerri@aol.com
TARGET: Families with children in Grades
1 to 6
TIME FRAME: 4-6 consecutive weeks in which
three 1½ to 2 hour workshops are
scheduled. Sunday mornings are a
typical time to schedule

OVERALL PURPOSES OF THE PROGRAM

"Torah B'Yachad" is a three-session workshop developed by Rabbi Jeffrey Schein and adapted by Judith S. Schiller. Its purpose is to provide parents with a foundation of knowledge, resources, and approaches to studying Torah together as a family at home. The rationale behind the program is that Jewish home life can be enriched by exploring the values, issues, and teachings of Torah. This program, which, in addition to the workshops, often includes informal coaching, enables families to engage in discussion about the weekly Torah portion or other Torah texts in ways that will engage children of different ages. Torah study is defined broadly and creatively, and is approached with a sense of exploration, openess, questioning, and discovery.

PROGRAM DESCRIPTION

When scheduling the three sessions, it is helpful to look at a Jewish calendar with the weekly Torah portions noted. It is recommended that this workshop series be introduced at a time of year when the *parshiyot* are accessible and user friendly (i.e., Leviticus may not be the easiest place to start). The three sessions should be spaced so that there is a week or two in between to allow time for families to do Torah study at home. The workshop sessions are designed to help parents prepare for this task. The three-part series is structured as follows.

Session 1 (Parents Only):

This parents only session focuses on the "why" and "how" of family Torah study. Parents imagine the possibilities of Torah study for their family, discuss the potential obstacles to engaging in Torah study, discover methods, approaches, and resources and prepare a study of the following week's *parashah*. This session includes the viewing of a videotape of a family studying Torah together. Excerpts from *Torah with Love: A Guide for Strengthening Jewish Values within the Family* by David Epstein and Suzanne Singer Stutman (Prentice-Hall, 1986) often serve as springboards to discussion. Chapter 1 of *Torah with Love* is helpful in launching discussion about the rationale behind family Torah study as a way to transmit and communicate values. Chapter 2 offers insights into the process of Torah study, managing family dynamics, and outlines some general approaches to study. Parents receive a packet filled with ideas, resources, and a bibliography. This information helps families get started in studying at home.

Key to the program's success is a set induction that allows a warm-up time for the group. To get started, the facilitator should give a brief introduction to the evening's agenda, and introduce himself/herself in order to model how the participants will do it — name, number and ages of children, experience with Torah study, and why he/she is taking this workshop. If the group feels sufficiently "safe," the participants can share their feelings and experiences regarding Torah study. This can be done in a playful way with metaphors, such as, "studying Torah as a family is like a (type of animal) because _____."

Session 2 (Parents and Children Together):

In this session, the Family Educator or program facilitator leads families in study using a variety of teaching/learning strategies. This session is an opportunity to model different approaches, such as questions for different ages, creative expression though arts and drama, debates, and games. Questions should be formulated for different levels. (See page 65, "The Ten Universal Questions," in *Torah with Love*. Also see Appendix B of Chapter 34.) Skits from *Sedra Scenes* by Stan J. Beiner or *Parashah Plays* by Richard J. Allen (A.R.E. Publishing, Inc., 1982 and 2000 respectively), charades, and story theater are some of the many ways to engage the younger participants. The latter part of the session involves feedback on the process and a discussion on preparing for the next *parashah*. It is helpful for the Family Educator to provide families with specific ideas and to recap ideas from group discussion. The Family Educator should be available for coaching families during the following weeks. A "walk-through" the packet will help parents identify readily available and accessible resources.

Session 3 (Parents Only):

This session is designed for evaluation of the workshops and feedback on the progress of the families in their efforts at home. Parents have an opportunity to share their successes and frustrations with the process and offer ideas to each other. The Family Educator can distribute evaluation forms to get written feedback. This meeting serves as a planning session for the next steps to be taken. Some groups often initiate their own regular Torah study group as part of their process of preparing to study with their families. Other parents may plan to work informally in *chevruta* (study pairs). Some families may join together for Torah study. Often, parents have suggestions for programming through the Religious School or synagogue that incorporates Torah study.

PREPARATIONS

If this program is being implemented in a Religious School setting, it is important to schedule it on the school calendar in advance of the school year, taking into consideration the other programs and events that go on in the school and synagogue. The workshops should be scheduled within a four to six week time frame. (In other words, it is not recommended that the first workshop be given in October and the second one in February.) If the program is taking place in a Religious School setting during school hours, the second workshop may require coordinating the logistics of having students join their parents. This may entail students leaving their classrooms for part of a Religious School morning. The Director of Education will need to communicate this to any teachers involved.

MARKETING AND RECRUITMENT

The program should be publicized in every possible communication vehicle in the school and synagogue for six or eight weeks prior to the first workshop. Recommended ways to advertise include: the school and synagogue bulletin, Shabbat program notes, and flyers sent home and posted at the synagogue or Day School. A registration form should be part of any flyer. It is helpful to get registrations in advance so as to be able to anticipate the age ranges of children and the needs of the parents.

In addition to written communications, personal contact and invitations are recommended for targeted families. Typically, educators and Rabbis are familiar with families who are likely to be interested in such workshops. Or, this program may be a strong complement to a specific grade level or Family Education curriculum. It is helpful to brainstorm a list of potential participants for more targeted recruitment efforts.

NUTS AND BOLTS

Room Set-up

The workshop sessions require a space that accommodates the size of the group. Typically, a classroom, youth group lounge, or library room will provide a workable setting. It is important to have a chalkboard or some other type of marking board on which to make notes and to aid in processing the discussions. The space should be set up so that parents are in a circle or around a table. A selection of books and resources should be available on a table for parents to browse. Suggested materials include different *Chumashim* and commentaries. *A Torah Commentary for Our Times* by Harvey Fields (UAHC Press, 1990) is a popular resource. Resources to help parents in their role as "teacher" are also useful. (See Appendix B of Chapter 34, *"Yom Iyun L'Mishpachah."*)

Hand-out Materials

Each participant receives a packet containing an agenda of the three sessions (see Appendix A), a bibliography, suggestions for getting started, a sample of different resources, e.g., *Teaching Torah: A Treasury of Insights and Activities* by Loeb and Kadden (A.R.E. Publishing, Inc., 1998), *Sedra Scenes* by Beiner, excerpts from *Torah with Love* by Epstein and Stutman, and a list of ideas (see Appendix B of Chapter 34, *"Yom Iyun L'Mishpachah"*).

FAMILY EDUCATOR'S REFLECTIONS AND EVALUATION

I have always found this to be a rewarding program because typically it attracts a motivated and interesting group of parents who are open to the possibility of enriching their Jewish home lives with Torah study. The role of the facilitator in this program is to ask good questions that invite responses, and then to listen and process the discussion.

Opportunities for parents to study need to be explored. Some additional synagogue-based programming may be helpful in getting families comfortable with Torah study. In one setting in which we did the three-session family Torah study program, the parents themselves formed their own support group. They decided to meet weekly on Shabbat morning while their children attended Religious School to engage in their own adult study, and then share ideas for preparing the family study session of the upcoming *parashah*. Brainstorming led to new approaches that were adapted to the style of the participating families. Although they met on Shabbat, they actually studied the next week's *parashah*, in order to prepare for Friday evening Torah study at home with their family.

The follow-up is the most challenging aspect of this program. Once the three sessions are done, the tendency is to feel finished with the program. In reality, this is a new point of departure for the families, a time when they will work on applying what they learned in the workshop sessions. The Family Educator needs to anticipate the needs for support and coaching of families after the workshop is completed. One way the Family Educator might do this is by making tangible his/her willingness to support them in this growth process. For example, he/she might give the family two Torah study coupons, one for a telephone consult as they prepare their study, and the second for a Torah study session the Family Educator might lead with this family and another family of their choice. In addition, the Family Educator should develop some home study guides for several upcoming *parshiyot*.

"Readiness" is a key factor in family Torah study. Parents who attended this program often came from a variety of backgrounds and familiarity with any type of Torah study. As educators and researchers, we wonder how "readiness" plays into the equation of successful family Torah study, and what we need to do to bring a family to a point of readiness. Our experience is that "readiness" moves along different planes. This is why honing in on the coaching and teaching needs of the individual families is so essential. We find the understanding of JFE helpful in getting a handle on the types of needs and issues that arise. For example, some families are very ready for the kind of discussions depicted in *Torah with Love.* They may be or have participated in book clubs or the Great Books programs. They may be educationally sophisticated and ready to facilitate discussions and yet, at the same time, feel intimidated by a page of Torah. For these families, their greatest area of need and support comes in regard to the *Jewish* aspect of JFE. Another family may be well grounded Jewishly, but hasn't yet learned how to carry on the best kind of educational conversations. They need a different kind of support that provides educational techniques and approaches. Last, but not least, we have families that have a fairly good grounding in both the Jewish and education aspects, but struggle with how to manage

family time, and how to gather everyone together on a regular basis. These patterns of individual families are also true for the group as a whole. Each group of families participating in the family Torah study process may need varying amounts of Jewish or family or educational support.

It has been our experience that families grow into this process slowly. For instance, one particular family first heard of this process as part of a parenting course they were taking. They watched the videotape of a family doing Torah study, with a sense of wonder and anxiety ("I could never pull this off!"). Two years later, the same family had become involved in a Havurah. Their home-schooled children had begun doing Jewish things. One of the parents had begun participating in the Havurah's monthly Torah study programs. As they view the same tape two years later, they seem less intimidated. They actually articulate, "I can imagine us doing Torah study now." Readiness had ripened.

COMMENTARY

- Try connecting families so they can experience Torah study as a family in a small group before doing it on their own. (SW)
- Consider finding "mentor" families from the congregation that have already engaged in significant family Torah study. (SW)
- Invite an individual or couple knowledgeable in Torah and empty nesters to guide new families in the process. (EC)
- Consider forming a Torah study Havurah after the families have completed their sessions together. (EC)

- Be aware of the need/desire of adults for ongoing Torah learning as a result of their experiences within the family. (EC)
- Mail or e-mail resources for weekly Torah study to the family. (EC)
- Give a copy of *Teaching Torah: A Treasury of Insights and Activities* by Sorel Goldberg Loeb and Barbara Binder Kadden (A.R.E. Publishing, Inc., 1997) to each family that completes the course to support them as they continue the process. (EC)

APPENDIX A
TORAH B'YACHAD
SAMPLE PROGRAM AGENDA

Sunday, January 29: Parents' Meeting
- Imagine the possibilities of Torah study for your family.
- Examine the ways of making Torah study part of your family, and discover methods and resources.
- Prepare for Torah study for the following week's *parashah, Terumah,* Exodus 25:1-27:19.

Sunday, February 12: Parents and Students Together
- Study together, as a group of families, the *parashah Ki Tisa,* Exodus 30:11-34:35.

- Share your insights and experiences.
- As a family plan to study next week's *parashah, Vayakhel,* Exodus 35:1-38:20.

Sunday, February 26: Parents' Meeting
- Evaluate how family Torah study can work best for your family.
- Provide feedback on how the program facilitators can help you further.

APPENDIX B
GETTING STARTED — SOME IDEAS TO CONSIDER

DIGGING INTO TORAH AS A FAMILY
By Judith Schiller and Susan Wyner

Helpful ideas as you begin:

• Establishing Torah study as a family is a process that takes time. There is no need to rush; go one step at a time.

• The more your family studies together and the more opportunities for positive communication, the more your family will grow to expect it and welcome it.

• Find a regular time to gather for Torah study. Often, Friday night dinner is a good time, but the time you pick depends on your family's schedule.

• You don't need to devote a tremendous amount of time to study. Fifteen to 20 minutes can be great for your family (especially with younger children), or there may be times when a discussion goes into the night.

• Older children may want to get involved in the preparation of studying the *parashah*. This can be a great opportunity to give them a special role.

• Questions that arise from the discussion may resonate with the other Torah portions, as well as current events in your home and in the news. You may want to keep a notebook of questions and issues discussed.

• Unanswered questions can become opportunities for some digging. There are resources within reach, starting with your synagogue. The Rabbis and Education Director can suggest sources in the library and offer their thoughts as well.

CHAPTER 34

YOM IYUN L'MISHPACHAH: FAMILY TORAH STUDY DAY

<table>
<tr><td>CONTRIBUTOR: SUSAN WYNER
ADDRESS: B'nai Jeshurun Congregation
27501 Fairmount Boulevard
Pepper Pike, OH 44124
PHONE: (216) 831-6555
E-MAIL: <u>swyner@ameritech.net</u>
TARGET: Families with students in Grades 3 to 6
TIME FRAME: Shabbat mornings, 9:00 a.m. to Noon</td></tr>
</table>

OVERALL PURPOSES OF THE PROGRAM

"Yom Iyun L'Mishpachah" evolved out of a pilot program of *"Torah B'Yachad"* (see Chapter 33). Over several years, B'nai Jeshurun Congregation has had interns training with *"Torah B'Yachad"* from the Cleveland Fellows Program (a graduate program in Jewish Education). These interns have helped to introduce and develop this program. Jeffrey Schein, an advisor to the Cleveland Fellows, and professor at the Cleveland College of Jewish Studies, was a key resource in helping to launch this program.

"Yom Iyun L'Mishpachah" is a dynamic program. Its purpose is:

- To provide an opportunity for parents to consider the benefits of Torah study as a family activity.
- To model techniques for examining Torah in a modern way using entertaining, intergenerational activities.
- To provide families with the opportunity for age appropriate Torah study through parallel learning.

- To bring families into the school as partners in their children's Jewish education.

PROGRAM DESCRIPTION

Two months prior to a *"Yom Iyun L'Mishpachah,"* teachers meet with the Education Director to study the *Parashat HaShavua* for the selected date. We examine the main themes, the language, and frequently used words in order to select the passages and ideas that we want to emphasize and study with our families. We draw ideas and background for this study from the *Chumash, Midrash,* and commentaries. A list of some of the supporting resources that we have found to be helpful are included in the bibliography for this chapter. As a team, we select strategies for teaching the *parashah.* We also choose an engaging family activity that reflects the themes and key words that the families will study. In our *Shomer Shabbat* setting, the selection and variety of family activities is challenging, and requires creative teamwork. The following are some of our favorite family activities:

- *Parashah Bechukotai* describes the blessings that the Children of Israel can expect if they follow God's commandments, and the curses to expect should they disobey. We constructed a board game entitled *Showdown at Bechukotai Pass.* By the throw of the dice, families move their pawns around a game board, landing on "blessings spaces," "curses spaces," and "*Bechukotai* spaces." They would then choose the appropriate card and either answer the questions related to the *parashah,* to traditions, and to Jewish values, or follow the directions to determine their next move. Values questions require a family discussion. The game is fast paced and fun. Each family takes home a game board and a set of cards.

- "The Oprah Show!": Using *Sedra Scenes* by Stan J. Beiner for a creative review of the *parashah*, family volunteers (adults and students) act out the scene. Then members of the "audience" ask the "characters" questions in a mock interview. The Education Director takes on an Oprah Winfrey-style role to facilitate the questions and answers. To keep the questioning lively, a few 3" x 5" cards with pre-written questions are passed out to students and parents. This guarantees that some of the key concepts are covered. The participants catch on quickly!
- Creation of age appropriate scenarios to facilitate family discussion of Torah values with the backdrop of modern situations.
- Torah Treasure Hunt: Using sticker signal dots and copies of the *parashah*, families are assigned repeating root words or statements to find. The search leads to a discussion of the concepts or values inherent in the roots and words found.

SET-UP, SCHEDULE, AND MATERIALS REQUIRED

About one month before the *"Yom Iyun L'Mishpachah,"* a letter of invitation is sent to parents. The letter describes the goals of the program, schedule of the morning, and includes a summary of the *parashah*, along with a list of themes to be studied (see Appendix A). A follow-up flyer is sent home through the school, and two weeks before the event, phone calls are made to any parents who have not responded. The school staff does everything in its power to try to assure that each student has a family member present.

The schedule for the morning is as follows:

9:00 a.m.-10:15 a.m. – Parallel Torah Study:

Students report to their classes to study the *parashah* with their teachers. Parents report to a room in which adult-sized tables and chairs are arranged in a large "U." There they study the *parashah* with the Education Director. They also review some of the reasons for modern Torah study. At the end of the session, each family receives a folder that includes handouts regarding Torah study, e.g., "Ten Universal Questions," adapted by Susan Wyner from *Torah with Love* by David Epstein and Suzanne Singer Stutman (see Appendix B), and a list of resources that are available from our synagogue library. A library cart is on hand so parents can examine some of these resources.

10:15 a.m.-11:45 a.m. – Family Activity:

Parents and students come together in a room big enough to create three large circles of chairs. Parents sit with their students to participate in the family activity, which is facilitated by teachers or the Education Director.

11:50 a.m.-noon – Family Worship Service:

The family service is led by the students in the class that is celebrating their *"Yom Iyun L'Mishpachah."* The students don't do any special preparation for this, as it is part of the morning's regular Shabbat service.

EVALUATION

Following the family activity, families complete a scaled evaluation using sticker signal dots, answering evaluative questions along a scale from 1 to 5 (see Appendix C). They evaluate the study sessions, family activities, and skill of the facilitators. The families have commented that our family programs are of high quality and well planned. Parent evaluation is limited because there is no writing on Shabbat, and individual opinions can only be offered orally. However, there are times when we receive phone calls from parents during the week following a *"Yom Iyun,"* during which they share their appreciation.

The staff of the Shabbat program of B'nai Jeshurun considers *"Yom Iyun L'Mishpachah"* to be the essence of quality Family Education programming. The parallel study allows us to reach parents and students at their own levels, providing them with the opportunity to discuss the *parashah* among their peers before sharing their ideas with each other. The family dialogues based on actual text are rich and relevant to their modern day lives. And best of all, parents who participate are empowered to guide the study with their children. The program promises that: "No prior experience with Torah study is needed." The study and support materials that parents take into their family session live up to that endorsement. From the perspective of the facilitators, the best part of this program is the look of pride and pleasure on the faces of the parents as they enjoy the "wisdom" of their children. Several parents have requested more opportunities for adult Torah study, and have purchased some of the support resources for themselves in order to gain more insight into the themes and values that Torah teaches us.

For the program planners, the biggest challenge is to reinvent the *"Yom Iyun"* experiences as the *parshiyot* are switched and changed from year to year. We want parents with more than one child in the school to attend engaging new programming each time they come to a *"Yom Iyun."* It has been challenging as well to provide the training and scaffolding for classroom teachers to become intergenerational facilitators in guiding the family activities. Based on the increasingly strengthened ratings that parents are giving our teachers as facilitators, these skills have become stronger each year. It is recommended that classroom teachers have some training and coaching as they learn these new skills.

Originally, we were concerned because approximately one-third of the parents arrive in time for the parallel study session, while the rest of the parents arrive in time for the family activity. We have come to realize that part of the beauty of the program is that parents can participate according to their own levels of comfort. Some parents are not yet prepared to study Torah with other adults. When we first began the program, it was fathers who felt most comfortable participating in the adult Torah study. We have watched this population change character, with more parents studying with

us on a regular basis, and a mixed father/mother attendance — even couples!

CONCLUSION

This is a program that can be replicated and adapted easily by other schools. Schools that meet on Sundays could enhance the programs with craft projects, using a variety of media. The possibilities for the program are limited only by the creativity of the planners. Most important, it's educational and entertaining in equal portions!

BIBLIOGRAPHY

Note: Each participant receives a copy of the *parashah* to be studied to facilitate their understanding and their participation in their parallel sessions. Teachers receive a resource packet created by the Education Director to assist their facilitation. The sources listed below are frequently added to these packets.

Beiner, Stan J. *Sedra Scenes*. Denver, CO: A.R.E. Publishing, Inc., 1982.

Epstein, David, and Suzanne Singer Stutman. *Torah with Love: A Guide for Strengthening Jewish Values within the Family*. New York: Prentice Hall Press, 1986.

Field, Harvey J. *A Torah Commentary for Our Times*. 3 vols. New York: UAHC Press, 1998.

Grishaver, Joel Lurie. *Torah Toons I*. Los Angeles: Torah Aura Productions, 1981.

———. *Torah Toons II*. Los Angeles: Torah Aura Productions, 1984.

Leibowitz, Nahama. *Studies in Bereshit*. Jerusalem, Israel: World Zionist Organization, 1980.

———. *Studies in Shemot*. Jerusalem, Israel: World Zionist Organization, 1980.

———. *Studies in Vayikra*. Jerusalem, Israel: World Zionist Organization, 1980.

———. *Studies in Bamidbar*. Jerusalem, Israel: World Zionist Organization, 1980.

———. *Studies in Devarim*. Jerusalem, Israel: World Zionist Organization, 1980.

Loeb, Sorel Goldberg, and Barbara Binder Kadden. *Teaching Torah: A Treasury of Insights and Activities.* Denver: A.R.E. Publishing, Inc., 1997.

Note: See also the Jewish Publication Society Torah Commentaries, available for *Beraysheet* through *Devarim.*

COMMENTARY

- Susan Wyner tells us that it took a long time for her to accept that not all parents would come to the adult learning beginning of the program. With that acceptance, however, she relates a great deal of personal and professional joy in seeing perhaps a third of the parents "choose" to come early for Torah study. (EC)

- See Chapters 38 and 39 on interactive homework as a way of enhancing the preparation for this program. (EC)
- Think about finding a group of dramatically inclined children and parents who might become the "Parashah Players," presenting a *Sedra Scenes*-type skit to begin each class's special *Yom Iyun.* (EC)

APPENDIX A
SAMPLE INVITATION LETTER TO PARENTS

Date

Dear Gimel Parents,

You are cordially invited to participate in an exciting family education program! *"Yom Iyun L'Mishpachah"* (Family Study Day) brings parents and their students together for Torah Study and prayer for a meaningful and enlightening family experience.

The Gimel class *"Yom Iyun"* will take place on Shabbat, December 10th. Please plan on joining your student for as much of the morning as possible. The following schedule will illustrate the variety of programming:

Shabbat morning, December 10th:

9:00   Students arrival. Parents are invited to the pre-program in Classroom 14. This program provides an overview of the concept of Family Torah Study, and a close look at the *parashah* of the week. Orange juice and *kuchen* will be provided.

10:15   Parents and students come together in Halpern Hall for a combined Torah study session.

10:50   Parents and students participate in the morning Shacharit service led by our Gimel students, and followed by a festive *Kiddush*.

We will be looking at *Parashah Vayigash* (Genesis 44:18-47:27). Our themes include the concept of forgiveness, the relationship between siblings, and the value of *Sh'lom Bayit* — peace within the family. A synopsis of the *parashah* is enclosed to give you insight into the depth of this portion. You are invited to bring your own Bible or use one of ours. Parents need not have prior experience in the study of Torah to get full enjoyment from this session. Your joy will come from sharing this morning with your child.

We look forward to seeing you at *"Yom Iyun L'Mishpachah"* on Shabbat, December 10th. Please indicate your attendance to our School Office.

Sincerely,

Susan Wyner
Education Director

APPENDIX B
SOME IDEAS FOR FAMILY TORAH STUDY

THE TEN UNIVERSAL QUESTIONS
(Based on the "The Ten Universal Questions" in *Torah with Love*, p. 65) adapted by Susan Wyner.

The ten universal questions that follow, focus on facts, action, and characters. They are the universal way of defining a topic, organizing thinking, starting or continuing a conversation, and stimulating imagination. A universal question is relevant in any discussion of the Torah, but it is not the only way to conduct a Torah Discussion.

- Who is in the predicament? This would include any person whose actions or mere existence influences the outcome of the predicament, as well as any person who is affected by the outcome.
- What is the predicament? What is the tug-of-war between personalities? What happened immediately before to lead to the predicament? What can we expect to happen as a result of the episode?
- What is the relationship between the people? Who are the parents? grandparents? children? siblings? spouses? What kind of interactions do they have? How do they interact with God? How do these people feel about each other?
- How is God involved? Does God communicate directly with anyone? Is God involved through intervention in the people's lives? Is God making demands on anyone? Do people react to God's actions? Why does God punish? Why does God reward?

- How is the predicament resolved? What actions lead to the conclusion? Is it resolved through the action of one of the characters or by God?
- How is the community involved? How does it affect the predicament? What are the cultural habits? Who are the leaders? How did things get done?
- Does the predicament illuminate our contemporary life? What can we learn from this passage? Have you ever had any similar feelings or experiences? Are you surprised by the resolution of the predicament?
- What ethical and moral principles are posed by how the predicament occurs or is resolved? Does the action harm or benefit someone? Is this good or bad? Does anyone else have to become involved to come to some resolution? Why did he/she decide to get involved?
- Does individual "free will" permit any other course of conduct? "Free will" means that an individual can make choices in how to act. Did the person choose to act? Why or why not? How does God feel about the outcome?
- How can you retell the story in your own words? If you could change anything in the story, what would you change? Why?

A dramatic reenactment is a good way to retell a story. Don't forget to have fun!

APPENDIX C
SAMPLE EVALUATION FORM
YOM IYUN L'MISHPACHAH

PROGRAM EVALUATION

Completed with parents _____
Completed by a student _____

Please place a sticker dot in the place that best answers the question. Your response will assist us in planning future Family Educational programming.

Expectations

The publicity and material which we sent to you accurately described this morning's program.

strongly agree	agree	disagree	strongly disagree
1_____	2_____	3_____	4_____

The program met our expectations.

strongly agree	agree	disagree	strongly disagree
1_____	2_____	3_____	4_____

This program was scheduled at a convenient time for our family.

strongly agree	agree	disagree	strongly disagree
1_____	2_____	3_____	4_____

Adult Torah Study (9:00-10:15)

I/We enjoyed the Adult Torah Study session.

strongly agree	agree	disagree	strongly disagree
1_____	2_____	3_____	4_____

The facilitator appeared to be well prepared.

strongly agree	agree	disagree	strongly disagree
1_____	2_____	3_____	4_____

Did you have adequate time to study the portion?   yes___ no___ unsure___

Did you learn any new skills at this session?   yes___ no___ unsure___

Would you like to see more opportunities for Adult Torah Study?   yes___ no___ unsure___

CHAPTER 35

SHARING SHABBAT

CONTRIBUTOR: SHARON HALPER
ADDRESS: Westchester Reform Temple
255 Mamaroneck Road
Scarsdale, NY 10583
PHONE: (914) 723-5224
E-MAIL: sharondin@aol.com (home)
TARGET: Families with students in Grades
K to 3
TIME FRAME: 2¼ hours weekly during the
school year

OVERALL PURPOSE

The aim of "Sharing Shabbat" is to help families to become more adept at studying Torah, and in worship, to feel a sense of community, and to come to appreciate what the synagogue can provide.

DESCRIPTION OF THE PROGRAM

"Sharing Shabbat" offers a family-centered worship option that is appropriate for young children. The service is music-based. It invites participation by families in ritual and conversation, and includes a story. Shabbat worship now occurs weekly, not merely when a scheduled "family service" or other special event seems appropriate for the age group. "Sharing Shabbat" has resulted in a group of families with Shabbat rituals who routinely act on their Jewish identity in a public forum.

This program has created a spiritual community, one in which family *simchahs* are shared with *Kiddush*, and family concerns are shared publicly during the

"*Mi Shebayrach.*" Families have continued this sense of community through potluck lunches after the service.

On a cognitive level, "Sharing Shabbat" has given participants a thorough knowledge of the Shabbat morning liturgy, including varied expressions of a particular prayer. Students of widely varied ages, from preschool siblings to third graders, now lead a visual depiction of the "*V'ahavta,*" much to the delight of all present. Through repetition, even non-readers have become fluent in the liturgy and music of the service. It is not unusual to hear the sound of a toddler's voice echoing a song that was sung ten minutes earlier.

Our "curriculum" is the weekly *parashah*. (The festivals are also taught as they occur.) Families engage in discussions of Jewish identity and values in ways that are non-threatening and non-personal. They have gained a greater sense of Torah as a living, guiding document.

Further, one of the goals of the concluding family activity was to enable parents to act as Jewish educators for their own families. This part of the program is designed to be totally parent run without reliance on staff members. We structured the activities to empower parents to feel confident in demonstrating to their youngsters their role as active Jewish learners and teachers.

This educational program has resulted in a far greater mixing of age and ability groups than would usually take place in a grade-sorted Religious School program. We have a teenage older sibling of participants who studies with the adult group There are mixed age classes, and we have a special needs student who will be mainstreamed with her peers for the first time this year in our program. Everyone's education has been enhanced by the opportunities to share with one another!

PROGRAM DESCRIPTION

Approximately one hour of each Shabbat morning session is spent in worship, followed by a *Kiddush,* which allows a brief opportunity for socializing. Another hour is spent in learning activities. The morning concludes with a family activity and closing song.

The family activity is introduced to the adult class just prior to the conclusion of the study time. While each such activity is designed to be user friendly, a brief rationale and an opportunity for questions is offered.

The staff determines the segment of each *parashah* to be highlighted and the specific concept on which to focus. This enables each family member to participate in the concluding activity.

NUTS AND BOLTS

Materials

Materials needed include copies of the liturgy used. We found that using a loose-leaf binder permited the addition of liturgy and songs as the year went on. We also provided Torah commentaries for adults, and this year will create a library of reference materials for them so as to foster more interactive Torah study.

No special materials were required for the children's classes, but we always provided an adequate library of Torah related books and teaching materials. The family activity required only a varied collection of papers and graphics in order to provide esthetically appealing materials.

Logistics

In terms of logistics, one large room is needed for worship and *Kiddush,* and several sites should be available for classes, baby-sitting, etc.

PROGRAM MATERIALS

Appendix A shows the concepts and concluding family activities that were the focus for several Torah portions. The main focus of each study session was an aspect of the relationship between God and people.

EVALUATION

This program has been one of the most rewarding of my professional life. It is designed to empower parents and families. We were correct in our assumption that a program such as "Sharing Shabbat" would attract a devoted and motivated following. These families, with all generations represented, are the most positively involved in many aspects of synagogue life. They form a cadre of people anxious to learn and do more of everything Jewish.

The outline and goals of "Sharing Shabbat" are easily adaptable for other audiences. This year, in response to participant feedback, we plan to modify some of the family activities into at-home discussion guides and suggested activities. (See participant feedback below.)

The most challenging aspect of the program is that posed by raised expectations. Now that families have become accustomed to an educational paradigm in which they are deeply involved with their children's religious education, the traditional model of "supplementary" education will most likely not satisfy their future needs. While that is a delightful consequence of our program, it raises the question of introducing varied tracks within our educational program. Further, one might anticipate similar consequences with respect to liturgy. Will these families be worshipers in the congregational Shabbat ("Bar Mitzvah") morning service, or will they want to introduce aspects of the worship to which they have become accustomed into the congregation's practice? These issues remain to be discussed.

Participant feedback, solicited through a questionnaire and a parent meeting, has been most positive. Adults want more — more study, more homework, more active participation in the learning. Parents reported difficulty in involving children in activities just when they returned from class, and were anxious to arrange play dates or find the *Kiddush* leftovers. As we try to respond to feedback, we will experiment with more modalities of learning, *chevruta* partnerships for adults and activities "to go" for families.

BIBLIOGRAPHY

Behar, Rivka; Floreva Cohen; and Ruth Musnikow. *First Steps in Learning Torah with Young Children.* New York: Board of Jewish Education of Greater New York, 1995.

Damon, William. *The Moral Child.* New York: The Free Press, 1988.

Fields, Harvey J. *A Torah Commentary for Our Times, Vols. I, II, III.* New York: UAHC Press, 1990.

Grishaver, Joel Lurie. *A Child's Garden of Torah.* Los Angeles: Torah Aura Productions, 1998.

———. *Bible People Book One.* Denver, CO: A.R.E. Publishing, Inc., 1980.

———. *Bible People Book Two.* Denver, CO; A.R.E. Publishing, Inc., 1981.

Kelman, Stuart, and Joel Lurie Grishaver, eds. *Learn Torah With . . . 5756 Torah Annual.* Los Angeles: Torah Aura Productions, 1999.

Kushner, Lawrence S., and Kerry M. Olitzky. *Sparks beneath the Surface: A Spiritual Commentary on the Torah.* Northvale, NJ: Jason Aronson Inc., 1996.

Steinbock, Steven E. *Torah: The Growing Gift.* New York: UAHC Press, 1994.

Plaut, W, Gunther. *The Torah: A Modern Commentary.* New York: UAHC Press, 1981.

Wolpe, David J. *Teaching Your Children about God.* New York: HarperPerennial, 1995.

COMMENTARY

- Add a Shabbat lunch to this program once a month or so to add an informal dimension. Also consider having such a lunch in the homes of participants on a rotating basis. (SW)
- Tape songs and liturgy for participants to take into their homes. (BDK)
- This program suggests an adult learning recipe. Take a motivated person, provide a significant educational experience, give him or her a learning community, and watch the adult learner grow. (BDK)
- Have a *siyyum/hadran* as each book of the Torah is completed in the cycle of *parshiyot.* (EC)
- Always be thinking of the next level of challenge for families. Now that they have become more comfortable with *Tefilah*, the Family Educator can begin seeking out the families who are ready to serve as *shlichim* and lead services. (EC)
- Watch for special opportunities to integrate older or younger siblings into the communal celebration. (EC)
- Think developmentally: What about this program needs to change as the eight and nine-year-olds you began with become ten and 11-year-olds? (EC)

APPENDIX A
SAMPLE CONCEPTS AND ACTIVITIES

PORTION: VAYAYTZAY

Concepts

God is apparent to those who are looking.
We can "see" God in many places.

Concluding Family Activity

"Seeing God" personal diary
Using stickers that represent the senses, participants will create a log of "God-sightings." ("I can see God when I _____ ; I can touch God when I _____")

PORTION: VAYAYSHEV

Concepts

God gives us gifts.
We decide how to use our individual gifts.

Concluding Family Activity

Make a family gift plan and/or gift certificates.
Some Ideas: Make a videotape for a family member who lives far away.

Make an audiotape of your children's favorite stories for a young family member. As a family, bake cookies for a family member, etc.
Children might give grandparents a supply of hugs and kisses, a sibling an opportunity to play with a toy or game belonging to him/her, etc.

PORTION: MIKAYTZ

Concepts

God provides food for all.
No one need go hungry in God's world.
We act Godly when we provide food.

Concluding Family Activity

Cooking for a soup kitchen (everyone brings an ingredient to add to our starter base)
Create a family action plan to help feed hungry people.
Give up a weekly treat.

CHAPTER 36

MI'DOR L'DOR: FAMILY TORAH STUDY IN HAVUROT

CONTRIBUTOR: TRICIA BERKE VINSON
ADDRESS: **550 West Crescent Drive**
Palo Alto, CA 94301
PHONE: **(650) 323-0867**
E-MAIL: **Trishbv@aol.com**
TARGET: **Families with young children in**
kindergarten to third grade
SUBJECT: **Jewish ethics/values as presented**
in the weekly Torah Portion.
TIME FRAME: September to June. Families stay
involved for two to three years.

INTRODUCTION

In September of 1994, six families came together to create Congregation Etz Chayim, a small, liberal congregation that emphasizes Jewish spirituality in a family-centered and participatory environment. The congregation grew rapidly, attracting a significant number of families with young children. In many of these families, one or both of the adults had a limited background in Jewish practice and theology, but all were eager to learn along with their children. We therefore decided that we would concentrate all of our congregation's resources on a Family Education program, rather than a conventional Religious School.

Early the next spring, we first connected with Vicky Kelman, the Coordinator of the Jewish Family Education Project for the Bureau of Jewish Education in San Francisco. She met with us on several occasions, assisted us in developing our program and in submitting an application for funding to the Jewish Community Endowment Fund and the Jewish Community Federation. In July, Etz Chayim was awarded a $3,000 grant from these institutions.) Ms. Kelman also helped find funding for my attendance at the Whizin Institute for Jewish Family Education at the University of Judaism.

For the first three years of its existence, *"Mi'Dor L'Dor"* continued to receive partial funding through the Jewish Family Education Project. Now, the program is funded entirely by Congregation Etz Chayim, and continues to provide a meaningful Jewish education experience for families with children in kindergarten through third grade.

GOALS

The overall goals for the *"Mi'Dor L'Dor"* program are:
- To create a sense of community among participants.
- To enable parents to learn about Jewish ethics and values and then to model those values for their children.
- To enable parents to explore Torah with their children in a supportive community with other families.
- To enable parents to gain familiarity and comfort with Jewish rituals and practices.
- To support carryover and continuation of Jewish practice and Jewish learning in the home.

Through *"Mi'Dor L'Dor,"* we hope that our participating families will gain an appreciation for the continuing vitality of Torah and its relevance to their lives. We want families to become familiar with previously unfamiliar aspects of prayer and ritual.

In addition, we hope they will be introduced to a broad range of Jewish children's literature and will gain ideas on how to use this literature effectively with their children at home. Finally, it is our goal that as families are introduced to new ideas for enhancing the celebration of Shabbat and the holidays, they will begin to incorporate many of those practices in their own homes. The Havdalah service is a case in point. We hope that families will so enjoy this service at the conclusion of our Shabbat afternoon sessions that they will have their own Havdalah service on the weekends we are not together. Audiotapes of Havdalah and other services are provided to help families learn the blessings and melodies of the service.

DESCRIPTION OF THE PROGRAM

The "*Mi'Dor L'Dor*" program consists of three basic types of activities: (1) Shabbat Family Education sessions, (2) Bagel Brunches, and (3) Shabbat Pot Luck Dinners. Each of these is described below.

Shabbat Family Education Sessions

The core "*Mi'Dor L'Dor*" program consists of Shabbat afternoon study sessions twice a month. These generally focus on the weekly Torah portions. Each session begins with ten to 15 minutes of singing. New songs, relating to the *parashah* or to an upcoming holiday, are taught, and favorite Shabbat songs are shared. This gives the group a chance to feel a sense of community while the stragglers arrive.

After singing, the 30 participant families break into two groups, and the *parashah* of the week is presented. We have selected *Being Torah* by Joel Lurie Grishaver (Torah Aura Productions, 1985) as our text, because it contains some of the actual passages of the Torah. Also, it presents the *parshiyot* in a way that most children are able to understand. (In addition, we have found the large print and arrangement of the text on the page particularly helpful.) Unfortunately, *Being Torah* covers only Genesis and Exodus. When we got beyond Exodus, I did my best to provide readable, large print excerpts of each *parashah* for the class.

Sometimes the selected part of the portion is read aloud with each member of the group who can read taking a turn. Sometimes the families will have already read the selected part of the portion at home. In either case, there will be an activity — sometimes a dramatization, sometimes an art project, sometimes a game, which is designed to focus the group on the particular value that we want to draw from the portion.

After this activity, the groups break for a snack. After break, parents and children assemble separately. The children are divided into two groups, depending on their age. In their groups they learn some Hebrew, and, using a variety of activities, build on the themes developed in the family portion. The parents generally break into two groups for discussions of Jewish issues raised by the Torah portions and additional readings which have been suggested to complement the text. On those occasions when the Rabbi is present to facilitate discussions, the adults meet together. During the last ten minutes of the program, the families reassemble for Havdalah and a friendship circle.

The Sunday Brunch Programs

"*Mi'Dor L'Dor*" sponsors four or five Bagel Brunches throughout the year, each of which focuses on an upcoming Jewish holiday. This is our chance to enjoy singers, storytellers, folk dancing, and other special events, as well as to learn about the various Jewish holidays and the rituals associated with each. One highlight of our holiday brunches has been baking *hamentaschen* together and assembling *Mishloach Manot* baskets that we then deliver to Jewish seniors at Lytton Gardens, a residence for the elderly in Palo Alto. As a result of the relationships formed during this activity, Congregation Etz Chayim held a special Shabbat morning service at Lytton Gardens in May, which was greatly appreciated by the many seniors who have difficulty attending services in the community.

Shabbat Pot Luck Dinners

Four or five Shabbat pot luck dinners are held throughout the year, giving families an opportunity to share in the traditional Shabbat blessings and songs and to develop friendships and a feeling of community. These dinners are held in parks, at people's homes, and at the facility where we hold our Friday evening services. After the dinners, the families all attend services together.

STAFF

For our first two years of operation, we had no professional staff. I, as one of the parents, coordinated the program and planned the overall curriculum and the family and children's activities. Another parent was responsible for choosing and coordinating the adult readings and overseeing the preparation of the adult discussion leaders. Two parents rotated as teachers for the group of younger children, while I was responsible for running the education programs for the older children. Each parent volunteered to lead at least one adult discussion and/or to assist in one of the children's classes during the year. Our Rabbi led several adult discussions.

After two years, we decided we were ready to hire a professional Jewish educator to continue the program. Our synagogue educator is now responsible for overseeing the development of the curriculum, which includes preparing the adult readings and planning all family and children activities. She and one teacher are responsible for teaching the children's portion of the program, but parent volunteers still run most of the adult discussions. The Rabbi continues to lead the adult discussions when the topic is of particular interest to him, or when a more knowledgeable leader is required.

PREPARATION

A great deal of the preparation for this program takes place during the summer months. It is then that the coordinator puts together the program overview, selecting the particular sections of the *parashah* to be focused on and the value to be highlighted at each session. After that outline is made, adult readings which complement the themes are explored and selected. During the summer, specific lesson plans for the family activities and children's

activities for the first few months are planned, and the coordinator meets with the children's teachers to review plans for the first several sessions. Every attempt is made to balance types of activities (drama, art, games, reading aloud, etc.) and to ensure sufficient variety to meet different learning styles and interests. Once the year is under way, planning sessions are held approximately every two months so that in designing future programs we can take into consideration which activities are working most successfully. The coordinator must also prepare or purchase necessary materials for specific programs.

COMMUNICATION

Despite the fact that parents are participating in this program regularly, we have found it to be most successful to send a bimonthly letter advising families of the topic for the upcoming session, reminding parents to complete their readings, and reminding parents who have volunteered to lead the adult discussion to prepare for this activity. Additionally, each session ends with a take-home activity — a chance to practice the value we have focused on, and to bring back some comments on their experience to write on a "leaf" for their family tree (see below). We have found it helpful to include in the bimonthly letter a gentle reminder about completing these activities.

NUTS AND BOLTS

Materials

At the beginning of the program, each family is provided with a copy of *Being Torah*, along with excerpts from a resource to be read as preparation for the adult discussions. Each family is also given a copy of the Havdalah blessings and a tape of someone singing these blessings, as well as some of the songs we regularly sing.

Prior to the first program meeting, we prepared a large cardboard cut-out of a tree for each family. At the first session, a Polaroid photo of each family was taken and pasted onto their tree, and the family added to their tree some words and pictures that symbolized their "root" values. These trees were hung in our meeting room each week, and "leaves," "flowers," and other symbols were added each week as the family practiced the values we explored.

We also had on hand several boxes of art supplies for the family and children activities and a large box of costumes, including headdresses, fake beards, crowns, and wraps to enhance the drama activities. Additional materials were required for some specific programs, such as *challah* dough for the program on blessings and packaged food for the *Kashrut* program. We purchased three Havdalah sets, and families took turns being Havdalah helpers, often in recognition of their help in leading a session, helping with a children's program, or providing a snack. Snacks were provided each week by participant families on a rotating basis.

Set-up and Logistics

Considerable time and effort is spent each week on set-up. Because we are in shared facilities, the materials need to be brought in and set up for each session, including hanging the family trees and making sure necessary supplies are available in each room. This program has extensive space needs as well: a room large enough to accommodate the entire group for singing and Havdalah, two medium size rooms for the large group to break into two groups for whole family activities, and smaller rooms for adult discussions and children's programming.

EVALUATION

In November 1995, a formal evaluation of *"Mi'Dor L'Dor"* was undertaken at our request. Riva Berkowitz, a professional Jewish educator who had reviewed our curriculum and observed one of our Shabbat afternoon family programs, conducted this evaluation. Ms. Berkowitz made some suggestions regarding better utilizing volunteers and increasing hands-on activities to reinforce the teaching of the Hebrew letters. She concluded her evaluation with these words: "All the activities and discussion questions were age appropriate and did involve both parents and children in an inviting, non-threatening manner. Newcomers were made to feel welcome. The amount of carryover into the homes was also very impressive. There was visible pride as each representative of a family or group of families described the production of their Midrashic work of art. Keep this wonderful program going! The level of enthusiastic participation by all age groups is a wonderful affirmation of the vibrancy of Family Education in our tradition."

In thinking back over the first years of *"Mi'Dor L'Dor,"* a number of significant successes stand out. The program seems to have been particularly successful in creating a feeling of community among participants. This was especially true in its first year when the program consisted of 16 families. As we grew to 32 families in our second year, the sense of community took a bit longer to build. By the end of the second year, however, participants consistently reported that they had found a supportive Jewish community in *"Mi'Dor L'Dor."*

The adult discussions also seem to be filling a need for families. Many of the adult participants had never experienced Jewish education as adults, and they were excited to get a taste of the richness of Judaism. Some were encouraged by this experience to take classes offered through our adult education programs, something they confided they had never before even considered.

A number of families reported that certain rituals introduced to them through the program have become part of their family lives, for example, blessing their children on Shabbat evening, ending Shabbat with Havdalah, and saying the *"Shema"* with their children at bedtime.

Finally, certain programs seemed to be quite successful in providing opportunities for parents and children to discuss significant Jewish issues such as *Tzedakah* and *Tikkun Olam*.

There have, however, been difficulties, as well as successes. One difficulty is found in the *parshiyot* themselves. In Genesis, each *parashah* is so rich with numerous opportunities for creating exciting programs that many aspects are left unexplored. However, as we move into Leviticus finding appropriate readings, materials, and ideas has become a constant challenge. In our third year, we solved this problem by not tying the curriculum so closely to the scheduled weekly *parashah*. This freedom has enabled us to do many more creative programs without making ourselves crazy.

There seems to be a continuing problem of creating a program that will be meaningful to all the participants, regardless of the level of their Jewish background. This problem was particularly acute in the adult discussions, especially when the lay leaders weren't particularly knowledgeable. In such cases, the more educated participants sometimes felt frustrated that discussions were at a low level and that occasionally misinformation was passed along.

Another ongoing difficulty is how to maintain the interest and involvement of the younger children in the whole family activities, especially for those children too young to read and write. Additionally, the whole family programs often depended on an underlying assumption that families had the ability and desire to interact and communicate with one another. Unfortunately, this assumption was not always valid. In general, while I believe that the whole family programming is the heart of *"Mi'Dor L'Dor,"* it has been the most demanding and the least consistently successful part of the program.

FUTURE DIRECTIONS

As their children reach fourth grade and enroll in our twice weekly program for Hebrew and Judaica instruction, many parents have expressed the desire to continue with a Family Education component of some type. This past year, therefore, we have been piloting a once a month program called *"B'Yachad."* Modeled on *"Mi'Dor L'Dor,"* this program brings the families of Hebrew school and Jewish Day School children from fourth through seventh grades together for two hours one Sunday morning each month for family learning and study. Our first year curriculum was *K'lal Yisrael* and the appreciation of Jewish diversity.

One of our major challenges is keeping up the energy required to run a comprehensive Family Education program. Family Education is extremely labor intensive. Planning the programs is time-consuming, as is the preparation of materials, set-up, and clean-up. While there are a number of sources of good ideas, the coordinator is constantly feeling as if she is in the position of designing things from scratch. We have yet to experience the luxury of reusing an already prepared program. Despite the difficulty of planning whole family activities that work for all families, we continue to believe in the importance of having the family spend some time engaged in Jewish learning together. When these experiences work, they are very powerful. Despite the difficulties of including families with all levels of Jewish background, such heterogeneity offers rich opportunities for meaningful sharing of knowledge with one another.

RESOURCES

As mentioned above, *Being Torah* by Grishaver is the text for our family programs. Adult readings were drawn from many sources and may be found in our schedule of readings. For planning purposes we relied on *Family Room: Linking Families into a Jewish Learning Community* by Vicky Kelman (Whizin Institute, 1995), *Teaching Torah: A Treasury of Insights and Activities* by Sorel Goldberg Loeb and Barbara Binder Kadden (A.R.E. Publishing, Inc., 1997) and *Teaching Mitzvot: Concepts, Values and Activities* by Barbara Binder Kadden and Bruce Kadden (A.R.E. Publishing, Inc., 1996). We are also deeply indebted to the Jewish Family Education Project, a collaborative program between the Jewish Community Federation and the Bureau of Jewish Education, funded in part by a grant from the Jewish Community Endowment Fund. This program provided us with funding, wonderful educational workshops, and also helped to fund our coordinator's attendance at the Whizin Institute for three years. We couldn't have done it without their help.

CHAPTER 37

FAMILY D'VAR TORAH PROJECT

CONTRIBUTOR: RABBI JOY LEVITT
ADDRESS: JCC in Manhattan
          334 Amsterdam Avenue
          New York, NY 10023
PHONE: (212) 580-0099, ext. 271
E-MAIL: joydevra@aol.com
TARGET: Sixth-Seventh Graders and Parents

OVERALL PURPOSES OF PROGRAM

For years, I have been frustrated by the way families prepare for the Bar or Bat Mitzvah of their child. Most parents dutifully drop their kids off for tutoring, but spend next to no time at all thinking about the service itself. True, in our synagogue, families do more than in many others — they prepare a supplement of readings to be offered by congregants and guests during the service, and they have the option of reading Torah as well. But for the most part, a family's preparation for their child's Bar/Bat Mitzvah revolves around party planning. Many families report a high degree of frustration at having to spend too much time and money on a four-hour extravaganza that has very little to do with the actual Bar/Bat Mitzvah ceremony.

The idea behind the "Family D'var Torah Project" came from my desire to give families something meaningful and productive to do in preparation for their child's Bar/Bat Mitzvah, something that might even set them on a course of continued study. This project is based on the assumption that Bar/Bat Mitzvah is not just an important time in the life of the child, but that it is also important in the life of the entire family. The project is especially helpful for younger siblings who sometimes feel left out of the Bar/Bat Mitzvah experience; it gives them something significant to contribute. Finally, the project has the potential of creating opportunities for meaningful family time, which is something of a rarity these days.

PROGRAM DESCRIPTION

Several events are held before a family decides to do a *D'var Torah*. One year before the Bar/Bat Mitzvah, we hold a general orientation for B'nai Mitzvah families, at which time we review all the issues regarding Bar/Bat Mitzvah preparation. Each family is given a loose-leaf binder containing several materials: the Torah portion to be read on the day of the child's Bar/Bat Mitzvah, an article entitled "How to Give a D'var Torah" (in *The Kosher Pig and Other Curiosities of Modern Jewish Life* by Richard Israel), an excerpt on their particular Torah portion from *Teaching Torah: A Treasury of Insights and Activities* by Sorel Goldberg Loeb and Barbara Binder Kadden, and the table of contents of articles found in the CD-Rom *Torah La'Am*.

Six months before the Bar/Bat Mitzvah, we hold an orientation specifically on the subject of presenting a *D'var Torah*. In this session, we review the article by Richard Israel, focusing on various approaches to writing a *D'var Torah*. We show people the library cart that contains a variety of resources, including Nehama Leibowitz, Gunther Plaut, Harvey Fields, the JPS five-volume *Chumash*, *Teaching Torah*, a collection of *Divray Torah* from Torah Aura Productions, and several other books we have found helpful over the years. We do the ten-minute tutorial from the CD-Rom *Torah La'Am* to acquaint people with how to use it. None of these materials leaves the building, but multiple copies of each book provide adequate resources for everyone. (The CD-Rom materials don't leave the building because they are so expensive. People come in to use it, and siblings who are in Hebrew School may use it during class.)

Then the family has to make a decision about whether this project is something they want to do. In the last three years, approximately 95% of our families have chosen to do it, which came as somewhat of a surprise to us. This, of course, has necessitated a serious commitment of staff time. Since the program's inception, we have had either three Rabbis or two Rabbis and an Educator working with each of the approximately 25 families that elect to do this each year. After the first year, we asked a group of family therapists to help train the staff regarding issues of family dynamics. We found that while the Jewish piece of the program was fairly challenging but manageable for most families, families often stressed over finding time to work on the *D'var Torah,* getting all members involved, and other issues around family dynamics. The training helped our staff to put families at ease and get them motivated and comfortable.

Once a family has made the decision to go ahead, their first task is to read the text of the Torah portion aloud at home as a family. We ask them to appoint one person as scribe to write down any and all questions, comments, issues, etc., which arise in the course of the reading. We also ask them to try to narrow down the issues that compel them. The next step is to call the Rabbi appointed to work with their family. A Rabbi then comes to their house to help further focus them and to suggest other resources. We help them structure the work as well. Generally, we ask the Bar/Bat Mitzvah child to write a summary of the entire portion (about a page in length). Then we help each member of the family decide how to proceed. Sometimes, the family decides on a single theme, which they attack from a variety of angles. Other times, they each work on a different section of the portion. We have

learned to be very flexible about this. Some families write plays or perform skits, while others prefer a more intellectual approach. We try to encourage families to understand their strengths and work with them.

We generally speak on the phone with one or more members of the family as they proceed. Usually, one person winds up taking charge of the writing process, although sometimes each member of the family writes his or her own section. We ask families to keep the length to about 15 minutes. We ask for a first draft to be given to us one month before the Bar/Bat Mitzvah. Then we rehearse the presentation, usually the week before the Bar/Bat Mitzvah. At the service itself, the family is called to the *bimah* right before the Torah reading. They sit on stools around the reader's desk for the presentation.

RESOURCES

Allen, Richard. *Parashah Plays.* Denver, CO: A.R.E. Publishing, Inc., 2000.

Beiner, Stan J. *Bible People.* Denver, CO: A.R.E. Publishing, Inc., 1988.

————. *Sedra Scenes.* Denver, CO: A.R.E. Publishing, Inc., 1982.

Berman, Melanie, and Joel Lurie Grishaver. *My Weekly Sidrah.* Los Angeles: Torah Aura Productions, 1986.

Chubara, Yona; Miriam P. Feinberg; and Rena Rotenberg. *Torah Talk: An Early Childhood Teaching Guide.* Denver, CO: A.R.E. Publishing, Inc., 1989.

Epstein, David and Suzanne Stutman. *Torah with Love: A Guide for Strengthening Jewish Values within the Family.* Upper Saddle River, NJ: Prentice-Hall, 1986, o.p.

Fields, Harvey J. *A Torah Commentary for Our Times, Vols. I & II.* New York: UAHC Press, 1990.

Fox, Everett. *The Five Books of Moses.* New York: Schocken Books, 1995.

Grishaver, Joel Lurie. *Being Torah: A First Book of Torah Texts.* Los Angeles, CA: Torah Aura Productions, 1986.

————. *Bible People Book One*. Denver, CO: A.R.E. Publishing, Inc., 1980.

————. *Bible People Book Two*. Denver, CO: A.R.E. Publishing, Inc., 1982.

————. *I Can Learn Torah*. Los Angeles, CA: Torah Aura Productions, 1992.

————. *Learning Torah: A Self-Guided Journey through the Layers of Jewish Learning*. New York: UAHC Press, 1998.

————. *Torah Toons*. Vols. I & II. Los Angeles, CA: Torah Aura Productions.

Israel, Richard. *The Kosher Pig and Other Curiosities of Modern Jewish Life*. Los Angeles, CA: Alef Design Group, 1994.

Kaplan, Aryeh. *The Living Torah*. Brooklyn, NY: Moznaim Publishing Corp., 1987.

————. *The Living Torah: The Five Books of Moses and the Hafarot*. Brooklyn, NY: Moznaim Publishing Corp., 1981.

Loeb, Sorel Goldberg, and Barbara Binder Kadden. *Teaching Torah: A Treasury of Insights and Activities*. Denver, CO: A.R.E. Publishing, Inc., 1997.

Rossel, Seymour. *Child's Bible: Lessons from the Torah*. West Orange, NJ: Behrman House, 1988.

Rosman, Steven M. *Sidrah Stories: A Torah Companion*. New York: UAHC Press, 1989.

Segal, Lore. *The Book of Adam To Moses*. New York: Alfred A. Knopf, 1987.

Singer, Ellen, and Bernard M. Zlotowitz. *Our Sacred Texts: Discovering the Jewish Classics*. New York: UAHC Press, 1998.

COMMENTARY

• Think about each family as a unique system in judging whether the family should be encouraged to undertake a family *D'var Torah*. For families that are well differentiated in their roles and personalities, doing a family *D'var Torah* is sometimes a wonderful form of togetherness. But there may be other families that have a cosmetic or plastic unity. Then allowing the Bar/Bat Mitzvah to take on the responsibility individually might be more helpful for the family system as a whole. (EC)

• Tape families who have done the family *D'var Torah* so that new families can have a picture of what it might be like to embark on this adventure/risk. (EC)

• A "Family D'var Torah Project" will happen best when there is a strong Torah thread running throughout the entire curriculum so that families have engaged in Torah study many times before the Bar/Bat Mitzvah. See Chapter 34, *"Yom Iyun L'Mishpachah"* as an example. (EC)

• Give *Teaching Torah* or an adult Torah commentary as Sisterhood/synagogue gift in acknowledgement of the family effort that goes into the *D'var Torah*. (EC)

• Think about the special role of siblings in this process. In one instance, we know that the younger sibling served as the computer editor of the *D'var Torah*, entering everyone's comments onto a computer file so that the Bar Mitzvah could then review and choose his favorite comments.

• Jo Kay and others have made this process of writing a family *D'var Torah* more communal by making it part of the broader process of guiding whole groups of families through the B'nai Mitzvah process. (EC)

FAMILY, SCHOOL, AND COMMUNITY PARTNERSHIPS

CONTRIBUTOR: Enid C. Lader
ADDRESS: Beth Israel–The West Temple
            14308 Triskett Road
            Cleveland, OH 44111
PHONE: (216) 941-8882
E-MAIL: eclader@aol.com

We cannot talk about educating the Jewish family without thinking about communication. As educators, there are two particular items on our agenda concerning communication. The first is ongoing communication with parents. Schools in general, and classroom teachers in particular, help keep parents informed through flyers, newsletters, bulletin articles, phone announcements, and e-mail. But, beyond the informational fliers, we want to help parents be involved in their children's education in deeper, more meaningful ways. When parents asked what would be more helpful to them in their role as partners with schools in their children's Jewish education, many parents answer that they would like to know more about the curriculum. The second item on the communication agenda is to provide opportunities for parents and children to communicate with each other about things Jewish. These opportunities enable them to talk and listen to each other, teach and learn from each other.

In Chapter 38, "The Joyce Epstein Framework for Family-School Partnerships," Meryl Wassner provides an exciting look into expanding the walls of the classroom to the living room (or dining room table) with discussion of her work on "Interactive Homework." Chapter 39, "TIPS: Interactive Homework in a Jewish Context," builds on Chapter 38, and offers examples of interactive homework created by teachers in the field.

Once a child becomes a teenager, the walls of communication are harder to scale. All the more reason to think creatively about ways to promote good communication. Chapter 40, "Connecting Parents To the Teen Israel Experience" by Joan Kaye and Jay Lewis, addresses this issue. As a result of the parent component, the teen Israel trip described in this chapter becomes an important vehicle for ongoing deepening Jewish identity both for the parent and the teen.

CHAPTER 38

THE JOYCE EPSTEIN FRAMEWORK FOR FAMILY-SCHOOL PARTNERSHIPS

CONTRIBUTOR: MERYL WASSNER
ADDRESS: 1524 South Gillette Avenue
Tulsa, OK 74104
PHONE: (918) 583-7121
E-MAIL: merylwassner@aol.com
TARGET: Principals and teachers of Grades 2 to 7

INTRODUCTION

The involvement of parents in their child's Jewish education is critical. Concepts, skills, and values introduced at school will more likely be mastered and internalized if they are reinforced in the home setting. Yet, parent participation in Religious School activities (as in public school activities) is problematic. Time and energy are limited resources for busy parents trying to juggle family, job, and perhaps other issues. Previous models of parent participation (the traditional room parent or parent serving on a school council) may not be feasible today for most families. Indeed, extended commitment requiring a specific time each week or month outside of the home may just not be possible to schedule. Religious School educators need to be sensitive to the parents' struggles. While it is appropriate to expect some level of parent commitment, we have to offer innovative ways to adapt to the outside challenges they face.

The model for parent involvement that follows was developed for at risk families by Joyce Epstein while she served as Co-director of the Schools, Family, and Community Partnerships progam of the Center for Research on the Education of Students

Placed at Risk at Johns Hopkins University. "TIPS" (Teachers Involving Parents with Schoolwork) booklets were created in various subjects for parents' use.

The Joyce Epstein framework features six types of parent involvement:

Type 1 – Parenting: Help families establish a home environment that supports children as students.

Type 2 – Communicating: Design effective forms of school-to-home and home-to-school communications about school programs and a child's progress.

Type 3 – Volunteering: Recruit and organize parent help and support.

Type 4 – Learning at Home: Provide information and ideas to families about how to help students at home with homework and other curriculum related activities, decisions, and planning.

Type 5 – Decision Making: Include parents in school decisions, so as to develop parent leaders and representatives.

Type 6 – Collaborating with Community: Identify and integrate resources and services from the community to strengthen school programs, family practices, and student learning and development.

In spring of 1996, I was approached by the Director of Professional Development for the Chicago Community Foundation for Jewish Education, Sara Shapiro. She charged me with investigating the potential for implementing in our Religious Schools the Joyce Epstein model Type 4 (referred to above as "Learning at Home," and identified in Epstein's subsequent writings as "Interactive Homework." Mrs. Shapiro and I discussed the findings of numerous studies, analyzing the merits of homework in general. It was agreed that expanded on-task time in all content areas, at whatever grade level, positively impacts the student's mastery and retention of materials. When schools bring the parents into the expanded learning process, the results are not only increased student mastery, but also parental empowerment and increased parental support of curricular goals.

Joyce Epstein's model for parent involvement with homework in public schools included the content areas of math, science, art, and social studies. She called the program TIPS: Teachers Involve Parents in Schoolwork. It focused primarily on the elementary grades. My charge was to transpose that model to Judaic content, and determine at what grades it would be realistic to involve parents in this format of learning.

The challenge of convincing parents to squeeze out extra time was made a bit easier when I began to examine parents' motivation for sending their children to Religious School in the first place. Families decide to join synagogues and get involved with a Religious School because they know that the schooling transcends cognitive knowledge. It isn't exclusively about "book learning." The mission of our synagogue programs is also to nurture souls, and to give our families the tools to carry on the traditions of our ancestors in their home practice. Our parents themselves often "hunger" to increase their knowledge and skills in Jewish living, and are therefore receptive to being involved.

On the other hand, the challenge of involving parents in Religious School homework is to eliminate the intimidating misconception that in order to help they must be *mavens* on a variety of topics. They are concerned they will fail in this partnership because they are not the repositors of facts and skills inherent in the school curriculum. It is is critical to the success of the program that the educator clarify the boundaries and logistics of the parents' role in this model. A significant amount of time orienting the teachers and students is also essential. With the Epstein model, the student becomes the transmittor of knowledge and skills. The teacher explains each specific Interactive Homework assignment that the students will be offering to their parents. This past year, the subjects for which the

exercises were developed included Hebrew, Bible stories, Jewish History, *Mitzvot,* and Holidays.

THE ORIENTATION PROCESS

Synagogue and School Board

For the Interactive Homework model to work in a synagogue school, there must be receptivity on the part of the synagogue Board of Directors and School Board. It is critical that such boards embrace the importance and value of parent participation in the learning process of the students. Lifelong Jewish learning has been a value/concept throughout Jewish history, and is articulated in current community development models. With the students as "transmitters of knowledge and skills," the Joyce Epstein model offers a vehicle for a dynamic parent-school partnership in learning, the benefits of which are wide-ranging for all participants.

It would be most appropriate to introduce the program concept during the early spring when budget and curriculum are reviewed. If it is in keeping with the synagogue's overall mission, the Board should appoint a project director to coordinate the Interactive Homework program in the school. Most frequently, this is the Education Director, but it can be a veteran teacher who is very articulate, knowledgeable, and prepared to make the time commitment to get the program off the ground. The project director would begin by planning the faculty workshops (for summer), at which the program is explained.

Faculty Orientation/Development
Part 1

It is desirable to have the entire faculty participate in the orientation process for the Joyce Epstein model of parent involvement, even if the decision is ultimately to have only selected grades develop Interactive Homework exercises. For the parent/school partnership to be viable, it is necessary to explore teachers' attitudes concerning working with parents on any number of levels. As a beginning activity, outline two columns on the board headed: "Challenges" and "Benefits." The faculty members discuss what they anticipate to be the challenges of having parents as active partners in the students' learning experience. They then reflect upon what they would see as benefits of this parent involvement/partnership and write down the salient points.

This exercise usually provides an animated discussion about parent participation. Teachers should be permitted to express concern and even frustration for past experiences that may not have been positive. It is the project director's role to assure the faculty that the Epstein model takes into account those concerns and offers innovative solutions to any challenges that might come up. It is recommended first to discuss the "Challenges" column, then the "Benefits." This can be an exciting and encouraging exercise for both new and experienced teachers. In sharing their views, they begin to see expanded potential for their own teaching and learning in the coming school year.

Next, the project director should present an overview of the Joyce Epstein model of parent involvement, explaining the other five types briefly, then explaining in more detail Type 4, Interactive Homework. He/she should share why the synagogue Board of Directors and School Board feel this is a valuable instrument for expanding learning and parent participation. At this time, it is useful for the faculty to review the school's present policy on homework in general, and how this new program builds on this policy. Any homework should be an enrichment and expansion opportunity for the students to master the materials offered in the curriculum. The students' role as transmitter of knowledge will be addressed later in this chapter.

A most appropriate next step in the faculty orientation is to have the project director present the faculty with an overview of the curricular focus of each grade in the school, as well as having the books and other reference materials available for examination. It is important for each faculty member to have an understanding that the content area he/she is covering builds upon what was taught the previous year, and serves as a foundation for what follows. Teachers should be given their texts to take home. They should be instructed to develop a lesson plan from one of their texts, and to bring it to the

second part of the faculty orientation (to take place within two weeks of this initial meeting). Two weeks allows them sufficient time to look over the materials, yet not so much time that the enthusiasm and momentum established in the first meeting diminishes.

Part 2

By the second orientation, the faculty has a familiarity with the curricular materials, and they have discussed the fact that the parents will be active partners in learning. Thus, it is time to introduce them to the process and components of the Interactive Homework exercises. A good interactive exercise should begin from a well written, age appropriate lesson plan, or series of lesson plans (study units). The goal here is to impart knowledge and skills recently learned in Religious School to family members. At the end of a unit of study, or midway through, depending on the length of the unit (and the grade), the Interactive Homework can be a fine vehicle to share with their parents.

A well structured exercise will contain the following elements:

- Statement of goals and objectives for this homework exercise
- Verbal instructions to the students on how to present the exercise to their parents (Grade 4 and up). Third graders should be given a written paragraph for their parents, explaining the approach to the assignment.
- A specific time frame given for completing the assignment, i.e., when the assignment will be given/due, and how much time the parent and student should spend on the assignment (in some cases, this can be left open-ended).
- A creative follow-up exercise to be done in class the day the homework is due, which allows students to share their family experiences (the teacher will then build on this in the next classroom lesson plan).

Faculty members should now pair off and be given an opportunity to create an Interactive Homework exercise from the lesson plans they have brought in. These exercises should represent an extension and expansion on the in-class lesson and be "doable" for the student and parents. Having the teachers work in pairs accomplishes many objectives, including:

- It facilitates teachers building a bond with one another.
- It allows each teacher to become more familiar with the curricular materials of another grade.
- It promotes teachers supporting one another as they attempt a new skill.
- Creative ideas for each interactive exercise are multiplied.

After the pairs have created the exercises from their respective lesson plans, they then share their products with the whole group. This can generate a good deal of excitement and appreciation for one another's work, as well as for this new school project. The project director now asks the teachers for feedback about creating the exercise, acknowledging that this is challenging, and that it will require additional time and effort on the teachers' part. It is important then to mention again the purpose of these exercises — to increase student mastery of the materials and parent participation in the learning process.

Each project director needs to begin to assess the receptivity of the faculty, and to be realistic when determining which grades will be involved in introducing this new concept to the parents during the first year of implementation. Another consideration is to determine how frequently the exercises should be assigned in each of the participating grades. A good deal of coordination among faculty is essential. It is not advisable to overload parents who may have two or three children enrolled in Religious School.

After the teachers have developed and shared their first exercises, they should work independently again, creating a letter to the parents of their students, explaining the project, and inviting them to the fall parent/teacher open house. Having to explain the project to the parents affords teachers the opportunity to clarify for themselves what this partnership will look like. The project director will see from teachers' first drafts whether or not they have a clear understanding of the purposes and implementation steps of the project, and can assist them by helping them rework the letters if necessary.

The final step of this second orientation session is to explain to the faculty how to gauge the efficacy of the lessons and the interest level of the parents as they participate. The project director explains that there is to be a book that goes back and forth between home and school with each assigned exercise. This enables parents to fill out a brief evaluation form and to make additional comments, thus helping a teacher to determine any necessary modifications of future assignments.

At this point in the orientation, the project director should now allow time for questions and initial thoughts about beginning this project. He or she can either ask teachers to think about whether each is willing to try this in his/her grade, or inform the teachers of the grades in which the School Board would like to see the project implemented It is important for the project directors to be familiar enough with their staff to know which alternative would be preferable in their school. A follow-up meeting can be set up for the appropriate teachers. This completes the second part of the faculty orientation is complete.

PARENT ORIENTATION

Although the fall open house does not occur until some weeks after the school year has been initiated, the parents will have received a parent manual during the summer. This outlines policies and procedures, philosophy of education, curricular focus for each grade level, introduces faculty, and explains hours of operation. Also contained in this manual is a brief description of the Interactive Homework model as one means of broadening parents' involvement in the school curriculum while expanding their own knowledge base. Thus, a seed has been planted in their minds. The fall open house is listed on the school and synagogue calendars. The project director should keep the School Board informed throughout the summer, and in the beginning month of school, regarding the faculty's ongoing work in preparation for the introduction of the project at the fall open house.

Parents will have received a flyer, sparking interest in the open house, and reminding them about ten days before the event of the time and location of the meeting. The purpose of the open house is not only to introduce the Joyce Epstein Model, emphasizing the Interactive Homework, but to facilitate the beginning of parent/teacher communication. In so many cases, the first time a parent has contact with their child's teacher (be it in secular school, Day School, or Religious School) is when there is a behavioral concern or repeated absences. Here is an opportunity to begin the year with a positive shared experience, facilitating school-home communication down the road.

There is no greater way to create a bond than to share the interactive experience of studying text together. After welcoming remarks by the project director and introductions of the faculty, the parents are divided into four groups, each of which will include at least one faculty member. They will engage in an exercise from *Targilon: A Jewish Family Education Workbook* by Leora W. Isaacs and Jeffrey Schein (JESNA and Jewish Reconstructionist Federation, 1996). The exercise explores the changing attitudes and roles of communities and families in educating their children. It takes participants through four Jewish texts and a period of 3,000 years. This activity not only expands the teachers' and parents' knowledge of various texts, but illustrates the challenge in every era of raising educated children who will ultimately become responsible members of the community.

After studying in small groups, everyone convenes and summarizes their understanding of the passages. Following this, the project director helps the parents explore their own concerns and thoughts about what their active participation in the school might require. Once again, a chart is used, and a discussion ensues regarding potential challenges and benefits (from the parents' perspective, now) from being involved in their child's religious education. This is an exceptional opportunity for teachers to hear how their students' parents see their role in the school, and it can allow for the building of a positive teacher/parent relationship. (It is useful to repeat this exercise at the end of the year, summarizing what were the actual challenges and benefits experienced.) An outcome of this initial discussion is that parents feel empowered to express their views, and they know that they are respected as vital partners in the implementation of their school program.

Following the chart exercise, the project director (or one of the teachers) gives an overview of what the interactive exercises will look like, how often these will be assigned, and the parents' role in completion of the exercises (including the evaluation sheets). It is explained that the teachers will be designing opportunities in class to share the family experience with classmates. Parents should be informed that a parent/teacher advisory committee will be formed to evaluate the project at the end of the year. Parents interested in serving on the committee should speak to their child's teacher in the coming weeks. After addressing additional questions, the formal program is concluded, and parents are invited to remain for refreshments and extended conversation.

STUDENT ORIENTATION

The stage has been set to explain this project to the students, who by now have gotten to know their teacher, as well as the curriculum they are studying. These factors should enable them to feel confident and capable enough to extend their learning by leading their parents in home exercises. (Refer to Chapter 39, "TIPS: Interactive Homework in a Jewish Context" by Enid C. Lader, which includes more details about preparing students for the home exercises.) Generally, it is advisable to send home more written instructions with younger children. Teachers can do more "coaching" of the older students so that they can explain the exercises themselves to their parents.

Teachers must take many variables into account as they prepare the students to "teach" what they have learned so far to their parents. These include:
• Students' verbal skills vary greatly.
• Students' academic motivation and proficiency vary considerably.

- Students' home environments may range from nurturing and stable to a home with internal conflicts and/or lack of resources. The latter may inhibit the student's confidence and competency in completing the assignment.

The project director should serve as a resource for the teacher, providing background information regarding home family dynamics and challenges.

It should also be explained at the orientation that if both parents are not available, then one parent, a close relative, or conscientious caregiver, may participate in the exercise. Each student must feel that he/she can share with those at home what is being experienced at school.

FOLLOW-THROUGH ACTIVITIES

Communication

Once the Interactive Homework exercises have begun, it is essential that the project director continue to generate enthusiasm and support to the faculty. It takes time and energy to develop these exercises, read parent comments, and reshape future exercises. Teachers should be given much encouragement and acknowledgment for their efforts.

The parents need to be kept informed of the frequency of the exercises and the initial feedback. Students will occasionally be absent on the day an exercise is assigned. In such cases, communication to the home should be sent in a timely fashion.

In the spring, after the grades participating in the project have completed a number of exercises, an open house should be planned. On this occasion, parents and students share with all the teachers and one another the innovative projects completed during the year. Each school can determine the criteria for selecting projects to be presented. During school parent-teacher conferences, all the other projects can be displayed. There should be an article in the synagogue and school bulletins highlighting the projects, and also featuring the reactions of parents and students to working with and learning together.

EVALUATION

As with all educational endeavors, documentation is critical so that future classes and future generations will benefit from what has been learned. Project directors would be wise to document the dates when exercises were completed, as well as conversations with parents, and should preserve copies of the written home-school sheets. Teachers might be expected to keep a journal describing how this process impacted their own teaching practice, and also the learning in their classes.

At the end of the school year, a series of meetings of the advisory committee (comprised of parents, teachers, Directors, the project director, and the Chairperson of the School Board, possibly the Rabbi) should be convened. It is advisable not to wait until summer, as momentum and reflections may have faded and fewer people will be available for the evaluation process. The objectives of the advisory committee are:

- Review all data (parent evaluation sheets, samples of completed exercises, teachers' journals, project director's data).
- Determine if the school wishes to continue the project the following year.
- Discuss which grades should participate in future.
- Assign a project director for the next year (could be the Education Director, a teacher, or a knowledgeable School Board member willing to attend faculty meetings).
- Set dates for summer planning sessions with the advisory committee alone, then together with faculty.

CONCLUSION

The Interactive Homework project, as well as the other five types of parent involvement outlined in the Joyce Epstein model, offers the potential of many benefits to a school community. Parents become more aware of school activities and curriculum. They are given an opportunity to experience the value in Judaism of being "lifelong Jewish learners," with the exciting twist that their own children become their teachers and "transmitters" of knowledge. The students have a concrete vehicle through which to share school experiences with their families.

The faculty develops a bond and increases communication with parents. Teachers come to understand that parent involvement is not a one-time activity, but an ongoing process. They develop an increased appreciation for the ideas, concerns, and talents that parents contribute to the school program. Teachers also gain a broader awareness and deeper knowledge of the school curriculum, having worked with their colleagues on developing the Interactive Homework exercises.

Through this program, the School Board and Education Director are able to share with parents the responsibility for and involvement in promoting the school's educational goals. The entire community will enjoy the fruits of this well structured, well thought out model which redefines what education and learning can be.

COMMENTARY

- For families that want to sign up for a once a month creative Jewish thought model (based on the Interactive Homework model), consider a *chug* based on the Olympics of the Mind. (EC)

- Bring teachers together across the school to design an Interactive Homework assignment that can be shared at an assembly for an upcoming holiday. (EC)

CHAPTER 39

TIPS: INTERACTIVE HOMEWORK IN A JEWISH CONTEXT

CONTRIBUTOR: ENID C. LADER
ADDRESS: Beth Israel–The West Temple
14308 Triskett Road
Cleveland, OH 44111
PHONE: (216) 941-8882
E-MAIL: eclader@aol.com
TARGET: Grades 2-7

INTRODUCTION

This chapter provides an explanation of how to use Interactive Homework in Jewish settings. For background on and a description of this model, see Chapter 38, "The Joyce Epstein Framework for Family-School Partnerships."

Each Interactive Homework piece has five sections:
- Letter to the family
- Background information that will be helpful for completing the assignment and/or materials needed
- An assignment which reinforces the classroom lesson and helps the students make a bridge to the next lesson
- A "family survey" that provides an opportunity for the student to interact with family members through interviews or conversation centering on the Jewish top
- A home to school communication that allows the parent(s) to give feedback to the teacher
    Each of these is explained more fully below.

Letter To the Family

The letter to the family is an explanation of the homework assignment. It usually includes: (1) a short statement about what is being studied in class, (2) how the family can help with this assignment, and (3) when it is due back to class. The letter is signed and dated by the student. It is important that the student understand the assignment so that he/she can further explain it to his/her family. With students of all grade levels, it is important that a clear and succinct statement is included so that there are no misunderstandings.

Background Information

The background information sheet includes information that will be helpful in completing the assignment. Background facts, data, or special readings to bring the family up to date with the topic are part of this section. If specific materials or supplies are needed, they are listed here. Try to utilize items readily available at home. If it is possible, send home a packet that includes any special supplies that are needed.

The Assignment

The assignment itself should be designed to reinforce the classroom lesson and to help the student make a bridge to the next lesson. It should engage the student and family in thoughtful creative work. This is a perfect time to offer the student an opportunity for higher level thinking — to analyze a text with his/her family, to create a new ritual, to make associations. It is very important to remember is that if there are "correct" answers, these should be made available. This is not the time for guesswork; it is not the time for parents to be teaching something new. It is the time to help parents feel comfortable with their child as they learn together.

The Family Survey

The family survey allows for going "beyond the text." Students have the opportunity to ask questions of family members. They can find out favorite holiday memories or rituals, and begin discussions that will help build Jewish connections. This activity offers time for meaningful Jewish conversation, something that is difficult at first for some families. But once this process begins, it can open the door to a better understanding of each other.

The Home To School Communication

In developing the partnership between the school and the home, it is important to keep the lines of communication open in both directions. This final activity allows parents to give feedback to the teacher. Was the assignment clear? Did the student understand what was going on? Was there enough time to complete the assignment? Are there other comments to add? Questions designed for yes or no responses with space for additional written comments and parental signature provide for the partnership and communication to come full circle.

CONCLUSION

When the five sections described in this chapter are followed, parents will become more deeply involved in their children's Jewish education. The bond with faculty becomes stronger, as both parents and teachers work toward the same goals. See Appendixes A through F for examples of Interactive Homework on a variety of topics for various grade levels.

APPENDIX A
TU B'SHEVAT (GRADES PK-2)

Name _____ Date _____

Dear Family,
We have been learning about Tu B'Shevat, the next holiday on our Jewish calendar. Even though Cleveland has a rather bleak look at this time of year, in Israel the trees are almost ready to bloom. We are learning about the fruits of those trees. Together, let's find out more about these fruits and I will write down what we discover. This assignment is due

_____.

L'shalom, _____
(Child's Signature)

WHAT WE HAVE ALREADY LEARNED IN CLASS:
- Seeds need special nutrients to grow, and they get what they need from earth and water.
- As seeds grow, they become seedlings, then saplings, then trees.
- Fruits and nuts which grow in Israel include: fig, date, orange, etrog, carob, apricot, olive, almond, and pomegranate.

LET'S FIND OUT MORE ABOUT FRUITS THAT GROW IN ISRAEL:
My class was divided into "Israeli fruit groups." I am in the _____ group. Please help me use a resource to find out about my fruit.
- How does it grow?
- What color is it?
- Does it have seeds or pits?
- Can you eat the seeds?
- What is the skin like — soft, hard, smooth, bumpy, hairy?
- What is this fruit used for — juice, canning, fresh, in recipes?
- Draw a picture — or find one — of this fruit

FAMILY SURVEY — FAMILY/PARENT CONNECTIONS
Interview several different members of your family and find out which fruits they like:

Fruit	#1	#2	#3	#4
Fig				
Date				
Orange				
Etrog				
Carob				
Apricot				
Olive				
Almond				
Pomegranate				

How would you prepare the fruit that you learned about? Please share a recipe for this fruit and bring it in for our class recipe book.

HOME-TO-SCHOOL COMMUNICATION

Dear Parent:

Your comments about your child's work in this activity are important. Please write yes or no by each statement:

_____ My child understood the activity and was able to discuss it.
_____ This activity helps me understand what my child is learning.
_____ I/We felt the amount of time suggested for this activity was realistic.

Other comments:

_____

_____

_____

Parent's Signature _____ Date _____

Dear Parent,

I hope you and your child enjoyed looking through resources together to learn about your fruit. Perhaps you have discovered a new and pleasing taste. Did you know that if you put parsley seeds in a styrofoam cup with a little potting soil, you'll have parsley by Pesach? Enjoy!

Name _____ Date _____

Dear Family,

We began learning about Shavuot today. We talked about many things that are associated with this Jewish holiday. Please help me sort through the list on this page, and then let's talk about the questions in the Family Survey section. I will write down our answers. This assignment is due _____.

Sincerely, _____
(Child's Signature)

DEFINITIONS

Shavuot – Means "weeks"; the Festival of Weeks occurs seven weeks after the second day of Pesach. Originally an agricultural festival, Shavuot became the time of *Matan Torah*, the giving of the Torah.

SHAVUOT HOLIDAY WEB

The holiday of Shavuot calls to mind many things. Fill in the spokes of a web with all the items below that are associated with Shavuot (see end of Appendix B for answers). Note: some of the items on the list are associated with other holidays and do not belong on this web. As you decide what belongs on the web, discuss your reasons.

1. Mount Sinai
2. *Matan Torah* (Giving of the Torah)
3. *Shofar*
4. Counting the *Omer*
5. The Book of Ecclesiastes
6. *"Na'aseh V'nishma"* (We will do and we will listen)
7. Wheat
8. The Book of Ruth
9. *Chag HaBikkurim* (Festival of the First Fruits)
10. Dairy foods
11. Hamentaschen
12. *Aseret HaDibrot* (Ten Commandments)
13. *Shalosh Regalim* (the Three Pilgrimage Festivals)
14. *Chanukiah*
15. *Machzor*
16. Flags
17. Flowers and greenery

FAMILY SURVEY — FAMILY/PARENT CONNECTION
Discuss the following questions with your family members. Write out your answers.

Shavuot celebrates the receiving of the Ten Commandments. What would you suggest as an eleventh Commandment?

_____

_____

_____

_____

How do we apply Torah in our lives today?

_____

_____

_____

_____

In the days of the Temple in Jerusalem, the first ripe fruits of the harvest were brought as an offering. What would you do with your offering today?

_____

_____

_____

_____

HOME-TO-SCHOOL COMMUNICATION

Dear Parent;

Your comments about your child's work in this activity are important. Please write yes or no by each statement:

_____ My child understood the activity and was able to discuss it.

_____ This activity helps me understand what my child is learning in Religious School.

_____ I/We felt the amount of time suggested for the activity was appropriate/realistic.

Other comments:

_____

_____

_____

Parent's Signature _____ Date _____

Answers to Shavuot Holiday Web:
1, 2, 4, 6, 7, 8, 9, 10, 12, 13, 17

APPENDIX C
TZEDAKAH (GRADES 5-7)

Name _____ Date _____

Dear Family,

Over the past few weeks, we have been learning about *Tzedakah*. In this week's *parashah*, *VaYakhel* (Exodus 35:5), we read about a *terumah* — a special offering — that is collected from the children of Israel. This activity will enable you to help me learn more about the differences and similarities between *Tzedakah* and *terumah*. We should talk about the questions, and write down our answers. This assignment is due_____.

Sincerely, _____
(Child's Signature)

DEFINITIONS:

Tzedakah – derived from the Hebrew root *tzedek*, meaning "righteous, just"; giving money and physical sustenance to those in need, as prescribed by Jewish law

Terumah – offering, gift, donation; contribution; choice, best part.

Rabbi Moses Maimonides – a great Jewish scholar who wrote many books. His writings help Jews apply the laws and teachings of Torah to the way they live and treat other people.

CLIMBING THE TZEDAKAH LADDER

Rabbi Moses Maimonides explained the different ways people can give *Tzedakah*. See if you can climb up and fill in the missing "steps" of the Tzedakah Ladder of Maimonides. Begin with Step 1. (Answers are found at the end of Appendix C.)

Step 8 – The best way of giving is to

_____

_____

Step 7 – The person who gives doesn't know who will receive, and the person who receives the money, doesn't know who has given it.

Step 6 –

_____

_____

APPENDIX C, CONT.

Step 5 – The person who receives the *Tzedakah* knows who is giving it, but the person who is giving the *Tzedakah* has no knowledge of the person in need.

Step 4 – _____

Step 3 – This person gives money directly to the person in need after being asked.

Step 2 – _____

Step 1 – This person gives *Tzedakah* with a scowl.

FAMILY SURVEY – FAMILY/PARENT CONNECTION

Discuss the following questions with your family member. Write out your answers.

How do we in our family give *Tzedakah* today?

_____

_____

_____

"It's also more than money. . . " In what other ways do we give *Tzedakah*?

_____

_____

_____

Do we give to particular organizations? How do we decide which ones?

_____

_____

_____

HOME-TO-SCHOOL COMMUNICATION

Dear Parent:

Your comments about your child's work in this activity are important. Please write yes or no by each statement:

_____ My child understood the activity and was able to discuss it.
_____ This activity helps me understand what my child is learning in Religious School.
_____ I/We felt the amount of time suggested for the activity was appropriate/realistic.

Other comments:

_____

_____

_____

_____

Parent's Signature: _____ Date _____

Answers to the Tzedakah Ladder of Maimonides:

Step 2 – This person gives directly to the poor person, but gives less than he/she should, even though the *Tzedakah* is given cheerfully.

Step 4 – This person gives directly to the person in need before the person has to ask.

Step 6 – The person who gives knows who will get the money, but the person who receives does not know who gave it.

Step 8 – The best way of giving is to help a person help himself/herself by entering into a partnership or by helping that person find a job.

APPENDIX D
HOLOCAUST STUDY (GRADE 6)

Name _____ Date _____

Dear Family,

While studying the literature of the Holocaust, we studied poetry which was actually "found" — words written on the side of a train car, poems written by people in concentration camps. For this homework piece, we will need to think and talk about what causes a person to create. Then we will write our own verse to add to the poem of our choice. This homework is due back one week from today. To help us, I have brought home the three poems we studied in class.

Thank you, _____
(Student's Signature)

REVIEW OF CLASS LESSON:

In class, we listened to songs created from poems written during the Holocaust. These include: "The Last Butterfly," "Dona Dona," "Birdsong." (The texts of these songs can be found in our class songbooks.)

As a group, we examined the lyrics to each of these songs. This helped us identify aspects of peoples' lives that they might have taken for granted, and that changed for them forever because of the Holocaust. We then discussed the various aspects of our own lives that might have been effected by the changes brought by a Holocaust experience.

We also touched on what causes a person to create — to write poetry, music, or stories, to paint or sculpt, etc. We surmised that the inspiration often comes from an emotional reaction, as opposed to a rational reaction, to an event, a person, a change.

HOMEWORK:

Together, please read the lyrics to all three of the songs. Feel free to include any explanation or observation as part of the discussion.

Select one song on which to focus and, together, explore other angles or aspects that might have been included in the lyrics. What must it have felt like? Have you ever felt this way, but over a different set of circumstances?

On a separate sheet of paper, write another verse for the song you chose.

FAMILY SURVEY – FAMILY/PARENT CONNECTION:

Do you have any relatives or friends who were somehow involved in the events surrounding the Holocaust? Describe.

_____

_____

_____

Has anyone in your family written music, poetry, painted, sculpted, or created in some other fashion? Find out what their inspiration was, or think about what it might have been. You can experience a deeper appreciation of a piece of creation when you discover a hint of the possible inspiration.

_____

_____

_____

HOME-TO-SCHOOL COMMUNICATION:

Your reactions to this homework piece are important. Please write YES or NO in the spaces before each of the following statements:

_____ There was enough time allowed to comfortably complete this homework piece.
_____ Your student was engaged by the activity.
_____ You learned something about what your student has been experiencing in class.

Do you have any comments or suggestions about this kind of family homework activity?

_____

_____

_____

Parent's Signature _____ Date _____

Name _____ Date _____

Dear Family,

In our Torah class, our focus has turned to Commandments and the concept of *Mitzvah* – what is means to be commanded. This homework piece will give us the opportunity to talk about this and what this means to me, as a teenager. Thanks for talking about this with me. This homework is due back on _____.

Shalom, _____
(Student's Signature)

WHAT WE'LL NEED:
• pencil and paper
• "tablet" materials, such as cardboard, fabric, clay, dough

HOMEWORK:
Please discuss and then put on paper the "Ten Commandments for Teenagers." Make your own decisions about stating them in a positive or negative way, and about their order.
After compiling your list, create your own "tablets" to display your commandments.

FAMILY SURVEY:
Using Leviticus 19:1-18, look at other commandments. Discuss their relevancy, timeliness, and applications. Which ones stand out to individual family members? Record their choices and reasons.

Family Member	**Mitzvah**	**Reason**

HOME-TO-SCHOOL COMMUNICATION:

Dear Parent,

Your comments are important. Please write YES or NO by each statement.

_____ There was enough time allowed for this homework piece.
_____ My child was engaged by the activity.
_____ This activity helps me understand what my child is learning.

Other comments:

_____

_____

_____

_____

_____

_____

Parent's Signature _____ Date _____

APPENDIX F
BERESHEET (GRADE 3)

Name _____ Date _____

Dear Family,

The book of Genesis begins with the story of the creation of the world. The understanding of the first story of Genesis — *Beresheet* — is very important to understanding the Jewish view of the world. This homework piece will give us a chance to talk about the story of creation and how we see evidence of God's creation around us. I will need to write things down, and we'll need to go for a walk. Thank you for helping me with this. This homework is due _____.

Shalom, _____
(Student's Signature)

BACKGROUND:
Things we have talked about in class:
- The first story of the book of Genesis introduces us to the understanding in Torah of the relationship between God, man, and the world.
- The story presents our ancestors' attempt to reflect on the concept of God as the Supreme Creator. It also expresses the sense of awe at the variety of God's creation in nature and the species of animals.
- The story introduces us to the role humankind must play as caretakers and nurturers of the world.

THE HOMEWORK ASSIGNMENT:
- God's world is marked by an astonishing variety. Help your child come up with a list of ten things God has created. Have your child tell you what are the three most important creations and why. (Write down all the responses.)
- Discuss together the ways the things your child named are the same, and the ways they are different from each other. (Write down responses again.)

NOW, LET'S GO FOR A WALK:
As a family, take a walk. Bring a bag to collect evidence of God's creation. When you come to school, you will have an opportunity to share your discoveries.

HOME-TO-SCHOOL COMMUNICATION:

Dear Parent,

Your comments about your child's work in this activity are important. Please write YES or NO by each statement:

_____ My child understood the activity and was able to discuss it.
_____ The activity helps me understand what my child is learning.
_____ I/We felt the amount of time suggested for this activity was realistic.

Other comments:

_____

_____

_____

_____

_____

Parent's Signature _____ Date _____

CHAPTER 40

CONNECTING PARENTS TO THE TEEN ISRAEL EXPERIENCE

CONTRIBUTORS: JOAN KAYE and
JAY LEWIS
ADDRESS: BJE
250 East Baker Street, Suite B
Costa Mesa, CA 92626
PHONE: (714) 755-4000
E-MAIL: joankaye@bjeoc.org
jay@bjeoc.org
TARGET: Parents of students going on a
community summer trip to Israel
TIME FRAME: September through the following
November (16 months)

TIES is Orange County's community "Teen Israel Experience." It is a Bureau of Jewish Education program co-sponsored by the Jewish Federation. The group of teens (approximately 60 per year) spends six weeks in Israel touring, hiking, and learning.[1] In addition, they meet locally for both pre-trip and post-trip programs.[2]

The experience that we design for the teens is good, but it is not unique, since many communities and youth movements offer six-week teen Israel trips. What makes our community's experience special is the extensive parent component that is woven throughout the entire process. Traditionally, the only contact during the summer between trip coordinators and parents concerns medical emergencies and discipline issues. As one colleague in

another community puts it, "Once we get the kids on the plane, we try to avoid the parents." Instead, with TIES, we bring the parents into the process before, during, and after the trip, enhancing the experience for the teen as well as the entire family.

GOALS

The goals of the parent component of TIES are:
1. To meet parents' needs

Our main goal in implementing an extensive parent component for TIES is to meet the needs of the parents. Most of the time, so much effort is devoted to the teens' needs that parents' needs are ignored. However, parents of Israel experience participants have their own sets of needs, especially since they go through the experience with their teen every step of the process, short of boarding the plane with them (and most would like to). The needs of parents of Israel experience participants include:
- To feel reassured that their child is safe and well cared for.
- To know more about what their child is experiencing than what is printed in the brochure or on the itinerary.
- To be able to share their emotions (excitement, pride, fear, etc.) with other parents who are going through the same experiences as they are, and who therefore understand what they are feeling.

[1] Young Judaea Israel Programs is the trip provider for TIES and along with the Bureau of Jewish Education, coordinates the six week Israel trip.
[2] There are four teen-only pre-trip sessions held in the spring, including a weekend retreat. These prepare the teens for their Israel trip, as well as for a number of teen-only post-trip, components of TIES. The details of these programs are beyond the scope of this chapter.

- To know that there is someone responsible whom they can trust and who will be responsive to them

"Caring for the needs of all age groups," as one parent explains, truly allows the teen Israel trip to be taken to a higher level. Not doing so misses an incredible opportunity.

2. To strengthen the Jewish identity of the entire family, as well as the family's ties to the Jewish community.

Educators and communal leaders need to see the teen Israel trip as a great opportunity for strengthening the teen's Jewish identity, as well as that of the parents. Sending a teen to Israel can impact the entire family. The desire to know more about what their teen is experiencing and to share in their child's adventure opens the way to include and educate the parents. As a result of the TIES parent component, the teen Israel trip becomes an important experience for the parents. Families feel much stronger ties to each other, to the local Jewish community through their involvement with the sponsoring organizations, and to Israel due to what they learn and experience through their children.

3. To enhance the teens' experience.

As with any educational experience, the teen trip to Israel is greatly enhanced by parent involvement. If a first grader learns to light Shabbat candles at the synagogue school, but the parents don't know how or don't care to light candles at home, the educational impact is minimized. The same holds true for teens traveling to Israel. For example, if upon returning home, a teen merely shows his pictures from Israel to his parents while his parents show him their pictures from their summer Hawaiian vacation, and then the family moves on as if nothing has changed in their lives, the impact of the teen's experience is lessened. On the other hand, if the attitude about Israel and involvement in the Jewish community is reinforced by the parents because their own connection has been strengthened and their knowledge about Israel has increased, the impact for the teen is that much greater. Parents are ready to ask higher level ques-

tions when their teens return and when they look through pictures together. The parent, as the child's primary educator, is given the tools to help extend the Israel experience beyond the six weeks in Israel.

PROGRAM DESCRIPTION

Pre-trip

Following are the elements of the parent program: pre-trip experiences, during the trip, and post-trip. Two events take place with parents before the trip: a Parent/Teen Orientation in March and a Family L'hitraot Picnic in June, one week before teens depart.

Our first contact with the parents as part of TIES, once the recruiting and registration processes are complete, is the Parent/Teen Orientation. The main goal of this gathering is to address family fears and concerns about the trip. Topics covered range from safety and security, to what to pack, to "will my child make friends?" The first meeting of the teens occurs a couple of weeks prior to the Parent/ Teen Orientation. At this session, we spend a great deal of time on mixers and ice-breakers. This ensures that when the families enter the Parent/ Teen Orientation, the teens have already met and gotten to know each other. They seek out their new friends, thus reassuring the parents that their teens are connecting with others going on the trip.

The Orientation begins with mixers and ice-breakers for both the teens and the parents. This is an important first step toward building a community of these families, who will be sharing this common experience in the following months. However, we quickly move to dealing with safety and security issues, the main topics of the evening. Extra care is given to detail the step-by-step procedures taken to ensure the teens' health and safety. Parents and teens are encouraged to ask any and all questions about the experience. It takes a huge amount of trust for a parent to send his or her child to the Middle East for six weeks. By covering these details thoroughly very early in the process, not only do we save ourselves from answering these questions individually for each family, but we also demonstrate to the parents that the teens' safety is our top priority.

Only after we address their concerns over security are the parents open to getting to know each other, and to learn more about Israel themselves. A simple, enjoyable get-to-know-you activity at the beginning allows the parents to introduce themselves to each other and to begin to talk about the trip in a very non-threatening way.

Following three more spring sessions with just the teens, the parents come together again as a group one week before the trip leaves for the Family L'hitraot Picnic. The first hour of the potluck picnic is left unstructured to allow parents the opportunity to share their anticipation with each other as well as to commiserate over the stresses of shopping and packing. A wonderful sense of excitement fills the air. We then bring everyone together for the climax of our pre-trip experience. After a short welcome, the custom of placing prayers in the *Kotel* is taught. Parents and other family members write prayers to send with their teen. Then, after explaining the custom of sending *Tzedakah* with someone traveling to Israel, we pass out envelopes for families to use. Finally, we teach *Tefilat HaDerech*. Each parent turns to face his or her teen, and sings the blessing together to Debbie Friedman's beautiful melody. There is not a dry eye as each parent blesses his or her own child before their journey. Many parents comment that they do not realize the emotional impact of their teen traveling to Israel until this very moment. At the end of the picnic, not only do the teens hug good-bye and say, "I'll see you at the airport," but many parents do as well.

During the Trip

While the teens are in Israel, here is how we stay in touch with parents:

- TIES Hotline (throughout the trip)
- Videos and pictures of the teens in Israel (throughout the trip)
- Two Parent Sessions, one in late June/early July — within the first week after the teens depart, and one in late July/early August — within a week of the teens returning home

To facilitate communication with the parents during the summer, we transform a voice mail box at the BJE into the "TIES Hotline." Parents can call 24 hours a day to listen to a recorded message, updated daily, of what is happening on the trip. The Hotline truly helps parents who want to know what their teens are doing thousands of miles away from them. It takes us only two minutes a day to update the message that parents refer to as "wonderful," "terrific," and a "godsend." The Hotline is called hundreds of times during the summer, and many parents go so far as to call it while on vacation. We have even received calls from as far away as Europe and Hawaii!

The daily updates also serve to assure parents that we monitor the group in Israel very closely. One parent wrote in her evaluation, "The most important part for me is that as a parent I felt very much at ease, always informed, and comfortable that my son was in good hands." In addition, parents can see even more first-hand what is happening on the trip thanks to videos (we send a camera with the group) and still pictures the group sends back during the course of the summer. Parents simply have to drop a blank video tape off at the BJE and our staff makes copies of the original tapes for them. An overjoyed parent told us, "I felt like I was on the trip with my son!"

In addition to being very accessible to the parents throughout the summer, we convene them twice as a group during the summer. The first time, soon after the group departs, is titled "Where Is My Child and What Is He/She Doing?" We provide the parents with a joint fax from the group to the parents, as well as pictures from the first few days of the trip. Also, we have a video camera set up so that parents can send messages to their teens. "It has been a fabulous experience for us to be so connected with our son while he was away," a parent commented.

For the first 20 minutes of the meeting, parents share what they have heard from their children in Israel. This allows parents to tell their own stories as well as to hear a wide variety of others' stories. This latter is especially important for the parents of teens who have not as yet called home. It also sets a very warm mood for the evening. We then follow with an interactive small group exercise during which the parents examine their own attitudes about Israel, and a map activity that helps them follow the group's itinerary.

The evening concludes with the distribution of a supplement to the itinerary. This includes a great deal of history and background information on places the teens are visiting. Many of the parents use the map and the itinerary supplement to follow the group throughout the summer. Sparked by their child's experiences, as well as their desire to know more about what their child is doing, the parents are open to doing some learning of their own. A parent explained, "Giving us information and the history of each place they visited made us feel that we were also part of the trip."

Then, with one week left in the trip, we bring the parents together again for a session entitled "What Might I Expect When My Teen Returns?" This is our opportunity to discuss the transforming nature of the Israel experience for a teen. Teens go through so much growth and change (physically, emotionally, and spiritually) that it is essential to prepare parents. We are also able to help the parents explore ways to capitalize on their teens' experience and keep the momentum going strong upon their return. These include encouraging participation in TIES post-trip programs, as well as in other Jewish organizations such as youth groups; subscribing to English periodicals about Israel; discussing Israel at home; and supporting teens' changes in religious observance. Parents and teens from previous years share their experiences, with the teens expressing what they want from their parents in the days and weeks after their return home. We stress that each individual teen will have a unique experience of Israel, and that each will come home with a unique set of needs. Many parents have told us that this program is the most helpful piece of the entire parent component of TIES.

Post-Trip

After the trip, we have two events that include parents: Welcome Home Picnic in August/September — within a month after the teens return, and, in November, a Parent Post-Program: "What Has Happened Since the Trip?"

Soon after the teens return, we bring the families together again for a parent-run Welcome Home Picnic. This serves as an opportunity for teens to share stories and pictures from the trip with each other, and for parents to continue the connection with friends they have made throughout the experience. As a parallel to the Family L'hitraot Picnic, it also provides a sense of closure to the summer experience. Then, later in the fall, we convene the parents again for a program entitled, "What Has Happened Since the Trip?" We discuss how the teens and families have changed as a result of the experience, and how they can best capitalize on the momentum that has been created as a result of their participation in TIES.

EVALUATION

Just as each TIES participant has unique needs and interests, so it is with each family. Therefore, the program must be able to meet a variety of different needs. For instance, parents who have sent older siblings to Israel on teen trips, or who have been to Israel themselves, generally need less reassurance about safety and security issues than parents for whom an Israel trip is truly an unknown entity. Instead, parents who have been to Israel often desire to know more specifics from the teens' itinerary. Families in which teens have been away before for long periods of time, such as at summer camp, generally do not require the same amount of support as families in which teens have not been away. In addition, some families look to the group of TIES families to be a *hevrah* for them throughout the experience. One single parent told us, "Thank you for providing me a family with whom to share this *simchah* of sending my child to Israel." Some parents even formed a TIES *havurah* as a result of this experience. And there are other parents who have no desire for anything deeper than simply meeting the other families.

In addition, we discovered that the needs of the group of families as a whole differ from year to year, depending on the families involved. The first year of the program, the parents developed very close bonds with each other. They enjoyed spending time with each other. In fact, many of the families took the initiative to get together during and after the summer in addition to the scheduled programs. We assumed that this would be a wonderful byproduct of the program each year. However, in the second year, the group of families did not bond. They still enjoyed coming to the scheduled programs, but there was much less of a sense of *ruach*, of this being a group experience for the families. There was little desire to get together outside of what the BJE offered. While we do want to devote more time to group formation with parents in future years, we also understand that not every group of parents will want that sense of a close *hevrah*.

One potential danger of bringing the group of parents together during the summer, especially the first week of the trip, is that a few parents sometimes raise complaints at the public forum, turning the evening into a destructive complaint session. Even with the best of Israel experiences, concerned parents have issues that they will raise. The key is to deal with those issues preemptively and keep individual issues out of the public forum. By carefully structuring parent meetings, we have found great success. For instance, at the first parent session after the teens depart for Israel, we address any issues that we know might be of concern (jet lag, food, homesickness, etc.). Then, we stress that if parents have any other issues, they should speak with us individually. We provide them with note cards on which to write their issues, which can be turned in to us if they choose. Finally, we ask parents to share the most positive things they have heard from their children. This formula keeps the parent sessions focused on the positive and allows us to cover other areas, such as learning about Israel.

FUTURE DIRECTIONS FOR TIES

To enhance the parent component of TIES, we would like to form *havurot* from the group of TIES families. Many families make social bonds with each other as a result of meeting each other at the TIES parent programs. While they all have a teen who has been to Israel in common, many families also discover other similarities and common interests. With staff support, we believe that enough families would be interested to make *havurot* viable. These families have children the same age, the children know each other and are friends from their Israel experience, and the families as a whole have shared a common experience. The sharing of holidays together as a TIES *havurah* could be well received since, as their children become teenagers, many families are struggling to find meaningful new ways to celebrate holidays as a family. Also, since Havdalah in Israel tends to be one of the fondest memories for the teens, families could meet together on a Saturday evening to share a Havdalah ceremony. Afterward, the group of teens and the group of parents and socialize separately.

On a grander scale, we would like to offer an Israel experience for parents of TIES participants. The families' interest in Israel is certainly raised as part of their participation in TIES. Even the families who have been to Israel comment that their itineraries did not include many of the exciting activities included in the teens' trip. Enough parents have expressed interest to make us believe that a parent trip to Israel would be successful. One parent suggested that we call the parent trip PIES: Parent Israel Experience. Offering a trip for the TIES parents every other year would double the pool of potential participants, but still capitalize on the energy of a recent teen trip to Israel and the social connections created among families.

OTHER COMMUNITIES

Even though TIES is a community Israel experience for approximately 60 teens and their families, other communities or synagogues should be able to offer a parent component similar to ours. The main difference is whether or not the teens participate in one single trip like TIES, or in multiple trips. The main variable in the single-trip model is the size of the group. This affects how close a relationship the staff can develop with each family, as well as the bonds formed between the group of parents as a whole. Obviously, with numbers smaller than ours, it is easier for staff members to form relationships with parents. As the number of families involved increases, the demand on staff time increases, making it much more difficult to have close relationships with many families. Also, it will be easier for the parents to get to know other families in a small group. While families will still be able to get to know some other families well in a larger group, they certainly will not be able to get to know a majority of the families in the same way they can in a smaller group.

Communities or synagogues that send teens to Israel on multiple trips should still be able to offer a successful parent component. All of the parent programs that we offer in TIES can be adapted for families of teens going on a variety of trips to Israel. Even though the teens and their families are not participating in the same trip, they are still sharing very similar experiences. All of the parents have the same need for comfort and reassurance about safety and security, a desire for a social network with other parents who are going through a similar experience, and a need to know more about their child's experience. Aspects of our parent programs, such as pictures and videos of the teens in Israel, as well as the Hotline, probably do not fit this model, but just about everything else does. In addition to meeting parents with teens in Israel the same summer, Israel trip participant families could be paired with families of teens who participated in previous Israel trips who could serve as resources and mentors.

MOST CHALLENGING ASPECT

The most challenging aspect of the parent component of a teen Israel experience is that it takes an enormous amount of staff time to do it well. The time that is spent planning and running the programs for the parents is very minor compared to the hours and hours spent before and during the summer on the phone with TIES parents answering questions, solving problems, responding to special requests, and responding to parents who need reassurance or simply want to talk. It is important that the parents know that staff is available to them throughout the entire process — from enrollment in the program to the return from Israel.

Generally, conversations with a participant's parents entail more than simple, quick answers. They tend to be fairly lengthy, with parents usually needing to get one thing off their chests or be reassured about another. As the summer approaches, these long conversations become much more frequent. During the trip itself, the time spent talking to TIES parents can become all-encompassing for a staff member, especially one who does not work on TIES full-time. However, the time spent pays off great dividends. It gives the parents a sense of confidence that they have a local person they can trust who is on top of what is happening in Israel and who is accessible throughout the summer. One parent explains, "We loved that you were available all the time and made the parents feel very welcome."

PARTICIPANT FEEDBACK

The best testament to the success of the TIES parent programs is the consistent 90-95% attendance by the parents. We were not surprised that the parents showed up to the Parent/Teen Orientation due to their concerns about their children's' safety and security. What stunned us was the response we got to the programs held for the parents while the teens were in Israel. Not only did parents make it a priority in their lives to attend these sessions, but some families even planned their summer vacations so they would be in town for them. The high attendance tells us that the parents have a thirst for these programs, and they feel that what we offer is of a high enough quality to make it worth their time.

Unlike any other program with which we have ever been associated with, the feedback was 100% positive. Neither in written evaluations, at parent sessions, nor in private conversations between parents and staff has there been any negative comment about the parent component of TIES. Comments from parents included, "I am happy to have been made a part of the whole experience. It has been very positive for our family," and "It was comforting for me not just to put my daughter on a plane and wait for her to return."

CONCLUSION

Based on the positive comments of parents and others, we believe that we were not only successful in meeting the parents' needs, but in exceeding their expectations. One parent beautifully summed up the TIES parent component by saying, "I know you're doing a good job of taking care of our kids, but I want you to know that you are doing a great job of taking care of us, too."

ISRAEL AND JEWISH FAMILY EDUCATION

CONTRIBUTOR: DR. JEFFREY SCHEIN
ADDRESS: Cleveland College of Jewish Studies
26500 Shaker Boulevard
Beachwood, OH 44122
PHONE: (216) 464-4050
E-MAIL: jschein@ccjs.edu

What is the particular promise and challenge of Israel in regard to Family Education? Long acknowledged as a source of inspiration for teens and the development of Jewish leadership, does Israel hold similar potential for our families? Let's check in with Howard Finklestein, a recent returnee from a family trip to Israel. When I asked Howard to share with me what impact he thought the trip had on his family, he answered this way: "The trip gave my family and me a context for everything Jewish. Our discussions about holidays, about Jewish identity, even about God somehow seem more rooted. Perhaps because we explored the roots of the Jewish people together, our own place as part of the Jewish tree has become clearer." This paean to the power of an Israel trip showed how significant the experience was for one individual. Still, such a trip may be a neutral experience at best when shared by those who do not or can not resonate to the rhythms of Jewish life, history, holidays, or culture.

So, a trip to Israel is no panacea; it cannot perform the miracle of *yesh mayayin* (creating something from nothing). Yet, a family that feels Jewish stirrings may well find in an Israel pilgrimage a more dramatic catalyst for Jewish growth and change within the family system than even the most care-fully orchestrated Jewish environments in the Diaspora. In Chapter 41, "Why Is This Trip Different from All Other Trips?" Sally G. Klein-Katz sets a standard for what counts as an excellent family experience while in Israel. Not satisfied with simply "being there in the Holy Land," she explores experiences such as a visit to Masada for their full educational impact. For instance, from a Jewish point of view it might well be *dayenu* to let families experience the drama of the Masada story. But if the Israel-based Family Educator is also concerned about promoting the "family-ness" of the experience, he/she will (as Sally describes) develop a family covenant regarding what in Judaism is worthy of great sacrifice. Further, if the JFE experience is authentically Jewish, it will not reduce martyrdom to its simplest Zionist/national affirmation of "Masada will not fall again." Instead, the full tension between *pekuach nefesh* (saving human life) and resisting national oppression will inform what families decide when they put themselves in the shoes of Eleazar Ben Yair and the martyrs of Masada.

Jewish Family Education means one set of things for Jewish families visiting from the Diaspora. Its import for Israeli families, however, is quite different. In Chapter 42, "Jewish Family Education Israeli-Style," Barbara Levine and Etti Serok describe their experiences in one school in Israel. Since Jewish Family Education is essentially a Diaspora concept, we watch with interest as these Diaspora trained educators seek to transplant Family Education concepts to an Israeli educational context. Here interesting contrasts emerge with Diaspora-based Family Education. The place, for instance, of Family Education within a Jewish community agenda of

"Continuity" and/or of "Jewish Identity" has no parallel in Israel. Israeli families live within a flow of "national" Jewish experiences that provide for a natural, organic Jewish identity. But the challenges of creating partnerships for Jewish education between parents and schools mentioned throughout this volume are certainly challenges for the Frankel School as well. Further, in Israel, Jewish Family Education also has an interesting relationship to matters of religious pluralism and diversity. The Jewish traditions of the various *edot*/communities that are part of the Frankel School all are given voice through opportunities created within the school's Family Education program. Finally, this program uniquely supports families as they develop new Jewish observances and celebrations sheltered from the crossfire of secular/ religious dichotomies in Israel.

Unfortunately, we were unable to discover a Family Education program that brings together North American and Israeli families to explore their common challenge of living in peace, to exchange understandings of the Jewish, Christian, and Islamic traditions, and to embrace and protect the land and environment which we all consider sacred.

CHAPTER 41

WHY IS THIS TRIP DIFFERENT FROM ALL OTHER TRIPS?

CONTRIBUTOR: SALLY G. KLEIN-KATZ
ADDRESS: 12 David St. Marcus Street
Jerusalem, Israel 92233
PHONE: (011) (972) 2-566-4925
E-MAIL: smk-k@netvision.net.il
TARGET: Educators working with families
going to Israel

BACKGROUND

"Mah Nishtanah"? Why should this trip be different from any other trip? The truth is, this trip *is*
different from any other trip. When Jewish people
think about coming on a visit to Israel, they most
often approach it with existential expectations.
Although the expectations are as varied as the
people who come, most often Jews come to Israel
on a kind of pilgrimage, whether it is to connect
with the ancient Jewish past, explore their Jewish
roots, experiment with their spirituality and rituals,
investigate the Jewish State, or for a number of other
reasons. This pilgrim approach influences everything about their experience, from the decision
to take a tour traveling with a group (even with
strangers) for the first time in their lives to their
willingness to experiment with Jewish ritual and
engage in Jewish study (which perhaps they have
not dared to do in their home environment).

I had been directing an ongoing think-tank that
explored the dynamics of the Israel experience on
Jewish families. The partner institutions included
Melitz, the Centers for Jewish-Zionist Education in
Israel, Project Oren, and Ramah in Israel. While
each of us are "trip providers" for various family

groups from the Diaspora, we have in our own
modest way tried to become reflective practitioners
and scholars of the Israel experience for families.
Support had been received for three years from the
Joint Program for Jewish Education of the State of
Israel-Ministry of Education and Culture, the Jewish
Agency for Israel, and the World Zionist Organization. Much of what follows in this chapter emerges
from the collaborative reflection of the think tank.

The caveat that precedes any of this analysis is:
It is common to think of the "Israel Experience" as
a must for Jewish teens. Such programs have been
offered since the early years of the State. A great
deal has been invested in developing, advertising,
and providing their programs. Most recently, the
Birthright Israel program has expanded the age of
participants in these programs to the early 20s, but
they still maintain the young peer group approach.
It is true that many who have been on a teen Israel
trip identify more strongly as adults with Jewish
causes or with the Jewish community (although for
the few teens who go on Israel experiences, the trip
is generally not the only Jewish influence in their
lives). However, it is also true that Jewish youth
returning from Jewish summer camps or Israel trips
may feel isolated or disconnected from the ways in
which Judaism is lived in their family or in the adult
community. This disjunct contributes to a quickly
diminishing impact of the potentially transformative powers of such an experience.

This brings us to our three *Mah Nishtanah*
points: (1) intensity of a family experience in Israel,
(2) potential transformative power of a family Israel
experience, and (3) growing together as a family.

Intensity of a Family Experience in Israel

Imagine a family sharing the most intensive experience of their lives in which everyone is an equally contributing participant (without the spotlight on one child, as in Bar/Bat Mitzvah). For most families, this is the most time they will spend together during the course of a year — and possibly ever, as the children grow older. This intensity creates a kind of "hot house" effect, encouraging a whole variety of interactions if the program is within a Family Education format.

Here are the things that make the trip intensive:
- The amount of time spent together (usually two weeks)
- The full program every day
- The group experience (as opposed to traveling as an individual family)
- The long flight to Israel
- The extensive variety of experiences
- The exotic nature of the experiences: the combinations of ancient and modern, east and west
- The vacation mode which allows people to "throw themselves into it"
- Everyone doing the same things together
- The openness to experiment away from home
- The connecting with our Jewish center — Israel
- The multigenerational interaction and learning
- The Family Education reflective and engaging programming

Other than a retreat or family camp format in their home community, no other Family Education program resembles the intensity of the Israel experience. One connects powerfully not only to one's own family, but to peers and other family units as well. The experience can lose intensity if guided poorly by educators. Or, the power of the experience can ripple beyond the short several weeks spent in Israel.

Potential Transformative Power of a Family Israel Experience

Once again, imagine a family sharing the most intensive experience of their lives and imagine that this experience is a Jewish one! Add to this the potential of what is referred to in the field of Sociology of Tourism as a serious search for authen-

ticity, and the potential transformative power of a Family Israel Experience becomes clear. Israel experiences provide opportunities for bringing both family and Jewish experience into a synergistic whole.

For our purposes, what is also significant is the element of the sharing of this experience as a family. One of the goals of Family Education is for the family to learn and grow together. An Israel experience that is developed with the principles of Family Education as the basis for its programming provides the family with multiple and powerful opportunities to reflect on the nature of their Jewish lives back home. It is also a chance to contemplate cooperatively and to program their next steps. A quote from a participant in a Family Educational Israel experience expresses succinctly what this means. "Seeing Israel through my daughter's eyes *made* this experience for me. Maybe it was the fact that the educational staff invested such incredible energy in both the adults and the kids, bringing the sites alive and making them meaningful simultaneously for all of us. This was no tour of Israel. It was an intense journey of exploration into our family roots. I have no doubt that our family life back home will be deeply affected. This program has helped us confront the issue of why we need to raise our kids Jewishly."

Growing Together as a Family

This third point relates to the side benefits of a family Israel experience. While we make it quite clear in our Staff Development Courses that the role of the Israeli staff is not to be therapists, still the opportunities for family growth on the trip are extensive.

First, because the generations are treated equally on the trip, each family member is empowered to explore his/her ideas openly. Each person's opinion has validity and needs to be considered by their family. The programmed activities and family discussions set out ground rules that allow for the full participation of each member of the family, while also preserving dissenting opinions. Although we recognize that each family has dominant personalities who generally take control of any process, the trip activities are designed to allow all family members to assert their ideas and to establish their sense of place in the family. In the end, we hope that parents, having been exposed to new models of family communication, will begin utilizing these techniques in the ongoing life of the family.

As each family's unique histories and beliefs form part of the content of the program, they are encouraged to explore the interplay between their stories and the master story of the Jewish people. Each day, they are examining other aspects of their values and beliefs, their family histories and identities. They are both the participants and the content, and the learners as well as the teachers. Rare is the opportunity for families to focus so intensely on who they are as Jews and as a family (standards, values, beliefs, lifestyles, etc.).

For all of these reasons, the Family Israel Experience, when it is programmed as a Family Education experience, encourages and supports growing together as a family.

MASADA: AN EXAMPLE OF A FAMILY ISRAEL EXPERIENCE

The best way to explain this process is to share an example of one program. Masada will be used as the example, as it is a powerful site for forming Jewish identification with very problematic Jewish content of its own (suicide is neither a Jewish value, nor something we want to set up as a model!).

It is important to clarify here that programming a visit to a site in Israel is no different from any other educational programming. It does have the advantage of a fabulous setting and very high motivation, but beyond that, the program must be focused in order for anything to be accomplished. As in the planning stages of every educational program about any subject, the planners must determine which of its aspects will be examined and which not. Every site in Israel could be used for various educational purposes. One must first determine what the focus of the content will be, and then stick to the plan. Otherwise, the group will be overloaded with every fact and date and name that is associated with a particular site.

At Masada, we use the context and content of the historical site to help the families make a connection between Jewish history and their own values. Basically, it becomes a values clarification exercise, both in terms of the historical context, as well as their own lifestyles back home. The basic content here is to demonstrate that the Zealots were zealous about their dedication and faith in the Creator, and this included their willingness to make major sacrifices to maintain this ultimate value. They were clear about their values and the sacrifices they were prepared to make because of them.

Goals of the Masada Program

The goals of the Masada program are to have the families:
• relate to a Jewish historic event as part of their own story.
• focus on their relationship with Jerusalem/Israel.
• contemplate their Jewish lifestyle within their specific Diaspora context.
• explore and record the values they collectively cherish.
• discuss and record the sacrifices and practical steps they are ready to make in order to preserve and actualize those values in their post-tour lives back home.

The Program Itself

We open the program on the top of the mountain by having the group tell the story. Everyone in the group regardless of age knows something about the Masada story, including the dramatic conclusion. Having the group tell the story reinforces their confidence in their abilities to recount historical happenings. Furthermore, it ensures that we are all working from the same historical context. Also, it allows the staff to highlight or supplement the significant points that will become essential to the program without using up the limited attention span for frontal speaking. Then we conclude by posing the guiding questions that will determine the group's journey on the mountain: (The parenthetical questions below were asked at four stations after the brief historical discussions at each spot.)
• What were the similarities and differences between the Zealots and the Roman cultures and

peoples? (Does this resemble anything in our own lives today?)

- What were the hopes and dreams of the Zealots for Jerusalem, and how did these contrast with their reality here on Masada? (In what ways does this relate with your own relationship with Jerusalem, living in the Diaspora?)
- What was the faith of the Zealots? (How does it contrast with our own?)
- Asked only at the end: What value(s) do you as a family cherish and what are you willing to sacrifice in order to maintain it (or them)?

Together, the four stations enable us to get at the core of the historical story. At the Western Palace or Bath House, we examine the clash between the culture of the Romans and the Zealots. At the top of the northern palace facing Jerusalem, we focus on the relationship between the Zealots and Jerusalem. At the synagogue, we explore the Zealots' fierce faith in God. And at the top of the Roman ramp, we examine the last evening of the Zealots on Masada, setting up the activities that follow. At each stop we discuss one of the questions above. (Depending on how busy the mountaintop is that day, we might use other site options as well.)

Each stop lasts a maximum of 15 minutes. At each, three activities are programmed. First, the telling of the story of that spot in a way that is interesting and accessible to all ages. The Family Israel Educator engages the group in exploring their responses to the question for that station. The whole group stays together, but when very young children ages four to seven are present, the Family Madrich works with them on the side, involving them in a treasure hunt. When the clue that he/she has planted is found, it serves as the focus of their short discussion, which parallels that of the rest of the group.

Following the dramatic recounting of the last night of the Zealots on Masada (see Josephus's version of Eleazer ben Yair's oration on that night), the group goes to a shady spot. There they are presented with an adapted version of Eleazar Ben Yair's final speech to the Zealot men on the mountain. For a copy of this speech, see *Josephus Complete Works,* translated by William Whiston (A.M. Kregel Publications, 1972, pp. 600-601). Then the participants are asked to break into four groups. These are based on the choice each might have made had he or she been on Masada on that last night: (1) try to escape, (2) surrender to the Romans and become slaves, (3) fight to the last person, or (4) take their own lives and die as free people. Each person in each group discusses and defends why they chose their option. Then each group reports briefly to the whole group as to their considerations and feelings about their chosen stance in a simulated Zealots' last night meeting.

Next, everyone regroups with their own family in order to identify a value they can all agree upon as a cherished family value. Once they have identified it, they are asked to clarify what they need to sacrifice or give up in order to maintain this value in their lives back home. Following this last step, each family is given a parchment paper text which they complete, describing their family value and the price they would willingly pay in order to maintain it in their real lives. (See the Family *Brit* found in Appendix A.)

At this point, the formal program has concluded. The emphasis on their family values is what differentiates this kind of Family Educational programming from more standard family tours. The essence of their experience is neither a detailed historical tour nor a dramatic drawing out of the story. Instead, they are the explorers of the site, they simultaneously examine the historical perspective with their own responses and explore within the context of their own lives the meaning of such a powerful example of cherished values and the price to maintain them. They themselves become the focus of the experience, rather than the history. In terms of educational method, they are partners in the telling and exploring, rather than receivers of information.

Again, a quote from one of the participants demonstrates the potential impact of such a program. "We have gone away before on family vacations, but this was different. We and our kids were involved because of the outstanding educational components. We became a family of Zealots on Masada, pilgrims from Alexandria coming to Jerusalem of the Second Temple, pioneers drying the swamps of Palestine. Never have my kids felt so totally connected to their heritage. I would recommend this experience to any Jewish family that cares about growing together as Jews. It was great."

Some of the participants indicated they planned to frame the parchment commitment page they completed on Masada, and refer to it at home around their Shabbat table as a family.

PROGRAMMATIC PRINCIPLES

It is important to make still another observation about the differences between Family Education programs and standard family tours and missions. Such programs take time. Family Education as an approach to visiting Israel means fewer sites and deeper experiences. It means taking the time for the families to interact with the site and its content. It means that their stories are of equal importance to those told by the guide. This can be challenging, as families do come with their lists of expectations, and often compare their itinerary with that of their friends. The task of the organizing group's leader/educator is to be clear about the benefits and differences of this kind of program.

A check list that I prepared for people developing such programs may be the best way to communicate the *"Mah Nishtanah"* of this kind of programming in Israel (the order does not reflect values or priorities).

- Does it involve the whole family, even though they may not always be doing the same thing at the same time?
- Does it allow for interaction within the family on the theme or content of the program?
- Does it have specifically Jewish content that allows participants to make meaningful connections between what they are experiencing and who they are as Jews?
- Does it allow for different levels of Jewish knowledge/observance/experience, providing for multiple entry points (not just allowing for the spread in ages, but also for the spectrum of Judaic knowledge, background, and interests of the adult participants)?

- Does it allow for building connections between families, leading to some aspect of community?
- Does it place primary responsibility for Jewish development and learning on the family? Does it potentially empower all of the participants to reflect on their roles as actively teaching and learning from each other?
- Does it allow for various family configurations, giving everyone access to finding (or to further strengthening) their active lives as Jews?
- Does it offer structure to support the family in being/doing Jewish, thus allowing further growth?
- Is the learning transferable back to their home environments? Does the program facilitate their considering how this can be done?
- Does the program draw from their resources and knowledge, facilitating their active participation and contributions?
- Is this program uniquely done in Israel (as opposed to in their home community)?

ROLE OF THE ACCOMPANYING FAMILY EDUCATOR

The ideal group leader for such a program is the community Family Educator. Ideally, the Israel program is an integral part of an ongoing Family Education program. At the very least, it should be planned with several pre-trip and follow-up sessions, each conducted by the accompanying staff person.

When the Family Educator participates in the Israel program as a member of the staff, continuity and context result. Continuity and context refer to a holistic view of the program as being part of a continuum within their lives back home. One of the problems of programming for educational experiences abroad is the lack of context within which the participants can continue to reflect, learn, and grow. In essence, each group develops its own codes during the Israel trip. It may be certain key words or names whose connotations are specific to what they shared, or it may also be jokes and stories that are only fully understood by those who were there. When these codes refer to new ways of Jewish thinking, feeling, and acting, then to build on these back in our Diaspora community requires someone who shares the codes and can refer to the shared references and memories.

OTHER ASPECTS OF GROUP FAMILY TRAVEL

There are other aspects of group family travel that are worth noting, although they are beyond the scope of this chapter. The adults need intellectual stimulation so that Family Education does not become a euphemism for parents tagging along while children engage in a pedagogic program. This applies to the Israel programmatic context in a couple of ways. First, each presentation or program needs to include content for the adults, yet be brief and clear so that the younger participants are not lost in the process. Second, some subjects are not appropriate for children (e.g., the political system of Israel and some current hot issues in Israeli society). These can be handled with some evening briefings that are set up for the older members of the group.

The contrasts in family lifestyles on such a trip make for many complications. For example, one family does not allow the children to eat sugar, while another may give the children a soda-candy-ice cream credit card at every kiosk. Other examples are: the degree to which parents protect, ignore, spoil their children, or the tone a parent uses when speaking with his/her child (or that the children use when speaking to parents). At times, there are conflicts within the traveling community. Some of these issues are best raised at a pre-trip briefing, so that families will be aware of the existence of differences and prepare themselves to deal with them.

The challenges to adults (i.e., parents) in this kind of program revolve around issues of authority and autonomy. The parents are the ultimate authority at all times, and the staff needs to be careful to consult with the adults before publicly announcing to the group (i.e., children) options that were not in the original plan. This is not to say that the program is a democratic process (definitely not!).

This means that the staff cannot announce to the whole group: "During free time tonight, there will be an ice cream party in town for any kids who want to come!" without first checking discreetly with the parents and receiving their approval. This has to do with issues of trust and empowerment. The staff needs to earn the trust of the adults (and the youth as well). The various family configurations also need to be provided for in the programming. These include: three-generations, single parents, intermarrieds, blended families, as well as cases in which only part of a family comes to Israel.

The ideal ages of the children for this kind of program, as a general rule, is from six or seven through teenagers. Certainly there have been groups with children of four and a half who have managed. Most often, however, the needs of these young children (slower pace, playground time, naps, etc.) have pulled one of the parents from part of a day's program or have even caused a parent to withdraw for the entire day. This kind of Family Education programming is not for families with children who are too young to participate in the full program and to join in discussions. On the other hand, 15 to 17-year-old teenagers who choose to come on this kind of program instead of a teen tour generally seem well suited. The spread of the ages of the youth in a particular group is not important, but teenagers need others around their age with whom to socialize. There are no camp counselors or babysitters at these kinds of programs. Rather, family time is maximized throughout the trip.

EVALUATION

Project Oren and Haifa University did a formal evaluation of the overall program, the results of which were very positive. We also heard very positive responses from some of the families upon their return home. They related how powerful the experience was in terms of its effect on their family life. Some of them changed Bar/Bat Mitzvah celebrations to reflect their new Jewish and family perspectives.

CONCLUSION

The major *"Mah Nishtanah"* of a Family Educational Israel Experience is its potential to transform the Jewish lives of participants in the program. The extraordinary and intensive experience of a family sharing a kind of pilgrimage to Israel can help to overcome the documented lessening of the impact six months after their return home. When families share in a serious search for Jewish roots and connections with an openness to experimentation, they are exploring the essence of who they are as a part of a people, as Jews, and as a family. Family trips to Israel provide multiple and powerful opportunities to reflect on the nature of their Jewish lives back home and, as a family, to contemplate together and program their next steps. Ultimately, this Israel experience becomes the next chapter in each participants' Jewish story, and the beginning of yet another chapter when participants return home.

For further information on family Israel trips, consult *The Ma Nishtana of Family Education Israel Trips,* edited by Sally G. Klein-Katz, co-edited by Roberta Bell-Kligler (Jerusalem, Israel: Melitz, 2000), or access info@melitz.org.il.

APPENDIX A
FAMILY BRIT

We, the _____ family, stand together on the mountain fortress of Masada on this day, _____(fill in date and Hebrew date)_____.

We learned today about the choice the Zealots made, to take their lives rather than fall into the hands of the Romans and live as slaves.

As a family, we cherish important values in our lives. For us, one of the most important values that we hold dear is _____.
We commit ourselves today to take concrete actions to maintain and preserve this sacred value. In order to make this value a regular part of our lives, we pledge to ourselves to:

_____

_____

_____

WE WILL NEVER FORGET THE PEOPLE OF MASADA!
WE WILL NEVER FORGET THE POWER OF OUR JEWISH PAST!
WE WILL NEVER FORSAKE OUR OWN FAMILY IDEALS AND DREAMS!

Signed by: _____

_____

_____

_____

_____

CHAPTER 42

JEWISH FAMILY EDUCATION ISRAELI-STYLE

CONTRIBUTORS: BARBARA LEVIN and ETTI SEROK

ADDRESS: 20 Etzel Street
Jerusalem, Israel
PHONE: (011) (972) 2-581-6955
E-MAIL: eserok@netvision.net.il
TARGET: The families of the Frankel
Elementary school (TALI) in
Jersualem, and schools and families
throughout Israel
TIME FRAME: Yearlong

RATIONALE AND DESCRIPTION

Family Education is critical if we are to enhance formal classroom education and make it pertinent to Jewish family life. By bringing the rich variety of family backgrounds, personal stories, hopes and aspirations into the ongoing Jewish story, we empower parents to regain their role as prime Jewish educators. Parents and children find themselves active players in this process.

Ve'Shinantam Le'Vanecha, the first and only center for Jewish Family Education in Israel, was developed in association with the Tali Frankel School in Jerusalem. The Center is a model for including families as authentic educational partners of the teaching of Jewish values, holidays, and life cycle events. Through their involvement, families are exposed to the wealth and diversity of various Jewish experiences. This promotes pluralism, sensitivity, and openness to others. It legitimizes different approaches to Jewish practice and Jewish and universal thinking. Further, it strengthens Jewish identity, creating a keen sense of belonging for all forms of families (secular, single parent, etc.).

BACKGROUND

The Frankel School was established in Israel in 1976, the first TALI school that was a result of parents' initiative. TALI is the Hebrew acronym for *Tigbur Limuday Yahadut* (Enrichment of Jewish Studies).

The TALI school system offers within the conventional school system a curriculum that presents a modern, liberal, non-compulsory approach to Jewish studies, along with Jewish practice (prayers and rituals). It is a blend of Judaism, Zionism, and modernity which preserves tradition while accepting a more liberal theology in keeping with the modern world. The school was conceived by parents who were either North American Conservative Jewish immigrants or native Israelis. The founding families were seeking a school that would reflect their ideology and encourage the same types of values and practices which they tried to provide for their children at home. Their experience proved that as a group of families, they could make a valid contribution to the school's curriculum and to the community's activities. That notion served as the basic concept behind the initiative to introduce a whole new field in Israel and to establish the Center for Jewish Education in the Family within the framework of public school. A new concept of parental involvement furthered the relationship between school and home, and helped to make the phrase "partnership" something more than an educational cliché. The school serves as a model for the entire school system in educational programming and in Jewish Family Education.

The Ministry of Education appointed Ve'Shinantam Le'Vanecha as the national training center for Family Educators. Schools in Tel Aviv, Jerusalem, and in the Galilee, as well as in Hadassah's youth villages, have benefited from the Center's workshops, consultations, and training. International delegations participated in training sessions, during which they learned how to use programs and materials developed by the Center.

GOALS

The Ve'Shinantem Le'Vanecha Center seeks to meet the challenges of Jewish education in Israel through its novel approach to Family Education. This approach is designed to engender interest among Jewish Israeli parents both to create more Jewish awareness and to enable schools to transmit pluralistic Jewish values more effectively.

The particular goals of the Center are:

- To strengthen Jewish identity and the sense of belonging to the Jewish people both historically and culturally by making the leap from the personal family story to the master story of the Jewish people.
- To enrich the school curriculum by using the culture, traditions, and values of the school's families as resources for learning.
- To create annual activities in which personal family stories — individual "spiritual journeys" of different ethnic and cultural backgrounds — can be documented and shared among families.
- To include in the curricular materials produced at the Frankel Center the varying cultural and religious values and practices of its families.
- To create family clusters or *havurot* that will function as mini-communities.
- To provide materials, workshops, and programs that have been tested by the Center to various educators and schools around the country.

THE CENTER'S PROGRAMS

Below are three examples of the Center's work, two brief, and one more comprehensive.

Ongoing Communication

During the year, communication with the families is done through letters, the weekly school newsletter, and questionnaires, which are prepared when input from the families is needed. Enrichment materials related to holidays, Shabbat, and Jewish issues are sent home periodically. Surprisingly, the responses to the questionnaires are very large in number. Phone calls are made by members of the steering committee and the class committee. The school staff is fully involved in the planning, as well as in the implementation of the various programs. Communication with parents for class projects is conducted through the homeroom teachers. Programs are initiated and planned according to the school calendar and according to the class curriculum. A teacher might, for instance, develop a unit around family communications as the class studies the Genesis narratives of the Patriarchs and Matriarchs.

Havurot

The Center initiated *Havurot* — a few clusters of families that joined together around a common interest and program. The families also share Jewish experiences, such as the Family Book Club and a hiking club with family history as the emphasis. In the former, families read the same book with their children and then participate in a monthly group discussion. Sometimes the author is present. In the latter, families meet monthly to join a Shabbat walking trip or a weekday hiking trip reached by bus. All their trips are history-oriented. Every program incorporates an element of Jewish celebration and ritual, e.g., a Shabbat *Shalosh Se'udot* and a Havdalah service, holiday learning, or discussion.

In light of the success of the *Havurot*, two additional groups were developed. "The Big Screen" brings parents and children together to view films on family related topics, followed by group discussion. "The Jewish Cooking Havurah" shares Jewish food rituals, recipes, and traditions.

Haggadah for Yom HaAtzma'ut

The Yom HaAtzma'ut *Haggadah* is the result of the initiative and work of parents, teachers and students, members of the steering committee of the Ve'Shinantam Le'Vanecha Center. The *Haggadah* exemplifies the Center's goal for a deeper and richer identification of the child with the concept of Zionism and for an understanding of the historical cultural forces that shaped the rebirth of the Jewish People in its Land.

The Yom HaAtzma'ut *Seder*, which borrows its form from the traditional Passover *Seder*, suggests that this important occasion of the rebirth of a Jewish homeland be commemorated by conducting a family, school, or community celebration. Various educational methods and activities have been combined, in the hope of triggering the participants' curiosity. The central focus of the Passover *Seder* is the telling of our ancestors' experience of leaving servitude to become a free nation. This pattern is mirrored in the Yom HaAtzma'ut *Seder* as we celebrate this day by relating the Zionist story of gathering the exiles to create an independent nation with its own land, language, flag, anthem, government, army, tradition, and culture.

Through the Yom HaAtzma'ut *Seder*, we accept the obligation to broaden our knowledge of our heritage, and to pass on to the next generation the Zionist legacy of the miracle of our national rebirth. Our goal is to emphasize the present relevance of past events and to build a bridge between the history of the individual or the family and our common story.

The Yom HaAtzma'ut *Seder* attempts to elicit a family's connection to Israel and Zionism, to link it to the continuity of the Jewish people, and to bring that connection forward into the next generation.

The *Haggadah* includes a guide for the *Seder's* instructor that details the preparation process for the student, the class, the family, or the entire community. This process includes:

- Decisions about the scope of the program and the time that will be devoted to it
- Instructions on how to form a steering committee that includes educators, parents, and students to oversee the event
- The "Israeli suitcase" is designed as a visual aid for presenting Judaica and those personal souvenirs with historical and emotional value brought by the participants.

- The Family's "Israel Memory Expedition," a questionnaire, is a means of collecting personal and family stories for the *Seder*, and provides a unique opportunity for discussion. Sent to all participants, it includes questions such as: Who visited Israel? When? Where? etc.
- During the *Seder*, one or more family members tells of their Israel experiences. These personal stories can be fascinating and generally have a strong and positive impact.
- A description of how to make a big, impressive exhibit called "Our Israel Experience," to be displayed where the *Seder* takes place. In addition to the family stories and their connection to Israel, the exhibit also showcases locations visited and/or relatives' hometowns.
- To emphasize the most important Zionist document, we reenact the establishment of the State of Israel by composing a "Community Declaration of Independence," which all the participants sign
- Like the Passover plate, the Zionist *Seder* plate includes a number of symbols central to Israel and Zionism (e.g., an olive branch, hummus, dates, and oranges). Each family designs and decorates a Zionist *Seder* plate on a blank plate placed at the end of the *Haggadah*.
- Yom HaAtzma'ut is always preceded by Yom HaZikaron, a day of mourning for those who fell in military service to Israel. Therefore, we begin the *Seder* with a short memorial ceremony. The following ceremonial objects are placed where all can see them: a black tablecloth, memorial candles, the word *"Yizkor,"* an album with pictures of IDF soldiers, the poem "On a Silver Tray" by Israeli author Nathan Alterman, and red flowers.

Preparing the Seder Table

There should be one central table with everyone seated around it as on Passover, with separate tables for one or more families. In the case of many participants, it is possible to set one central table with all of the *Seder* objects. The leader raises one cup to include everyone. Every participant, or at least every family, should have a *Haggadah*. Students may create table decorations and design the menu and name tags. On every table, place an Israeli flag and two holiday candles.

Songs

It would be best to teach the songs in advance. Singing together adds to the festive atmosphere of the experience. Copies of both the cassette and the actual Yom HaAtzma'ut *Haggadah* can be obtained from the Frankel Center in Israel and from the JNF-KKL U.S. office, 42 East 69th St., New York, NY 10021, (212) 879-9300, fax: (212) 879-3980.

Israel Blessing Box

On a special box decorated with the *Menorah*, the Western Wall, or a *Magen David*, the participants write their own blessing or good wishes for the State of Israel. Decorations hang on the wall: a map of Israel, an Israeli flag, children's paintings, an Israel photograph exhibition, an Israeli poster. Israeli songs play in the background. After the *Seder*, Israeli folk dances can be organized.

EVALUATION

The Center benefits from the professional consultation of highly esteemed scholars, including Professor H.J. Leichter of Teachers College, Columbia University, and Professor J. Lukinsky of the Jewish Theological Seminary in New York.

Informal evaluations include written evaluations by participants following every program, which are reviewed by the Center's Steering Committee. Words used to describe the program included "great," "fabulous," "wonderful," and "impacting." Other recent comments: "Thank you for giving us exciting new tools and insights for involving and empowering our families." "[Participants] took away both philosophical concepts and practical advice."

CONCLUSION

Ve'Shinantam Le'Vanecha continues to catalyze new learning about Jewish Family Education within the Frankel School and throughout Israel. This is done through a *"nusach Israeli"* — goals and methodology uniquely suited to the Jewish and educational needs of Israeli families committed to Jewish peoplehood and pluralism.

Concepts were adapted from guidelines developed at the School for the Study of the Family as Educator at Teachers College, Columbia University.

The Center responds to the pressing needs and challenges of the field by developing ongoing creative and innovative programs and materials. Professionals with further interest are warmly welcome to contact The Frankel Center for Jewish Family Education.

INTERGENERATIONAL JEWISH EDUCATION

CONTRIBUTOR: DR. JEFFREY SCHEIN
ADDRESS: Cleveland College of Jewish Studies
26500 Shaker Boulevard
Beachwood, OH 44122
PHONE: (216) 464-4050
E-MAIL: jschein@ccjs.edu

In recent years, there has been an explosion of new dimensions of Jewish Family Education. Accordingly, Family Educators have become much more aware of how broad a rubric JFE actually is. Many different understandings of the nature of the Jewish family, the functioning of Judaism in our lives, and the dynamics of family life parade under this broad banner. Vicky Kelman is particularly helpful when she reminds us that Jewish Family Education can be *Jewish* Family Education, Jewish *Family* Education, or Jewish Family *Education*, depending on a complex web of assumptions that undergird our practice of JFE.

A live, but often unexplored, issue in the field is the relationship between JFE and intergenerational religious education. JFE most often nurtures the unique relationship between members of a family system (as in grade level programs with parent[s] and the child in that grade), while intergenerational religious education tends to define the family as the *"ganze Mishpoche,"* and welcomes grandparents, other siblings, and extended family into the programming mix.

Jewish Family Education is often linked to a sociological analysis of the nuclear family as the center of Jewish life. Such analysis points out the frayed fabric of the nuclear family. Advocates of intergenerational religious education, however, often argue that the nuclear family may be stronger now than it ever was. Indeed, the argument runs, it is not the nuclear family that needs to be recreated for Jewish learning and living to thrive, but rather the extended family and supportive community. (See Arnold Dashefsky's analysis of this in *Families and Religions: Conflict and Change in Modern Society* by William V. Dantonio and Joan Aldous, Sage Publications, n.d.).

While there are strengths in each approach, my own personal understanding is that there is greater Jewish promise in making intergenerational religious education the organizing frame for our work with Jewish families. One individual who has explicated this framework quite extensively is the Christian educator James W. White in *Intergenerational Religious Education: Models, Theory, and Prescription for Interage Life and Learning in the Faith Community* (Religious Education Press, 1988). In this volume, White defines and analyzes intergenerational religious education (IGRE) from a number of different perspectives. The volume includes an analysis and a critique of "ageism" in contemporary society. It also includes (in Chapter 8) a discussion of what the author calls a "Total Parish Paradigm." In this chapter, what he has laid out programmatically in the first seven chapters becomes the living vision of a religious institution, operative not only in programs, but in its structures, values, and decision making processes.

For the Family Educator, White's most valuable contribution (which is also the focus of this section of *Growing Together*) is his description of the four phases of an effective IGRE program. These are:

- All-inclusive, in-common community building activities
- Parallel learning for each of the multiple generations involved
- Creating together
- Sharing life cycle experiences

Here, in Part XI of this volume, you will find several examples of intergenerational programs based on the White model.

Chapter 43, "Teaching the Ketubah: An Intergenerational Event" by Tziporah Altman-Shafer, is an example of an intergenerational program that is focused on the White model. Chapter 44, "Council of Sages: The Aytzah Program" by Lynn Liebling, features a staged conversation between me and the creator of that program, which explicates how a program developed for one generation (senior "sages") might create a richer intergenerational weave for the entire congregation. In Chapter 45, "Tashlich for All Ages," I show how the ritual of *Tashlich* can be adapted to the rhythms of an intergenerational event. In Chapter 46, "Chaverim BaTelefon," Elissa Kaplan demonstrates how strong links are established between fourth grade students learning Hebrew and their non-familial senior tutors.

CHAPTER 43

TEACHING THE KETUBAH: AN INTERGENERATIONAL EVENT

CONTRIBUTOR: TZIPORAH ALTMAN-SHAFER
ADDRESS: 632 E. Orangewood Avenue
Phoenix, AZ 85020
PHONE: (602) 674-9462
E-MAIL: tziporaha@aol.com
TARGET: Fourth-Sixth Grade, Middle-aged
Adults, Senior Citizens
TIME FRAME: 3 hours

INTRODUCTION

This program was created for a class on intergenerational education as a part of the Cleveland Fellows Program. We were asked to use the model of William White in designing an intergenerational program on a Jewish topic. In choosing a theme, I recognized that oftentimes children know little about Jewish weddings. I also thought that adults would enjoy talking about their *Ketubot*.

The program utilizes a flexible lesson that could take place in any number of educational settings. It is a stand-alone, one-time program, but it could be incorporated into a unit on life cycles. Although the program has never been conducted in its entirety, parts of it have been used by me and by other educators in Cleveland.

DESCRIPTION OF THE PROGRAM

This program provides an opportunity for children in fourth through sixth grades, middle-aged adults, and senior citizens to explore together the meaning of Jewish marriage through an examina-tion of the *Ketubah*, the Jewish marriage contract. The learning process is thereby enhanced as different ages are provided with different ways of looking at the same issues. For people with little background about Jewish weddings, the introduction to the *Ketubah* will also teach them about the central values emphasized in Jewish marriage. For those with greater background knowledge, the program will provide the opportunity for them to deepen their understanding of *Ketubah* and Jewish marriage.

The children will grow from this intergenerational experience for several reasons. First of all, developing a relationship with adults other than their parents in a learning environment provides them with role models they might not otherwise have discovered. Although children often come in contact with adults of different ages in their daily lives, when they are placed in a setting in which they come together as equals for the purpose of learning, their relationship will be significantly different. Given enough opportunities to study together, this new type of relationship provides the opportunity for friendships to develop.

Second, the children will have the chance to learn from the experiences of people older and wiser. Since children have not experienced the life cycle of marriage, they can learn something from the anecdotes of the adults participating in the educational program. Although they may have heard stories about marriage from their parents or grandparents, hearing such stories in this setting may be more profound. The children are less likely to disregard the stories as just more boring droning by relatives, and therefore will learn something from their elders.

Finally, the children will benefit from this intergenerational program because it provides an alternative to their regular classroom setting. This change, in and of itself, makes the activity more interesting to them. In this setting, the children may also develop friendships with children other than classmates, as the program does not separate children according to their ages.

The middle-aged adults in this program also derive special benefits from their participation. Because adults in this stage of life often neglect their own education because they are so busy taking care of others, this program provides them with the opportunity to learn from and to teach others through a sharing of experiences. Finally, the interaction with different generations provides insight into how different age groups see the world. Such insight may allow for better understanding of themselves, their children, and their parents. Adults may also discover they have developed new friendships during the learning process.

Senior citizens in this program also benefit from the interaction with other generations. It is well known that spending time with younger people often revitalizes the elderly. Not only does the experience bring back memories about the past, but it also reminds the seniors of their community's future. Listening to the idealistic attitudes of children can be inspiring to seniors who remember all too well the challenges of earlier times. Such an intergenerational educational program also allows the seniors to share their experiences with others. This process of sharing not only teaches the younger generation, but also fulfills the need for seniors to remember and to be remembered. Finally, seniors benefit from the opportunity to make new friends through interactions that might never take place without this type of intergenerational program.

THE LESSON PLAN

Following is an outline of the intergenerational lesson.

Introduction: Discussion/Lecture
(Whole group together, 25 minutes)
Ask participants:

- What is a contract?
- What does it mean to be married?
- Why do people getting married need a contract?

After eliciting responses from people of different ages, explain that a *Ketubah* is a Jewish wedding contract. Tell them that the history of the *Ketubah* goes back to the first century C.E. Explain that the *Ketubah* was originally intended to protect women in case of divorce. If a woman had a *Ketubah*, her husband had to support her if he left. She was also guaranteed a certain sum of money if he died. Explain that, at the time, this tradition was very progressive, because women in other cultures were not so protected. Tell them that the *Ketubah* was written in Aramaic, the language of Jewish legal codes, and that it became the property of the bride after the wedding ceremony.

Next, ask: How do you think *Ketubot* have changed over time? Tell the group about egalitarian *Ketubot*. Tell them that today many *Ketubot* are written not in Armaic, but in Hebrew and English (or the vernacular of the country in which it is written).

Parallel Learning Experiences: Introduction to the Ketubah
(Small groups of 5-10 people each and a facilitator, 35 minutes)

Kids

Brainstorm about what responsibilities husbands have to their wives and wives to their husbands. Hand out worksheets introducing the group to the key promises which the bride and groom make in the *Ketubah*. Discuss similarities and differences between the list they made and the one on the handout. Ask if they would add any responsibilities from their list to the K*etubah*.

Middle-Aged Adults

Hand out the English texts from five sample *Ketubot* that represent different traditions and styles (see *The New Jewish Wedding*, by Anita Diamant, Schocken, 1991).
- Ask the group to describe similarities and differences between the texts.
- Ask which ones they like and which ones they don't, and why.

- Discuss how the content of the *Ketubah* reflects or does not reflect their personal experiences with marriage.

Senior Adults

Hand out copies of a traditional and an egalitarian *Ketubah*. Discuss how *Ketubot* have changed, and how this change mirrors the changes they have witnessed in society at large during their lives. Two valuable resources are *Mazel Tov: Illuminated Jewish Marriage Contracts* (from the Israel Museum Collection, Shalom Sabat, Jerusalem), and *The Ketuba* by David Davidovitch (Tel Aviv, 1968).

Collaborative Experience
(10 minutes in small groups)

Form small groups of five to ten people of all ages. Have each group share briefly with each other what they learned during the parallel learning experience.

Whole Group Experience
(15 minutes)

Show a few slides or overhead projections from various volumes which depict the artistic nature of *ketuvot*. Discuss the importance of *Hiddur Mitzvah* — the obligation to beautify ritual commandments. Ask participants for other examples of *Hiddur Mitzvah*.

Collaborative Project
(One hour, small groups)

Form small groups of ten people each, with mixed age groups in each. Each group will create a *ketubah*. They can use any text they wish, making alterations if they so choose, or they can write an original text. They might also decorate the *Ketubah*. Provide pictures of *Ketubot* to help in this process.

Interactive Sharing
(25 minutes)

Form groups of three to five people, with each age group represented in each group. Have the adults (who have been invited to bring their *Ketubot*) show them to the group. Allow the discussion to expand to people's individual experiences with

Jewish weddings, their own, or others. Give them the opportunity to ask one another questions.

Whole Group Experience
(10 minutes)

During the earlier sharing time, facilitators hang the finished *Ketubot* on the walls. As a concluding experience, have people walk around the room and look at each group's *Ketubah*.

EVALUATION

Since this program was never comprehensively conducted, there is no evaluation to share. I would certainly suggest that participants be given evaluation forms at the end of the morning. You might consider offering a prize as an incentive to return the evaluation, or someone could stand at the door to collect the forms as participants leave. Feedback from people who utilize this program would be welcome.

CONCLUSION

William White's model (see Introduction to Part XI) was an immense help in the design of this program, as it gave me the tools to envision a program that addressed the need to create different types of learning experiences. This program differed from the White model in that three whole group experiences are included (at the beginning, middle, and end) instead of just one. The program is arranged in this way so that a sense of community develops. The whole group experiences allow the program to flow better, because the group is together for the introduction to the program, their experiences are integrated in the middle of the program, and there is closure at the end. Finally, an extra contributive piece is added in order to give the different generations the opportunity to interact with each other in multiple contexts

Although this program was originally developed as an assignment for a Family Education class, I have used various components of it in different settings.

CHAPTER 44

COUNCIL OF SAGES: THE AYTZAH PROGRAM

CONTRIBUTOR: LYNN LIEBLING
ADDRESS: Temple Emanu El
2200 South Green Road
Cleveland, OH 44121
PHONE: (216) 381-6600
E-MAIL: lliebling@aol.com
TARGET: Senior citizens
TIME FRAME: 8 1½ hour weekly or biweekly
sessions (except for *Shabbaton*
(Session 2) and Shabbat Service
(Session 8)

INTRODUCTION

The Council of Sages (Aytzah group) engages elders in the congregation in a special program of study, group discussion, and personal exploration. The program is open to members who are at least 60 years of age. According to the Mishnah, 60 is the age of maturity and wisdom, when life's experiences are worthy of being shared with others and one is truly ready to become a sage. As noted in a recent book on the process of spiritual eldering, "... an elder is a person who deserves respect and honor and whose work it is to synthesize wisdom from life-long experience and formulate this into a legacy for future generations" (from *Age-ing to Sage-ing* by Zalman Schacter-Shalomi and Ronald S. Miller).

Begun as a program for "sages" (seniors) at Temple Emanu El, Albuquerque, New Mexico, "Aytzah" was originated by Rabbi Paul Citrin, adapted by Rabbi John Spitzer of Canton, Ohio, and has been further modified for Temple Emanu El in Cleveland. (For a more extensive description of

this program, see *A Heart of Wisdom: Making the Jewish Journey from Mid-Life through the Elder Years*, edited by Susan Berrin.)

GOALS

The Council of Sages program has four goals:
• Each participant will embrace the process of becoming a Sage through study, self-examination, and discussions of values.
• Each person will create his/her own ethical will.
• The group will share their experiences with the congregation at a special Shabbat service.
• The Sages will form the core of an active and ongoing group which continues to study and act as a resource for advice and support for the congregation.

DESCRIPTION OF THE PROGRAM

The initial part of the program is a course of eight sessions as follows:
Session 1 – Introduction: Getting to know you and the program
Session 2 – Shabbat retreat: Encountering the book of Kohelet (Ecclesiastes)
    This is a six-hour session on a Saturday which includes a creative Shabbat morning service, lunch, and extended study.
Session 3 – Jewish Ethical Wills
    The group reads and discusses various ethical wills from the medieval period to modern times (see *So That Your Values Live On: Ethical Wills and*

How to Prepare Them, edited by Jack Riemer and Nathaniel Stampfer.

Session 4 – From Age-ing to Sage-ing

Here we engage in a discussion of the challenges and rewards of aging through articles from *The Courage to Grow Old,* edited by Berman, and selections from From *Age-ing to Sage-ing* by Schachter-Shalomi and Miller.

Session 5 – Priming the Pump

This consists of guided discussion and exercises that lead toward the writing of each participant's own ethical will.

Session 6 – Shabbat Dinner and Sharing the Wills

Session 7 – Planning a Creative Shabbat Service

Session 8 – Shabbat Service

Ethical wills are read and *Av/Aym Aytzah* (father or mother of counsel) certificates are presented.

The group continues to meet monthly to study and work on issues that affect the congregation. They have spent a year studying Zionism, and are currently researching the experience of retirement. The goal is to gather resources for members of the congregation approaching this milestone, and to create a retirement ceremony for those who wish to celebrate this transition.

EVALUATION/CONCLUSION

The Sages program has become an important part of the senior adult learning at Temple Emanu El. It appears that, as the Jewish demographers have it, "more" does equal "more" equals "more." Participation in the Sages program has lead to more active involvement for these elders in many other arenas of Temple Emanu El life.

The potential for even greater impact can be seen in these suggested new directions:

• Sages can be invited as special guests to participate in family days when a parent is unavailable.

• Sages can sit down with the seventh graders who run the school's Beit Tzedeck to offer perspective on the ethical dilemmas about which these students need to make decisions.

• Sages can become storytellers and share life experiences related to Jewish holidays, prayers, etc., as these fit into the curricular structure of the school. Sages can share the *bimah* with Confirmands on Shavuot. Their presence and sharing of sections of their ethical wills helps the congregation underscore that the "first fruits of wisdom" (Confirmation) and the ripened fruits of wisdom (Sages) are part of the same continuum of Jewish living and learning.

• Sages can become the added third generation in the student-parent forums for seventh to ninth graders in the exploration of various Jewish issues.

• Sages can be the teachers at various programs falling between Pesach and Shavuot when *Pirke Avot* is studied.

• The Sages are presently planning a "retirement" ceremony during which they will share with the congregation the challenges, joys, and frustrations of this stage of life. The symbolic and real value of this event are both significant. Shared as it is with the congregation, younger adults have an opportunity to look ahead and begin to think (if only subconsciously) about a life stage event that all too frequently takes us by surprise.

BIBLIOGRAPHY

Berrin, Susan, ed. *A Heart of Wisdom: Making the Jewish Journey from Mid-Life through the Elder Years.* Woodstock, VT: Jewish Lights Publishing, 1999.

Riemer, Jack, and Nathaniel Stampfer. *So That Your Values Live On: Ethical Wills and How to Prepare Them.* Woodstock, VT: Jewish Lights Publishing, 1991.

Schachter-Shalomi, Zalman, and Ronald S. Miller. *From Age-ing To Sage-ing.* New York: Warner Books, 1997.

CHAPTER 45

TASHLICH FOR ALL AGES

CONTRIBUTOR: DR. JEFFREY SCHEIN
ADDRESS: Cleveland College of Jewish Studies
26500 Shaker Boulevard
Beachwood, OH 44122
PHONE: (216) 464-4050
E-MAIL: ischein@ccjs.edu
TARGET: Intergenerational Groups – Families

There is power in brevity. There is rich meaning in the telescoped, nonverbal language of Jewish ceremonies. These two features together make Tashlich a ceremony that can be particularly meaningful for Jewish families.

Below you will find the script of the Tashlich ceremony which I have used for many years. I present it in an active voice, much as I would guide any intergenerational group through Tashlich. It reflects both the developmental stages of children and adults and the context of families being part of a larger congregational community.

THE CEREMONY

We begin by singing a *niggun*.

Leader: Gathered by waters, we anticipate a happy ending not only to this day of Rosh HaShanah, but to the string of holy days that extend through Sukkot and Simchat Torah.

We sing *"Shavtem Mayim."* As an optional activity, discuss: Why does our tradition liken Torah to water? Share responses to "Torah is like water because both Torah and water _____.

Leader: We take further note of the special setting in which we have gathered for Tashlich. We sing *"Ehsah Aynei"* (in San Bernardino where mountains are visible) or *"Al Shloshah Devarim"* (in Philadelphia at Valley Green, where the many paths of the Wissahickon can be likened to life's paths/twists and turns).

We now hear readings from our prophets Micah and Ezekiel, both of whom alluded to the healing power of water (and/or selections from Herschel Matt's Tashlich service that appeared in the fall 1985 issue of the *Reconstructionist* magazine). We ask our children to add their voices to the voices of tradition.

We listen to a story about a family walking up to the edge of a stream as they prepare to throw bread into the water: *A Rosh HaShanah Walk* by Carol Levin (Kar-Ben Copies, 1990). Each child reads a paragraph. (Unfortunately, this is out of print. However, it is available in many synagogue and central agency libraries.)

Leader: In a moment, we are going to throw a piece of bread into the water. Each piece of bread stands for an occasion on which we have missed the mark (sinned), a time when we have failed to do a *mitzvah* that we might have done. Holy days are awesome, but they are also optimistic and healing. The message of Judaism on this day of Rosh HaShanah (and Yom Kippur) is that we are (or can become) at our core decent human beings. We can always do *teshuvah*.

So we want to be very sure as we gather here for Tashlich that we don't throw away the very good things about ourselves along with our sins. We're going to take a few moments now and ask parents to share with their children something they love very much about them — something that absolutely should not be thrown away into the stream. Children do the same with their parents. [Participants who are not part of family units can share with one another in the same way, or individuals can be asked to focus on what they most like about themselves.]

Leader: Many of the prayers in our prayer books on Rosh HaShanah are an acrostic — a prayer whose first verse begins with *aleph* and whose last verse begins with *tav*. When we do an acrostic, we have used all our resources of language to praise God or do *teshuvah*. We're going to create an acrostic together of the sins we want to cast into the water. (The *kahal* [community] creates an acrostic together. A might be anarchy, B badness, etc., whatever the group comes up with.)

We now have a prayer our adults will read. At the end of each verse, everyone will call out "Tashlich," and we will all throw a piece of bread into the stream. (Option: If there are ducks around, talk about what it might mean that our symbolic short-comings — the bread — might actually nourish another part of creation.) Please save one large piece of bread for the end.

Leader: Each of is a very unique individual. Having thrown away our collective shortcomings, we each pause for a moment to think about something we, as an individual, would really like to change about ourselves. Think quietly, in this very peaceful environment. (Softly sing or hum a *niggun*.) Now, on the count of *shalosh*, we will all call out "Tashlich" one more time, and each of us will throw our last piece of bread away.

Teshuvah is a process, just as this whole period that runs from the beginning of Elul to Shemini Atzeret is a process. We take the next step in this process as we prepare for a second day of Rosh HaShanah and for Yom Kippur. Let's recognize here and now that we need help, that as powerful as we are in doing *teshuvah*, we still need the help of a greater power, God.

We're going to sing *"Aveenu Malkaynu"* (our Parent our Sovereign). Here in nature we have a little more room for physical as well as spiritual stretching than back in the synagogue. As we sing *"Aveenu Malkaynu,"* you may want to add the motions we have learned: *Aveenu Malkaynu* — hands stretched up toward the sky; *chanaynu v'anaynu* — shuckling or other prayer motion; *ahsay imanu tzedakah v'chesed* – a rocking, lullaby motion as if in the end we all need to be rocked and cared for by God like a baby; *ki ayn banu ma-asim* – turning hands over and shrugging shoulders as if to say our basket of good deeds is empty.

Let's end by asking everyone to connect with at least a *minyan* (ten) of people from among our *kahal*, shake their hands, and wish each a *"L'Shanah Tovah Tikatayvu."*

We end with the same *niggun* with which we began.

EVALUATION AND CONCLUSION

The flow of this 20-minute Tashlich service is designed to give different age groups a special place in the ceremony. The very active nature of being outside and moving about is great for younger children. The throwing of bread and the calling out of "Tashlich" are elements designed to engage the two to five-year-olds in the group. (All of this is, of course, done within the constraints of safety and common sense. For example, when I did Tashlich near ledges overlooking creeks, I shortened the service because it was so difficult for parents to watch their kids.)

The book *Rosh HaShanah Walk* provides a special role in the ceremony for young readers, children in the six to nine-year-old range. (Unfortunately, this book is out of print.) The creation of an acrostic is something with which older elementary students (nine to 14), as well as adults can get very involved.

The intergenerational Tashlich ceremony described here has been replicated in the many communities in which I have served. It has been particularly rewarding to watch the leadership for the Tashlich service transfer from Rabbi to lay leaders. Its simplicity can indeed be very empowering.

CHAPTER 46

CHAVERIM BATELEFON

CONTRIBUTOR: ELISSA KAPLAN
ADDRESS: Congregation Har Shalom
11150 Falls Road
Potomac, MD 20854
PHONE: (301) 299-7087, ext. 7
E-MAIL: ekaplan@harshalom.org
TARGET: Third or fourth grade students and adults
TIME FRAME: 15 minutes per week, plus a beginning workship, a Family Education progam, and an ending ceremony

OVERVIEW

"Chaverim BaTelefon" is a program involving adults from a congregation (and/or from a *havurah*, from the alumni of the school, or even from the general community) and students who are beginning to learn Hebrew, usually in the third or fourth grade. This simple program operates on many levels: the home and the school, the congregation and the school, the adult and the child, and the mentor and the mentored. Students bring Hebrew work home and do it over the telephone with a mentor. Thus, parents see and hear what is going on at school. Members of the congregation call students to help with Hebrew homework, thereby enabling congregants to interact with the school and its curriculum, and to feel like stakeholders in the school. Children talk to adults over the telephone and learn how to communicate with people outside their family or school settings. Adults who may not have considered themselves mentors give advice on a wide range of topics, and they discover that children are interested in what they have to say.

This program is also "bifocal," that is, it operates through two different lenses. Through the adult lens, this program tutors students in Hebrew, guides them toward communication and respect, and opens a path toward mutual understanding and friendship. Through the child lens, this program facilitates doing homework, offers a grown-up activity on an ongoing basis, and opens a path toward mutual understanding and friendship. Through both lenses, this program is actually fun!

GOALS

Here are the Jewish goals, the family goals, and the educational goals for *"Chaverim BaTelefon."*

Jewish
- To teach and learn Hebrew language decoding and prayer.
- To impart and glean wisdom that is important to meaningful Jewish living.

Today, each school determines how much and in which ways Hebrew and prayer are taught. This goal is both general in nature and specific in setting. The goal of giving and receiving wisdom is both ancient and modern. The Book of Proverbs is an example of this kind of wisdom literature. In the Talmud the Sages were known as the *Chachamim*, the wise ones. It is in the spirit of the *Chachamin* that the program *"Chaverim BaTelefon"* was originally begun. Adults in the congregation become the teachers of practical wisdom to the students in the school. This ancient goal indeed becomes modern.

Families

- To encourage families to commit a specific time and place for Jewish education in the home.
- To place in parents' hands resources that can be used at home to reinforce and deepen lessons from the classroom.

Educational

- To develop skills in the fluent reading and comprehension of Hebrew prayers and blessings as part of *Tefilah* — prayer (taken from the Jewish Reconstructionist Federation Education Commission Statement of School Goals).
- To promote the Jewish value of honoring and respecting older people (*Kibud Zekaynim*).

Homework is a challenge for both children and parents. Since many students have a great deal of secular homework, they often put off or ignore homework from Hebrew School. Since Hebrew School teachers know that their homework will be largely ignored, they often refrain from assigning needed home practice. A program that allows an "outsider" to set the time and scope of such homework takes the burden off both parents and children. Homework is thus a non-issue. In fact, since it is part of a phone call, it is special, rewarding, and fun. In terms of resources for Hebrew education, parents can use all the help they can get. Many parents do not know enough Hebrew to help their children with their homework. The friend at the other end of the telephone line is a "live" and fully interactive resource.

Many Jewish schools begin their Hebrew reading programs in the third or fourth grade. Whatever method is used — from full language immersion to simple phonetic decoding, those years are the years to "get with the program." Most students and parents are delighted to be doing the "real thing," at least at first. Study that begins rather easily, however, can soon become difficult. Having a personal tutor on hand on a weekly basis can make all the difference in learning a new skill, and perhaps a new language, too. Having an adult friend to help with study, and being able to discuss important matters with him or her, is much like having an extra aunt or uncle. Intergenerational learning is an exciting

and underutilized educational tool, one that is quite powerful.

DESCRIPTION OF THE PROGRAM

"Chaverim BaTelefon" is an intergenerational mentoring program involving adults and students. Once a week the *chaver/ah* (friend) calls the *talmid/ah* (student), and spends ten to 15 minutes coaching and listening. Both the *chaver/ah* and the *talmid/ah* have the same text and assignment. *Chaverim* attend an introductory workshop at the beginning of the year. Before the program starts, there is a demonstration at a Family Education program during school time. At the end of the year, the *talmidim* honor their *chaverim* at a special Shabbat ceremony. *"Chaverim BaTelefon"* is one of the simplest of educational programs, while at the same time it is a powerful educational experience for everyone involved.

The story of Ruth and Valerie is a case in point. Ruth, a parent of two grown children, attended synagogue regularly and was curious about what children were learning in the school. She was easily persuaded to take part in the *"Chaverim BaTelefon"* program. Ruth started calling Valerie once a week when this student was in third grade. Valerie performed her homework tasks very well and asked many questions, which sent Ruth to the dictionary, the encyclopedia, and to other places as well for information. The families, who had not previously known each other became friends. At the end of the year, Ruth decided to continue as Valerie's *chaverah*, promising to stick with her until Valerie's Bat Mitzvah. Ruth even took Valerie to work on Mother-Daughter Day. This story is typical of the "rest of the story" consequences of this program. Some families have invited mentors who are single over for Shabbat dinners. Some families and mentors met at synagogue. Some students gave gifts or made donations in honor of their *chaverim*. Some mentors improved or learned more Hebrew, and had useful input into the school curriculum. Once begun, it seems, *"Chaverim BaTelefon"* develops a life of its own.

QUESTIONS AND ANSWERS

Following are the questions most frequently asked about the programs and a brief answer to each.

How do we find adults who are willing to be chaverim*?*

The best candidates for the adult mentors are single people of any age or empty nesters, people not involved with the school, and people with a working knowledge of beginning Hebrew or those willing to learn. Letters and announcements in bulletins are a good first step. The best way to secure *chaverim*, however, is the personal invitation delivered face-to-face. And the best sales pitch is the most genuine one: congregant and school have a common goal. We want to provide the best Jewish education possible for our children. You as a member can play an effective role.

What if people say that they don't know enough Hebrew?

It is important to know if potential mentors can tutor the students. The best way to find out is to evaluate their actual knowledge with non-threatening questions. It is also a good idea to show potential mentors the material used in the classroom. Many adults remember the textbooks they used in Hebrew school. They are usually delighted to discover that not only are the texts colorful and inviting, but they are practically self-programmed, especially when viewed through the eyes of an adult.

Which grade is the best to target for the program?

It is best to begin the program at the beginning of the formal Hebrew teaching. That way, the mentors and students can grow and develop together. Students in third or fourth grade have secular homework, so they are ready to be responsible for Hebrew homework, too. These students also like receiving telephone calls, and are willing and able to talk purposefully on the telephone.

How do the mentors know what the students are doing?

The mentors have copies of the texts that the students are using in class. Before the beginning of the school year, the Program Coordinator (the Principal, the Family Educator, or the classroom teacher) briefs the mentors about the class curriculum and procedures. About once a month, the program coordinator sends out a mini-syllabus so the mentors know where the students are in the curriculum. Surprisingly, students are quite reliable about knowing what their assignments are. Mentors keep simple journals so that they know what the students are studying at any given time.

How do chaverim *arrange their telephone calls?*

As soon as a mentor receives his/her student's name from the Program Coordinator, the mentor talks first to the parents to arrange a day and time to call the student. For example, it might be arranged to call every Tuesday night at 7:00 p.m. The night before Hebrew school usually becomes a popular night to do homework. When calling the student, the mentor first talks to him/her about general topics. Then they discuss the Hebrew homework. They end with a reminder about next week's call.

How can we afford to buy extra texts for the mentors?

Allot dollars for one set of texts for the mentors that can be reused as necessary. If there is no money in the budget, ask other arms of the synagogue (e.g., Sisterhood, Brotherhood, educational funds, or the PTA) to help. If no money is available there, try to get a small Family Education grant from a local Jewish agency or an "angel" in the congregation. Do not photocopy pages for the mentors. Not only is it difficult to distribute these materials to tutors in a timely manner, it is illegal and immoral to do so.

How do parents and students react to the weekly phone calls?

Once the routine is established, they really look forward to the weekly call. Occasionally, it is difficult to establish a set time, especially if the mentor or the family has an irregular schedule due to work or travel. It is important for the program coordinator to keep on top of situations such as this, and to intervene personally so as to make the program work. On rare occasions, the *shidduch* (match) does not work out between the mentor and the student.

Again, the Program Coordinator has to be alert to these situations, and change the combination.

NUTS AND BOLTS

Following are ten steps for a successful *"Chaverim BaTelefon"* program.

1. Select a Program Coordinator. This person can be the Principal, Family Educator, classroom teacher, or interested volunteer. This person's job is to be in charge of all aspects of the program: the staff, the volunteers, the materials, the pre-program workshop, the Family Education program, and the end of the year ceremony. He/she orders materials, including textbooks and folders for journals.

2. Recruit potential mentors. Call people, interview potential mentors, and sign them up for the program.

3. Arrange a pre-program workshop for all staff, both volunteer and professional. At this get-together, engage the staff in interactive exercises about mentoring. Role play phone calls. Get mentors excited about the year ahead. Be sure to include the classroom teachers as part of the program. Keep them up to date every step of the way. Serve good food. Make the workshop first class.

4. Plan a Family Education program for parents, students, and mentors during school time. Do activities together and actually stage the first phone call. Serve food. Generate enthusiasm for this fantastic program.

5. Prepare journals for the mentors. Ask each to record the date of their calls, the pages covered, the material covered, and one sentence about what they would do differently next time. The Program Coordinator should keep in touch with the mentors regularly, about once a month. The journals augment that communication. If there are problems, these should be fixed on the spot, if necessary changing around the mentors and students.

6. Check regularly with the classroom teacher on the progress of students. Make sure all the stakeholders keep up with class assignments.

7. Have faith that adults and children who never met each other and never worked together can create friendly, empowering, working relationships. Laugh at the unexpected. Enjoy the praise you so richly deserve for producing such a great program in your school. To document the program, take pictures and publicize the program throughout the synagogue and the community.

8. Plan an end of the year ceremony at a Shabbat service. Create a program at a Shabbat dinner with "Academy Awards" for *"Chaverim BaTelefon"* service. These awards might include such things as most phone calls per year, most concerned *chaver/ah*, most improved *talmid/ah*, most supportive family, etc. Give *aliyot* to *chaverim*, *talmidim*, and families at a Shabbat service. Have *talmidim* present flowers, poems, or songs to their *chaverim*. There will not be a dry eye in the synagogue.

9. Plan for next year. Ask *chaverim* to continue and recruit new ones.

10. Conduct a formal evaluation of the program. This is an important aspect of any program. Regretfully, we didn't do this. Instead, we relied on immediate personal feedback from participants, which we found to be very helpful.

LOOKING BACK/LOOKING AHEAD

I have run this program at Adat Shalom Reconstructionist Congregation when it was located at the JCC in Rockville, Maryland, and made plans to introduce it at Shaare Tefila Congregation (Conservative) in Silver Spring, Maryland, where I was the Education and Youth Director. In my second year there, I wrote a grant proposal for the program to the UJA Federation, and was awarded a Family Education grant. With this grant, I was able to hire a Program Coordinator. The need for someone other than the Principal to run the program cannot be overstated; the Program Coordinator's job takes a lot of time. Also included in our grant is money for the production of a video to explain the program. We also plan to use the video to publicize the school and the congregation in general.

This program operated the best during its first year. I would like to expand the program to continue through the B'nai Mitzvah year. I also hope to create a *"Chaverim BaTelefon"* handbook that explains the program to mentors and families. This would provide many suggestions to families about how they could become involved with their child's mentor, and how to include the mentor in the family.

Getting started is the hardest part of doing this program. Finding enough mentors and keeping all the stakeholders informed are challenging tasks. Monitoring what happens is crucial to the progress of the program. However, watching it shape the lives of so many people is incredible and awe inspiring.

The mentors and families enjoyed all aspects of the program. They were dissatisfied only if they had difficulties connecting with each other on the telephone. Some mentors who worked with children with special needs felt that they needed some extra guidance, but they loved being part of the program. Everyone — teacher, mentors, and families — wanted more of the program, that is, more time, more materials, more involvement. It has been a fantastic success.

RESOURCES

Since this program is original to this writer, there are no sources to cite. However, two very important people served as resources. Jeffrey Schein was the inspiration for the program. When I was the Education Director of Adat Shalom Reconstructionist Congregation, I was fortunate to be part of the original Cooperating Schools Network, which he led. Our mission was to create Family Education programs for specific grades around specific themes. *"Chaverim BaTelefon"* was a program that Dr. Schein called a "Wrap-around Project for the Entire School." During the formulation and execution of the program at Adat Shalom, he was the "on call" mentor.

I also met Dr. Michael Zeldin, Professor at Hebrew Union College, Los Angeles, at a CAJE at the University of Indiana. I participated in his workshop on mentoring. Learning about the art, science, and craft (moral craft) of mentoring validated the *"Chaverim BaTelefon"* program. Further, the ideas from those classes became the basis for the pre-program workshop.

COMMENTARY

- Think about pairing the tutors so they can discuss different strategies for tutoring their students. (EC)
- Utilize *chaverim* for the study of other Jewish subject matter. (EC)
- Put photographs of the student and his/her *mentor* in the synagogue newsletter. (EC)

- There are possible links between the *"Chaverim BaTelefon"* program and the "Council of Sages" program discussed in Chapter 44. The former might actually feed into the latter. (EC)
- Use e-mail to communicate between mentors and the program coordinator. That would save numerous phone calls. (EC)

FAMILIES AND PRAYER

CONTRIBUTOR: DR. JEFFREY SCHEIN
ADDRESS: Cleveland College of Jewish Studies
26500 Shaker Boulevard
Beachwood, OH 44122
PHONE: (216) 464-4050
E-MAIL: jschein@ccjs.edu

This section of *Growing Together* reads differently from the more programatically grounded previous sections. Here the overarching concern is with the set of relationships that create the triangle of children, families, and prayer rather than the content of a given program. Concomitantly, the setting for Family Education here switches from the classroom to the sanctuary as we glimpse families engaged in Jewish worship.

Perhaps we are well guided here by the Rabbinic understanding of prayer as a form of complete service to God. The full, natural spirituality of young children is contagious; contributors to this section, such as Lyndall Miller and Marilyn Price, hope that parents will quickly "catch this" if the right atmosphere is established for family prayer. Chapter 47, "Young Parents, Their Families, and Prayer" by Lyndall Miller, and Chapter 48, "Staging Family Prayer: Breath, Story, and Symbol" by Marilyn Price are both full of examples of how the child's openness to prayer can significantly affect the parents and the family as a whole. Here one is reminded of Rabbi Mordecai Kaplan's suggestion that asking the question "why pray" is like asking someone "why breathe." Both are deeply engrained functions of healthy human existence. The real question worth

asking is "How did we forget to do what otherwise comes so naturally?"

Helping parents and children share a language of Jewish spirituality is the subject of Chapter 49, "Creating Family Dialogues around Prayer" by Barbara Carr. The author shares her well thought-out methodologies for creating family dialogues across a variety of subject matters.

Chapter 50, "Family Conversations and the Siddur" by Jeffrey Eisenstat, reminds one of a long-standing *machloket* (debate) among Family Education practitioners. Some early advocates for Family Education termed this emerging field Jewish Family Life Education. The goal was to improve the quality of family experience for Jewish families. Others argued that the real goal was Jewish knowledge and achieving the more formal goals of the Jewish curriculum in different ways. Here I work from the interesting hypothesis that there is an intricate parallelism between the structure of family life and the *matbeya shel tefilah,* the core structure of the prayer service. The *"Barchu"* is about our most "blessed" moments shared as a family: the *"Avot/ Imahot"* is about the strongest personality forging a link between our family story and the story of Judaism, etc. As Joel Lurie Grishaver likes to put it, the master story of the Jewish people and the story of each family are refractions of one another: each has its own exodus from Egypt, its own *ma-amad Sinai* (moment of standing at Sinai), etc. Reading Chapter 50 is a little like watching a master detective. Always there are hidden clues linking the core meaning of a given *brachah* to an important conversation that a family has yet to experience about its Jewishness and familiness.

As is often the case in JFE, one is left with a challenge, as well as a stirring sense of achievement. One is struck in surveying these chapters as to how much "younger is better" in regard to family and prayer. The set of prayer experiences for families with older children in which there are sophisticated conceptual maps for prayer is yet to be written.

CHAPTER 47

YOUNG PARENTS, THEIR FAMILIES, AND PRAYER

CONTRIBUTOR: LYNDALL MILLER
ADDRESS: 7114 McCallum Street
Philadelphia, PA 19119
PHONE: (215) 247-2333
E-MAIL: lyndallmiller@compuserve.com
TARGET : Early childhood children and their parents
TIME FRAME: One hour every Shabbat morning during the school year

INTRODUCTION

The children come in, clutching their parents' hands, skirts, pant legs, anything within the three-and-a-half-foot range that they can reach. They keep their distance from me as they find a spot behind the children's *Siddurim* that are laid out carefully on their mats in a semi-circle. I, the *Shaliach Tzibbur* of this interesting congregation, sit in front of our beautiful wood *Aron*, observing the prevailing mood. Parents get closer to the size of their youngsters as they settle down with them on the floor. And then we begin.

THE SERVICE

It's time for the *Ginat Shabbat* service at Germantown Jewish Center in Northwest Philadelphia.

We start with a Shabbat song. The adults, concerned that the children have not "warmed up" to the service yet (I am not bothered in the least), participate with hearty vigor, performing actions and singing lustily. Sometimes, in fact, it is difficult for me to keep control of the tempo. The parents go on enthusiastically after I am ready to start the service itself! It is fascinating to experience the adults singing loudly while the children sit quietly, watching and listening and preparing themselves as young ones must to participate in a group. Parents, who at this point could have taken a more reserved role, act instead as they suppose their children should.

We move on to the singing of *"Mah Tovu,"* and the taller family members often form a tent for the smaller ones, who now start to come alive, giggling and pushing into the tent formed by loving arms and smiling faces. As we start *"Birkot HaShachar,"* the adults now begin to recede into the background. Now they are the ones who sit and listen and absorb, while the children become involved in the prayer concepts. "What are we thankful that we can do?" I ask. The children and I move together as we act out the various *brachot* while we say them. Parents watch with intense looks on their faces, but sometimes do not even get up from the floor. When we come to *"HaNotayn L'Ya'ayf Koach,"* I ask if anyone has a problem that has made them feel "bowed down" during the last week. Now the adults are truly fascinated as the children bring up all kinds of problems. We all find out together what has troubled the children recently, and there are frequent surprises. It is also interesting for me to watch the adults as they see how open the children are in bringing their problems to the prayer experience.

In *"Hallel,"* we move in many different ways — most suggested by the children themselves — to demonstrate how prayer can have many different forms. We are all entertained as we try to fit our song into the various motions, from "the turning around way" to "the jumping way." In how many ways do the parents allow themselves to pray? In our service, it depends on how vigorous they feel on that particular Shabbat morning! Next, we all go to *Bayt HaMikdash* to take part in the "orchestra." At one point, everyone chooses an imaginary instrument and we "play to God" — another way to pray.

We move, sing, and talk our way through the rest of our Shacharit prayers. We create our own religious poetry during *"Nishmat,"* and feel close to God in our own space as we say the *"Shema."* We also note as we turn to the *Avot* and *Imahot* sections of the *"Amidah"* that we have mothers and fathers of the whole Jewish people, as well as some of our own.

Finally, we reach the Torah service. We pass the student Torah from hand to hand to every person in the room — the Torah is not just for boys or girls, children or adults, but for all of us. Then, we "do" the story. This is often the favorite part of the service for adults and children alike. Props and costumes come out as the story is brought to life, often with players chosen from the *kahal*. I love to see the looks on the parents' faces as the children become Avraham, Sarah, Moshe, and Miryam. Scenes which have remained words on a page spring up in front of us and become real. And who knows what abilities of biblical proportions abide in our children?

We end our service with a very short Musaf, and then join together in a *"Kiddush."* There is grape juice and *challah*, with hand washing in between. At the end of our *Kiddush*, we say a very short children's form of *"Birkat HaMazon."* We may have as many as 30 members of our "Shabbat family" around the table as we finish our time together.

EFFECTS ON FAMILIES

I often have as many adults as children in our *Ginat Shabbat* service. The "family" is often the extended family; the *ganze mishpoche* includes parent figures, grandparents, aunts, and uncles who have joined us. I know that I enjoy my time in this partic-ular *"davening* group" very much, and often feel that I have had a more spiritual experience than at an adult service. The intergenerational character of *Ginat Shabbat* is unmistakable. When I started doing this service, however, I was unaware of the effect it would have on the adults who come with the children.

I have been told by adults that this is their favorite service — and this in a building where there are three adult *minyanim* going on at the same time! For several parents, *Ginat Shabbat* provides a gateway into the prayer experience in terms of knowledge. They say that they did not understand the structure of the service until they started attending this children's service. In the adult groups, they felt intimidated and acutely aware of their lack of knowledge. These are feelings that we know are impediments to participation in prayer. A level of comfort is necessary before spiritual exploration can take place.

Even more surprising to me, however, is the reaction of some knowledgeable Jews. They claim that in our service, there is a *ruach* that they do not often find in services geared only to adults. After considerable thought, I have come to the conclusion that this added spirituality in the children's service may be due to the spiritual gifts of the young children themselves. These gifts are quite profound. Because they are intuitive rather than analytical, children five and under tend to "feel" their way into situations rather than trying to dissect them. Therefore, they respond to the emotions of prayer without lowering the cognitive screen that adults use to filter experience. The children participate directly, and bring their parents along with them. Almost unsuspecting, the adults feel the child's emotional response through the parenting bond, for which there is no filter even for adults.

Also, children are highly imaginative, and their imaginations have a vivid sensory aspect. Adults can "imagine" a scene almost as an abstract idea. Children imagine the scene in terms of sights, smells, sounds, actual experience. As a result, when they reenact a scene, they truly take us there. Our ideas become freer in the wonder of children's spontaneity.

Young children are also intensely interested in God and want to learn more. They have not learned that this subject is fraught with all kinds of contradictions and difficulties. They approach God with all of the openness and energy with which they investigate the rest of the world. Adults in this setting can regain some of the interest that they lost when their questions were ignored or repressed.

Finally, adults can learn from the children that prayer is not a passive experience. Children *must* participate in order to stay engaged and part of a group. They have to respond verbally, move physically, and interact with the concepts. Often, adults look at prayer as something that they go to hear, rather than do. In the process, what prayer can do for them remains unrealized.

It is possible that the openness and spontaneity of the children reawakens the spiritual development of their significant adults. As the parents go back to childhood with their own offspring, they can recapture these feelings and explore them in a safe setting. This setting is enhanced by the joy of sharing with a group of children for whom the miracle of awareness and growth is unfolding as a living reality. And somewhere in the garden known as *Ginat Shabbat*, is the deepest possible connection to the special flower they know as their own child.

EVALUATION

Up to this point, there has been no formal evaluation. While this would unquestionably be of value, it is sometimes difficult to get the physical arrangements in place, to say nothing of the kind of surveys, interviews, and focus groups that are ordinarily a part of a formal evaluation. Families do, however, provide useful anecdotal comments. Occasionally, a Bar or Bat Mitzvah will mention the service (which is now in its sixteenth year). And I have had other educators observe me. Additionally, many of the parents who attend are Rabbis, and their feedback has been overwhelmingly positive.

CHAPTER 48

STAGING FAMILY PRAYER: BREATH, STORY, AND SYMBOL

CONTRIBUTOR: MARILYN PRICE
ADDRESS: 2430 Prairie Avenue
Evanston, IL 60201
PHONE: (847) 869-6360
E-MAIL: marilynlprice@aol.com
TARGET : Families with children in grades
PK-4

INTRODUCTION

Every good story (and experience) should prepare us for what is to come. So, too, with prayer. To get into the prayer experience, we need to prepare ourselves, to get an idea of what is to follow. It is difficult to get into prayer if we jump right in cold without any mental preparation.

In this chapter, I offer three different suggestions to use with families to help prepare them for prayer. The first of these is "breathing" our way into prayer. The second is thinking about the prayer service as a story. The third is connecting to the *Siddur* as a symbol. A fuller explanation of each of these suggestions is found below.

All activities that involve families should be participatory and should be conducted in an atmosphere of calm and order. If the leader establishes a relaxed atmosphere, it will carry over into the rhythm of the prayer service. The breath should be natural, and can eventually lead to song if you so choose. The stories can be the leader's or the participants'. The visual aids can be actual (e.g., a prayer book or ritual symbol), or can be described through visualization. The use of these "prayer starters" will enrich future attempts at prayer on the part of the families.

BREATH

In a Friday evening Shabbat service, the *entire* Kabbalat Shabbat is a set of warm-up prayers. In theatre language, the overture; in sports and aerobics, the stretching, the limbering up. When we allow ourselves to "get into" the warm-up, we leave behind physically and mentally where we came from, and make ourselves ready for prayer.

The simplest (and quickest) exercise to accomplish this is to ask everyone to exhale and remove the space they brought in from the outside world, and then to deeply inhale the new space in the sanctuary. The exhaling removes thoughts of the week, the outside world that affects our secular actions. The inhaling makes us come together as a unit as we draw in our communal space. You might want to discuss the things that could be left behind: the week with its problems, school and too much homework, the squabbles, the bus that forgot us, the annoying sibling, or the friends who didn't act like friends. Make sure to include as many issues as possible without turning it into a gripe session or an overlong segment. Allow room for silent thoughts, especially if the numbers are too great to let everyone speak, or create a beat to let everyone chant together. In other words, let everyone express all the things that characterize "the worst week ever" in the way that works the best for your group.

Now it is appropriate to think about the *best* things ever. Children are always ready to talk about places they like to go, people they like to have with them, things they particularly enjoy doing. Around a Shabbat dinner table, as well as in the sanctuary, there are good opportunities to initiate conversation, often missed because of a heavy weekly schedule. Before Havdalah as well, this is an excellent way to summarize the things that made Shabbat — your day as well as God's day — special, and a time to reenter the following week by taking Shabbat with us into the week ahead.

STORY

Story and narrative give structure to a child's experience of holiness. The abstractness of prayer and the relentless complexity of the structure of the *Siddur* distance children and many adults from prayer. When families can experience prayer in story form, hundreds of chunks of random information begin to cohere as an integrated whole.

Find ways to illustrate how the service is formatted like a story. The opening (*"Birchot HaShachar"*), the introduction of theme (*"Pesukay D'Zimra"*), the drama/the listening (the *"Shema"*), the body of the story (*"Amidah/Tefilah"*), the gradual softening of the prayers as we reach conclusion with a song (*"Alaynu"*), a blessing, and in general, a happily ever after (*"Kaddish"*).

Another nice and effective approach is to tell a continual running story about fictional characters who live parallel lives to the children in your community. These serial Jewish stories might tell of children who are solving problems with Jewish solutions in the everyday world, and how the values of the *Tefilah* guide them in meeting these challenges. Use examples of *Tzedakah* and *mitzvot* by actions that these children do — extraordinary, yet cool children who could be anybody's friends, and who "belong" to the community. Have the children in the congregation begin to make up stories about these wise, imaginary Jewish friends: stories about listening, about conflict, about prayer, songs, identity, the holidays — anything related. Have these "artists in residence" draw pictures of the kids to accompany their stories.

SYMBOL

As a Jewish symbol, the *Siddur* carries a spiritual weight greater than the totality of all the individual *tefilot*. A beautiful story illustrating this is I.B. Singer's "The Old Siddur." My retelling of this story is available in written form, as well as in video format, through the Jewish Reconstructionist Federation's *Puppets and Paradigms as the Guide: A Journey through the Jewish Life Cycle* (JRF, 1990).

"The Old Siddur" is a "lost and found" story of a *Siddur* that is almost trashed, but then miraculously ends up being found by the grandson of the grandmother who had used it for decades. During the story, the *Siddur* "talks" with other Jewish texts (Tanach, Gemara) in an old, abandoned Jewish library. In so doing, it educates the readers both about family history and prayer.

This is an easy story to retell through drama. Adults and children can take appropriate parts in the story. Questions follow naturally:
- What would it be like to discover a precious object previously owned by a beloved grandparent?
- If the "object" is a *Siddur*, what is added to its value?
- What prayers do we imagine Rachel the grandmother might have prayed?
- Does the *Siddur* being "old" make it "better"? (Usually, in our society, newer is better.)
- What do you think your own Grandmother would have inscribed in a *Siddur* she might have wished to pass on to you?

Perhaps the greatest value of this story is the invitation it provides to give voice to the *Siddur*. If the *Siddur* could talk, what would it tell us about:
- The value of prayer in general
- When it's easy to pray/when it's hard
- The meaning of particular prayers (*"Barchu," "Shema," "Amidah,"* etc.)
- What is different about *davening* in the morning, afternoon, and evening?
- What feels different about being on a bookshelf (or prayer book cart) and in the hand of a human being?

CONCLUSION

This chapter has concerned itself with the entry point in the worship service. Just as important is the conclusion. The same three elements can be used at the end of the service, further enticing the participants to return. Before they reenter the secular world, suggest that they take that important breath, and fill themselves up with the peace of the service. Singing a song together is an uplifting way to end the service. Tie things together with a theme, perhaps Torah. There are many outstanding stories related to the *parashah* of the week. Find one, and relate it to the personal experiences of participants to make Torah pertinent to their lives. For an effective beginning of the service, we have suggested three different things to use. It would provide a wonderful balance to use one of these to close as well. Through the use of these modalities, you will be able to create a family prayer experience of substance.

CHAPTER 49
CREATING FAMILY DIALOGUES AROUND PRAYER

CONTRIBUTOR: BARBARA CARR
ADDRESS: Congregation Dor Hadash
4858 Ronson Court, Suite A
San Diego, CA 92111
PHONE: (858) 268-3674
E-MAIL: brcarr1@cts.com
TARGET : Supplementary school children in
Grades K-9 and their families
TIME FRAME: Six times a year

INTRODUCTION

Family Education models have grown up all over the country in response to the very real concern about Jewish identity. Some of these programs are outstanding. Others, however, do little to foster quality Jewish learning. Congregation Dor Hadash, in San Diego, California, has created a Family Education model with the primary goal of developing dialogue about religion between parent and child. Our congregation is 40% interfaith, so our task is made more intriguing by our commitment to making the Family Education program a comfortable learning experience for both Jews and non-Jews. The program takes participants out of the classroom and puts education where it thrives best — in the heart of the family. Our families learn together, pray together, and grow together in this process.

DESCRIPTION OF THE PROGRAM

Six times a year, parents are required to attend school with their child in the same classroom. This means that every week, somewhere in the school, parents are learning with their children. The schedule of classes is given to them as part of the overall school calendar in September, and we continually stress the importance of attendance. Letters from the teacher and phone calls from parent representatives serve as timely reminders. Missing parents are phoned and reminded of their commitment if the child arrives unaccompanied on a scheduled date. Signs are posted, with the parent-child class of the day listed in bright colors. Parents are our students as well, and they know that they will be on site, learning with their students, if they want their children to attend our school.

Under the Education Director's supervision, each teacher is charged with developing lesson plans that can "go home" for these special classes. We compensate our teachers for a half hour prep time for each class session throughout the year as a way of acknowledging that we are asking something special from them. They seem to respond to our trust in them. Advice and guidance for our newer teachers is available from their peers, and from the Director as well, since creating these plans can be complex. Every lesson plan assumes a zero knowledge base, since many parents have little or no Jewish education. That these families participate together is every bit as important as the information they absorb. For many of the participants, these classes are the first time they have ever talked about significant religious issues together: Do they believe in God? Why are they Jewish? Why did the Holocaust happen? Is there any reason to pray? In what ways are Jews different? By setting up the classroom as a safe space to discuss these kinds of questions, we foster family dialogues that continue at home.

Most important, we need to have families talking about religious moments at home. We need families to bring their religious practices out of the closet and into the living room. We need families talking about God, talking about tradition, and talking about why they are Jews. Here are some models that have worked in creating this journey and this precious dialogue.

PRAYER MOMENTS

The most successful of all our models requires nothing more than a teacher who can see the presence of God in the everyday. I have had teachers who cringe at this idea, and so teacher training on the topic is always in order. Over the life of the program, we have found that the most effective approach with staff has been to open up the same dialogue with them as we ask them to undertake with the parents. They need to take a look at the incredible richness of commentary and text on God and prayer; finding their own voice is essential. We allow teachers the freedom to explore Harold Kushner's wonderful "When is God?" idea. We encourage them to be able to say they aren't sure about their own prayer voice. And we tell them again and again that the only thing that guarantees failure on this topic is apathy. All of these things together liberate the teachers and make for exciting dynamics when the time comes.

The teacher must be willing to act as facilitator for the families, to guide their thinking without squashing it. We merely act to help our families find moments when they might find a "yes" or a "help" or a "thank-you" in their daily lives. This can be extremely difficult to get started, but once it begins, it's almost impossible to shut down.

I often start families off by turning to the many *brachot* in the tradition. I will usually get a chuckle quoting the Rabbi in "Fiddler on the Roof" with his blessing for the Czar ("Keep him far, far away from us . . . "), but my point is to prove to them that blessings are everywhere. I also talk about the

"*Shehecheyanu*" moments which we have all had, but have not necessarily identified. I use the example of a very observant friend who was about to run his first marathon. A group of us were sitting around offering encouragement when he said he needed a blessing. We fooled around with various possibilities and then realized that that was certainly a "*Shehecheyanu*" moment. Now, ten years later, he still talks about how the memory of our chanting with him strengthened his legs. Too often families fail to utilize the spiritual resources of Judaism in ways that are connected to their own experience.

The easiest way to focus attention on blessing is to ask the adults to tell about a moment with their child when they could have uttered a prayer of thanks. They are comfortable talking about the moment of birth, or the first step, or the first time they heard the child say their name. Having focus on their own daily lives is a bit more difficult. We ask the parent to use "prayer language" — to find an opening and closing phrase with the middle being unique. A simple prayer such as, "Thank you God for allowing Aaron to be such a wonderful son. I am grateful. Amen," works really well and is actually quite a wonderful prayer. One parent told me that for the first time, at age 50, he was watching the sun set at the beach with his daughter and he grabbed her hand and said a blessing for the moment. He laughed when he told me — said he always knew the sunset was a prayerful moment — but actually to say a prayer made the sun setting more significant that day than it had ever been before. Without that class with his daughter, that moment would never have happened.

Children have more of a struggle with personal prayer because they lack a sense of the extraordinary. Every moment of their lives is new and fresh, and so they struggle to distinguish "prayer moments." They often begin with "Thank you for letting me win the soccer game." This is where the facilitator can be most helpful. The prayer moment needs to be broken down. "Is it appropriate to give thanks for winning?" one can ask. "What about the kids who lost?" Eventually, over the course of several weeks, the prayer evolves into something like "Thank you for the health of my body which has allowed me to play sports, Amen." The whole class will then burst into applause at the successful "prayer moment."

An additional twist on this can help to refocus on traditional prayer. We ask the families to identify moments in their lives when they actually did pray. These responses are fascinating. Some responses are wonderfully predictable: prayers for health, good grades, a safe journey, etc. But then a hand is raised and I hear, "I pray after I get a good grade." What? A prayer of thanks? Then a father says quietly, "When I was a child, when I would go to bed, I always had a conversation with a benign presence before I went to sleep. I wasn't raised to believe in God, but I guess maybe I was talking to God." His daughter's eyes look at him in surprise. He hugs her, and I want to offer my own prayer moment. The logical next step is to move into a discussion of the *"Shema"* as a bedtime prayer, and its sense of affirmation as opposed to the terrifying "Now I lay me down to sleep . . ."

By focusing on when people actually do pray outside the sanctuary, we can then talk about the content of prayers within the sanctuary. We can look at the wisdom of our liturgists who have "covered all the bases." We can talk about prayers for health, a traveler's blessing, the *"Hashkivaynu,"* and all of a sudden the *Siddur* comes alive, full of relevance, and parent and child alike are exploring the idea that there are fundamental truths which are addressed by our tradition.

EVALUATION

Formal evaluation of the Dor Hadash Parent-Child program has been undertaken every few years since the program began. The evaluations have been embedded in a general questionnaire about the entire school program. Parents and children are given separate forms with age appropriate questions, some open-ended, and some on a 1 to 5 scale of like/dislike. The evaluations, like our program, are full of abstract notions, such as comfort level and increased parent-child communication. Overall, the responses are enthusiastic. Over the years, more than 90% of our families have found the program worthwhile or highly worthwhile. The narrative responses have been the most helpful in reshaping our program, and it continues to evolve as the families become more sophisticated participants.

My personal belief in Family Education as the cornerstone for modern Jewish education has grown stronger over the years. At Dor Hadash we have used this model since the school began 15 years ago. When parents enroll their children, they enroll themselves. They embrace the learning model, and in some ways are more inspired than the children. I can't count the number of times we hear something like: "I went for four days a week to Religious School, and no one ever told me before why we say the *"Baruch Shem"* quietly!" Or even more important, "This was the most serious discussion I ever had with my child. Thank you."

There have been naysayers, most often parents, who believe that a school's job is to teach data not feelings. More poignant, others say that they can't talk to their children about religious "stuff." There have been classes that don't work, either because the subject matter was too complex or the teacher underestimated the level of sophistication of the families. This program requires incredibly brave facilitators — teachers who are willing to take risks and to put in hours of uncompensated preparation because they are inspired to teach a particular subject to their families. In the final analysis, the success of the program rests with the families. If they believe that what they are doing is worthwhile, it becomes worthwhile.

CONCLUSION

Our families today have a number of difficulties as they strive to become more committed and observant Jews. They are all, in reality, Jews by Choice. Assimilation and intermarriage have made the traditional patterns of communal support and isolation from the secular world a thing of the past. Every parent chooses to affiliate. Many parents know they want something religiously different for their children — something more meaningful, more relevant than what they themselves experienced.

By creating new educational models that encourage questions and new answers, we make our religion and our history accessible. By acknowledging that Jewish education is a lifelong process which we model by teaching the whole family, our children do not look at their Bar or Bat Mitzvah as the exit door from the synagogues. By affirming that religion belongs in the home, at the kitchen table, and in the car, as well as in the *shul*, we are ensuring a new generation of thinking, caring Jews, who look to their synagogues and their educators as essential resources for their personal journey toward creative and meaningful Jewish learning. What a joy that is for everyone involved!

CHAPTER 50

FAMILY CONVERSATIONS AND THE SIDDUR

CONTRIBUTOR: RABBI JEFFREY EISENSTAT
ADDRESS: **Ramat Shalom Synagogue**
               11301 West Broward Boulevard
               Plantation, FL 33325
PHONE: **(954) 472-3600**
E-MAIL: **rabjeff@aol.com**
TARGET : **Families**

OVERVIEW

The following activities have been adapted and refined over years of conducting family services. Common to all is (1) the search for engaged *davening*, and (2) the intersection of family experience with the core meaning of each prayer.

These prayer activities are designed to provide *Kavanah* — a spiritual mindset — to a family engaged in Jewish prayer. The activities are staged much like the mini-dialogues described in Chapter 49, "Creating Family Dialogues around Prayer" by Barbara Carr. However, the activities in this chapter focus less on general prayer concepts and values and more on the content of a particular *Tefilah*. The activities described in this chapter reflect the work of Rabbi Devora Bartnoff [z"l], Rabbi Jeffrey Schein, and me, as we led worship services at Reconstructionist family camps and at the National Havurah Institute.

PROGRAMS

Here are short summaries of the connection between the core idea of the *Tefilah* and the family life issue. The challenge of adapting these suggestions to a particular group of families is left in the hands of the readers.

Mah Tovu:
- Creating our tents — each family spreads a *tallit* over their heads to create the sense of a tent.
- While singing *"Mah Tovu,"* adults hold a large *tallit* like a *chupah* so that children can walk through the "tent."
- Using crepe paper, each family unit creates its own tent and leaves it up throughout the service.
- Discuss: What is your home like? If you lived in a tent with the Israelites, what would it be like? What are the special elements of your home today, and what would you want to have in your biblical tent?

Birchot HaShachar:
Divide up the blessings so that each family will act out one of the individual blessings of the morning. The task is to find a body movement that matches such key phrases as "gives strength to the weary," "opens my eyes," "clothes my body," etc.

Pesukay D'Zimrah: "Ashray" (Psalm 145):
- Discuss the concept of an alphabetical acrostic, as demonstrated in the *"Ashray"* prayer.
- Create an acrostic listing from A to Z of those experiences that bring happiness to your family.
- Use your family name as an acrostic for words that represent your family. Or, create an acrostic out of the words Jerusalem, Israel, Havurah/Congregation name.

"Kol HaNeshamah" (Psalm 150):
- Review the different musical instruments of the psalm and ask if family members play instruments. Drums, cymbals, tambourines, and horns are distributed. As that phrase appears, those members will play in the "Temple band."

Barchu:
- Explain the reasoning for bowing. Families may create some other movement for this blessing, e.g., a circle with arm around each other to represent community.
- As a family, repeat the chanting of the *"Barchu"* a number of times, each time with greater force and conviction.

Yotzer Or:
- Discuss: What are the things that you have created as a family?
- List some projects that you would like to create together in the coming year.
- Think and talk about the most beautiful sunrise your family has ever seen.

Ahavah Rabbah:
- Read together the second paragraph of the prayer, beginning with *"veha'ayr aynaynu"* (light up your eyes). If you had been blind and had your sight restored, would this prayer have exceptional meaning to you?
- What are some ways we should be considerate of those members of our community who have visual disabilities?
- Read together the last paragraph of the prayer, focusing on the phrase, *"May arba kanfot ha'aretz"* (from the four corners of the earth). On what part of the earth does your family live? With a map, place stickers on the cities and regions of the world where your family lives and where they came from.

Shema:
- Listening is important in our tradition. What about those who are hearing impaired, and cannot hear the words of the *"Shema"*?
- Teach the signing of the *"Shema."*

Ve'ahavta:
- Discuss: What are some ways that kids love parents and that parents love kids? How is this like God's love?
- What does it mean to do something with all your soul and all your breath? Use all of your breath in reciting each of the words of the *"Shema."* What does breathing and chanting feel like in this important prayer?
- Discuss the phrase, *"veshinantam levanecha"* (teach them to your children). What is something that you learned from your parents? What is something you learned from your children?
- Find the phrase, *"ukshartam le'ot"* (bind them as a sign). Strap crepe paper on your arm and your head, like *tefillin*. For the arm, list ways in which you use your physical strength. For the head, list ways in which you use your mind.
- Find the phrase, *"uchtavtam al mezuzot baytecha"* (inscribe them on the doorposts of your house). Fold a large sheet of paper in half. On one side, make a list of all the items a visitor to your home would see that would show it is a Jewish home. On the opposite side, make a list of all the Jewish values that are in your home and how these are displayed.

Mi Chamocha:
- This is a prayer that represents great triumph. Discuss the times in your life when you have overcome adversity and triumphed.
- Have adults stand on opposite sides as kids walk through the center singing the *"Mi Chamocha."* What might it feel like to walk through the water of the Reed Sea?
- Invite people to share the victory moments in their lives when they have overcome worry, fear, or disease. Ask the group to yell out *"Mi Chamocha"* as they finish their "moment of redemption."

Amidah
Avot V'imahote:
- Name one thing that you appreciated this past week from your parents. Parents mention one thing they appreciated from their kids.
- Mention someone who was a great teacher and model in your life.

Blessing for Healing:

- Sing *"Mi Sheberach"* by Debbie Friedman and her song "The Angels' Blessing."
- Was there a time when you or someone you love were in need of healing? What were the things that helped?

Prayer for the State of Israel:

- Discuss the importance of "land." Remember a place outside the home that was a beautiful and meaningful place for you as a family. Draw a picture of this space.
- How is the Land of Israel a special place for the Jewish people?

CONCLUSION

These activities have been developed and applied and refined over many years of Family Education and *Tefilot* learning. Using different activities at varied times has been most effective in an ongoing course for family development.

The use of these activities has an enriching way to create an engaging family *davening* experience. But equally important is the matter in which families can truly understand, at many different levels, the core meanings of each prayer. The above programmatic devices for prayer have been a new and spiritual approach through which families can experience engaged and meaningful *davening*.

RITUAL FOR THE JEWISH FAMILY

CONTRIBUTOR: DR. JEFFREY SCHEIN
ADDRESS: **Cleveland College of Jewish Studies**
26500 Shaker Boulevard
Beachwood, OH 44122
PHONE: **(216) 464-4050**
E-MAIL: jschein@ccjs.edu

As was made clear in the previous section of *Growing Together,* Jewish Family Education may be viewed through a wide lens. Here, in this final section of the volume, our concern is to broaden our understanding of the role of the Family Educator to be as much "coach" and "trainer" as he/she is "teacher." The Family Educator must think of the individual family as a *Mikdash Ma'at* (a replica of the ancient sanctuary), and must provide service for the specific needs of the family. Boilerplate programs won't do in this arena of Jewish Family Education. Personal support and new skills are what families need here as they cautiously approach a threshold of adopting and adapting ritual.

As Rabbis, Family Educators, and leaders, our essential mantra rarely changes: Judaism is a home-based tradition. Jewish identity is formed primarily by the Jewish home. Although this assertion runs throughout this volume, we have waited until this section on Jewish ritual to assert it in a prayer-like fashion.

Enhancing the capacity of a Jewish family to incorporate Jewish rituals is perhaps the most important single task for the Jewish Family Educator. Empowering the family to act Jewishly is what we are all about. Here we have the opportunity to learn how masters of the art engage our families in magical weaves of Jewish ritual. In Chapter 51, "Rituals for Our Time: A Book Review," Carol Freedman Wolf helps us understand some of the powerful uses of ritual within the family system. She reviews *Rituals of Our Time* by Evan Imber-Black and Janine Roberts, which has proved immensely helpful to Cleveland-based Family Educators as they have tried first to imagine, then understand, then master the dynamics of families as they incorporate more ritual into their lives.

Chapter 52, "Oneg Chochmah: A Celebration of Turning Seventy" by Julie Jaslow Auerbach, reminds us that ritual does not stop with the celebration of the obvious life cycle events. In her description of a new ritual created for the seventieth birthday of her parents, Julie demonstrates a model for families to create rituals that honor important life transitions. Finally, in Chapter 53, "Around the Family Table," I return to the *Mikdash Ma'at* theme and describe how my family works toward expanding our ritual repertoire.

CHAPTER 51

RITUALS FOR OUR TIME: A BOOK REVIEW

CONTRIBUTOR: CAROL FREEDMAN WOLF
ADDRESS: 23700 Halburton Road
Beachwood, OH 44122
PHONE: (216) 591-9653
E-MAIL: cwolf@jfsa-cleveland.org
TARGET : Family Educators

The book *Rituals for Our Times* by Evan Imber-Black and Janine Roberts is filled with information on ways to make rituals an important part of our lives. This is not a book specifically about Jewish rituals. However, through a general understanding of how rituals function, we can apply the concepts to Jewish life. Through this volume, Family Educators will learn about ritual as a useful tool for teaching Jewish life and encouraging families to grow together as they develop unique ways to celebrate, mourn, pray, heal, separate, and reunite.

Drs. Imber-Black and Roberts introduce us to rituals by showing us how much they are a part of our everyday lives. They divide rituals into four categories. The first category is the "Day-To-Day Essentials." Such rituals take place each day, and may involve something as simple as brushing our teeth in a certain way. They may seem insignificant, but try telling a two-year-old that her favorite "blankie" cannot be found at bedtime, and you will see just how important daily rituals are! Daily rituals involve the most basic parts of our lives, including waking up in the morning, eating breakfast, going to work, coming home, eating dinner, relating to family and friends, and bedtime. Each of us has certain rituals that we go through each day, although we may think of them simply as habits.

The second category of rituals, the "Inside Calendar," is about ritual for special days that are meaningful only to a certain family or group. These include birthdays, anniversaries, births, family reunions, vacations, and any other special family occasions. Some have universal symbols attached to them, such as birthday cakes, but others may have symbols unique to a particular family. On the surface, these may not seem like the kind of religious occasions that a Jewish educator would teach about, but there is much opportunity to add a spiritual aspect to almost any family event.

The third category of rituals is the "Outside Calendar." These include holiday celebrations that link the family to the outside community. Such special occasions bring people together, but also create pressure for those who have uncomfortable relationships with family or who have unpleasant memories. Family Educators can provide their students with opportunities to enrich individual family holiday celebrations so that they have more comfort and meaning.

Finally, there are the "Life Cycle Rituals." These are the milestone events that are celebrated by family and community together. Individuals must decide how these celebrations fit their lives and who to involve in each of the occasions.

As well as giving us the varied forms of ritual, Roberts and Imber Black provide the Jewish Family Educator with an in-depth view of the dynamics of ritual. Ritual is important to us because it facilitates relating, changing, healing, believing, and celebrating. Every time we peer beneath the surface behaviors of a given ritual, we see the profound transformations occasioned for the individual, the family, and community through ritual. Embedded in particular traditional rituals, these same dynamics provide the raw materials for creating new ritual as illustrated in many of the chapters in this section of *Growing Together.*

Another part of *Rituals for Our Time,* a part which is of most interest to Jewish Family Educators is a discussion of the creation of new rituals to help families deal with difficult dilemmas. Abounding here are descriptions of rituals that help blended families bury (sometimes literally) the unhelpful part of their old relationships so they can move into their new situations.

Balanced and blended rituals within intermarried Jewish-Christian families are also explored. The volume, written by therapists, forms no moral or Jewish judgment about situations such as these. The Jewish Family Educator will undoubtedly hold specifically Jewish positions, yet he/she will still learn an enormous amount from the authors of this book about family dynamics and systems.

The process by which rituals are established within a family also says a great deal about the teamwork needed to create effective Jewish Family Education programs. As stated elsewhere in *Growing Together,* Vicky Kelman asserts that JFE really goes by three different names: *Jewish* family education, Jewish *Family* education, and Jewish Family *Education,* each emphasizing one of three distinct dimensions of the work. To the extent that we engage in Jewish *Family* Education, we need the expertise of those who understand family dynamics and systems.

Individuals — often found in Jewish communal agencies and family services — with competency in each of these areas ought to be joining with Rabbis and educators who can bring Jewish knowledge and pedagogic creativity into the design of Family Education programs.

BIBLIOGRAPHY ON RITUAL

Biziou, Barbara. *The Joy of Family Rituals: Recipes for Everyday Living.* New York: St. Martin's Press, 2000.

Drucker, Malka. *The Family Treasury of Jewish Holidays.* Boston, MA: Little Brown & Co., 1994.

Imber-Black, Evan, and Janine Roberts. *Rituals for Our Time: Celebrating Healing, and Changing Our Lives and Our Relationships.* Northvale, NJ: Jason Aronson Inc., 1998.

Orenstein, Rabbi Debra. *Lifecycles Vol. 1, Jewish Women on Life Passages & Personal Milestones.* Woodstock, VT: Jewish Lights Publishing, 2000.

Robinson, George. *Essential Judaism: A Complete Guide To Beliefs, Customs and Rituals.* New York: Pocket Books, 2000.

Shendelman, Sara, and Avram Davis. *Traditions: The Complete Book of Prayers, Rituals and Blessings for Every Jewish Home.* New York: Hyperion, 1998.

Weber, Vicki L., ed. *The Rhythm of Jewish Time: An Introduction To Holidays and Life-Cycle Events.* West Orange, NJ: Behrman House, 1999.

Wylen, Stephen M. *The Book of the Jewish Year.* New York: UAHC Press, 1998.

CHAPTER 52

ONEG CHOCHMAH: A CELEBRATION OF TURNING SEVENTY

CONTRIBUTOR: JULIE JASLOW AUERBACH
ADDRESS: Solomon Schechter Day School
19910 Malvern Road
Shaker Heights, OH 44122
PHONE: (216) 751-6100
E-MAIL: julirene@aol.com
TARGET : Seniors turning 70 and their families, or could be adapted for other age groups

INTRODUCTION

Like the intergenerational Tashlich service found in Chapter 45, this chapter utilizes a narrative format that invites the reader to participate in the *"Oneg Chochmah"* ceremony which the author developed for her own parents. After reading the chapter, Rabbis and Family Educators will need to unpack the ceremony and think about how it might be utilized in different contexts and with non-parent populations.

THE CEREMONY

Julie: Terach was 70 years old when Avram, later known as Avraham, was born. Avraham was 75 years old when he left Haran. Moses was 80 years old when he returned to Egypt to lead the Jews out of slavery.

In the book *Marriage and Family Life*, Jacob Milgrom writes: "For Abraham, life began at seventy-five. At this advanced age, tradition tells us, he uprooted himself from home, his friends, his busi-

ness, and his community, and undertook the perilous journey across the desert to start a new life in Canaan — to found a family and a faith, a new idea of God, and a new people to transmit it" [p. 254].

Similarly, although less confident and sure of himself than Avraham, Moses uprooted his family and left his business and community to return to Egypt on a daring mission of rescue at the age of 80. Moses went from shepherd of Yitro's flock to the shepherd of God's flock, and, in the later years of his life, became their greatest teacher. Perhaps the stories of Avraham and Moses, and even Terach, have something to tell us beyond the story of a people. Perhaps there is an additional underlying message our literature longs to share: that most elder statespeople and retired or semi-retired persons cling to the familiar, the old ways, and are reluctant to try new things and meet new people. That is precisely the time to take adventures, to try a new road, go somewhere different, dare to be, as Gail Sheehy called it, a "pathfinder." With the wisdom of their years as their primary resource, the elderly have everything to gain.

And so, Mom and Dad, as you begin your journey into your eighth decade and beyond, we your family, friends, and community bless you with these eight *brachot*:

1. The Blessing of Distinction
    Julie: "Until Abraham's time, the young and old were not distinguished from one another. A man could live a hundred or two hundred years and not look old. Abraham said, 'My son and I enter a town, and nobody knows who is the

father and who the son.' So Abraham said to God, 'Sovereign of the universe, there must be some outward sign of distinction between a father and a son, between an old man and a youth.' And God said, 'I will begin with you.' "Abraham went to sleep and when he awoke in the morning, he saw that his hair and beard were white. He said, 'Sovereign of the universe, You have made me an example.'" (*Tanhuma*, on Genesis, *Chayay Sarah*, from *Voices of Wisdom* by Frances Klagsbrun, New York: Pantheon Books, 1980, p. 196)

May your white hair be a mark of distinction as it was for Abraham, and may you, too, be a shining example to others.

2. The Blessing of Heritage
(Song: "Standing on the Shoulders" by Doug Cotler; *The Doug Cotler Songbook*, Woodland Hills, CA: Wail & Blubber Music, 1992)

Julie: In the late 1800s, my great grandparents on both sides made journeys across the sea. My mother's maternal grandmother, Rebekah Horowitz, brought with her some things that remain in the family even today. What is an inheritance? A European *menorah* or *chanukiah*? A tray from a saloon (one of the first family businesses)? a saying? a story? a teaching? The family folklore says that great grandmother Rebekah raised ten children on her own in the Lower East Side of New York. My aunt Bessie, Anna's sister, saved these things, as well as others, such as the samovar that stands in the dining room in the house of my cousin Cindy, Bessie's granddaughter, in Los Altos, California. These objects were passed on to us so that future generations of this family could make Rebekah Horowitz a part of their lives. My father maintains that it was the specialness of my mother's family that made him the *mensch* he became. Here to share a story from my parents' heritage is Rebekah's daughter, Bessie and Anna's younger sister, my mom's Aunt Roz.

(Roz speaks.)

All: May you continue to be a source of stories, memories, traditions and inspiration as your lives build upon the inheritance of the past and create the inheritance for the future.

3. The Blessing of Generativity
(Song: "*L'chi Lach*" by Debbie Friedman; *Blessings,* San Diego, CA: Sounds Write, 1990)

The grandchildren relate a *midrash* from *Song of Songs Rabbah:*

Grandchild 1: We are taught in a *midrash* that when the people of Israel stood at Mount Sinai ready to receive that Torah, God said to them, "Bring me good securities to guarantee that you will keep it, and I will give the Torah to you." The people responded: "Our ancestors will be our securities." Said God to them, "I have faults to find with your ancestors. What else can you offer?"

Grandchild 2: They said, "Sovereign of the universe, let our prophets be our securities." God replied, "I have faults to find with your prophets. What else can serve as securities?"

Grandchild 3: They said to God, "Let our children be our securities." And God replied, Yes, these are good securities. For their sake I will give you the Torah."

Grandchildren: Therefore, it is written: "From the mouth of babes and sucklings you have found strength" (Psalms 8:3).

All: May your "securities," your children and grandchildren, be a source of great pride and strength to you.

4. The Blessing of a Strong and Noble Spirit
(Song: "Get Up and Go" by Pete Seeger; *Bits & Pieces*, Ludlow Music, Inc. and Sanga Music, Inc., 1965)

Julie: In the thirteenth century, Immanuel of Rome said: "Old Age is a natural disease." Rabbi

Joshua ben Levi said: "Honor and respect the aged and saintly scholar whose physical powers are broken, equally with the young and vigorous one; for the broken tablets of stone, no less than the whole ones, had a place in the Ark of the Covenant." Alas, your bodies often feel like they cannot endure the rigors of past years. Dad, you probably couldn't deliver a mail route in one day. Not only because it would be physically taxing, but because you'd spend too much time chatting at each house. And Mom, you worked full-time, caring for me and Nanny, and attended volunteer meetings. This might be really hard to do today, not only because your digestive system might want to rebel against those necessarily hasty meals, but also because you'd much rather be taking the time to enjoy the company of the people with whom you're eating! The energy you two would like to have has been replaced with the patience Irv and I would like to have!

All: May your beautiful spirits forever prevail.

5. The Blessing of a Community of Friends
    (Song: *"V'ayzeyhu,"* Music by Karen Ezcovitz, *NFTY's Fifty Songbook*, New York Transcontinental Music Publications, 1989; words from *Pirke Avot* 4.1)

Julie: We read in *Midrash Rabbah*, Exodus 3: "When does Israel stand upright? When they have their aged with them. One who takes counsel in the old will not falter." Perhaps this is so because, as Job tells us, "With the aged is wisdom, and length of days brings understanding." (Job 12:12)
  Not just your family has benefited from your wisdom and example, but your friends, apartment house, synagogue, and community as a whole.

(Friends share what they have brought.)

All: May you continue to serve as good counsel to all of us — your family, friends, and the community as a whole.

6. The Blessing of Each Other
    (Song: *"Dodi Li."* Music by S. Sher, words from Song of Songs 2:16, 3:5, 4:9; or, *"Dodi Li,"* original music and lyrics by Joel Sussman of Safam.)

(Story: *"The Three Brothers."* In *Stories One Generation Tells Another* by Penninah Schram, Northvale, NJ: Jason Aronson Inc., 1987, pp. 15-17.)

Julie: Having wealth or knowledge without compassion for others is useless in Elijah's eyes, but a good spouse is worthy of everything. You have been good *to* each other and good *for* each other, nurturing, enabling, and supporting each other throughout the years.

All: May you continue to share, nurture, enable, and support each other in the decades yet to come.

7. The Blessing of the Future
    (Song: *"Ashrey Adam."* Music by Donald Rosoff, CAJE Conference, 1990; words from Proverbs 3:13-18)

Julie: In the article "To Grow in Wisdom" in *Judaism* (Spring 1977), Rabbi Abraham Joshua Heschel says: "According to all the standards we employ . . . the aged person is condemned as inferior . . . Conditioned to operating as a machine for making and spending money, with all other relationships dependent upon its efficiency, the moment the machine is out of order and beyond repair, one begins to feel like a ghost without a sense of reality . . . Regarding himself as a person who has outlived his usefulness, he feels as if he has to apologize for being alive. May I suggest that man's potential for change and growth is much greater than we are willing to admit, and that old age be regarded not as the age of stagnation, but as the age of opportunities for inner growth. The years of old age . . . are indeed formative years, rich in possibilities to unlearn the follies of a lifetime, to see through inbred self-deceptions, to deepen understanding and compassion, to widen the horizon of honesty, to refine the sense of fairness."

All: May you be blessed with many formative years, rich in opportunities, and new roads yet to be discovered and tried as you enter this eighth decade of life. May you live to *ein hundert und tzvanzig* (to 120 and beyond).

8. *"Shehecheyanu"* (led by relative)

Julie: According to the *Sefer HaChinuch*, *mitzvah* number 257 requires that one rise before the aged. "The rationale for this *mitzvah* is that the purpose of one's life in this world is to acquire more and more wisdom *(chochmah)* in order that we should come to know our Creator. Therefore, it is appropriate to honor one who has attained (such wisdom) so that others will be encouraged to do the same." We therefore ask all those who are here with us tonight to rise as we all recite together the *"Shehecheyanu.*

CONCLUSION

"Oneg Chochmah" was a very uplifting event for all. It came at a time of life when celebrations are often fewer than funerals or hospital visits. The ceremony reenergized my parents, refocused the family on who we all are, and enabled friends and family alike to give testimonials to the living and to the wisdom of those who have reached the "Age of Wisdom."

In addition to the ceremony as presented in these pages, Dov Peretz Elkins, my parents' Rabbi at Park Synagogue in Cleveland, helped me to format some original Hebrew blessings. Distinguished Service Rabbi Armond Cohen, also of Park Synagogue, provided the stirring conclusion with the priestly blessing. Eyes were moist, hearts were full.

The ceremony can be easily adapted to any age. Just follow *Pirke Avot*, Chapter 5, *Mishneh* 25, and provide one blessing for each decade of life.

CHAPTER 53

AROUND THE FAMILY TABLE

CONTRIBUTOR: DR. JEFFREY SCHEIN
ADDRESS: Cleveland College of Jewish Studies
26500 Shaker Boulevard
Beachwood, OH 44122
PHONE: (216) 464-4050
E-MAIL: jschein@ccjs.edu
TARGET : Everyone living with families

INTRODUCTION

In this chapter, I share a set of traditions that have enriched my own family's holiday celebrations. In general, there is a wealth of Jewish traditions for the home and family (e.g., the Pesach *Seder*). Yet, I have found that these traditions are distributed unevenly across the holiday cycle (think of the frequent complaint that there is "no good ritual" for Shavuot). Yet, we can never accomplish even a third of what we might want to do at a Pesach *Seder*. Here I try to even the playing field a bit by exploring new rituals for the "under-ritualized" holidays. The setting for most of these is the *Mikdash Ma'at*, the miniature sanctuary of the family meal table. Rabbis and Family Educators can certainly transfer these ritual experiments to the classroom and synagogue. Many of these will work particularly well at Religious School assemblies and celebrations.

ELUL

When our children were younger, my wife and I composed a *megillat teshuvah* scroll on which each of us wrote one way in which we could contribute to a happier, more productive, Jewishly engaged family. We created the *megillat teshuvah* at the beginning of Elul. During Elul, we follow a custom of allowing the Havdalah candle to burn for five minutes in brandy while we talk about the *shavua* (week) ahead. At our Havdalah ceremony, we added this twist: we revisited the *teshuvah* scroll to talk about how well we were doing in realizing our *teshuvah* goals for ourselves. This gave us a way, as a family, to be doing our High Holy Day preparation.

ROSH HASHANAH

- Ask each member of the family (and, of course, guests) to share something new that happened to them in the past year. Other people sitting around the table respond with *"titchadesh"* or *"titchadshi"* (may you be renewed) as each person concludes.
- The pomegranate is often used as a symbol of the many *mitzvot* available to us. We cut up small pieces of pomegranate, give one section to each person at the table, give them a few moments to think about the special *mitzvot* they would like to perform during the upcoming year, and then eat a pomegranate seed together.
- For the Rosh HaShanah *Kiddush*, when we come to *"melech al kol ha-aretz mekadaysh yisrael v'yom hazikaron"* (the God of all the earth, the Sanctifier of Israel and the day of remembrance), we chant this phrase 13 times. Why? To indicate that the God we call upon during the High Holy Days through the selection from Exodus 34 ("God is a compassionate God . . . ") has 13 different attributes. If we understand God in these broad ways,

we have more of an opportunity to connect God to our own lives.

YOM KIPPUR

- From the "Holiday Workshop" series of Patty Golden, we learned another tradition. As one leaves for *"Kol Nidre"* on *Erev* Yom Kippur, we place a *Tzedakah* box, a *Machzor*, and a small Torah scroll under a *challah* cover. The family has then made a statement that in this home these objects will constitute our "food" on this very special day.

- Each member of the family asks the forgiveness of the rest of the family for any wrong deed — intentional or unintentional — they may have committed. The rest of the family responds to each individual, *"Salachti kid'varecha"* (I will forgive you as you have requested). This is from a line in the Yom Kippur liturgy, and is what God says in response to the petition of the Jewish people for forgiveness.

SUKKOT

- Sukkot is a *yom hoda'ah*, a day of Thanksgiving and joy. Thus, creating a Hebrew or English acrostic of the things in life for which we are appreciative seems quite natural for Sukkot. The process of creating it is fun, and posters listing the collective "thank-yous and appreciations" of the family can be hung in the *sukkah*.

- As the children have grown older, we study something from Kohelet (Ecclesiastes), either in our own Sukkah or while on some nature expedition.

- For reasons perhaps idiosyncratic to our family, Sukkot is never complete unless we have gone on one canoeing trip. There we deeply appreciate the beauty of the change in seasons.

THANKSGIVING

- The Jewish connection to Thanksgiving can be enhanced by reading selections from such stories as *Molly's Pilgrim* by Molly Cone (Beech Tree Books, 1998) and/or the selections for Thanksgiving at the back of *Kol Haneshamah*, the Reconstructionist prayer book. These various selections emphasize our Jewish status as pilgrims, searchers for religious and cultural freedom, who have found a special place for ourselves in America. A favorite story of mine (now out of print, but still available from libraries) is *The Lekachmacher Family* by Carol Richmond (Bonim Books, 1970). This story traces a family from its shtetl in Russia to its new home in America. When our children were younger, it made wonderful reading in the living room before proceeding into the dining room to enjoy our Thanksgiving meal.

- A fuller set of Jewish Thanksgiving celebrations is available from the Jewish Reconstructionist Federation in Philadelphia (215-752-8500).

CHANUKAH

- Chanukah becomes a family time to count and consider. We count the money we have collected for *Tzedakah* and consider to which causes the money ought to be "dedicated." Sometimes the tradition is enriched by hiding *gelt* (usually silver dollars), and letting the kids split the *gelt* they find between themselves and *Tzedakah*.

- We reverse roles and get on the "receiving end" of *Pirsum Hanays* (the broadcast of the miracle). On one night of Chanukah (usually when the candles burn most brightly), we walk outside and marvel at our five *chanukiot* glowing. Another night, we walk or drive to the area of greatest Jewish density in the community in which we live and see how many "miracle pronouncements" (lit *chanukiot*) we can spot.

SHAVUOT

- Shavuot makes most Jewish sense as the completion of the 50-day cycle that begins with the first day of Pesach. It represents the promise of responsibility delivered at Sinai in response to the gift of freedom. We underscore the connection between the two holidays by focusing on the *Aseret HaDibrot*, the Ten Commandments. We read each of the commandments. After each is read, family members respond, *"Na'aseh V'nishma"* (we will seek to do and understand these *mitzvot*).

- For each of the Ten Commandments we can affirm, we place a drop of wine back in the Shavuot *Kiddush* cup. We think of these lost drops of wine as the ones we emptied at Pesach at the reading of the ten plagues. At that time, we removed the drops because we could not completely rejoice in the drowning of the Egyptians at the sea. Now, our joy can be more complete, because the Torah disciplines us and teaches us to act ethically even in times of great stress and tension.

CONCLUSION

Family system theorists often comment on how "under-ritualized" North American families are. It is hard to think of Jewish families in this light because of the very richness of our home-centered celebration. Yet, even beyond the fact that the availability of rituals doesn't ensure that families utilize them, I have suggested that Jewish family rituals are unevenly distributed over the holiday cycle. Some of the holidays themselves are "under-ritualized" from the standpoint of home celebration. I hope these various ideas will help Rabbis and educators think of innovative new ways to provide rich and "fattening" new home celebrations for some of our "thinner" Jewish holidays.

CONTRIBUTORS

JANICE P. ALPER is Executive Director of Jewish Educational Services of Atlanta. She is the editor of *Learning Together: A Sourcebook on Jewish Family Education* (A.R.E. Publishing, Inc., 1987). Ms. Alper is the author of a number of articles about Jewish education, and has extensive experience working with families, training Family Educators, and writing programs and curricula.

TZIPORAH ALTMAN-SHAFER is Director of Education at Congregation Beth El in Phoenix, Arizona. She is a graduate of the Cleveland Fellows program and has a Masters of Judaic Studies with a Concentration in Jewish Education. She also has served as Family Educator for several schools in Cleveland.

JULIE JASLOW AUERBACH is the Director of Family and Adult Education at the Solomon Schechter Day School of Cleveland. She is the former Project Coordinator for Numbers 2000 North America, a senior educator position with Melitz Centers for Jewish Zionist Education. She has taught Family Education extensively throughout the Cleveland area, and earned her Masters Degree in Jewish Studies with an emphasis on Jewish education from the Cleveland College of Jewish Studies. Ms. Auerbach provided musical contributions to *Jewish Every Day: The Complete Handbook for Early Childhood Teachers* (A.R.E. Publishing, Inc.).

ELLEN ABRAHAMS BROSBE has been a Family Educator in Northern California since for more than a decade. She has an M.A. in Human Develop-

ment and teaching credentials from Pacific Oaks College. She has been on the adjunct faculty of the Whizin Institute for Jewish Family Life in Los Angeles, and worked at the Jewish Family Education Project of the Bureau of Jewish Education in San Francisco.

BARBARA CARR is Education Director, as well as a longtime teacher, at Congregation Dor Hadash in San Diego. She serves as the President of San Diego County's Agency for Jewish Education Principals' Council, and is a member of the RRA-JRF National Education Commision. Ms. Carr was honored with the Reconstructionist Movement's Master Teacher Award in 1996.

TREASURE COHEN is the director of J.E.F.F. (Jewish Experiences for Families) at the Jewish Education Association of MetroWest. She has been a family educator for almost 30 years — as a parent; as a leader in developing meaningful and joyful Shabbat and holiday services for young families; as a trainer of Family Educators; and as a creator of school, synagogue, and community programs that touch and teach the Jewish family.

MARK DAVIDSON is Family Education Director at The Agnon School, a community Day School in the Greater Cleveland area. He also implements informal educational programs for middle school students.

ELLEN CHENCHINSKY DEUTSCH has taught preschool through third grade at a Jewish Day School, and is currently director of Curriculum and

Family Education at Suburban Temple-Kol Ami in Cleveland, Ohio. She was the teacher on the interdisciplinary team for multi-handicapped toddlers at the Achievement Center for Children in Cleveland. Ms. Deutsch is currently completing her Masters Degree in Jewish studies at the Cleveland College of Jewish Studies.

DR. SANDY WALDMAN DASHEFSKY is a Jewish educator/consultant who served as Assistant Director of the Commission on Jewish Education of the Jewish Federation of Greater Hartford for 11 years. Currently, she is the Consultant/Education Director of two synagogue change initiatives in Hartford, the Academic Director of Certificate Programs at Hebrew College-Hartford Branch, and an adjunct staff memeber of JESNA (Jewish Education Services of North America). She has authored many articles and serves as presenter/consultant throughout North America.

RABBI DAN EHRENKRANTZ, a 1989 graduate of the Reconstructionist Rabbinical College, has been the Rabbi of Bnai Keshet in Montclair, New Jersey since he began there as a Student Rabbi in 1988. Rabbi Ehrenkrantz has written commentary for the Reconstructionist prayer book, and has authored several articles on a range of subjects. He is a past President of the Reconstructionist Rabbinical Association.

HEIDI B. EICHAKER devised and implemented the "Family Involvement Time" program at a synagogue in Milwaukee, Wisconsin. Currently, she resides in St. Louis, Missouri, where she is an educator in a public school.

DR. RELA MINTZ GEFFEN is a Professor at Gratz College where she also has served as the Academic Dean. She is currently the acting President of the Baltimore Hebrew University and is a noted authority on the Jewish family.

SHERI GROPPER is a consultant for the Orange County Bureau of Jewish Education. She co-developed the Jewish Discovery Zone for J.E.F.F. (Jewish

Experiences for Families) at the Jewish Education Association of MetroWest. She has been in the Jewish Family Education field for over ten years.

SHARON HALPER is Director of Education at Temple Beth El of North Westchester. She was a contributor to the ZIV Giraffe Curriculum, and is the author of *Mishpacha* (CAJE), *B'shivtekha B'veitekha — When You Sit in Your House* (Torah Aura Productions), and *To Learn Is to Do: A Tikkun Olam Roadmap* (UAHC Press).

ELISSA KAPLAN is the Director of Education at Congregation Har Shalom in Potomac, Maryland. She has served as both a Principal and Family Educator in Conservative and Reconstructionist congregations for the past ten years. Elissa is currently a doctoral candidate in Educational Leadership at George Washington University.

JO KAY has an M.A. in Jewish Education from N.Y.U., and is the Director of the New York School of Education at Hebrew Union College-Jewish Institute of Religion. She served as the Director of Jewish Studies at the Rodeph Sholom Day School in New York, and most recently as the congregation's Religious School Director. Ms. Kay created the PACE (Parent and Child Education) model of Family Education, and is a consultant to the Whizin Institute for Jewish Family Life at the University of Judaism in Los Angeles. She also serves as chair of the editorial board of CAJE's *Jewish Education News.*

JOAN KAYE is Executive Director of the BJE of Orange County and an adjunct faculty member of the University of Judaism, serving as a consultant at the Whizin Institute for Jewish Family Life. She is the co-author of "The Parent Connection" and several high school curricula, including "Why Be Good?" and "The Power to Lead."

VICKY KELMAN is the Director of the Jewish Family Education Project at the Bureau of Jewish Education, San Francisco Bay Area, and a member of the faculty of the Whizin Institute for Jewish Life. She is author of "Together 1: A Child-Parent Kit,"

"Together 2: Windows" and *Jewish Family Retreats: A Handbook* (all three published by The Melton Research Center); *Family Room: Linking Families into a Jewish Learning Community;* and three chapters in *First Fruits: A Whizin Anthology of Jewish Family Education* (both published by Whizin Institute for Jewish Family Life). The latter won the National Jewish Book Award in education.

BARBARA HARRIS KLARISTENFELD has been working as the Family Education Coordinator at Heschel Day School for six years. With an elementary school teaching background and a Masters Degree in Educational Psychology, it is her love of people and Judaism that fuels her enthusiasm for her work. In her spare time, she calligraphs and illuminates *ketubot*.

SALLY G. KLEIN-KATZ is an Israel-based private consultant for groups of educators, community leaders, and families seeking a unique and customized educational Israel experience. Ms. Klein-Katz is the editor of a new book for Melitz Centers for Jewish-Zionist Education, *The Ma Nishtana of Family Education Israel Trips*. She is a former Jerusalem Fellow.

BEN ZION KOGEN is Head of School at Kellman Academy in Cherry Hill, New Jersey. Formerly, he served as Principal of the Los Angeles Hebrew High School. Mr. Kogen has served as a member of the Board of the Jewish Educators Assembly and CAJE.

ENID C. LADER is a graduate of the Cleveland Fellows Program, with a Masters Degree in Judaic Studies from the Cleveland College of Jewish Studies. She also holds a Bachelor of Music degree in Music Therapy and a Masters Degree in Music Education from Florida State University. She is presently the Director of Congregational and Family Education at Beth Israel–The West Temple in Cleveland, Ohio, and is the Cleveland Community Associate in Family Education.

BARBARA LEVIN has a B.S. from Columbia University and a Bachelor of Religious Education from Jewish Theological Seminary. She made *Aliyah* to Israel in 1969. From 1969 to 1971, she worked with the Department of Jewish Education in the Diaspora at Hebrew University. She is one of the founders of the Frankel Tali School in Jerusalem, and its Principal from 1976 to the present. Ms. Levin was a recent recipient of the Israel Prize in Education. Prior to moving to Israel, Ms. Levin had 15 years of experience in a variety of Jewish educational settings in the U.S.

RABBI JOY LEVITT is the Associate Executive Director of the Jewish Community Center in Manhattan. She served as a congregational Rabbi for 20 years on Long Island and New Jersey. She is the co-editor of *A Night of Questions: A Passover Haggadah* (Jewish Reconstructionist Federation).

JAY LEWIS is currently the Assistant Director of the Bureau of Jewish Education of Orange County. He is a graduate of the Masters program in Jewish Communal Service of the Hornstein Program at Brandeis University.

LYNN LIEBLING is currently Director of Community and Family Enrichment at Temple Emanu El in Cleveland, Ohio. She works with the Religious School on family study days and projects, and leads a monthly study group for elders in the congregation and a weekly Torah study group for women. She earned a Masters of Jewish Studies with a concentration in Jewish Education from the Cleveland College of Jewish Studies.

JILL JARECKI MAINZER received a B.A. from Columbia University and a B.A., M.A., and Principal's Certificate from the Jewish Theological Seminary. She has developed Family Education programs and curricula for Camp Ramah in New England and The Epstein School in Atlanta, Georgia. Ms. Mainzer currently educates families as the Associate Director of Ramah Darom in Georgia.

DR. SHARON SEIDMAN MILBURN is currently a faculty member in the Department of Child and Adolescent Studies at California State Univerity,

Fullerton. Dr. Milburn's expertise addresses both parents' and children's responses to different educational strategies, with an emphasis on children's self-concept and motivation to learn. Dr. Milburn has worked with synagogues and community institutions to evaluate educational priorities and perceptions of existing educational approaches. Currently, she is helping the Jewish Reconstructionist Federation with their national educational survey.

LYNDALL MILLER is an Early Childhood Consultant for the Auerbach Central Agency for Jewish Education in the Greater Philadelphia area. She also consults nationally for various professional development programs in Jewish early childhood education. She is the author of a manual for leaders of Shabbat morning services for young children.

ESTHER NETTER is the Executive Director of the Zimmer Children's Museum of Jewish Community Centers of Greater Los Angeles, an innovative and interactive museum for children and families. Ms. Netter received her undergraduate degree in Jewish Studies from UCLA and her Masters Degree in Jewish Education from the Jewish Theological Seminary.

SARA LYNN NEWBERGER plans programs and teaches at the Talmud Torah of St. Paul Day School. She is a co-founder of the St. Paul Coalition for Jewish Family Education. Her background includes a B.S. in Ornamental Horticulture, an M.A. in Jewish Communal Service and Jewish Education, the Jerusalem Fellows, and the Teacher Educator's Institute of the Mandel Foundation.

MICHAEL OPPENHEIMER, D.D. has served as Rabbi of Suburban Temple-Kol Ami in Cleveland, Ohio since 1976. He is also Lecturer in the Department of Religion of Baldwin Wallace College and the Department of Religious Studies at John Carroll University, member of the Board of the American Jewish Committee, active with the Campaign Cabinets of Cleveland Jewish Community Federation and Cleveland United Way, past President of the Greater Cleveland Board of Rabbis, and recipient

of the earned title Reform Jewish Educator from the National Association of Temple Educators.

ELISE PASSY has a Masters Degree in Jewish education from University of Judaism. She served as the Family Education Director for the Houston Bureau of Jewish Education, and currently teaches for the Robert M. Baron Academy, an Orthodox Day School in Houston.

AMY GROSSBLATT PESSAH graduated with honors from the Hebrew Union College–Jewish Institute of Religion with a Masters Degree in Jewish Education. She served as the Pearlstone Director of Jewish Family Education at the Center for Jewish Education in Baltimore, Maryland, and is presently an educational consultant in Boca Raton, Florida.

MARILYN PRICE is a professional storyteller, puppeteer, and Jewish educator. She has designed and run a Family Education school, published books on puppetry, and has written extensively on a variety of subjects, including Torah commentary for educators.

LOREE BLOOMFIELD RESNIK has been a school psychologist in public schools, as well as the Principal of Suburban Temple-Kol Ami in Cleveland, Ohio. She is presently the Executive Director at that synagogue. An officer of the National Association of Temple Administrators, Ms. Resnik is also a past chair of the Jewish Educator's Council of Cleveland.

SELMA R. ROFFMAN was educated at Columbia University and the Jewish Theological Seminary, and received her M.Ed. from Beaver College (now Arcadia University). She is a Jewish studies teacher at the Perelman Jewish Day School in Melrose Park, Pennsylvania, and serves as the coordinator of Jewish Family Education programs at the school. Currently, she is the Principal at the Forman Center, and has published *HaSiddur Sheli*, an interactive prayer book for primary grade students.

ELLIE ROSENBERG has worked for numerous Jewish institutions in the Bay Area. She is currently the Assistant Director of Early Childhood Education and Family Services at the Peninsula Jewish Community Center in Belmont, California.

BARBARA ELLISON ROSENBLIT is currently a humanities teacher at the New Atlanta Jewish Community High School and instructor in the Melton Adult Mini-School in Atlanta, Georgia. She been a curriculum coordinator, middle school director, teacher in the Negev development town of Yerucham, and recipient of the Teachers Forum Award presented by the Department of Education in Washington, D.C.

RISA SHATZ ROTH, M.A., M.J.S. is a graduate of the Executive Educator Program at the Cleveland College of Jewish Studies. She serves as the Family Educator at Congregation Shaarey Tikvah, a Conservative synagogue in Cleveland, Ohio.

ORNA S. SCHAFER studied education at the Seminar Hakibbutzim, which is affiliated with Tel Aviv University. She received a Bachelors Degree from the Cleveland College of Jewish Studies, and is working toward a Masters Degree at that same institution. She teaches Hebrew and Jewish studies throughout the Cleveland community.

BENJAMIN SCHEIN is a graduate of the University of Pennsylvania. He has worked with B'nai Brith Youth Organization doing alumni organizing, and serves on their national advisory board. He is currently mentoring teen leaders within the Reconstructionist Movement.

DEBORAH SCHEIN has been a teacher for 30 years. She has a Masters Degree in Early Childhood Education. Ms. Schein has been an Early Childhood Coordinator, has taught college child development courses, and is presently teaching pre-kindergarten at The Agnon Jewish Day School in Cleveland.

MONA SENKFOR is the Educational Director of Temple Emanu El, Cleveland, Ohio. She has her B.A. from Case Western Reserve University, and an M.A. from John Carroll University. Ms. Senkfor is a

member of N.A.T.E., CAJE, and A.S.C.D., and is a former board member of N.A.T.E.

ETTI SEROK is the founder and, since 1994, the Director of the Frankel Center for Jewish Family Education in Jerusalem — Ve'Shinantam Le'Vanecha. She is the author of several publications on Jewish Family Education. Ms. Serok has served as Director of the Department of Jewish Education in the U.S.A. for the WZO, the first Director of the Tali Education Fund in Israel, and an Informal Education Supervisor at the Municipality of Jerusalem. She is a graduate of the Hebrew University, and is currently a doctoral candidate in Jewish Family Education at the Jewish Theological Seminary.

CAREN SHILOH, M.A. is an artist/educator/consultant specializing in informal Jewish education. Accessing traditional Jewish texts through art, storytelling, drama, and physical initiatives, she helps learners of all ages to reach deeper levels of understanding and connection.

ROB SPIRA is a graduate of the Cleveland College of Jewish Studies Fellows Program, where he received his M.A. The recipient of a Covenant Fellowship from the Covenant Foundation, he has served in a number of community leadership positions in Cleveland. Presently, Mr. Spira is the Madrich Ruchani at the Pardes School, a new community Day School in Cleveland.

RABBI JEFFREY SULTAR is the Hillel Campus Rabbi at Cornell University in Ithaca, New York. He previously served as Rabbi at Choate Rosemary Hall, a college preparatory school in Wallingford, Connecticut, and at Reconstructionist Congregation Am Haskalah in Allentown, Pennsylvania.

ELLEN R. TILMAN is currently the Associate Director of Admission at Perelman Jewish Day School, Forman Center, in Melrose Park, Pennsylvania. She has B.A. from Goucher College, an M.S.W. from Bryn Mawr College, and an M.B.A. from Northwestern University. She has held a variety of positions within the Jewish Community, and has been a Religious School teacher for more than 25 years. At the inception of the adult learning programs described in Chapter 21, she served as president of the PTO of the Forman Center of PJDS.

MARILYN VINCENT is currently the Director of the Department of Family Education at the Community Foundation for Jewish Education of Metropolitan Chicago (CJFE). Ms. Vincent's experience includes development of JFE curricular materials and the creation of the CFJE Family Education Program Bank. She is also responsible for the administration of community-wide grants to Religious/Hebrew and Day Schools. She has a B.A. from Northeastern Illinois University in Education and a Masters Degree of Judaica from Spertus College of Judaica, Chicago, Illinois.

TRICIA BERKE VINSON is a fifth grade teacher at the Mid-Peninsula Jewish Community Day School in Palo Alto, California. She was a co-founder of Congregation Etz Chayim and the creator and original education director of its Family Education program, "Mi'Dor L'Dor."

MERYL WASSNER is presently doing independent consulting in the areas of Family Education, curriculum development, teacher training, and storytelling. She has served as the Director of the Columbus Family Jewish Education Project in Columbus, Ohio and as the coordinator of the Cooperating Schools Network in the Reconstructionist Movement.

DAVID WEINSTEIN is the Education Director of the Jewish Foundation for the Righteous. For the past seven years, he has been the Family Educator at Bnai Keshet, a Reconstructionist synagogue in Montclair, New Jersey. Mr. Weinstein has also taught high school history and sociology for ten years in public high schools.

CAROL FREEDMAN WOLF, LISW is the coordinator of the HIV/AIDS outreach and education program at Jewish Family Service Association of Cleveland. She has taught child development and facilitated support and education groups for new parents. She holds a Masters Degree in social work.

DR. RON WOLFSON is the director of the Whizin Institute for Jewish Family Life and the principal instigator of Synagogue 2000: A Transdenominational Project for the Synagogue of the 21st Century. He is the author of *The Art of Jewish Living*, a series of books on the celebration of Jewish holidays in the home, sponsored by the Federation of Jewish Men's Clubs and the University of Judaism.

SUSAN WYNER received a B.S. in French and Education from Beaver College (now Arcadia University), and a Masters Degree in Judaic Studies in Education from the Cleveland College of Jewish Studies. She has taught grades pre-kindergarten to high school in Jewish and public schools. She has been Education Director at B'nai Jeshurun in Cleveland, Ohio since 1989 and is a former chair of the Jewish Educators Council of Cleveland.

DR. LOIS J. ZACHARY is the principal of Leadership Development Services, a consulting firm located in Phoenix, Arizona, that offers leadership, coaching, education, and training for corporate and not-for-profit organizations across the continent. Dr. Zachary, a specialist in adult development and learning, coaches leaders and their organizations in designing, implementing, and evaluating learner-centered mentoring programs. She is the author of *The Mentors Guide: Facilitating Effective Learning Relationships* (Jossey-Bass Publishers, 2000), and is a National Lecturer for Programs for Higher Education, a doctoral program of Nova Southeastern University.

EVE JOAN ZUCKER is the creator and teacher of "The PAK-Parents and Kids Learning Together." She also serves as the Family Educator at Congregation Sinai and the Milwaukee Jewish Day School. She recently received her Masters Degree in Jewish Education from the Cleveland College of Jewish Studies Distance Learning Program.

SELECTED RESOURCES FOR JEWISH FAMILY EDUCATION

Compiled by Dr. Rela Mintz Geffen, Benjamin Schein, and Dr. Jeffrey Schein

NOTE: This annotated bibliography comes from three different resources, each reflecting how quickly a new field of educational endeavor evolves: the Internet (Benjamin Schein), books and articles about the Jewish family that have developed over the last ten years (Rela Mintz Geffen), and selections from Jeffrey Schein's bibliography for a course entitled "Jewish Education for Tomorrow's Families" at the Cleveland College of Jewish Studies.

INTERNET RESOURCES

Jewish Search Engines and Information:
Shamash; http://shamash.org
Maven; http://www.maven.co.il/
> Big search engine for Jewish stuff. Good place to look for something specific.

Virtual Jerusalem; http://www.virtual.co.il
> Judaism and Jewish Resources.
> http//shamash.org/trb/Judaism.html

Professional Organizations:
http://www.jesna.org
> Lots of good resources for Jewish educators. Has a list of Central Agencies for Jewish Education under their Resources section, each of which is likely to have resources for Jewish Family Education.

General Jewish Family Web Sites:
http://www.jewish family.com/
http://www.jewishteens.com/
http://www.jcn18.com/
> Jewish Communication Network – has both a "Parenting" section and a "Kids" section.

http://www.jajz-ed.org.il/
> The Jewish Agency for Israel
> The Department for Jewish Zionist Education Resources, games, and other information on Israel.

http://www.sparksmag.com
> An e-zine written for Jewish kids, ages 9 to13 — "a hip, hot, outrageous" collection of stories, articles, games, interviews, and activities. Features a "Teachers Talk" section, and a Sephardic emphasis.

http://www.zigzagworld.com/
> Best Jewish games on the web. Also good for learning Hebrew applications.

Web Sites Recommended by the Whizin Institute for the Jewish Family
www.JewishFamilyLife.com
"The Jewish Internet Consortium"
> Excellent, comprehensive resource linking to the newest Jewish lists, events, and web sites.

www.Mishpacha.com
"A virtual community for real Jewish families"
> Provides an introductory guide to the most important ideas of Jewish life, beliefs, practice, culture, and community. For parents who find that what they learned as Jewish children isn't enough to build their own Jewish families.

www.JewishFamily.com
"Online Community of Jewish Family and Life"
> Provides family chat, Q & A, and holiday talk. Regular columns include "Dear Rabbi," "A Mother's Muse," and "Parenting from Jerusalem." Great link to more information

and Jewish sites on holiday, food, travel, love, and sports

www.Family.com
"Brought to you by Disney . . . "
Learn what experts have to say about children, relationships, pregnancy, arts and crafts, and household pets. Features include celebrating your family history, ultimate boredom buster activities, and all-inclusive family resorts.

www.parentingproject.org
"The Parenting Project"
Preparing tomorrow's parents today. A not-for-profit organization dedicated to addressing our nation's crisis of child abuse, neglect, and abandonment, teen pregnancy, and overall violence by making parenting education part of the curriculum for all school children.

www.CSOS.JHU.EDU/P2000
"National Network of Partnership Schools"
Established by researchers at Johns Hopkins University. Brings together schools, districts, and states that are committed to developing and maintaining comprehensive programs of school-family-community partnerships. Log on to this web site for ideas on how to develop promising partnerships.

Jewish Movements

Note: All of these sites offer various education resources.

Reform – http://www.uahc.org
Reconstructionist – http://www.jrf.org
Orthodox (Orthodox Union) – http://www.ou.org
Conservative – http://www.uscj.org
Jewish Renewal Communities –
    http://jewishrenewal.org

Buy Jewish Online

http://www.judaicagiftstore.com/
Good place to buy Judaica on line.
http://www.amazon.com
Buy Jewish books online. Look for Judaism section, under "Religion and Spirituality."

The Jewish Family Today

Cherlin, Andrew J. and Frank F. Furstenberg, Jr. *The New American Grandparent – A Place in the Family,*

A Life Apart. Boston: Harvard University Press. 1992.
A discussion of the ambiguous and ambivalent role of grandparents in America.

Fishman, Sylvia Barack. Chapter 5 in *Forming Jewish Households and Families in Jewish Life and American Culture.* Albany, NY: SUNY Press, 1999.
A Volume in the SUNY Series on American Jewish Life in the 1990s.

———. "The Changing American Jewish Family Faces the 1990s," pp. 51-88 in a new reader from Brandeis and University Press of New England, 1999, entitled *Jews in America: A Contemporary Reader,* edited by Roberta Rosenberg Farber and Chaim Waxman.

Geffen, Rela Mintz, and Egon Mayer. *The Ripple Effect — Interfaith Families Speak Out.* B'nai Brith International and the Jewish Outreach Institute, 1997.
Reports the results of a qualitative study through focus groups around the US. Both spouses in mixed marriages and parents of Jews who have intermarried (who are also the grandparents of Christian grandchildren) speak frankly about their experiences.

Goldscheider, Frances K., and Linda J. Waite. *New Families, No Families? The Transformation of the American Home.* Berkeley: University of California Press, 1991.
Provides the American context for study of the Jewish family.

Keysar, Ariela; Barry A. Kosmin; and Jeffrey Scheckner. *The Next Generation — Jewish Children and Adolescents.* Albany, NY: SUNY Press paperback, 2000.
A volume in the SUNY series on American Jewish Society in the 1990s. Series editors Barry A. Kosmin and Sidney Goldstein.

Linzer, Norman; Irving N. Levitz; and David J. Schnall, eds. *Crisis and Continuity — The Jewish*

Family in the 21st Century. Hoboken, NJ: KTAV, 1995.
Edited by professors of social work at Yeshiva's Wurzweiler School of Social Work, this volume contains various aspects of clinical issues and how to deal with them from a Jewish perspective. Considers spousal abuse, caring for incapacitated parents, stress points in the contemporary Jewish family; self and other — the Jewish family in crisis.

Phillips, Bruce A. *Re-examining Intermarriage: Trends, Textures and Strategies*. Los Angeles, CA: The Wilstein Institute of Jewish Policy Studies and The American Jewish Committee, 1997.
A nuanced analysis of the impact of interfaith marriage on family life and especially transmission of Jewish identity to the next generation. (Phillips went back to the 1990 National Jewish Population Survey of interfaith families and did in-depth interviews with several members of each household.)

The Winter/Spring 1996/97 issue of the *Journal of Jewish Communal Service* on "Jewish Family Service: Looking Back, Moving Forward," many articles on various aspects of Jewish Family Life. Guest editors – Sherry Rosen and Lucy Y. Steinitz. An article entitled "The Jewish Family: An Institution in Transition," pp. 116-122, synthesizes in short form much of what we know about the Jewish family today.

Selections and Reflections from "Jewish Family Education for Tomorrow's Jewish Families"

For engaging the interest and enthusiasm of lay leaders, the clear writing of Leora and Ron Isaacs in *Jewish Family Matters: A Leader's Guide* (United Synagogue of Conservative Judaism, 1994) and Harlene Appelman in *Jewish Experiences for Families* (Jewish Experiences for Families, 1995) is very helpful. A different media for the same purpose: the video *Gefilte Fish*, available from Ergo Media. This is a terrific trigger film of three generations of Jewish women preparing gefilte fish. There is a set of discussion questions in *Targilon: Charting a Course for Jewish Family Education* (Isaacs and Schein, JESNA and JRF, 1999), designed to help participants respond to "Why the need for Jewish Family Education today? My *bubbie* certainly didn't need it."

The richest exposure to Jewish sources and perspectives on the family comes I believe from David Biale's article "Classical Teachings and Historical Experience" in *Jewish Family and Continuity* by Steven Bayme and Gladys Rosen (KTAV and AJC, 1994). I have found that after reading this article, educators are able to ground their intuitions about the Jewish family much more firmly in both a traditional Jewish and historical/sociological perspective.

Two wonderful volumes for raising issues about the changing configurations of the family in our contemporary society are *Free to Be Family* (Bantam, 1987) by Marlo Thomas and *The Notion of Family* (Orange Frazer Press, 1999) by journalist Eleanor Mallet. The former is full of playful contemporary retellings of such classics as Cinderella (will we ever forgive the wicked stepfather?). Eleanor Mallet's book is a compilation of short essays she wrote as her own children grew up. While the essays often move the reader to much laughter and tears, they also raise critical points for discussion about the evolving (Jewish) family.

When I want my students to develop a deeper appreciation for the *family* in Jewish Family Education, I think there is no better volume than *Rituals for Our Times* by Roberts and Imber-Black (reviewed in Chapter 51 of this volume).

In order better to understand the most critical issues today in JFE, I turn to two sources. One is the rich and varied set of essays in the *First Fruit: A Whizin Anthology of Jewish Family Education*, edited by Ron Wolfson and Adrienne Bank (Whizin Institute, 1999). I am also very excited about the upcoming publication of a set of case studies about Jewish Family Education edited by Vicky Kelman and available through the San Francisco BJE. I had the privilege of serving as the "Rashi" to one of these case studies, and have found very impressive the collective *chochmah* emerging from a group of

Jewish Family Educators. The various case studies truly trigger critical reflection.

While there is a wealth of emerging literature on adult learning, I find the most accessible material for those in Family Education comes from an unexpected source, Lee Meyerhoff Hendler's *The Year Mom Got Religion* (Jewish Lights Publishing, 1998). Her self-portrait of her own struggles to transcend a limited, pediatric Jewish education are so vivid and honest that they quickly generate the right kind of discussions about adult learning. I have also found the Fall 1998 edition of *Agenda* magazines (JESNA) on adult learning to be very helpful in this context.

I often think of professional development as mirroring the Maslow hierarchy of needs (survival, competence, self-realization), which so many of us studied in our college psychology classes. With a group that is beginning to feel confident and competent in their JFE understanding, I think it is critical to turn to issues of vision, goals, and evaluation. *The Targilon: Charting a Course in Jewish Family Education* by Leora Isaacs and Jeffrey Schein (JESNA and JRF, 1996), and the 1998 publication *Pathways: A Guide for Evaluating Programs in Jewish Settings* (JESNA, 1998) have been very helpful tools for Family Educators in this aspect of their work.

Greater confidence and competence naturally evoke the issue of greater Jewish depth. A particularly useful volume in this regard is *Torah for the Family* by Ned Epstein and Suzanne Singer Stuttman (Prentice Hall Press, 1986). This book chronicles the journey of a once secular family into the tradition of weekly family Torah study with great passion and Jewish erudition. While intimidating to a family beginning study or to a novice Family Educator, veterans will find it deeply challenging. Unfortunately, the book is out of print. However, most BJEs and the Cleveland College of Jewish Studies have several copies. A videotape of a family having come through the process of studying *Torah for the Family* and engaged in their own Torah Study is available by contacting Dr. Jeffrey Schein, Cleveland College of Jewish Studies (jschein@ccjs.edu, 216-464-4050, ext. 123). In a different way, Vicky Kelman's *Jewish Living Room: Linking Family into a Jewish Community* (Whizin Institute for Jewish Family Life, 1995) addresses this same "what is my next step in JFE" question.